The Rockefeller Women

Dynasty of Piety, Privacy, and Service

ALSO BY CLARICE STASZ

The Vanderbilt Women: Dynasty of Wealth, Glamour, and Tragedy

American Dreamers: Charmian and Jack London

The Social Control of Deviance: A Critical Perspective
(with Nanette Davis)

The American Nightmare: Why Inequality Persists

Female and Male: Socialization, Social Roles, and Social Structure

Sexism: Scientific Debates

Simulation Games for the Social Studies Teacher
(with Samuel Livingston)

Simulation and Gaming in Social Science
(with Michael Inbar)

The Rockefeller Women

*Dynasty of Piety, Privacy,
and Service*

Clarice Stasz

St. Martin's Press / New York

LIBRARY OF CONGRESS CATALOGING-IN-PUBLICATION DATA
Stasz, Clarice.
    The Rockefeller women : an intimate portrait of an American
dynasty / Clarice Stasz.
        p.   cm.
    ISBN 0-312-13156-9
    1. Rockefeller family.   2. Women—United States—Biography.
3. Upper class families—United States—Biography.   4. United
States—Social life and customs—20th century.   I. Title.
CT274.R59S73 1995
973.9'092'2—dc20
[B]   95–2826
                                                                            CIP

First Edition: August 1995

10 9 8 7 6 5 4 3 2 1

To my sister, Cathy,
and my husband, Michael

CONTENTS

THE FOUNDING OF THE LINE

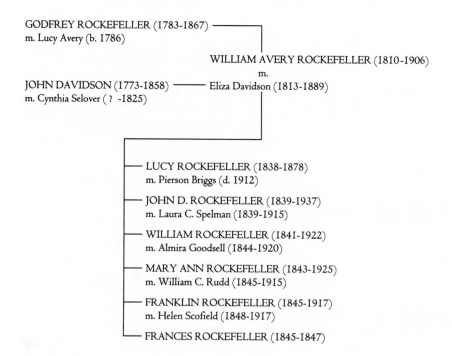

GODFREY ROCKEFELLER (1783-1867)
m. Lucy Avery (b. 1786)

WILLIAM AVERY ROCKEFELLER (1810-1906)
m.
JOHN DAVIDSON (1773-1858) ——— Eliza Davidson (1813-1889)
m. Cynthia Selover (? -1825)

LUCY ROCKEFELLER (1838-1878)
m. Pierson Briggs (d. 1912)

JOHN D. ROCKEFELLER (1839-1937)
m. Laura C. Spelman (1839-1915)

WILLIAM ROCKEFELLER (1841-1922)
m. Almira Goodsell (1844-1920)

MARY ANN ROCKEFELLER (1843-1925)
m. William C. Rudd (1845-1915)

FRANKLIN ROCKEFELLER (1845-1917)
m. Helen Scofield (1848-1917)

FRANCES ROCKEFELLER (1845-1847)

JOHN D. ROCKEFELLER LINE

JOHN D. ROCKEFELLER (1839-1937)
m. Laura C. Spelman (1839-1915)

ELIZABETH ROCKEFELLER ———— MARGARET STRONG (1897-1985)
(1866-1906)   m. Jorge (George) de Cuevas (1885-1965)
m. Charles Strong (1863-1940)   m. Raymundo de Larrain (b. 1937)

ALICE ROCKEFELLER
(1869-1870)

ALTA ROCKEFELLER ———————— JOHN R. PRENTICE (1902-1972)
(1871-1962)   m. Abra Cantrill
m. E. Parmalee Prentice
(1863-1955)   MARY ADELINE PRENTICE (1907-1981)
                                m. Benjamin D. Gilbert

                                SPELMAN PRENTICE (b. 1911)
                                m. Dorothy Jean Ryan
                                m. Lola Pierce

EDITH ROCKEFELLER ——————— JOHN D. ROCKEFELLER MCCORMICK
(1872-1932)   (1897-1901)
m. Harold Fowler McCormick   H. FOWLER MCCORMICK (1898-1973)
(1872-1941)   m. Anne "Fifi" Potter (1880-1969)

                                MURIAL MCCORMICK (1902-1959)
                                m. Elisha Dyer Hubbard (1880-1936)

                                EDITHA MCCORMICK (1903-1904)
                                MATHILDE MCCORMICK (1905-1947)
                                m. Max Oser (1875-1942)

JOHN D. ROCKEFELLER, JR. ——— ABBY ROCKEFELLER (1903-1976)
(1874-1960)   m. David Milton (1900-1976)
m. Abby Greene Aldrich   m. Irving Pardee (1892-1949)
(1874-1948)   m. Jean Mauze (1903-1974)
m. Martha Baird Allen
(1895-1971)   JOHN D. ROCKEFELLER 3RD (1906-1978)
                                m. Blanchette Ferry Hooker (1909-1992)

                                NELSON ROCKEFELLER (1908-1979)
                                m. Mary Todhunter Clark (b. 1907)
                                m. Margaretta Fitler Murphy (b. 1926)

                                LAURANCE SPELMAN ROCKEFELLER
                                (b. 1910)
                                m. Mary French (b. 1910)

                                WINTHROP ROCKEFELLER (1912-1973)
                                m. Barbara Sears (b. 1916)
                                m. Jeanette Edris (b. 1918)

                                DAVID ROCKEFELLER (b. 1915)
                                m. Margaret McGrath (b. 1915)

THE ROCKEFELLER-STILLMAN FAMILY CONNECTIONS

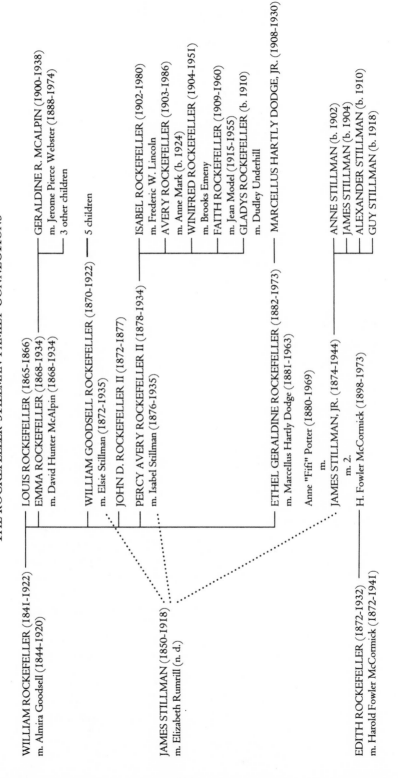

FOREWORD

*I*n October of 1864, John D. Rockefeller took his bride Laura Spelman to their new home at 29 Cheshire Street in Cleveland. When he went to work the next day and closed the door on the house, he could just as well have closed the door on her history. At least, that is what his many biographers would have us think. Allan Nevins's remarks are characteristic: "Mrs. Rockefeller was essentially a homemaker. While she took a keen interest in her husband's business labors, she never took an active share in them, and realizing their complexity, seldom gave him any advice."[1] Closeted in her home, wise enough to leave "complexity" to men, she need no longer interrupt the flow of the real story, the remarkable rise of Standard Oil and, later, of the Rockefeller philanthropies.

In one sense it is correct to exclude her. She played no formal role in Rockefeller's public life. She viewed homemaking as a woman's royal robe, borne proudly, signifying duty that bore rich rewards. She would approve her public notice being limited to the wedding, the births of their children, and her own funeral. It was John D. whose imagination and energy forged the great corporation and charitable foundation; it was John D. who suffered the calumny of vicious attack during the years of trust-busting, whose money was condemned by ministers as "tainted." Laura had no desire to participate in that public battlefield, for the home offered more than enough opportunities for expressing her talents.

More to the point, she would add, the results of her housebound acts were no less significant than his, for the value of one's deeds is relative. She would note how often Jesus reminded the Priests, Pharisees, and Merchants that their acclaim and wealth were meaningless when placed beside the kind act of a beggarly leper or prostitute. She would have enjoyed many of the biographies of her husband. Yet she would have been secretly amused at how some missed the point: that fame and fortune were not the final measure of a life.

Still, to close the door on Mrs. Rockefeller, as she might prefer, would be to diminish the life of her husband, to say his meaning is bound only in his large-scale social contributions. John D. Rockefeller was as much a family man as a man of industry. To neglect his domestic life is to caricature him as a dry, remote, methodical, perfectionist—in modern metaphor, robotic. One might suspect him of being a cool husband and absent father, or an intrusive and commanding biblical patriarch. He was neither. He was both a man of his era and a man ahead of his age, in his private life as well as public.

His conventionality made him appear safe, unthreatening, part of the crowd; his scruples kept him true to what his contemporaries expressed only as rhetoric. A Gilded Age baron, he rejected Society. He was a multimillionaire who lived comfortably, but never ostentatiously. (Had Thoreau gained such a fortune, one could imagine him living likewise.) He vacationed in Cleveland, the city where he gained his wealth, and his closest friends included less wealthy congregants of the Baptist church he attended there. When other men rushed after work to lodges, clubs, and saloons, he hurried home to the company of his wife and his four children, three of whom were daughters. For long periods his mother and his sister-in-law lived with him as well.

Some historians refer to the nineteenth century as a period of the "feminization" of church and home, that is, the subversion of male values in these settings. John D. Rockefeller came of age when this process was in full current. Unlike the Colonial period, where a man ruled steeple and parlor, and passed his craft and authority on to his sons, now the woman took his place. After the Civil War, the home, under woman's rule, was indisputably the center of refuge and morality. For John D. Rockefeller, fate exaggerated this feminization. First, his mother, more than others in her community, was forced to raise the family on her own. Second, his adult household, apart from his youngest child and only son, consisted entirely of female relatives. Rather than rebel against this "excessive" female influence—as many contemporaries did—he welcomed it. He was not a "man's man," nor was he in need of a "bully pulpit." He seemed simply to love and respect women, although he never fully understood them.

This side of John D. Rockefeller was a complete surprise. When I began this project, my inclination was to do a study parallel to my earlier work on four generations of women in the Vanderbilt family. During my research on Gertrude Vanderbilt Whitney, I kept crossing the path of Abby Aldrich Rockefeller, wife of John D. Rockefeller, Jr. She was one of the founders of the Museum of Modern Art, a leader in the YWCA with regard to working women's housing, and a pioneer collector of American folk art. The daring and creative women in the Vanderbilt line often contributed to society in order to express personal rebellion or to transform private tragedy. The Rockefeller women, I suspected, contributed out of other motives. I also expected to find women other than Abby whose contributions to social or cultural history had been expunged.

What I did not anticipate was the commanding participation of John D. himself in shaping the tale. He lived almost a century and, once his business was underway, he used his office facilities to prepare, copy, and file family correspondence. Even telegrams were preserved, both in his pencilled hand on scraps of cheap paper and in final Western Union paste-ups. He had copies of his letters to family members, and he preserved their replies.

Further, the trove of correspondence included letters from his sons-in-law. This meant I could view the daughters' husbands firsthand, and not, as was necessary in the case of the Vanderbilts, through the perceptions of the wives. Also, the children's letters remarked (or even tattled) on one another to their father and gave insight into the sibling relationships. These resources promised a more balanced examination of the women's history.

Although the papers give John D. a central role, that of his wife could not be diminished. Unfortunately, through both purpose and accident, much of Laura's correspondence with him and with their children vanished. After her death, her sister destroyed letters Laura's daughters had written to her. Since Laura did not have the benefit of Standard Oil clerks to type and copy her letters to others, few remain. Exceptional are the dozens of letters she sent to her son John Jr. when he attended college. It says something about her relationship with her children that he alone of the four siblings kept all of her messages. Fortunately, journals hint at her activities with her three daughters, if not the values she directly passed on to them.

John Jr. went on to a remarkable life. He built a well-known career in philanthropy and social service. Through his marriage to a strong woman with her own interests, he reared his six children; the most noted, the five "Rockefeller Brothers," continued the family commitment to service. I was fortunate that Bernice Kert completed her study of his wife, *Abby Aldrich Rockefeller*, as I was beginning mine. Her careful investigation filled a gap that would have added several years' labor to my problem, and did much to illuminate John Jr.'s private life. Those familiar with Kert's study will find I have introduced some new information about this extraordinary woman, and a somewhat different interpretation of her role in the family.

But what of John Jr.'s sisters? Bessie remains a ghostly figure despite extensive attempts to capture her in print. Alta became a partner with her husband on a New England farm and assisted his many significant contributions to agriculture. Still, she strove continually for her father's approval, and no amount of reassurance on his part could sate her need. Edith became an extravagant hostess, traded religion for psychology, and made a lasting imprint on Chicago culture. But only Edith, the youngest, became known in her day; after her death, history recorded lies that distorted her contributions.

How could a family that was so home-centered, so rich in women's influence, reap in so much female anonymity and discontent? Why were the three daughters in the family—equal in energy, drive, and intelligence to their baby brother—unable to find the peace of mind and self-expression he was able to achieve? Why did they seem more fragmented, less able to sense themselves whole? Such questions propelled my study.

With information from so many family members, it was possible to see how men who admired women, who would have been disgusted by the denigrating stereotypes of today's media, would nonetheless restrict them. The family offers a case study of how sexist practices need require neither an individual's awareness of what he or she is doing, nor malicious intent. In most cases the Rockefeller women's autonomy shrank as a result of society's ways of doing things, the assumptions that blind even thoughtful observers to the consequences of their actions.

A related set of questions concerns the influence of the women upon the men. Would John D. and John Jr. have acted differently had this particular female influence been absent? For example, would they have placed their philanthropies behind such controversial areas as birth control and "Negro" rights at a time when both implied the breaking of laws? Would the remarkable art collections now gracing many museums have been gathered? Would Williamsburg now be the site of a shopping mall, the Blue Ridge Skyway cluttered by interstate malls and motels?

It happens that a comparison line was available to explore this question, that of John D.'s brother and partner at Standard Oil, William Rockefeller. The women in William's family tree are little known, but so are his male descendants. They are the "other Rockefellers," few of whom retain the name. Both temperament and circumstances pulled William Rockefeller away from a life of Christian service toward the materialism of the Gilded Age. Consequently, despite amassing great wealth, William was little involved in philanthropy. Only one of his children, Ethel Geraldine, left the bulk of her estate to social causes, a decision shaped partly by her having no living children at her death. William's line also reminds how significant marriage is for the shaping of family culture, for it introduced a strain from a troubled family, the Stillmans.

Another gap in other biographers' writings on the family is the failure to take their Baptist convictions seriously. The Rockefellers' piety was profound and sincere, and cannot be brushed off as Sunday-go-to-meeting ritual. What may be more surprising is that some of the family's more liberal social leanings relate directly to their Baptist convictions. It is also through the gospels that their way of parenting can be understood.

Yet it is the women who most concerned me, and here again other puzzles occurred. Why did John D.'s God-fearing mother choose a roustabout husband? Why did his three daughters fall away from a spiritually guided life, while his son continued the tradition? How is it that loving, supportive and, most of all, forgiving parents did not raise children in their likeness? To understand these actions, one has to let go of the twentieth century and examine these people by their own values and the historical conditions they experienced.

Few secret heroines reside here—women who deserve an entry in *Notable American Women*. Yet that very normality makes them more accessible. Despite their coming from great wealth, the Rockefeller women braved challenges familiar to women of more modest means today. Though seeming passive or housebound, the wives were slyly powerful and self-directed. Though deeply loved by John D. and Laura, the three sisters were not taken as seriously as their brother, whose role in life was so much clearer and more honored. Crisscrossing the women's issues are more universal currents: the negotiation of parent-child relationships from birth to late life, the maintenance of humane values in an increasingly indifferent world, the sculpting of a philosophy of life.

Another theme concerns the effects of fame on private life. The Rockefeller fortune was made at the same time that technology and transportation created a national media. Reporters could move more freely, telegraphs and telephones sped news, and printing became cheaper. Consequently, the lives of elite families became more than a matter of local gossip. With the "golden age of the magazine," the 1890s, editors demanded lengthy and well-illustrated accounts of personalities. This shift, along with the rise of muckraking, focused a bright spotlight on John D. Rockefeller. Thus a man who had not sought fame found he had gained notoriety. The impact of that public excoriation permanently impressed the patriarch and his son John Jr. in a way that later biased some of their actions within the family. For this reason, I have provided more information on the patriarch and his son than might normally be done in a book focusing on women's lives.

Reflecting on the impact of fame reinforced my own concerns about the ethics of biography and the invasion of privacy. This work is essentially a family history, one whose information concerns descendants still living. Most surviving members of the clan prefer anonymity, avoid publicity, and even eschew awards when deserved. It should be remembered that some incidents, albeit occurring decades ago, happened to the grandmother, aunt, or cousin of someone living today. I could have filled out information on current generations through extensive interviews with anyone who crossed their paths, but the more I read studies based primarily on such research, the less valid they appear. My hope is that some of these later Rockefellers will follow their ancestors' model and file private papers at the Archives for the use of some historian decades from now.

Whenever I mentioned the topic of my book, an almost universal response was "Are you going to write about Happy?" I even heard this from an elderly relative who was in a very conservative religious order. This question astutely captured how notions of fame and repute have changed in our society. (No one cared about Nelson Rockefeller's public record, whether good or bad.) Accordingly, whenever I discussed the many significant consequences of Rockefeller decisions, both economic and philanthropic, people were taken aback by their ignorance. So at the risk of losing some readers hungry for sensationalism, I warn ahead that this book will not talk about Happy, at least not in the way they anticipate. Human nature does not change, and one benefit of history is the opportunity to learn from others without injury to people still alive.

Finally, despite my quarrels with some earlier biographies, I do not mean to discredit them. Many offer dramatic and compelling stories atypical in the normally dry field of economic history. I recommend these works, which so ably augmented my understanding of the time and economic tides. My intent is rather to supplement, and to remind later biographers of noted men that their subjects' lives do not begin once they leave the house in the morning. Furthermore, one has to appreciate the men's public lives to make full sense of their behavior toward their wives, daughters, and sisters. Finally, I hope this narrative honors the curious hubris of these early Rockefellers, who preserved both their private affections and squabbles for us to spy upon. They challenge us with their purity of intention, their being "united in love," as the patriarch often closed his correspondence, and all the complications that inevitably follow.

Praise ye the Lord. Blessed is the man that feareth the Lord, that delighteth greatly in his commandments.

His seed shall be mighty upon the earth: the generation of the upright shall be blessed.

Wealth and riches shall be in his house: and his righteousness endureth forever. . . .

He hath dispersed, he hath given to the poor; his righteousness endureth for ever; his horn shall be exalted with his honour.

—Psalm 112

The trouble with looking at the Rockefellers is that most people either try to describe them as billionaires with diamond-studded fly swatters, or else "Just plain folks in spite of it all." The truth is, of course, that they are civilized human beings who fully appreciate how to use and enjoy their wealth wisely. On the other hand, a man who maintains five homes, most of them stocked with butlers and original Picassos, can't claim to be just another ordinary American wage earner. Not that he tries to, of course.

—anonymous family friend

1

Eliza Davison,
a Good Woman

"And God said unto them, Be fruitful, and multiply, and replenish the earth,
and subdue it."

Genesis 1:28

S he was conceived under portents of misfortune. Meteors fell
from the sky. Earthquakes emanating from Missouri broke
pottery in Boston. Rivers reversed their courses, forests were
uprooted, clouds of dust smote the sun.[1] The British held Detroit, while
Indians, encouraged by the French, massacred more than nine hundred
Americans in another settlement. Ministers warned that such catastro-
phes were signs from God of the waywardness of the people.

John and Cynthia Selover Davison lived in Niles Township, above Lake
Owego (today's Oswego) in western New York, and were little touched
by these cataclysms. Nonetheless, they must have felt some misgivings to
bring forth a child during that tumultuous time. Then, just before her
birth on September 12, 1813, Oliver Hazard Perry led a makeshift naval
force to defeat the British on Lake Erie. Fighting would continue, and the
enemy would even burn down the White House the following August.
Yet by the time Eliza Davison could walk, peace reigned.

Indeed, by the time Eliza was five, the nation was in the midst of what
it proudly called the "era of good feelings." Kentucky hemp, Vermont
wool, and Pittsburgh iron supplanted their imported British equivalents.
Roads and canals sped trade; easy credit fostered new business. Such
commerce would favor farmers such as the Davisons, who now more
readily sent their produce eastward to New York City and westward to
the Ohio frontier.

In their subduing of 150 fertile acres, the Davisons were typical of
western New York settlers. Such adventurers fled the worn-out earth of
New England, bringing little more than their Puritan views for capital—

ideas better than gold for investing in their future. They were patient and tenacious, sober and modest. They honored community, the setting up of rules and order in their families and towns. Above all, they honored God, who had made a covenant with His followers and was their source of mercy and compassion during difficult times.

The difficulties were mostly natural in origin. God had promised thorns and thistles, sorrow and sweat, and these were abundant to the newcomers. Forests must be razed to make plowing room, a backbreaking job even with the aid of an ox or two. A series of hot, dry summers seared crops, forcing smaller landholders into starvation. While the Iroquois were seldom a threat anymore, the wolves upon whose lands the settlers also encroached were aggressive, though their pelts brought sumptuous bounties of ten dollars apiece. Infection following child-birth struck down women; ague (malaria), consumption, and diphtheria plagued those of all ages. These were the tribulations that sent the people to the Bible: Exodus for the reminders of promise, Psalms for hope, Job for deeper consolation.

The Owego Lake settlers quickly established churches to bind people together; they formed local governments to discuss basic needs. They were in the part of New York known as the "infected" or Burned-Over District, an area given to unusual religious beliefs and crusades devoted to the perfection of humanity on earth. It attracted younger sons from scrabby, worn-out New England farms. A typical migrant had grown up in the atmosphere of the Second Great Awakening, and brought with him or later married a professing Christian woman. Her task was to warn him of temptations, his temporary violations of the Sabbath, his dalliance with a poor farmer's daughter, his sipping of too much whiskey. Methodist, Baptist, Disciples of Christ, Universalist, and other denominations reinforced the New England piety. The emotional fervor and optimism of the religions stimulated wide-ranging social reform, including utopianism, women's rights, abolitionism, and temperance. They were among the first Americans to turn taverns into nonalcoholic gathering places. With the elimination of excessive drinking, problems common to other frontier areas—fighting, wife beating, needless accidents—were infrequent.

Like many of this stock, the Davisons and the Selovers were hardy lines, long-lived and resourceful. Cynthia may have been less robust, for daughter Eliza was her third and last child. When Eliza was twelve, Cynthia died, leaving the girl to be reared by her nineteen-year-old sister Mary Ann while her father and brother worked the fields. John Davison never remarried, and showed special attachment to his youngest child.

All we know of this time in the lives of the Davison women are the bare facts one would find in a family bible. No written records were passed on by Cynthia, Eliza, or Mary Ann. Neighbors did recall John Davison being one of the most successful farmers in the region; consequently, the women must have played their roles well, for his reputation represented the efforts of the family in concert. Fortunately, we can easily imagine the seasonal and daily activities Cynthia Davison taught to her daughters, for such labors were the rituals of four-fifths of womankind in this infant nation with its agrarian promise.[2]

Farming absorbed society. Virtually every chore depended upon human muscle. When youngsters were physically able to handle a chore, it would be assigned to them. Men's work was variable by season, from tilling soil and planting in the spring, to weeding the crops and watching the livestock through the summer, to harvesting in the fall. Winter was for repairing tools, and a time of rest. The rhythms on any one day could change from the next, since some tasks, such as calving, did not occur to schedule. Men saw more of the land, got out of the house beyond the barnyard, into woodlands and fields, and suffered the consequences of harsh elements in turn.

Though women's work circled broadly with the seasons, most tasks marched to tight weekly and daily cycles. Seasonal chores included tending the kitchen garden that provided the family's subsistence, preserving of vegetables and meats, blending of medicines, soap making, and production of clothing. Surrounding these particulars was the everyday work of the household: cooking, scrubbing, mending, feeding poultry, churning butter, grinding grain, and baking. The work continued whether one was heavy with child and had two toddlers pulling at one's skirts, or whether one was sixty years old and arthritic. With so much to do, Cynthia Davison would soon have her daughters checking hens' nests, pounding corn in the hominy blocks, and mending small tears in a shirt. A pious woman, she could soften the work with proverbial reminders that a "wise woman buildeth her house" or that "in all labor there is profit."

One chore made ironic the implication of Genesis that it was man who would bear sweat on his face for the sin of Eve, for it was woman who would labor supplying the most life-giving of substances, water. She needed water to prepare foods and clean the house, to satisfy the thirst of her hard-working husband and sons. She must carry it from somewhere, from a spring or creek, nearby the house if she were fortunate, and drag it out when soiled. On an average day she hauled the heavy pails eight to ten times, through heat, rain, or snow. On the first day of the week, laundry day, she lugged an additional fifty gallons (four hundred pounds) to fill the wash and rinse tubs—and then refilled the pails and carried out the dirtied leavings. In winter, she cut the ice to reach it. Cynthia Davison could ask her small children to bring in tinder or a log for the stove, but she could not have them haul buckets of water until they were nearer full-sized.

If men's work ended with sunset, women's work continued, for cooking, kitchen cleaning, and mending remained. It may have been less lonely for these settler women than for modern day, however, because the family would gather in the kitchen around the stove and by the tallow or sperm candle. There would be singing or reading aloud, or declaiming of poetry to lighten the atmosphere, then a Bible lesson and prayer before bed.

Because the Davison farm was so productive, and the family small in number, other females probably helped in the household. Poor families would "put out" their daughters to labor in more affluent homes until they married. Even with an extra hand or two, the Davison women found a few hours' rest only on the Sabbath. Consequently, Eliza had little schooling, if any, and although able to read the Bible, did not learn to write with correct grammar and spelling.[3] She would not be ignorant, however, for many of her day could read yet not write. Her knowledge was more practical, gained through experience, and she would always value doing and trying out over talking about or mulling over a problem.

Church provided the one regular social event with women from other families. The building would rattle not only from the hymn singing and the preacher's declamations, but from the scuffle of family dogs dashing about the pews, or the momentary visit of a rooster stepping in to crow a few arpeggios. Tobacco chewing being a requirement of masculinity, the floor grew sticky of spit, to which stuck the shells of the nuts members brought to sustain them through the long services. As a pious family, the Davisons attended two services, with a sedate noontime dinner between. Toys were put away, voices hushed, joking forbidden, and only religious reading allowed. While these restrictions seem harsh to modern sensibilities, they were welcome relief to bodies and nerves exhausted by the toil of farm life.

Of course, these tapestries of rural life cannot contain the shifts and richness brought on by challenge, caprice, tragic circumstance, and miracle. As we have seen, in 1824 the death of Cynthia Davison suddenly changed the patterns in Eliza's life. In 1836, another sudden shift came about with the appearance at the front stoop of a tall, broad-shouldered, brown-eyed, story-telling, card-playing stranger. His name was William "Big Bill" Rockefeller.

✳   ✳   ✳

A more incompatible attraction is hard to conceive.[4] Where others always remarked on Bill Rockefeller's roguery, they spoke of Eliza Davison's goodness. Yet this coupling is odd only for modern readers; it was a natural one for people of their day. Thus, before examining this unlikely pairing, it helps to understand the larger context of their lives.

Both had come of age during the Age of Jackson. Spindly Old Hickory presented himself as a common man and hero of the underdog. Although he was a wealthy slave owner and decidedly undemocratic, he convinced voters he was a backwoodsman eager to let the majority, not a monied elite, govern the young nation. Following his inauguration in 1829, cheering mobs crushed into the White House, breaking furniture in their scrabble over food and whiskey. Their boisterous enthusiasm reflected the average person's hope to share more in the riches of western expansion.

The other influence, one that developed in objection to some of Jackson's fiscal policies, was Whiggery. A new political party, Whigs originated among urban businessmen who wanted a stronger federal hand in developing transportation systems, securing a national banking system, and creating protective tariffs. They opposed the conservative Democrats, individualists who wanted to preserve the old agrarian economy, prevent the development of large commercial farms, and limit the role of manufacturing. Despite the elite origins of the party, it eventually attracted those rural residents who understood the tide was turning toward an economy dominated by industry.

Whigs tended to be evangelical Christians who wanted to reform people and society as well as hasten economic growth. They believed in the perfectability of humanity through self-discipline and self-control. Whigs sought to inhibit slavery, to eliminate such social evils as drink and prostitution, and to educate the citizenry through public schools. Thus Whigs, not Democrats, were the liberals of their day, albeit their reform interests were grounded in Scripture.[5] This moral base naturally attracted devout Protestants of all social classes.

The Whigs as an effective political party would not last many years, but their influence as an ideology would come to pervade nineteenth-century thinking. Whiggery was the unspoken credo of all who rose to the call of the steamboat and train whistles, who saw romance in these behemoth machines as symbols of the nation's advance. They were the restless, the challenged, the inspired. Moving ahead, getting on in the world, was a patriotic act, a means to show up the dissolute and corrupt European nations.

Bill and Eliza clearly took to these new ferments. As a forward-looking couple of the 1830s, they made a perfect whole, a fusion of material and spiritual optimism. Through the assistance of science, technology, and religion one could attain heaven on this earth as well as in the afterlife. Unlike their respective parents and siblings, who seemed content with the slower agrarian life, they were ready to prove the truth of these new beliefs.

Bill's parents, originally of Massachusetts stock, were recent migrants to the area. Godfrey and Lucy Rockefeller had nine children, of whom Bill was the oldest. Taller than her sturdy husband, Lucy had wide-set blue eyes and a bright smile. She was known to be highly competent and courageous. A family tale told of how she heard a noise in the barn late one night, ran to find a man who was stealing oats, grabbed him, whipped out her scissors, and cut a piece out of his coat. She then let him slip into the darkness. A few days later during dinner Lucy noticed that one of the men hired to help with the threshing had a hole in his jacket. She brought in the piece of cloth she had cut from the thief and pleasantly offered to repair the gash. She said nothing about the oats, but the man knew he had been found out. Bill inherited her salty courage.

The Rockefellers owned a farm fifty miles south of Lake Owego near Richford on the slopes of Michigan Hill, which was so steep that people joked about cows there being roped together like Alpine climbers. Pine, hemlock, and maple—a primeval forest from which the Iroquois had recently been routed—covered half the land; cleared meadow comprised the other half. The thirty tillable acres were poorer than the Davison spread, so eking out enough wheat, potatoes, and cattle for the family of eleven was strenuous. Fortunately, the boys were crack shots and could be counted on to bring in a steady supply of game. Although the children attended the religious services held at the log cabin school, the family was less pious than the Davisons. Neighbors remarked on the Rockefeller men's boisterous, frontier ways, their preference for turkey shooting, raccoon hunts, games of chance, and barn dancing over church attendance, self-discipline, and frugality.

When Eliza Davison met Bill Rockefeller, she was unsure of exactly what he did to earn a living. That he went away for periods and returned with pockets full of money was evident. In going into trade, he was presumably a man who questioned the common belief that "agriculture is the great wheel which moves all machinery of society."[6] More apparent as she came to know him, Bill Rockefeller exemplified a new idea introduced into popular thought, one that resolved the conflict between the Life of Virtue, where character and principle reigned, and the tempting material opportunities of a burgeoning industrialism. As Reverend Thomas P.

Hunt explained in *The Book of Wealth*, "From this common desire [to possess more property], may it not be presumed that it is a duty to be rich? And one thing is certain: no man can be obedient to God's will, as revealed in the Bible, without becoming wealthy."[7] That Christ and capitalism could be united was the essential bond between Eliza and Bill.

In a farming community, however, Bill's commercial absences fed rumor, including stories of horse thievery, a most despicable crime for a people dependent on the beasts for transportation. That he was sharp at cards and the best shot in the region did not always aid his reputation. Nonetheless, people praised Bill Rockefeller for his intelligence, his high spirits, his readiness to identify a need and fill it, as when he stocked a local lake with pickerel. Despite his hanging about saloons, he was also a teetotaler.

In truth, he was a traveling salesman who could likely flimflam if need be. In later years he would call himself a "doctor" and create timely "cures." While this seems quackery today, it was not necessarily so. Formally trained medical doctors were few and had brief education, primarily in healing wounds, setting bones, amputating limbs, and dispensing herb-based drugs. The drawing of copious amounts of blood, or "bleeding," was still a favorite treatment. The self-proclaimed itinerant doctors like Bill were really pharmacists providing remedies the women of the households would need in their role as major healers. Certainly they inflicted less harm than the physicians operating under unsanitary conditions without anesthesia. Most illnesses are self-limited, and much healing depends upon the placebo effect, whether a laying of hand or a pill that is believed to have curative powers. Thus men like Bill Rockefeller were valued resources to homesteaders.

One story further elucidates the importance of these travelling men to the local women in particular. Among Bill's remedies were certain red berries that he hawked as a cure for "female problems."[8] In explaining their use, Bill would whisper that women should never eat them when pregnant, else they miscarry. Because birth control was virtually nonexistent, women sought out abortifacients of this type. (Informed that long spells in hot water would cause miscarriage, wealthier women visited spas with hot springs to end unwanted pregnancies.)

Some of the gossip attached to Big Bill Rockefeller may have resulted from neighbors' envy or personal grudges. He would return from his travels with thick wads of bills, and pay up his debts immediately. His physical dominance and charisma surely intimidated some. That he would intermittently take charge in the community must have frustrated those leaders who volunteered year-round to oversee small squabbles and larger crises. Nonetheless, rarely does so much discredit attach to a reputation without some truth being present.[9]

On the other hand, neighbors always described Eliza as a "good woman," which then meant one who was pious, prim, devoted to home and to unselfish Christian service to others. She was frugal, austere, not given to smiles or laughter. A slender redhead with blue eyes and a gaunt face, she could appear hawkish, alert for indiscretion, and be severe in response to it. Where it is easy to imagine a man such as Bill—charming, dominating any scene, garrulous, entertaining, handsome, skilled in manly ways—one glimpses only shadowy portraits of Eliza. Perhaps she was so conforming to the model lady of the day that her individuality was quashed, unrecognized, Perhaps in later years people thought it unwise to criticize the mother of one of the nation's most successful men. Perhaps she was adept at disguising forbidden desires—through Bill Rockefeller she could vicariously engage secret passions without losing her reputation.

The story concerning their first encounter lingered in neighborhood gossip for a century afterwards, and while it may be apocryphal, its persistence shows Bill's impact upon others. It was said that one day he appeared at the Davison door with chalk and slate, the pretense of a deaf-and-dumb peddler. Smitten, Eliza purportedly exclaimed that were the handsome man not deaf and dumb, she would surely marry him. When Bill revealed his ruse, she welcomed his courting. Her father was not pleased with the smart-talking, easy-going young man, but he had no legal power to block twenty-four-year-old Eliza. Consequently, just a few months after meeting, on February 18, 1837, Eliza wed Bill in her family's parlor.

Bill took Eliza to the old homestead house on his family's farm, for his parents had built a larger house farther upslope. What Eliza saw that day was a typical farmhouse, a three-room clapboard cottage with attached stable and woodshed. She walked into the main bedroom, behind which was a kitchen/living room area and a smaller bedroom with an attic loft above. The ceilings were low, and the windows few and tiny to keep out the cold. Conveniently, a well stood near the door, so there would be no hauling water from the nearby brook, and both the kitchen and main bedroom had stoves. With Bill's friendly parents and many siblings living nearby, Eliza would not be isolated during his long absences.

✳   ✳   ✳

To add to Eliza's comfort, Bill hired Nancy Brown, a poor, beautiful young woman from Harford Mills to help about the house, an unusual provision for a young trader's wife. In 1838, Eliza gave birth to a daughter, Lucy, and a few months following Nancy bore a girl, Clorinda. In 1839, Eliza's first son, named for her father, John Davison, was born, and a few months later Nancy's daughter Cornelia arrived. Although Nancy Brown was not married, it was not unusual then for even pious people to engage in premarital intercourse. The most likely father could have been a poor farmer who could not offer Nancy the security provided by the Rockefellers. But neighbors, even relatives, identified Bill as the father, and Cornelia, who lived to maturity, developed into a tall, handsome, intelligent, and commanding personality. Bill, they said, though in love with Nancy Brown, had married Eliza for the five hundred dollars her father had promised upon her marriage.[10]

After several years, Nancy's brothers confronted Bill and forced him to send her away. Eventually she married and had other children, but until then Bill supported her family. Neighbors claimed that throughout this remarkable episode Eliza was tolerant of Bill's infidelity, and that she sent clothes and other goods to Nancy after she had moved out. (Rockefeller infidelity reappeared several years later. Bill's younger brother Miles left his wife and deserted to the West with another of Eliza's household help, Ella Brussee. He may even have married her bigamously, using the last name of Avery.)

If the story is true, Eliza's behavior is most curious. The community's explanation is simply that she loved Bill so much, and he was so much a law unto himself, that she tolerated whatever he did. As the aggrieved wife, she could have returned to her father for his protection. She could have called in her brother or local churchmen to defend her. She could have ousted Nancy Brown when Bill was on one of his trading jaunts. Were Nancy Brown pregnant from another man, she could have defended her reputation by appealing to her neighbors' Christian compassion toward a woman defiled. What is odd about the tale is that afterwards the community did not damn either Bill or Nancy in the retelling, but offered it matter-of-factly. Evidently, the norms of sexual behavior in the rural communities of the 1840s did not match the prevailing moral literature. Lacking direct proof, it is unwise to choose from the many explanations for this possible menage.

If the story is not true, one must wonder what so convinced Bill's own family and townspeople of its veracity. Had he been womanizing with someone else, and that fact later been confused with the situation of

Nancy Brown? Were perhaps Bill and Eliza protecting Nancy's reputation at the cost of their own?

Whatever, Eliza's intimacies with Bill continued. In 1841 she bore a son named William, and in 1843 another daughter, Mary Ann. During the latter pregnancy, Bill was gone for months, and the bill at Robbins general store reached nearly a thousand dollars. Even with in-laws close by, and hired hands, managing the household alone through the winter with four toddlers may have tested her fortitude. Or maybe not—for having grown up under hard conditions, she was well-prepared for the physical and emotional demands of such a life. Furthermore, current beliefs about good parenting assisted her, for she could set up strict rules and expect ready obedience from her children. The stories she told them urged respect of elders and conformity to their wishes, and any playmates they encountered were being raised similarly.

When Bill returned in 1844, with pockets full, as usual, he announced they were leaving the area. Following a three-day journey, the family arrived thirty miles north at the more fertile lands near Lake Owasco and the more populous town of Moravia. Named for the United Brethren who settled it, Moravia was a conscience-driven community, strong on temperance and antislavery. Eliza felt at home in this atmosphere.

The Rockefeller house, situated on a grassy knoll, overlooked pine trees and barns to a commanding twelve-mile view of the lake below. A charming tree-shaded brook, which John always recalled playing near, ran down the slope. Bill renovated the five-room cottage into a spacious kitchen and storeroom, and attached a two-story structure with living room below and three bedrooms above. Again, Eliza's domestic convenience was considered, for he constructed a flume to carry water from the brook to the storeroom, and put two stoves in the home.

Nonetheless, what was comfort in the 1840s seems rough today. One has only to read Lydia Maria Child's *The American Frugal Housewife* to realize how hard life was in middle-class households like the Rockefellers'. She reminded readers to throw a horse blanket over the pump in winter, lest it freeze. John and William recalled how they lay abed listening to the wind whistle through the hemlocks, and in winter shook off snowflakes falling through the roof cracks. In the morning, the icy cold brook water stung as they splashed their faces. In summer, because heating water, cooking, and baking kept the stove going all day, the kitchen was never the pleasant domestic setting idealized in artwork.

When Bill was away, Eliza was alone in protecting the household from vagabonds and thieves. John remembered how one day when she was abed with whooping cough, she heard sounds of rifling about the back of the house. Unable to get up and chase the intruders, she stood by the open window and sang "some old negro melody" to warn that the family were awake. The robbers ran off, taking only a set of harnesses from the carriage house.[11]

During visits home, Bill worked on the house and participated in the larger life of the community. When he saw the need for a school in Moravia, he surveyed the land, counting the buggy wheel revolutions to make his measurements, and rallied support for the project. Perhaps because of his commanding ways, he was chosen tax collector, a duty he enacted scrupulously. Decades later John spoke admiringly of how his father had taken a man's cow and kept it until the man paid the charges. During these visits he instructed the boys in the practical skills of business. For example, he taught them how to identify a cord of good wood and bargain hard for it.

Bill's presence also brought liveliness into the household. Fond of music, he played the melodeon in the evening to accompany the others' singing. When old enough, son John took piano lessons.

In 1845, Eliza bore twins Franklin and Frances. Six-year-old John was already helping with household and farm chores. In the garden, for example, Eliza set up string to parcel out the plot, and assigned each child an area to weed as he or she became old enough. By age seven John was up before dawn to milk the cow, and by age eight he could drive a horse. Like many successful men, late in life he described these experiences as exceptional, a basis for shaping his character and explaining his good fortune. Actually, he grew up little different from other farm boys, most of whom did not become millionaires.

Nonetheless, the elderly John D. Rockefeller recognized that he was not a self-made man, but had been cradled in capitalism by his mother. "I had a peculiar training in my home," he once remarked. "It seemed to be a business training from the beginning."[12] However much Eliza impressed outsiders with her piety, at home she discounted the biblical warning that money was the root of all evil (as would many of her day). To the contrary, she inspired love of its capture, of its doubling and tripling through thoughtful management. When their father was around, the children eavesdropped while she discussed various business decisions with him. She paid the children for chores, but it was John who developed a hoard, who sought ways to add to the glint of gold and silver coins. She encouraged his first business venture, turkey farming. The free-range, crafty hens hid their nests in brush. Eliza told John he could have the profits from any hidden broods he raised to maturity. To do so required him to track a hen for days to locate her nest, which, given his patient temperament, was congenial work.

Bill reinforced Eliza's materialism by introducing the boys to the tactics of commerce. He lent the boys money and called in the loans without warning to see if they had kept a reserve. He instructed them in earning and charging interest, a lesson John particularly appreciated, because it taught a way to multiply coins without hard labor. When John was eight, Bill took him on a business trip to Syracuse. There his first view of paved streets, wooden sidewalks, and marbled hotel lobbies thrilled rather than intimidated him. Although it was much smaller than the cities Bill had spoken about, John suddenly understood how much opportunity awaited from beyond the peaceful Finger Lakes farmlands.

Like other middle-class mothers of her time, it was Eliza who inculcated the habits that fostered success in nineteenth-century business. She was the disciplinarian, who ruled through force of personality most of the time, and with a switch "for love" when need be. Neighbors noted she never scolded her children or shouted at them, but patiently ruled. One visiting youngster said he felt like a "tame cat" anytime he was around her, that he never saw others disobey her.[13] Her rules emphasized order and respect for others. They were not to trim their nails in the house because inevitably some scraps would remain for someone else to pick up, and that was inconsiderate. Similarly, they knew to wipe their feet at the door to reduce others' labor. Their lives ran on schedules, as was happening in offices and factories. Although they learned farming skills, it was the form and style of their work that mattered—that it be done, and done well. Eliza was not raising her boys to become farmers.

As in any family, due to temperamental differences the children responded in varying ways to the demands made upon them. Of daughters Lucy, Mary Ann, and Frances hardly any history remains. Little more is known of Franklin, apart from his hot-headedness and rebelliousness. More outgoing and free-spirited, William took after his namesake father, yet did not seem as troublesome to raise as quiet, secretive John. On the one hand, John shared his mother's attentiveness to detail and frugality, and her religious devotion. But he was also a dreamer who avoided work. Eliza would complain, "John, if you don't wake up and set to work with a will, you'll find yourself in the county house."[14] She often had to stand at the bottom of the loft stair and call up in the morning, "Come, my son; time to get up and milk your cow!" What appeared sloth—a major sin of the day—was really the use of cleverness to avoid work. It was this "laziness" that would nurture John D. Rockefeller's later achievements, for he would always think of new ways of doing things with the least effort. His sister Lucy captured his manner perfectly: "When it's raining porridge, you'll find John's dish right side up."

Much as he adored his mother, John was not above some deviousness. One day, when Eliza was bedridden and discovered he had failed to do his chores, she told him to bring in a switch. He did, but he nicked it first so it would break while she hit him. When she realized what he had done, she sent him out for another branch.

Behind John's cleverness was his endless curiosity. Although both parents required that the boys have good schooling, they treated education more as a necessary step in the forging of a career than an inherent value. John was not as good a student as William. He demonstrated no particular intellectual talent, although he loved number games involving mental calculation. Yet he was more earnest than William, and so spent hours exploring books. Eventually Eliza concluded that she "didn't know what John is going to do when he grows to be a man, but I'm sure of one thing—he won't want. He is always studying."

John was also a terrible tease, particularly toward his siblings. His position as eldest son was so significant to him that in old age he reminded an interviewer that William was "one year, one month and eight days younger than I." Consequently, William was the brunt of most of the jokes, until one day when he finally struck back at his tormenting older brother. Mary Ann hated the way John would appear with a solemn, straight face, pull a trick, then smile impishly in self-congratulation over his accomplishment. Teasing was the only form John's hostility or aggression would ever take, and by adulthood he learned to control even this expression of negative feeling. Consequently, he grew unaware of his hostility and his devious expressions of it. This blind spot was to assist his later corporate leadership, for he could order devious acts against competitors without recognizing his actions as ruthless.

One of John's most curious memories of his mother concerns the death of his baby sister Frances. In November of 1846, Dr. William Cooper began to make frequent visits to the household to treat Frances, who was ailing of later undisclosed illness. His ministering could not prevent her death the following summer. When it came time to bury the toddler, Eliza sent John out to the field to clear it of stones. It was not until later that he understood that the purpose of her orders had been to protect him from witnessing the interment. Her behavior is odd for a time when death of family members, children in particular, was a common occurrence. It is stranger still in light of the then Christian emphasis upon children becoming angels in heaven, the wrapping of youthful death in a vision of pleasantness and beauty. The story of this deception is the closest John ever came to implying that Eliza ever did anything wrong in raising him. She was the Mother Perfect.

To appreciate Eliza's complex character, one must look at her choice of the Baptist faith and its place in the culture. Today "Baptist" popularly conjures a fundamentalist Bible-directed Christian of reactionary bent. This stereotype overlooks the many disagreements among church members on key matters, such as the primacy of the Scriptures or the autonomy of congregations. Baptists cannot even agree on the roots of their movement. Since the Bible lends itself to many interpretations, its adherents are diverse. Debates and schisms characterize Baptist history, and its members are strong individualists. It was this individualism that, prior to the American Revolution, provoked condemnation and persecution of Baptists, particularly in New England. Since the Revolution stood for the triumph of liberty, Baptist thought gained in acceptance afterwards, despite the often ornery temperament of its adherents, who continued to argue among themselves and against other churches.

Nevertheless, certain themes united Baptists during the early 1800s. One was the belief that one's life choices must be tested against the Old and New Testaments. The metaphors, symbols, and stories of the Scripture ran through everyday conversation. From earliest days, Eliza's children would hear her explain or instruct through reference to the wisdom of the Proverbs, the trials of the Israelites, and the parables of Jesus. They learned to examine their experiences in light of biblical wisdom. John found The Book to be a steady beacon lighting the best pathways to take in life. (His brother William was not so convinced, and while not quitting religion, did not treat it as the foundation for his actions.)

Another unifier among Baptists was the local congregation as the living expression of Christian community. Each individual church embodied the Church at large, and was thought spiritually endowed to govern itself. Church members not only claimed Jesus Christ as their Lord and Savior, but covenanted to practice their faith diligently. Baptism by immersion, though not required in all congregations, was a believer's sign to the congregation of ultimate obedience to Christ. Baptists also encouraged the visible demonstration of faith to nonbelievers.

In recent years, Baptists who witness for Christ are more biblically focused than in Eliza's day. Their public actions are narrow and center upon individual morality, specifically with regard to the family and sexuality. In the 1840s, the Baptist witness incorporated many social causes, including the control of alcohol, antislavery, and education—in other words, aligned with other denominations that supported Whiggery. Baptists in cities joined in campaigns against prostitution and for public health. The strife over slavery would eventually split the denomination, with the Southerners separating into a Convention of their own. Given this involvement of their church in social causes, the Rockefeller children learned that Christian service extended beyond the church walls, into the community at large.

By the time Eliza was raising her children, the Baptists had established preparatory schools and colleges. The initial impetus for such schools (which include Brown, Colby, Baylor, Bucknell, and Colgate) was the education of ministers; it soon expanded to incorporate the notion of universal education. Baptist success in education was remarkable because the church attracted more rural, less affluent members than did the Episcopalians or Presbyterians. Consequently, it offered its families religious support for economic mobility. A poor Baptist boy then had a better chance for a church-sponsored scholarship than a poor boy of any other denomination. Although the Rockefeller children did not attend Baptist-founded schools, because none were in the immediate area, during Sunday School they found an emphasis upon literacy and learning.

A key feature of Bible study was assimilating recent scientific discoveries into interpretation. Baptist children studied the geography and history of the Holy Lands, along with the culture of the ancient Israelites. They were taught to place biblical events within the known chronology and politics of the era. The better-educated ministers and Sunday School teachers knew Greek, and discussed the fine points of word meanings in translation to English. Since this was pre-Darwin, the discoveries of archeologists and classicists were thought to illumine, not threaten the validity of Scripture. John and his siblings were aware, for example, of patriarchal rule and slavery because comparisons were often made between such practices in ancient times and in the American South.[15]

Others have noted the Baptist roots of Eliza's condemnation of alcohol, but nothing has been said of the feminist leanings of the denomination. Baptist schools were among the first to venture into coeducation, and even some of their colleges had "Female Institutes." Women's causes were especially strong in the Burned-Over District. (The first women's rights convention was held in 1848 in Seneca Falls, New York.) The Baptists even had someone analogous to a female saint. Her story would be well-known and held up as an example to Eliza and her brood.

She was born Ann Haseltine in 1789 in Bradford, Massachusetts, of parents who recognized her intelligence and nourished her interest in learning.[16] Although Ann attended Bradford Academy, which fostered the Christian life, she went to balls and parties, enjoyments that took time away from daily prayer and Bible reading. One day she accidentally took up Hannah More's *Strictures on Female Education,* and was captivated by its first words: "She that liveth in pleasure, is dead while she liveth." A few months later she read John Bunyan's *Pilgrim's Progress,* which inspired her with his vision of the challenge of the narrow path. Despite attempts to quit the social crowd, she remained preoccupied with "vanity and trifling."

At sixteen, during a revival, Ann was thrown into a turmoil about her life, and she grew hateful of God for daring to throw people into hell. With further reflection she identified with Christ, for she concluded that God offered justice through His son, who promised salvation to those who followed His way. She found the knowledge empowering, for it gave direction to her own purpose, that she could save souls from damnation by saving sinners through the message of Christ. This was not a simplistic conversion, for her journal continued to mark thoughtful questions on theology and the temptations to forego her chosen path. She became an informal home missionary, going into people's homes and instructing them of her belief.

When she was twenty-one, Ann met Adoniram Judson, a graduate of Baptist-supported Brown University. Lacking any clear religious convictions, he went to Andover Theological Seminary out of curiosity, although some might say he was unconsciously following a call. In his senior year, a course on Eastern Missions inspired him to "rescue the perishing millions" of Asia. With several like-minded friends, he helped organize the first American Mission Society. He and Ann found much compatible in their beliefs, which had originated in doubt. Following their marriage, in 1812 they travelled to Calcutta, India where, after much study and debate, they formally became Baptists.

At a service honoring and praying for the couple before their departure, the Rev. Jonathan Allen expressed a view of women indicative of the liberal thinking among Ann's religious circle: "It is remarkable, too, that Jehovah has thought proper to mention, in his word, with honorable commendation, many 'holy women,' . . . The Bible, though written in a part of the earth where the female character is undervalued, is full of testimony to the moral and intellectual worth of woman. It is no small evidence of its divine origin, that it thus rises above a prejudice which seems to be universal, except where the Bible has dispelled it. Christianity alone teaches the true rank of women."[17] Ann Judson would rise to this call to prove his interpretation correct.

The Judsons did most of their missionary work in Burma. Unfortunately, in 1824, a British invasion provoked the Burmese to imprison and torture all English-speaking men, and Ann, then pregnant, spent her days seeking food to take to her husband. A year and a half later, British victory resulted in freedom for the missionaries. Ann returned to Rangoon to revive their work there, while Adoniram went to the States on missionary society business. There he received word that both Ann and his infant daughter had died of fever.

Ann Judson's story inspired Baptists for more than its lesson of Christian martyrdom. From her first encounters overseas, she was sensitive to the situation of women and published reports of their subordinate position. She was the first traveller to alert American women to such practices in India as men's referring to wives as "dogs," forcing them to eat separately, and suttee (the widow's pyre). In Burma, she observed, the women's material conditions were better, and they could eat in the company of men, but they essentially suffered "under the tyrannic rod of those who should be their protectors."[18] Consequently, she recognized the need for female education, not only that women be able to study the Bible, but that they find some amelioration of the degradation of their sex.

Judson proposed a model of political participation slowly emerging in the young democracy with its egalitarian aims. "Shall we [women] sit down in indolence and ease," she wrote, "indulge in all the luxuries with which we are surrounded, and which our country so bountifully affords, and leave beings like these, flesh and blood, intellect and feeling, like ourselves, and of *our own sex*, to perish, to sink into eternal misery?" Judson was speaking of more than Christian salvation. Just as slaves and abolitionists invoked Scriptural metaphors of deliverance to refer to their earthly liberation, so she used them to write of secular as well as spiritual freedom. The two were not separate: Church and politics were one.

Ann Judson was one of many devout Christian women now forgotten, who planted the seeds for the more assertive women's rebellions of the 1840s. Though Eliza Rockefeller never participated publicly in woman's rights activities, she was embedded in a religious culture that nurtured independence for women as well as men. Eliza's spirit readily gained obedience from the children, and garnered respect throughout the community. When Bill's behavior was egregious, she needed not feel victimized, for her Baptist beliefs emphasized the imperfection of humanity. His transgressions gave opportunity for her to show mercy and compassion, further occasion for her to bear witness to her Christian faith.

*   *   *

Eliza had little opportunity to mourn the death of Frances. She still had five children of very different personalities to nurture, farm hands to direct, and household helpers to manage. Bill continued to disappear, and during this time stories of his horse thievery grew. Eliza endured the gossip, which could not have been easy for such a virtuous person. As far as neighbors could tell, her loyalty to Bill was absolute.

That trust became most difficult in 1848. Early that year Bill hired a new domestic, Ann Vanderbeak, and neighbors gossiped that he was having improper relations with her.[19] The matter became public in an indictment entered on July 26, 1849, in the city of Auburn, in Cayuga County:

> That William A. Rockefeller late of the Town of Moravia in the County of Cayuga, on the first day of May in the year of our Lord one Thousand eight hundred and forty eight, with force and arms at the Town of Moravia in said County, in and upon one Ann Vanderbeak in the Peace of God with the People of the State of New York then and there being, violently did make an assault on her, the said Ann Vanderbeak, then and there violently and against her will feloniously did ravish and carnally know . . .

Four days later, Eliza's father sued Bill in the Supreme Court of Cayuga for failure to pay a debt of $1,175 owed him on two promissory notes. His plea stated that Bill had asked him for assistance in bail on the rape charges, to which he had responded that he "was too old a man to become bail for anybody." He also stated that he had not seen Bill since then, and that Eliza informed him that her husband had "absconded and cannot now be found within the state." Davison added that Bill's disappearance was motivated by Bill's "intent to defraud his creditors." Sheriff Joseph P. Smith certified that he had seized some of Bill's property on July 1, and that on August 1, the defendant was nowhere to be found. A few months later Eliza's father changed his will, directing that executors would oversee her interest in the estate. He left it to them to contribute annually to her welfare as they saw fit. In this way he made certain that Bill could never control the money—unless, of course, Eliza handed it over to him.

The Rockefeller family doctor, William Cooper, had also been indicted for assault and battery with intent to ravish Ann Vanderbeak. He appeared at the courthouse and placed five hundred dollars bail. On the other hand, Bill neither appeared nor did the sheriff apprehend him. For reasons unknown, neither case made it to trial, so no review of the official evidence is available.

In 1917, when the family hired William Inglis to write a biography of John D. Rockefeller, his interviews with many people in the community resulted in contradictory accounts of this episode. One respondent said he often heard unkind gossip about Bill, though none of the stories convinced him of Bill's wrongdoing; another said the rape charge had been brought by the brothers of Charlotte Hewitt, with whom Bill had been having an affair for several years; another said Bill was "always a gentleman." These inconsistencies are not surprising given that the informants had been children at the time of the indictment. In his notes, Inglis systematically discounted those who supported the indictment. The most telling weakness in the charge, he observed, was Ann Vanderbeak's waiting of more than a year to bring the indictment. Yet the date of the indictment may not reflect her initial communication with authorities. At that time, a woman had to present overwhelming evidence, preferably witnesses, to press a rape charge. In cases such as Ann Vanderbeak's, where the alleged assailant was her employer, getting authorities to act upon her claims would have been even more difficult. Other indirect evidence leans the judgment in favor of Ann Vanderbeak: John Davison's hostile lawsuit and will, Bill's disappearance, and talk of his involvement with other women.

Whatever the truth, the charges placed Eliza in disgrace. It was one thing for a man to dally on the side, especially with a woman of lower class, but the double standard of the time did not tolerate rape. Many in town sympathized with Eliza. Others held her complicitous in Bill's repeated embroilments, for the proof of a saintly woman was her reining in of her husband's lust and immorality. Clearly, Eliza had failed on that account. Through such legerdemain of logic, the wife, also a victim, became identified with her sinful husband.

Apart from brief and surreptitious visits from Bill, Eliza was left alone with the children through the long winter. It semed as though the curse of the stars had finally struck.

2

Cradled in Capitalism

"A wise man will hear, and will increase learning; and a man of understanding shall attain unto wise counsels."

—Proverbs I:5

Married to a fugitive, Eliza prepared her household to flee the region. Her father had come out publicly against her husband, and in so doing forced her hand to choose between the two. To return to her father would be to admit defeat, as well as place her under his rule. It would also limit her children's opportunities to remain in that isolated farming region. To go on her own and move to a town or city with better schooling and job prospects for her sons was not an option either. Women like Eliza had little likelihood of earning a comfortable wage. The result would be not only impoverishment, but worse, the exposure of her children to the temptations of the streets—hooliganism, tobacco, liquor. Anyway, divorce was an anathema, something hardly to consider. Worse for Eliza, who wrapped her life in motherhood, the children could become the custody of their father.

All these practical reasons aside, a simpler reason may account for Eliza's fidelity to her wayward husband. She loved him, and in his odd way he gave what affection he could in return. Much more commonly of men of his ilk, those wanderers for fortune, those rebels to constricted domesticity, deserted their families completely. All over New England and the mid-Atlantic states, husbands were forgoing their vows and disappearing. In a day without computers and paper trails, vanishing and starting a life elsewhere was for men at least relatively easy. Thus credit must go to Bill as a provider and a father.

In April of 1850, Bill Rockefeller arrived with a wagon to move the family south to Tioga County. Because this placed him out of the Cayuga court jurisdiction, some neighbors believed he was escaping the short arm of the law. Within several months, Bill leased a house about three miles east of town on the old River Road. From there Eliza and the children

looked out across the open fields of buckwheat and hay to the Susque-
hanna River below. Close by lived the family of Marcus La Monte, whose
children became playmates for the Rockefeller brood.

As a river town, Owego was a commercial center, more of a small city
than the village of Moravia. Barges and steamboats moved lumber and
farm produce south, trading goods north. Settled by New Englanders
following the Revolution, Owego had the pristine, orderly, and bustling
appearance of Yankee practicality. There were lumber mills, a foundry,
and soon to be, a shoe factory. A new jail and sheriff's residence were
under construction near the county courthouse. The noise of carpenters
sawing and hammering added to the cacophony. They rushed from sunup
until nightfall six days a week to replace seventy buildings recently destroyed in a disastrous fire. Another reason for the optimistic rebuilding
was the recent arrival of the Erie Railroad line, which now connected
Owego to New York City over two hundred miles to the east. Walking
about the streets of this vibrant town, young John and William would see
the future, the certain winning out of industrial over agrarian interests. In
Owego, the family no longer farmed to sell a surplus; it grew food only
for its own consumption.

Owego also reflected the cultural and spiritual preferences of the
transplanted Yankees. Literature and the arts were everyday concerns, and
furthered by improvements in publishing that made books and magazines
cheap. Lithography allowed reproductions of Renaissance masterpieces,
sentimental American scenes, and western landscapes. Readers could buy
sermons and tracts, novels and travel stories. Several Owegans were in the
process of forming *St. Nicholas Magazine,* which would grow to national
prominence. Among the many churches was a Baptist congregation, and
Eliza offered to pay a Presbyterian neighbor to drive the family to a
church different from his own.

In its early years Owego had been typical of American communities, a
place where whiskey flowed easily—provided free by merchants to encourage trade and by politicians to lubricate the voters into action. During the 1840s, however, the Washingtonian Total Abstinence Association
took hold; it forced almost all liquor licenses withdrawn and the bars
closed. While Owegans dressed fashionably and knew the latest ideas
from New York City, they guarded against "urban sin." No prostitutes
walked among the proper ladies out on their daily shopping promenades.
No counterfeit beggars wore reversible signs, with "Paralyzed since 39"
on one side, and "Blind since 44" on the other. No pickpockets roamed
the streets—because no crowds existed to make easy pickings. No bands
of rowdy and drunken immigrant boys taunted the pedestrians. Gentility

marked public life. Regardless of income, citizens strained to portray themselves as "middling sort," the civilized backbone of the young democracy.

Propriety began at home, of course, but unlike smaller towns in frontier New York State, Owego offered advanced schooling to inculcate the values of proper citizenship and life success. Certainly this opportunity to improve the children's education motivated the Rockefellers' choice of a new home.

Established in 1827, Owego Academy occupied a three-story brick building adorned with spire and bells. Its director was Reverend William Smith, a noted classical scholar who taught Sunday School from a Greek Bible. Typical of such institutions of the time, the curriculum included English and mathematics, various sciences, Latin, Greek, French, political economy, and moral science. Besides taking classes, a student attended daily devotions and exercise periods, turned in an original essay every two weeks, and regularly practiced oratory. Less typical perhaps was the emphasis upon independent, pragmatic thought rather than memorization. As the catalogue noted, "the analytic method of instruction is especially employed, leading to an investigation of every rule learned, and of every scientific operation performed. The student is thus enabled, not only to acquire a knowledge of facts, but also the methods by which they can be applied to the practical business of life." None of its pupils would take this pedagogical philosophy to greater height than John D. Rockefeller.

Fellow students noted John's enthusiasm for anything scientific and mechanical. The telegraph was just coming through the region then, and he had many questions when it was demonstrated in the school laboratory. (After school, he may have joined the townspeople who sat on fences below the wires in hopes of spying an electric message twitch by.) Similarly, he looked forward to Saturday mornings, for it was then the entire student body gathered in the principal's room on the top floor to watch various experiments. It was well-equipped with a Galvanic battery, an electric generator wheel, an orrery (mechanical model of the planets), and a human skeleton.

Teachers were stern and demanding. Most terrifying of all was Mr. Coburn, the mathematics instructor who snapped his finger off his thumb to thunk the head of any child who failed a memorization exercise. Of all his studies John preferred mental calculation, and enjoyed working the most complicated problems out in his head. Yet his skill here, so often noted later in life, was due more to his persistence and to Mr. Coburn's finger than to inborn talent. Mr. Hardy, the grammar teacher, threw his ruler across the room at any inattentive pupil. John, who may have been dyslexic, found spelling difficult and thus faced Mr. Hardy with trepidation.[1] To compensate, like many with that malfunction, he developed a prodigious memory and ability to analyze complex problems without benefit of paper.

Owego Academy was also unusual in its being coeducational. Support for the education of females outside the home had been growing since the Revolution. Nevertheless, girls attended school for fewer years than boys, and private schools such as this one were more commonly all-male. Owego used religion to argue the contrary. "[Coeducation is] the powerful stimulus which has been found by experience to be more efficacious in developing the intellectual capacities than all others combined, simply because it is the plan by God designed, as is evident from the family relation of sisters and brothers." John's being among females that were treated as peers may have shaped his later attraction to self-assured women.

Of course, Eliza most influenced his attitude toward women. Freed from overseeing a farm, in Owego she had more time to attend to Christian duties. Townsfolk grew accustomed to her going out in the afternoons in a black silk dress, never in casual calicos, to visit neighbors and attend to others' needs. She paid her bills promptly and hired the less fortunate to do sewing and other domestic chores. She no longer feared robbers at night, for she hired railroad worker Hiram Odell to live with the family for protection as well as to handle the heavy work. As her life grew easier materially, she did not ease the demands she made of herself. If in Owego no gossip passed concerning the Rockefellers, it was much due to the visibility of Eliza's dignity and charity.

Many middle-class American boys in the 1840s and 1850s had parents similar to Bill and Eliza: fathers away for long periods of time, mothers dominating the discipline and moral instruction. So feminine was the home atmosphere that boys wore dresses and smocks during their early years. Once freed from the constraints of gowns after age six, most such boys ganged together to create a world apart from the influence of their mothers. So common were these groupings that writers such as "Mrs. Manners" in 1853 deplored the "disagreeable cubs" and asked why gentle, polite boys were such rarities.[2]

Away from the female realm of the home, boys established places where dirt, noise, and roughhousing supplanted gentility. They hiked, swam, and skated together; they played leapfrog, tag, and marbles. They taunted one another, played mean tricks, beat each other up and, at their worst, tortured animals. Proving one's aggressiveness was so important that the preferred side in games of Settler-and-Indian was that of the supposedly more barbaric Indian. Although the boys spoke of loyalty, friendship, and brotherhood, close ties were short-lived, for a new contest could realign the status of the gang's members. Gangs formed and set against one another: Protestant on Catholic, Yankee on Irish, railroad workers' sons against shop owners'. Such experiences eased the transition to the world of adult masculinity, where social skills, competitiveness, and self-confidence were assets to success in business. Boys taught each other mastery over nature and stoicism in the face of pain—very different lessons from the ones their mothers were trying to teach.

Strikingly missing from John D. Rockefeller's early history is any reference to such boy playmates, partly because Eliza's reach on her eldest son was too long. Before school the children had chores, such as milking the cow, and afterwards they joined the La Monte children for studying. John also liked to add to his penny supply by working for others, and he practiced the piano for hours at a time. Partly, too, John felt the responsibility (and never the burden) of being the oldest male in the household when his father was away. His solitary temperament also set him apart. He lacked his brother William's gregariousness and physical agility. While others competed, John sat on the sidelines and kept score with notches on a stick. He was happier on his own, lost in thought, and as a result he developed little inclination for rough-and-tumble competition.

Accordingly, his outbursts against female-enforced confinement were few and quickly ceased. His notion of bad behavior was clambering up to the school roof, where he could rest on the ridge pole and read. Thus, more than other young men of his time, John D. Rockefeller incorporated feminine ideals into his notion of masculinity. A good man honors the Lord, is temperate in mind and body, works industriously, and shares his comforts with others less fortunate. Christian men of the day revered these principles as well, but seldom expressed them in the free-for-all economic battle that the boys observed from afar. Most Owego observers looked at the skinny lad and saw nothing particularly remarkable in this rule-minded, colorless boy whose most notable quality was not intelligence or manly drive, but doggedness. What would prove to be John D. Rockefeller's uniqueness as a businessman and philanthropist was his remaining a Mama's Boy.

John also impressed neighbors with his love of beauty, both visual and musical. His appreciation was sensual. His awe of a stand of trees and the rhythmic splashes of a brook rushing alongside suggests exposure to the Transcendentalist essayists. He would agree with Ralph Waldo Emerson that "Most persons do not see the sun," and the "true lover of nature is he . . . who has retained the spirit of infancy even into the era of manhood."[3]

Perhaps it was her recognition of John's unusual sensitivity that had led Eliza earlier to protect him from the burial of his little sister. One day the La Montes sent a message for Eliza to come to their house to fetch John. That morning, upon learning that one of their young daughters had died, he appeared in their front yard, where he threw himself down prostrate and refused to move or eat. It was a sight that another La Monte daughter would never forget. It was an act that would prove to Eliza the depths of John's compassion, and validate her effectiveness as a mother who had taught her eldest son Christian virtue.

Eliza was greatly contented with such a son. His disobedience, which was seldom, had an impish element and he was quick to accept his punishment. When she tied him to a tree for a whipping, he went willingly. She must have sensed he sympathized with her having to raise three independent boys and two daughters without much help from his father.

Some neighbors suspected that John held a large grudge against his father for neglecting his mother, and that he felt compelled to compensate for her unrequited love. For no matter how badly Bill Rockefeller behaved, people noted that Eliza was endlessly faithful. She once remarked to a friend how at night she would go out and look at the moon and imagine Bill, hundreds of miles away, looking at the same moon. Her son John could not imagine the pull of such passion on his mother, and possibly never would.

In 1853 Bill Rockefeller arrived and moved his family again, this time to the Western Reserve of northern Ohio. Although some biographers suggest escape from the law was once again behind the migration, more likely it was the pull of the West. During these years, American families were on the move, tempted by California gold rushes, Iowa farm lands, Midwestern factories. This "Great Restlessness" made a virtue of mobility. Forced migration, sheer neglect, and outright genocide had eliminated much Native American resistance to settlers. The Mexican-American war freed the continent from coast to coast for exploration, and the call of Manifest Destiny propelled a patriotic as well as economic imperative to pack up a household and start off westward.

The Western Reserve had once belonged to Connecticut, and in 1792 had been assigned to those inhabitants of that state's towns who had suffered losses inflicted by raids of the British army during the Revolution. Little settlement occurred, however, until canals in the 1830s and railroads in the 1840s provided better transportation. By the 1850s, with only 25,600 in population, Cleveland had become a focal point for commercial development. Developing transportation put the city at the cross-roads to Pittsburgh, Cincinnati, Detroit, Chicago, and frontier areas of Indiana and Illinois. Its foundries processed the iron and copper ores from the mines of Michigan; its traders shipped in furniture, stoneware, dry goods, livestock, and whiskey to supply the frontier explorers and set-tlers; its bankers extended credit to merchants and entrepreneurs. While Bill Rockefeller could not have known it at the time, certain discoveries in the mountains of Pennsylvania would mean that his sons' move to the Western Reserve would situate them within reach of unimagined wealth.

The family moved in with one of Bill's sisters, a Mrs. Huniston, in Strongsville, Ohio, but John and William took a room at Mrs. Woodin's boarding house on Erie Street in Cleveland so that they could attend high school. Boarding out was a common rite of passage for young men, who would use their landladies as maternal substitutes to ease the final separa-tion from their real mothers. The brothers paid a dollar a week each for their lodgings, meals, and informal guidance about the city's temptations which any Christian lad should eschew.

The Rockefeller brothers found the city's setting dramatic, a visual metaphor for progress and promise. Most of its buildings sat upon a high bluff and plateau running along Lake Erie, while the Cuyahoga River snaked through a deep ravine at the western end of the develop-ment. The homes were spacious with rolling green lawns and so tree laden that residents referred to the town as the "Forest City." Church steeples were many and dominated the vista. Yet smoke and coal dust choked the lungs, and smeared the whitewashed houses with soot. Busi-nesses, stores, and factories formed a crazy quilt mixed up with resi-dences. For country boys, the evidence of the vigorous economy and ready moneymaking provided thrill and challenge. Employment in such a city meant freedom from the vagaries of agriculture, the insistent physical demands of working the land.

By completing Central High, the only high school in the city, the boys knew they would be much better educated than the average American man of the day; fewer than two in a hundred accomplished so much. The principal, who was later to head a theological seminary, was a courteous man who did not believe harsh treatment necessary to motivate students. There, John in particular applied himself in his solemn, persistent man-ner, and continued his narrow interest in mathematical topics. Based on the opening lines of a speech he made, classmates nicknamed him "Old-Pleased-Although-I'm-Sad." Despite courses in the classics, literature, science, and art—at both Owego Academy and Central High—John D. Rockefeller would complete his education with little understanding of culture, history, and politics. Such lack of breadth was common in a country where a man was judged by his occupation.

If Eliza was no longer present daily in her elder sons' lives, her influence remained strong. John's major diversions were two: music and religion. He continued his piano lessons, and joined a church choral group as well. One of his favorite songs, which others heard in the mornings throughout his life went:

> *I'd be a butterfly, born in a bower*
> *Where roses and lilies and violets meet!*
> *I would not struggle for place nor for power,*
> *Nor sigh for wealth and slaves at my feet.*

His major enthusiasm was for church activities. He and William joined the recently formed Erie Street Baptist Church, where both signed up for the Sunday School class taught by William J. Sked, a stern, knowledgeable teacher of Scripture. In 1854, John came forward for public baptism, and became a clerk of the church. There he quickly proved himself adept at stirring up contributions from men much older than himself. It was not so much his salesmanship as his earnest sincere model of stewardship that convinced others to give more generously.

Out of the New England origins of its settlers, the Western Reserve manifested the social values as well as religious fervor of its Congregationalists, Baptists, and Methodists. It boosted educational opportunity, so that believers could study religious and moral works alongside the Bible, and be thoughtful in their individual spiritual development. Public schools in America then were really quasi-religious schools, where Protestant themes were inculcated, and where prayer meetings were held before and after class. (Considerable anti-Catholic prejudice wracked the nation at the time, a particular fear being that Papal influence would contaminate the classrooms.)

As in the Burned-Over District, the majority of the denominations fostered temperance, woman's rights, and abolitionism. By the time the Rockefellers moved to Ohio, the slavery debate overwhelmed other reforms. The state was a major conduit for the Underground Railroad, the Ohio River being the "River Jordan" in slave songs that spoke of a yearning for release. The counties just above the river held many poor white people who had fled the South because they realized slavery restricted their own economic gain. Consequently, they did not mind the fleeing slaves—so long as they moved on. In the central and northern counties, the numerous New England immigrants imported their abolitionism.

Oberlin, with its fervid Congregationalist citizenry, was the nucleus for this activity. Nonetheless, the majority of Ohioans were opposed to the Underground Railroad.

Despite neighbors' disapproval, many citizens were willing to break the laws and face attack from roving slave hunters. They clothed and fed the escapees, tended their injuries, made secret rooms to hide them, prayed with them, transported them under cover of hay in wagons, and passed them on from one safehouse to another until a Lake Erie port was reached. Towns competed with one another to keep bounty hunters from succeeding. As one frustrated slave capturer observed of one Ohio community, "Might as well hunt the devil there as to hunt a nigger!"[4] Of all Eliza's children, her oldest son, used to responsibility for his younger siblings, most absorbed a sense of compassion for the slaves.

While he was attending Central High, John made several lifelong friends. One was a stocky, square-shouldered boy he met on the high school debating team. His name was Mark Hanna, a youth who would also find great business success and political influence in the Republican Party. At critical moments in adulthood the two would support one another.

The others were two sisters who had grown up in a pious family fervent in its support of social causes. Lucy "Lute" and Laura Celestia "Cettie" Spelman were petite, dark-haired, dark-eyed daughters of prosperous businessman Harvey Buel Spelman and his wife Lucy Henry. Lute, who was two years older than Laura, had been adopted. The story is vague, with hints of her being the child of an impoverished relative, but she was so much like Laura that no one guessed at their different parentage. The third child in the family, Henry Jennings Spelman, was two years behind the girls at the high school.

Both Harvey and Lucy Henry were born in Massachusetts, but met in Ohio, where they married in 1835. They first settled in Kent, where daughter Laura was born, but soon moved in 1841 to Akron. The Spelman house was built of sandstone, only one room deep, with a large two-story porch of massive oaken timbers. Harvey Spelman kept a store near the Ohio Canal, and prospered for much of the time. Consequently, the children's lives were more stable and secure than that of the Rockefellers' offspring. Their father's reputation was not only spotless, but admirable.

Both Spelman parents were exemplars of Congregationalist activism. Lucy Henry was a committed abolitionist. Once she remarked that the only time she had ever cooked on Sundays was when she was hiding runaway slaves. Among those who stayed with the family was Sojourner

Truth, the great African-American orator and defender of both abolition and women's rights. Harvey organized Congregational churches in several communities. As a member of the Ohio State Legislature, he made establishing a system of public education his major goal. Consequently, the Spelman daughters had a richer view of Christian service than did John D., whose mother was less given to consideration of issues beyond the concerns of her family and circle of friends. (Having no legal or civil status, American women seldom voiced strong political and social opinions. Lucy Henry Spelman was an exception.)

When Laura was eight, her parents entertained a prominent foreign missionary, who impressed her with his stories of "the heathen gods." When he departed, he wrote out a statement that she pasted in one of her books: "I promise, by the help of God, to go as a missionary to the heathen, if God permits."[5] Several years later she confessed her faith in Christ, and asserted this promise as her guide. For many years she waited for the call to become a foreign missionary, but it was never to come.

As a result of wildcat banks and panics, Harvey Spelman's business fell bankrupt in 1851. Seeking new opportunity, he packed the family off to Cleveland, where he readily built a new business, possibly because he was well-known among men of means, and could get loans on the basis of his trustworthiness. He recovered quickly, and the family eventually settled into a substantial two-story home on Huron Street, whose rooms furnished a comfortable stop for runaway slaves. (Cleveland was distinguished as a final terminus because freed black men there provided passage across Lake Erie to Canada.)

While attending Central High, Lute Spelman befriended John Rockefeller.[6] She shared his interest in mathematics, and found him attractive. Unlike his brother William, John was "studious, grave and reserved . . . never noisy or given to boisterous play," Lute observed in admiration. Despite his seriousness, "he was soberly mirthful. His eyes lighted up and dimples showed in his cheeks when he heard anything amusing." He also shared her antislavery beliefs, for he argued in a school assignment how it was "a violation of the laws of our country and the laws of God that man should hold his fellow man in bondage." Although the Spelman sisters lived only three blocks away from Mrs. Woodin's boarding house, John did not visit them. He later reflected that he was too busy with lessons, music, and church to think about female companionship. Perhaps he felt too humble in background to appear at their well-appointed home with its cosmopolitan manners.

On June 16, 1855, the Spelman sisters graduated from high school, where Laura gave a forthright valedictory address that reflected her parents' nurturing of her own views.[7] It began with a staunchly American theme, that "we are formed dependent yet independent." The dependency is upon fellow human beings and upon the material world. The independence is to find that "our chief source of happiness is in ourselves." She cited a wise man of Greece, who took no trouble to save his valuables when his city was being ransacked by enemies. "Riches are but playthings; my only real treasures are my own thoughts." Few of us can be original thinkers on the level of Locke or Newton, she explained, but "we may nevertheless be independent thinkers" who do not submit automatically to the arguments of others.

At this point, the audience may have begun to drift off, as it is wont to do during such oratory, until Laura unexpectedly shifted her theme in a more controversial direction. "The independence of woman in thought, deed, or will is one of the problems of the age." Woman is silent because she has "been regarded incapable" and all attempts otherwise "have been ridiculed and discouraged." She has been spoken to in "baby phrase." The world's view of a perfect lady was "angelic silliness," a frilly figure of passive deportment uttering a smattering of French and slight knowledge of the arts. Laura challenged this ideal, urged that women be allowed in the laboratories of science and mathematics, in the halls of literature and culture.

The one ability women have not been denied developing, she averred, was "the power and right to suffer. Man often complains of the manifold causes of his suffering, but woman is not excelled." Indeed, woman "is continually, silently suffering." To soften her conclusion, Laura left her listeners with a light yet effective message, that "woman, even as man, can paddle her own canoe."

John, who should have been sitting among the graduating class of ten, had dropped out several weeks before the course of study ended, and did not hear this eloquent plea. Having watched his own mother's accomplishments in keeping the family together through difficult years, he would not have disagreed with Laura's conclusion. But because Bill was having a rough patch financially, John was forced prematurely into the work world. Thus, he had no opportunity to learn of the speech until later in life. For now, the Spelman sisters passed out of his interests. Making his way as a man took precedence, and that meant striving for success in work.

Unable to go on to college, John enrolled for a crash course in banking, business, and bookkeeping at E. C. Folsom's Commercial College. During the rest of that hot summer, the thin, serious lad walked the newly paved streets seeking work. In late September, after repeated rejections, he found a position with Hewitt & Tuttle, commission merchants and produce shippers. It was his penmanship that won the job, for in a day when all transactions were by hand, employers prized legible writing. At Hewett & Tuttle, John sat like Bob Cratchett at a high clerk's desk, where he was to help the bookkeeper. Unlike Cratchett, he had no Scrooge for a boss. More important, he found the method and system of the office delightful and had no regrets about missing further education: He was working with those beautiful numbers.

In 1856, Eliza moved with daughters Lucy, Mary Ann, and son Frank to Cleveland. Bill had shifted the household four times in the past three years, and she must have been gratified to learn he was planning to build a home in the city. Apparently such nostrums as "Doctor William Avery Rockefeller's Celebrated Cancer Treatment for $25" and his Seneca Oil were once again selling well. Bill bought a lot on Cheshire (later East 19th) Street, and asked his eldest son to oversee the building of a house there. Since residential architecture was not yet an established profession, most houses were selected from a book of designs, and the building overseen by family members. Thus after work, John pored over plans, sought bids, went to the site, and ensured that every detail match the particulars of the drawings. John's sister Mary Ann felt guilty afterwards, because the contractor lost money as a result of her brother's demanding supervision. On the other hand, John always took pride in his efficiency and cost-cutting on the project, and would tell the story as proof of his early promise. He was learning to separate religious morals from business, a necessary component of success in a day of free-for-all, no-holds-barred capitalism.

What is less clear is whether John knew of his father's motive for the grand new home—to situate the family permanently so he could go on with his other life. For in 1855, then middle-aged, Bill Rockefeller apparently decided he wanted a more settled homelife. Consequently, he married twenty-year-old Margaret Allen of Ontario, who knew him as Dr. William Levington. He moved in with her family, and was able to deceive them as he had Eliza by explaining his absences as the call of commerce. In time, his son Frank, and possibly William, would know of this arrangement, but for some years Bill successfully concealed his bigamy from any of his first family.

Eliza Davison Rockefeller must have found some irony in moving into the comfortable brick abode, for such a structure was the most visible proof of family prosperity. However comfortable and secure the surroundings, she would find her life remained troubled. Her husband was gone for such long periods that she realized he had essentially deserted her. Her youngest son, Frank, had the wild and unpredictable ways of his father, and her favorite son, John, was openly disapproving of that brother's impetuosity. Somehow her home had not become the heaven-on-earth claimed by Catherine Beecher, Lydia Maria Child, and other writers on women's domesticity.

From that point, Eliza further withdrew from public view. One solace proved to be the Erie Street Baptist Church, where she was elected vice president of the Society for Women. Although no evidence exists, one hopes that among that female companionship she found succor for her unhappy fate. Her main comfort, however, was with her children. She would see her daughters married to suitable men and observe her sons advance to unimagined wealth. More important to her, each child kept close to her, so that as the years advanced she lived less on Cheshire Street. Instead, she became a nomad travelling from one child's house to another, where she was treated with the honor due her as a devoted mother.

In 1856, while Eliza and her youngest children settled in comfortably on Cheshire Street, Lute and Laura Spelman haplessly searched for teaching positions in northern Ohio. Raised to be of service to others, they were disappointed, but soon found other diversions. They left Cleveland with their parents and settled in Burlington, Iowa, a community on the Mississippi River. Harvey Spelman bet that this booming frontier region would bring opportunities to replenish his fortune. There his wife and daughters met other devout Congregationalists around whom to structure their daily activities. Lucy and Laura grew especially fond of their music teacher, Mrs. Hawley, who fostered the young women's moral and artistic values.

Eighteen fifty-seven was not a provident year for the family. In March, fifteen-year-old Henry Spelman died, probably from scarlet fever. Death was still a frequent guest in American households, where almost one out of three females died before the age of twenty, and almost half of all deaths were children under five. Yet the Puritan vision of death—skulls on tombstones—had been replaced by the cherub's head of sweet deliverance. The Spelmans could express their grief through following elaborate mourning rituals prescribed by the culture. Though the women were no longer limited to wearing only black, they would don simple, dark clothes as a public expression of the loss. Their mother may have placed a lock of Henry's hair in a brooch. Weeping over the dead was considered evidence of Christian piety, and the mourning literature used Jesus's weeping at the tomb of Lazarus as an example. Furthermore, explained one advice writer, "the chain of family love on earth becomes much more strong and enduring, when some of its precious links are in heaven."[8] For the Spelmans, bound to faith in resurrection, Henry's death reminded of God's promise of later reunion.

Eighteen fifty-seven was not a provident year for most Americans. An insurance company collapse in New York City set off a financial panic throughout the nation. More than five thousand businesses failed that year; eight thousand more would fail the next. In early 1858 the Spelmans returned to Cleveland—possibly the panic had stifled the family's chances for success in Iowa. In April, Lute and Laura wrote Mrs. Hawley of their pleasure that a religious revival was taking over the Lake Erie city, as it was much of the nation. They were delighted that even little boys were attending church and prayer meetings.

John D. Rockefeller must also have noted the new evangelical fervor. Since he did not attend the same church as the Spelman daughters, he likely did not see them during this time. When not at home with his mother or at church, he was busy at Hewitt & Tuttle, where he handled complicated negotiations with suppliers, railroad managers, ships' captains, jobbers, warehousemen, and merchants. Besides learning about transportation and the commission business, he oversaw the firm's real estate holdings of houses, office buildings, and warehouses. Where the middle-aged Harvey Buel Spelman foresaw continued trouble ahead, Bill Rockefeller's son "was preparing, getting ready for something big."

The Spelman sisters' stay in Cleveland was brief, however. On April 29, they arrived in Worcester, Massachusetts to attend Oread Collegiate Institute.[9] Founded in 1849, Oread was one of the first schools to provide a college education for women. It was founded and run by Eli Thayer, a direct descendant of John and Priscilla Alden, who held the then queer opinion that young women should have the same opportunity for college education as men. On a hilltop above Worcester, he designed "Oread Castle," a stone building with the round towers and crenellations of a feudal lord. The name Oread referred to Virgil's lines concerning the mountain nymphs who followed the goddess Diana of the Hunt. The school's board included scholars, a Congregational minister, and Lydia Maria Childs, the noted author and antislavery champion. Thayer had originated the New England Aid Society, whose activities ultimately resulted in Kansas becoming a slave-free state. Consequently, the students were steeped in an atmosphere of fervent abolitionism.

Upon arriving, the Spelman sisters first met with the head matron, a Miss Dodge, whom they soon dubbed "Miss Prim." As they amusingly explained to Mrs. Hawley, "We live constantly in fear and trembling lest one commit some atrocious crime which shall outrage her sense of propriety . . . I guess you think we are in a *straight jacket.*"[10] Another time they described Miss Dodge as "so cold that when Lute sees her in the morning she develops shivers, then sneezes, then chills down her back, then her blood begins to congeal, but she manages to sit up demurely as a Quaker, or she should say, a Shaker."[11] They also made mocking horror of the fact that the only church close enough to attend was Baptist.

Lute and Laura readily fit in with their eighteen schoolmates and their instructors. The clockwork schedule invigorated them: up at 5:30, breakfast from 6:30–7, classes from 7–1, then dinner (the largest meal of the day), a walk until 3:30, study until 5:30, tea, a walk or music practice, more study from 7–8:45, and then to bed. On Friday afternoons they were free to go into Worcester; Saturday mornings were for study, the rest of the day unscheduled; Sunday was for two church services and quiet Sabbatarian pleasures.

The courses available included classical writers such as Virgil, Tacitus, and Cicero (in Latin), mathematics through calcus, French and German, philosophy, history, chemistry, theology, astronomy, ethics, rhetoric and English literature. It is unclear which of these courses the Spelman sisters took, for they wrote Mrs. Hawley mostly about their favorite activities: art and music. Both studied piano and voice, the two musical expressions recommended for women of the day. (Public opinion held that practicing orchestral or band instruments required too much time, which females could better use for domestic purposes. Singing lessons were essential training for future mothers, who would be expected to teach hymns to their youngsters.) For Lute and Laura these lessons were not duty, however, and they admired their teachers, who were demanding perfectionists. They sent Mrs. Hawley reports of concerts they had attended, and astutely criticized the skills of the performers. One young singer had "a very soft and flexible voice, but the way the words were murdered . . . one might imagine them to have been a mixture of different languages."[12]

For ten weeks during the summer of 1857 the young women travelled about visiting relatives in Albany and Massachusetts, for there was "no home to go to"—a suggestion that the Spelmans had rented out their Cleveland home. Their father was taking a water cure, a popular form of healing, and their mother was also recuperating from some unstated ailment. The sisters carefully observed and judged the lifestyles of the various cities they visited: the rich-and-fast ways in Albany, the economical-and-slow tempo of New England cities, the "dandified exquisites" and "richly dressed ladies (per steamer in Paris)" of Fifth Avenue in New York.[13] Overall, the trappings of wealth left them without any twinge of envy, for their values were by then fixed upon simplicity and service. Consequently, they most liked the restful Hudson River village of Dobbs Ferry and a visit to the modest, charming home of Washington Irving, and certainly never expected they would someday live nearby on hundreds of wooded acres on rolling hillsides.

That summer the sisters announced a most private celebration to Mrs. Hawley: Twenty-one-year-old Lucy "has arrived at the climax of her expansion—in other words, she has *busted.*"[14] This reference to final physical maturation is the only reference to their bodies in any of their many letters. Accordingly, their accounts never discussed their clothes, hair designs, or other expressions of conventional feminine beauty. Character was what mattered.

Just before the fall term began, the sisters returned briefly to Cleveland to see their parents. Their father was not working at all. Lucy remarked, "Father thinks his ship has been out so long that it is nearly time for it to come in. I tell him every day that he is a perfect McCawber."[15]

Harvey Spelman's ship would never again find a major port, but unknown to him, it would not matter. For several blocks away, young John D. Rockefeller was planning to leave Hewitt & Tuttle to form a partnership with Maurice Clark, an Englishman interested in starting a commission business dealing in grain, hay, meats, and miscellaneous goods. While Harvey Spelman lay awake wondering about his family's future, John D. Rockefeller lectured himself on how "pride goeth before a fall" and about "nothing in haste, nothing ill-done." These admonitions to himself engrained a humility and patience that women like the Spelman sisters would find irresistible.

The fall of 1857 brought a new matron to Oread, one who had spent eight years as a missionary in India, and had travelled in Europe. She was cosmopolitan, and kinder than "Miss Prim." That semester the sisters added bookkeeping to their course schedule, an unusually practical course for a woman's school, for only men held jobs in offices as secretaries, clerks, and account keepers. Indeed, few states gave women any property rights, so women's knowledge of finance seemed superfluous. In offering this course, Oread was hinting to its pupils that they deserved more, that rights were due.

The sisters' feminist leanings were made explicit in the school's student paper, *Vox Oreadum.*[16] As president of the literary society, Laura was responsible for editing and producing the work. It consisted of a single copy of sixteen pages of material written out in Laura's and Lucy's neat handwriting, on paper fine enough to be passed about the students without undue wear. The sole surviving issue suggests that the sisters wrote most of the material, for the voice echoes that of their letters, particularly their wry humor. One piece imagines the stories received by a telegraph in the editorial office:

> Midnight—Omnia Scio University. The Prof. of Mathematics states, that the problem of squaring the circle has been solved by his little son, only six years of age. The circle was made of a slender wire, and was placed by the boy over a square pyramid, and pressed downwards, until the circumference became the perimeter of a square, which can be easily measured. . . .
>
> *Another click*—Half-past moon-rise—Madame De Rose's Pavilion of Cultivation, New York. With the accustomed promptness and foresight of this institution, upon the advent of the first springlike day, the young ladies began their *Fan-practice*, and have already arrived at the *languishing department*, which although difficult of attainment in its full perfection, is at once graceful and effective.

That Oread students would not indulge in such "languishing" is evident. It was clearly a school that encouraged a woman to paddle her own canoe.

In an article pretending to tell of students' activities ten years in the future, one is said to have been appointed postmaster general of the nation, another was "star of the European courts," two were nurses in Cuba, one was a successful lawyer "on the Pacific Coast," and one was writing happily from a log hut. A classmate who returned to the family plantation with its "many thousand negroes" was chastised for losing her antislavery principles. Lute was described as being an artist with a studio in Massachusetts, and Laura, having studied voice in Europe, was a prima donna at Drury Lane Theatre in London. Such rich aspirations would never be met, for no matter the liberalism of their parents, or the independence of their women teachers, society would realign these ambitions toward other spheres.

Gradually, the sisters' letters to Mrs. Hawley expressed awareness of their approaching adulthood and the adoption of conventional adult attitudes. Nineteen-year-old Laura reflected on how she "must not shrink from meeting the future, but now prepare for it. I have assurance that I shall have help from above, and that I shall not be tried, above that I am able to bear."[17] They were dismayed to learn that some Iowa Baptists allowed dancing, "so unworldly and sinful an object."[18]

They commended Mrs. Hawley for her economy, it being "an exceedingly desirable trait in a good wife." When Mrs. Hawley referred to herself as a "trifle lazy," they demurred, and insisted that laziness was no part of her busy nature. Thus in condemning waste and sloth, the Spelman sisters expressed the same capitalism-nurturing values that the Rockefeller boys had been taught.

Before the spring term of 1859 ended, the Spelmans called their daughters back to Cleveland. Laura immediately registered at the Cleveland Institute to study French, Latin, piano, and voice. She hoped to continue her schooling for two or three more years, but lack of money would soon curtail this plan. After classes she helped her mother in the kitchen, evidence that the family was not doing well financially, for they would have had a servant otherwise. Her father returned to Iowa to attend to his real estate and business interests there. Given the political turmoil around the irrepresible conflict of slavery, the national economy continued to heave and stumble.

In the fall, Lute found a position as a primary school teacher, but was sick so often with bronchial problems that Laura stepped in to teach the "sixty little dirty-faced angels." When she tried to get private students for music instruction, Laura discovered that people did not have the money for such extras. She preferred to teach older children, and eventually won a position as music teacher at an academy twenty miles away. To her disappointment, her mother made her turn down the offer for it would mean leaving home.

The Spelman women continued to serve the Underground Railroad, a commitment that was even more risky now that the Supreme Court had upheld the Fugitive Slave Act, which ordered the return of escapees. They wrote Mrs. Hawley of a "little darkey girl, a regular daughter of Africa" they were protecting. To them, beliefs were a directive for action, and one must follow the path of righteousness, no matter how uncomfortable or treacherous.

The capture and hanging that winter of slavery fighter John Brown was one of many events to reflect the growing instability of the country. "The cross of a martyr," northerners said of his gibbet. Poet Henry Wadsworth Longfellow warned that the execution was "sowing the wind to reap the whirlwind, which will soon come." In early 1860, other sources of conflict appeared as Charles Darwin's *Origin of Species* was circulated and fomented strife concerning the accuracy of the account of creation in Genesis. Also, when women workers participated in a shoemaker's strike in Lynn, Massachusetts, newspaper editorials bewailed the dangerous consequences of the feminist movement and its fomenting "Revolution at the North."

Laura Spelman eventually found her own teaching assignment in

Cleveland, at the East Fourteenth Street Grammar School with its "well-governed" pupils. Among them was John Green, son of a slave whose father had purchased the family's freedom. John's father died soon after, and he and his mother despaired over the loss. Laura's steady encouragement boosted the boy's resolve to remain in school. He did so, and went on to become a lawyer and Ohio's first black member of its State Senate. Known as the "Father of Labor Day" for introducing that holiday's legislation, he attributed much of his success to Laura, who became a lifelong friend. Decades later other students recalled her as fondly.

To continue as a school teacher, Laura had to remain single, for married women were forbidden to teach, a rule meant to prevent children from seeing a pregnant woman—as though they would never be exposed to one in their homes! "I seem to have no anxiety about leading a life of single-blessedness," she explained to Mrs. Hawley, although a "gentleman told me not long ago, that he was in no particular rush to have me get married, but he hoped that in the multitude of my thoughts I would not forget the subject."[19] The "gentleman" was John D. Rockefeller.

3

The Storm King
and the Zephyr

"Who can find a virtuous woman? for her price is above rubies."

—Proverbs 31:10

*L*aura's male friend, John D. Rockefeller, was too consumed with work and church for serious courtship. His agreement with Maurice Clark seemed an unlikely partnership, yet their very differences dovetailed precisely to form a sturdy bond. Rockefeller immediately demonstrated a trait that was common to other nascent millionaires, that of tracking every penny, claiming each one due, and giving out each one owed. He had a thorough understanding of commission transactions, and knew how to run the office reliably and efficiently. Introverted, he was content to work with correspondence and account books, while his jovial and outgoing partner bargained easily with suppliers and shippers, and brought a steady stream of customers to the young firm. Since he was thirty-one, and well-known about the business community, portly Clark also presented an image of maturity which the gaunt, taciturn young Rockefeller could not manage on his own. Clark smoked and drank, though in sufficient moderation as not to repel his sober partner. If different in many ways, both men agreed in the need to make the company's success their first priority.

Despite the stumbling economy, within a few months the partnership turned a profit. In fact, business grew so rapidly that they sought loans from Bill Rockefeller to increase their capital during emergencies. John's income at the end of the first year was $2,200, equivalent to several times that of the average working man. He was twenty-one.

John's brother William was also showing promise for commerce. Upon finishing high school, he joined his brother at Hewitt & Tuttle, starting out as a bookkeeper. In time, his financial acumen caught the eye of a prominent miller, who hired him away. By 1859, William was earning one thousand dollars a year at the forwarding and commission house of Hughes & Lester, and he would soon rise to partnership in that firm. Although William was more sociable and less pious than John, he shared the Rockefeller exactitude about money, and was quietly building up a stash of capital that would prove most useful to the brothers in a few years.

By February 1861, seven Southern states had split off to form the Confederacy. The three Rockefeller sons were all of age to fight for the Union, but only the youngest, sixteen-year-old Frank, put on a uniform. Even then, to enlist he had to lie about his age as well as defy his father's orders against signing up. John and William did not want to leave their businesses, and they had no compelling reason to participate. They were abolitionists, but the war was not being fought to end slavery (a cause that would arise only later in the conflict). They were Republicans and Lincoln-supporters, yet not so fervid as to take up rifles.

Long afterward, John rationalized his decision to remain a civilian. He explained that he had wanted to fight, but had his mother and sisters to support, an assertion that is not fully credible. If his father had money to lend John's partnership, he was obviously still making visits to Cleveland and leaving household money with Eliza. Furthermore, John Davison had died in 1858, which meant Eliza would be receiving an annual annuity from her father's estate. A group picture taken about this time reveals an affluent family, for the sons all sport large watch chains, and the daughters wear fashionable jewelry.

John later claimed to have participated in the Union effort by helping out soldiers and their families: "I was represented in the Army. I sent more than twenty men, yes, nearly thirty!" To supply a volunteer was to outfit him with clothing and a weapon, and to supplement the soldier's meager pay so the man's family would not suffer. However, Rockefeller's account books show he spent only $138 on such contributions, a miniscule amount that casts doubts upon his memory of generosity. He did, however, contribute to war causes by attending such activities as the Northern Ohio Sanitary Fair, which raised money for what was a forerunner of the American Red Cross.

Nonetheless, it is remarkable that John felt *any* discomfort over his not fighting, for most Northern businessmen felt guiltless about exempting themselves. Among the business community a family like the Vanderbilts was exceptional. Seventy-year-old multimillionaire Commodore Vanderbilt badgered President Lincoln to let him captain a ship on the Chesapeake, and his favorite youngest child, George, went to West Point, only to die of tuberculosis caught in an unsanitary Civil War Army camp.

More typical were the businessmen and their sons—from Astors and Wanamakers in New York to the mine owners in Michigan—who bought their way out for three hundred dollars and left the fighting to poorer or more ideologically committed men.

Consequently, the war provoked a battle on the Northern home front concerning American values, specifically sacrifice versus greed. The sacrifice was men (and women disguised as men) dying in battle; people like Walt Whitman nursing wounded comrades; an elderly woman carrying spy messages in her underskirts; and children rolling bandages by the hour. The greed was cheating for more profits; watering old horses to sell them beyond their worth; using shoddy cloth to make uniforms; and adulterating wheat with cheaper grains, even dirt. Perhaps one of four dollars paid by the Union treasury went to swindle, historians later estimated. Some businessmen, like Stephen Harkness in Ohio, took advantage of the war to cheat competitors and corner a market, as he did in whiskey, a troop necessity.

Worse, those benefiting from the wartime economic boom grew lavish in their display of wealth. Before the war, wealthy families in New York City—the staid Knickerbockers—condemned luxury and ostentation. "Upstarts" now were building showy mansions and entertaining with fancy multicoursed dinners based on European cuisine. The evil rooted in money was visible and abundant, the Scripturally minded would intone.

Sometimes the same individual played both sides. The patriotic Vanderbilt who searched hopelessly for a sea battle was the crafty Vanderbilt who put fresh paint on hull-rotted ships and leased them to the Union at top dollar. John D. Rockefeller evinced less contradiction; for him, war meant profit, but won honestly. Wealth meant neither mansion nor gold-trimmed walking stick, but more coins to contribute to the Erie Street Baptist Church and local charities.

John's pattern of giving hinted at his growing open-mindedness. Where before the war his donations went mostly to his church and Baptist missions, he now recorded gifts to a black church, a Catholic orphanage, a society for mute and blind "Africans," a Swedish mission in Illinois, a German Sunday School, and an industrial school to train the poor in a craft. He gave a black man in Cincinnati the money needed to buy his wife out of slavery. Rockefeller was a Christian before he was a Baptist, and gave away an increasing proportion of his income as it grew.

Much known of these early days comes from a document he started in 1855, *Ledger A*, a thin duodecimo book bound in leather. It shows he spent the minimum on clothing, always buying a cheaper cut; and that he took his lunch to work rather than buy one at a nearby eatery. Some months he gave away as much as he spent on himself. Few young adults were so generous with their small salaries, and he longed to be able to give more than ten cents to a poor man or woman at church, twenty-five cents to the deacon.

Ledger A in later years achieved hallowed qualities, both for Rockefeller himself and for his biographers. They wrote as if he had invented the idea of recording one's expenses, that this account book was a key to his success. Accordingly, he passed the sacred method on to his son, who passed it on to his children. A flaw in this theory is that ledger-keeping was a common practice in a time when pennies held value and the average person did not use checks. From tramp to washerwoman to lawyer, Americans were jotting down the outflux of their coins, tying money to particular goods and services, and demonstrating an appreciation for the flow of the nation's economy through an individual's life.

If keeping a ledger was not unusual, John D.'s posting in it so precisely and regularly was. Of more significance is his own interpretation of the document, for it was to him more than the measure of his wealth or poverty. He perused the accounts as a form of conscience-keeping, just as Ben Franklin had done decades earlier with his daily checkoff list of virtues. Both men kept their ledgers as forms of self-discipline, meditative practices to inculcate order, regularity, precision, and attention to detail—qualities valuable in a capitalist. Unlike Franklin's notebook, *Ledger A* laid out Rockefeller's return to society in the form of transfer of wealth, however meager in the early years. A penny saved was a penny earned for another's salvation, earthly and otherwise.

When Civil War battles cut the Mississippi River as a trade route, the cities of Cleveland, Toledo, and particularly Chicago boomed as the major trade connections with the Western frontier. Chicago became the key transportation hub, a place where railroads and shipping lines converged. Cleveland transformed itself into the key industrial core. Its iron, steel, and copper mills grew in number and size. New factories, such as textile works and paint companies, joined alongside. Shippers and commodity suppliers like Rockefeller and Clark thrived, and not just because of the increased military demand. In the early 1860s, winters were harsh in England and Europe, so demand for foodstuffs was greater than ever from overseas. Consequently, their profits multiplied without the partners' necessarily resorting to the more despicable practices of some other businessmen. Even given an opportunity to cheat, these biblically governed partners were unlikely to do so. (The more questionable practices would arise in Rockefeller's future.)

Had it not been for John's imagination, what he envisioned upon hearing certain stories, the name Rockefeller today would be little known. The first rumors came from Titusville, Pennsylvania. On August 21, 1859, when Billy Smith, a blacksmith turned driller, looked down the tube of a shaft he had cut, he saw a thick, dark liquid: oil. The owner of the well, Edwin Drake, never appreciated its promise, but instead got himself a commission as justice of the peace. While Drake oversaw the legalities of land sales and oil leases, more adventuresome men set up derricks, tended the roaring drills and chugging engines, and, if they were lucky, and many were, filled the barrels. Despite the flow of black gold, smarter money was placed on barrel making and teamstering, for the drillers and speculators were a brawling sort who prevented any order of rationality from shaping production.

After joining with some other Cleveland businessmen to gather some intelligence on the oil boom, Rockefeller concluded that were there money to be made, it would be in refining. Depending upon the vagaries of the market, a refined gallon sold for up to four times the cost of the crude used to produce it. Rockefeller's expectations were confirmed in April 1861. That month a gusher exploded in flame and incinerated some of the bystanders. The disaster provoked a sudden drop in the price of oil, and many adventurers left. For those who remained, new strikes brought a flood of the fuel, so much so that even the war-torn nation could not absorb the overflowing stream. Barrels that had brought one dollar at the start of the year earned barely ten cents by the end.

That instability would change during the next few years. Since most of the fortune hunters eventually left the oil fields for war profiteering, what resulted was a shakeout of producers, a survival of the fittest. Those remaining saw value in organizing and protecting their mutual interests. Consequently, an informal alliance developed to control prices and return higher rates. New demand increased profits as well. Chemically inclined inventors were finding new uses for petroleum, such as turpentine for cleaning paint and a safe, purer kerosene for fueling lamps. Europeans, who lacked a continental source of oil, clamored for these products. In a final boost to business, the oil was transported less by teamsters—driving horses strained by barrel-laden wagons through creekbeds, muddied roads, and mountain passes—and more by steady, reliable locomotives. Increasingly those heavy barrels of thick crude rode the rails not southward, toward Pittsburgh's refineries, but to those in Cleveland, with its more abundant labor, cheap coal, and commodious port facilities.

Among John D. Rockefeller's clients and Baptist church friends was a candlemaker turned refiner, Samuel Andrews. An astute experimenter, Andrews had devised a method for getting more kerosene from crude oil, and was possibly the first to use the residuum of the refining for fuel. Andrews, however, was a poor man, whose wife took in sewing to help support the family. Always quick to judge talent and character, Rockefeller overlooked the man's ragged clothes and in his patient, dogged way gleaned from Andrews a technical understanding of refining methods. Noting that oil production was coming into the hands of more sensible people, he was ready to make his move.

Early in 1863, John Rockefeller, Maurice Clark, and Clark's two brothers underwrote a refinery, with Andrews managing its technical operation. For some unknown reason, Rockefeller's name was absent from the firm's title, Andrews, Clark & Company. Although others were building refineries at the same time, few chose so good a site as this partnership. The bluffs on Kingsbury Run linked directly to both the Atlantic and the Great Western rail lines; and to Lake Erie, by way of the Cuyahoga River. In addition to stills and furnaces, the partners built a barnlike cooperage to produce their own barrels (and thus be free from the demands of outside suppliers). The company's strategy was soon bringing Rockefeller, Andrews, and the Clarks profits to add to those of their thriving commission business.

While other men went off after work to saloons and men's clubs, dance halls, and theaters, Baptist Rockefeller dined at home with his mother and siblings. If he went out afterwards, it was to church for a meeting or worship service. Sometime during the early 1860s, however, he allowed himself one other frequent evening diversion, that of visiting the Huron Street home of the Spelman family. The war economy once again brought some affluence to this family so devoted to one another and the cause of the slaves.

Although John enjoyed the company of both daughters, he eventually showed a preference for Laura. Unpracticed in wooing, he brought his account books over and spread them out before her on a table. Huddled together by the oil lamps, they discussed the meaning of the numbers in the same way that other courting couples would discuss a novel or musical composition. When their examination of the books was finished for the night, they played piano together. Very likely Lute or Laura's parents were present during these meetings as chaperones.

John's courting may have been spurred by that of his younger brother

William, who had announced he would marry Almira "Mira" Geraldine Goodsell in May 1864. Mira was from a prominent Cleveland family whose origins were Yankee; consequently, the ceremony took place in Connecticut. Taking more after his father, William proved a handsome groom whose looks would gain dignity with age. Mira was a pleasant-looking brunette who would pass her distinctive square-jawed face on to several of their children. She shared with her husband a more secular outlook toward life.

Because John and Laura never went to dances or to the theater together, and attended different churches, their friends were amazed when the couple announced their engagement. They could understand John's devotion to Laura, but not the reverse. He was somewhat homely, countrified, a bit peculiar in his habits. She was the daughter of a prominent businessman and Ohio civic leader, whereas John's father was usually absent. Her grace and warmth more than made up for her less than beautiful face. Other young men, more handsome and sociable than John, were making hopeful visits to Laura at the time. When her girlfriends expressed surprise at her choice, she noted simply that she loved John better than she would ever love anyone else.

On April 8, John spent $118 on a diamond ring, an extravagant amount for that era. As part of the engagement process, John likely visited alone with Harvey Spelman to give an account of his financial condition and expectations. If parents no longer directly controlled courtship, they yet retained considerable power over the outcome of an engagement. A disapproving father sent his daughter away to travel or to live with a relative; she had no recourse, for she was fully dependent upon his economic support. Fiction in ladies' magazines emphasized the tragic effects of such interference, and in turn reminded their readers of their subordination to their fathers. Laura Spelman had no such interference from her father, who can only have been extremely pleased by her choice of a young man who was both deeply religious and successful in business.

Engagements then also signified that the woman no longer answered to her father, but to her betrothed. As part of this transition to his rule, Laura expected visits from John almost nightly, and she could no longer see or even correspond with other men without his approval. It was a custom that could foster autocratic men, but we must not assume all men dominated as a result. Certainly nothing in John Rockefeller's later actions suggest he would have been anything other than thoughtful and respectful of Laura's needs and preferences. If anything, she would have held sway over this reserved young man. In matters apart from business, she was better educated and held strong opinions. Her sister summed up her character best: Laura was "gentle and lovely, but resolute with indomitable will."

Ledger A now documented John's comforming to the attentiveness expected by a fiancée. He scribbled in the expenses for "Bouquettes" and "Vignettes," appropriate gifts for Laura. He noted the expenses of "drives," the rentals of rigs from a livery stable. As the wedding date approached, he bought himself a new umbrella, a valise, and opera glasses.

Long engagements were to be avoided for fear that sexual intimacy might develop. "There must be no rough freedom, no romping caresses, no behavior that you would be ashamed of if the engagement should be broken," women were warned. Another worry was that a couple would be too "apt to find out each other's imperfections, to grow exacting, jealous, and morose." Consequently, on September 8, 1864—two days after General Sherman occupied Atlanta—John scheduled a special dinner for his twenty-six refinery employees, who had known nothing about his plans. After working part of the day, he appeared at the Spelman parlor for the two o'clock wedding ceremony.

It may seem odd that given the great religiosity of the time, parlor weddings were common. In fact, the home was held to be as sacred a place as the church, and had not acquired the purely secular meanings attached to it years later. If the Spelmans followed convention, the public area of the house was laden with floral decorations, transforming it into a lush, fragrant garden. Festoons of greenery ran down the entrance stairway; large vases of rose displays stood about; smaller bouquets adorned mantels, sideboards, and end tables. Scented candles added to the romantic atmosphere. The parlor organ or piano provided the hymnal music to further remind the couple of the connection between the home and the church.

White, with its symbol of virginity, was the traditional wedding dress color, but many women then were turning to colored dresses, for they could be reused for other social events. Laura's choice here is unknown. Nor do we have a record of whether Lute was her official attendant, for no newspaper announcement was printed. Nor were photographs taken, for wedding portraits had not yet entered tradition. The witnesses included members of both families, and perhaps a few very close friends.

Both Laura's Congregational pastor and John's Baptist minister administered the ceremony, but from this day forward Laura would be a Baptist in practice, if not always in creed. John paid twenty dollars to each of the two men for their services.

When the short event ended, the newlyweds climbed into a shiny rented brougham which carried them to the Union Depot at the foot of

Bank and Water streets. John paid ten dollars for their train tickets to Buffalo to visit Niagara Falls, even then a favorite honeymoon destination.

Their first intimacy must have been clumsy. Doubtless both were virgins. Since discussion of sexuality was virtually nonexistent for young women, Laura particularly would be ignorant. Having grown up in a rural area, John was familiar with the biology of sex, if not the art of loving. Still, if ignorance brought confusion, the culture of high eroticism present a century later was also absent, so expectations were not overblown. Popular medical advisors such as Sylvester Graham were certain that men had only a limited supply of spermatic "vital fluid" and thus they should avoid frequent intercourse and all masturbation. To fumble or fail during early encounters would be viewed as a matter of course, and of no significance for estimating the participant's worth. In fact, awkwardness was proof of one's chastity. So, left alone in the hotel room, one imagines that the two were nervous, and grateful to have body-disguising bedclothes, yet boosted by God's assurance that they were fulfilling His wishes. It was after all, a Sacred Act.

The route of the honeymoon trip snaked through Montreal and Quebec, down through New England, including Boston, to New York City. In Massachusetts, Laura took John to Oread Academy, and explained how much that one year of education among other women had meant to her. Oread had just hired Sophia B. Packard as principal, and her friend Harriet Giles as teacher of music. Packard was, in the words of a contemporary, "a woman of powerful intellect and strong will ... with almost a masculine genius for business ... a thoroughly consecrated and devoted Christian."[1] These qualities impressed both Laura and John, and as a result the meeting would have beneficial consequences for generations of African-American women. The fruits of this encounter were some years off, however, and could not have been imagined by the participants.

The couple returned by way of Niagara Falls for a second look. John had set aside one month for the honeymoon, and they returned to Cleveland precisely on October 8, 1864.

The couple moved in temporarily with his mother. The next day he introduced Laura to the Erie Street Baptist Church, where she signed up to teach a children's Sunday School class. On Monday, John returned to work, and on Tuesday he was off to Chicago, where he stayed on business matters for the rest of the week.

*　　*　　*

Reality quashed Laura's adolescent fantasy of becoming a famous singer in Europe, yet she knew all along it was merely a dream. Fantasies were for literature, and she had no aspirations in that direction. To say she sacrificed, that she failed to fulfill herself, misreads her character. She had grown up watching her father battle for success, suffer defeat, then pick himself up and start over. The Underground Railroad visitors dramatically reminded how blessed had been her fate: to be born into a relatively affluent, loving, free family. She understood loyalty and commitment and compassion for others. She would not belittle the woman who left all behind to become an artist, but that path was not hers. As for her teaching career, marriage closed that door.

Laura's choice of her conventional path was forecast in a story she wrote in *Vox Oreadum*. Titled "The Storm King and the Zephyr," it expressed a common romantic plot of her time.[2] The Zephyr, a modest, unassuming young female, breaks the rules and speaks to the Storm King, who invites her to his palace to see his resplendent wealth and jewels. She decides to "play the Coquette," which means to hold back and feign disinterest. She hints of another male Zephyr in her life. The Storm King grows angry with jealousy, then notices a "glimpse of roguery in her eyes." He laughs, sweeps her up, and carries her to his palace. "And when the bright sunshine comes after the storms and tempests, one may know that the Storm King has listened to the gentle Zephyr, that her influence has prevailed over him."

Striking about this story is the control the female exerts. The Storm King sweeps the Zephyr off her feet because she wants him to. Her flirtatiousness brings about the desired end, the abduction. Once in the palace, she is the power behind the throne. She moderates violent, destructive masculine impulse, and feels superior as a result. While subduing the Storm King, she retains a submissive demeanor. This simple story illustrates the complexity of gender relations then, for what appears at first victimization is otherwise. The female achieves what she desires, sexual fulfillment and power, despite society's apparent proscription. She casts what has been forbidden her—aggression, sexual potency, greed, pride— upon the male, yet ultimately shares these qualities through her binding to him. He has not been deceived here, for he welcomes her playful deception and damping of his cruel impulses. He is redeemed by her love.

The value of these romances was in offering women a script for conforming to the demands of purity and piety, while incorporating forbidden desires. The disadvantage was that not all men turned out to be as tameable as the Storm King. Laura's fortune was in finding a man who already had the darkest part of his masculinity leashed. The couple settled into a folie à deux, in which they saw their life was a pure expression of Christian goodness, which for the most part it was. Yet they deceived themselves nonetheless. For when they sat together with the business ledgers, they transformed their inadmissable desires—their avarice, their will to power—into a matter of numerical calculations.

The burning issue for middle-class women like Laura then was not their exclusion from employment; it was their lack of the most essential right, that of full citizenship and the vote. The concept of "home" held a different meaning from today. Each spouse had his or her allotted duties: the husband to go off daily and battle in the world of business, the wife to create a "happy home" for his respite and for the healthy raising of their children. This arrangement was readily reinforced by religion, through such biblical passages as Proverbs 12, with its warnings against the imprudent and slothful man or the unvirtuous woman. The portrayal suggested women were fortunate to be isolated from the degradation and depravity of business and politics.

This concept of "separate spheres" did not mean a housewife was condemned to a life of "angelic silliness." Middle-class women saw much benefit from the arrangement. The husband might be the patriarch in theory, but he was not around much. Her daily life was in the company of other women—her servants, relatives, and friends. So completely female-related were her days that a woman like Laura used the word *home* to include this larger circle of women—neighbors, church members, club members—who lived outside her household. She was not isolated the way suburban wives would be a century later.

Furthermore, although women and men were to rule separate arenas, their relationship was not so unequal as the separation implies. The most common word in advice books to young husbands was *mutuality*. He was to love his wife "as Christ loved the Church," confide in her, respect her opinions, defend her honor, and always treat her kindly. He was not to undertake any major decisions, such as moving the family, without consulting her. While not having the same duties in life, they were "like the different parts of a wisely constructed and well-regulated machine designed and calculated to act in perfect harmony."[3] Condemned was the "domestic despot," the man who tyrannized "the weakness and dependent condition of his wife." In other words, a man had to earn his place as the head of the family through his right actions.

The wife had reciprocal obligations to respect and confide in her husband. Her "weakness and dependent condition" was only with regard to external affairs of business and politics. In the home, she was in charge, so long as she, too, met her responsibility to run domestic activities with discretion. And in the area of morality and spirituality, one might say the husband had a weak and dependent condition, for she was considered superior.

The couple's mutuality then was based upon complementarity. Each had their realm of expertise to manage effectively for the welfare of the family. Child rearing was to be a joint activity, not left solely to the mother. Above all, they were to nurture one another's spiritual development, a role that implicitly gave more authority to the wife.

While advice books from a period can never be taken as typical of how people actually behaved, Laura and John Rockefeller followed the prescriptions closely. Advisors then were ministers, not psychologists or sociologists, so the couple readily accepted the Christian rationale underlying this relationship of mutuality. When it came to choosing a branch in a river, Laura always paddled her canoe along the Christian current, and carried her family along with her.

The couple let a two-story brick house at 29 Cheshire Street, close by his mother, with whom Laura shared many beliefs. Her sister-in-law Mira Goodsell Rockefeller also lived on Cheshire. Her parents and sister lived a short walk away. Her husband was gone long hours, and when home, was content to stay there, napping in a rocker after dinner.

With its double row of overarching trees and well-built homes, Cheshire Street was one of the most beautiful in Cleveland. City houses were more substantial than country dwellings—no cracks in the roof to let in the rain and snow—yet they were not much easier to keep clean. The main reason was the slow development of municipal services.

In the 1860s, cities like Cleveland provided few of the amenities taken for granted fifty years later. Most streets were unpaved, and thus became muddied streams during springtime showers, and ice-skating rinks in winter. Piped public water supply was just starting, so most homes still depended upon hand-pumped wells. Municipal sewage disposal was in the future. No trash collection existed (hence the ready availability of old bottles today for those who know where to dig in yards.) Fire protection was left to either competing commercial companies or to volunteer brigades. The absence of zoning meant homes could reside in the same block as a small slaughter house, a tannery, or other noxious industry. With horses providing the major intracity transport, stables filled the alleyways. Horses meant manure, manure meant flies, flies meant disease and nuisance.

Consider this situation, and the resulting labor for a middle-class household is evident. The house may have a bathroom upstairs, but someone, namely a servant, must heat water and carry it up to the tub and back down again. Because toilets with plumbing do not yet exist, someone must empty chamber pot slops down the outhouse pit. (In 1869, Catherine Beecher recommended that homes no longer follow her previous design for the backdoor two-person privy, but now have full bathrooms connected to indoor plumbing.) People coming in bring dust or mud, which collects not on bare flooring, but on rugs and heavy carpets that need frequent scrubbing and beating to keep clean. Soot deposits from factories, oil lamps, and mischievous stoves laid a black film over wallpaper, drapes, upholstery, and countertops. Since so much soot came from indoor sources over the winter, "spring cleaning" became a hated two-week ritual, "a general housewrecking process . . . an abomination of desolation . . . that breaks women's backs and causes men to break the Ten Commandments," remarked one diarist.[4]

Until electricity became widely available, household inventions did not much reduce the physical labor of this cleaning. "Washing machines" were merely mechanical devices that depended upon strong arms and shoulders to crank the agitator. Sewing machines seamed quickly with the help of foot pedalling, but fashion demanded much additional handiwork before a garment was completed.

One of the few significant technological developments was related to that crude oil flowing from the rigs in Pennsylvania, clean kerosene. The new illuminant inspired safer design of glass lamps, with more efficient wick composition. Good oil and safety-glass lamps reduced fire danger and brought much brighter light, from three to four times more candlepower than the earlier camphene, castor oil, or cottonseed oil lamps. Nonetheless, to perform well and safely these new lamps were as demanding as the older kind. The wicks must be kept trimmed, the bowls filled with oil, and the mantles regularly cleaned of soot.

Women like Laura and her sister-in-law Mira were not likely to lug water, empty slops, beat carpets, or grind the washer agitator. Unlike their mothers in earlier years, they could buy clothes or soap, rather than having to make each from scratch. This does not mean they spent their days shopping or lunching after giving the maid the orders for the day. For one, more work needed to be done than a daily helper and weekly laundrywoman could complete. Diaries of middle-class women like Laura and Mira recorded the numerous chores to be done each day: cooking, baking bread and sweets, sweeping, dusting, cleaning and filling lamps, washing dishes, making beds. Because Sunday was the Sabbath, when housework was taboo, Saturday meant preparing six meals for two days instead of three for one. Sweeping rugs was "the hardest torture of the week . . . prosecuted until every nerve is throbbing in fierce rebellion at the undue pressure to which it is subjected."[5] Less frequent chores included stove cleaning, rug mending, mattress cleaning, and furniture cushioning.

Furthermore, despite the availability of such consumer goods as canned foods and clothing, "good" housewives felt compelled to continue producing these necessities at home. Sewing was the most frequent domestic labor for middle-class women. They made their everyday clothes, undergarments, blouses, bonnets, pillowcases, towels, handkerchiefs, shirts, cuffs, and collars. They knitted socks, stockings, scarves, and caps. Popular magazines provided fashion plates with colored steel engravings of beautiful ladies in stiff brocades, cloaks, ruffles, and tilted hats. If readers were not skillful at copying such designs, they could order paper patterns from the firm of Madame Ellen Curtis Demorest, whose magazine brought Paris fashions to the middle class. A related project which the magazines encouraged was to make over old dresses into more "comely" ones. (These same publications also carried articles that criticized women for spending so much time bent over their sewing to add the complicated fashionable embellishments touted in their own illustrations!) Keeping one's hands busy with a needle was visible proof a woman was not commiting the heinous sin of sloth.

Thus the day would start at 29 Cheshire Street before sunrise, with Laura up to set the fire in the kitchen stove and bedroom grates, while John enjoyed some final slumber. Before dressing, she ran a soapless wet towel over herself as a form of bath. Her long hair must be brushed and swept up into a net to form a "waterfall." She was not the sort to paint her face, but likely used such skin conditioners as concoctions of lemon, cucumber, horseradish, honey, almond oil, or even mutton suet. Her undergarments were complex, as the model figure of the day was a well-developed bust, a tapering waist, and huge hips. This ideal called for artifice: whalebone corsets, corset covers with flounces to increase the appearance of the bosom, and either a small bustle or crinoline petticoats made of scratchy horsehair and linen. Laura's dresses were not as fancy as those of her friends, but they kept up with the styles. Her leather-soled, high-topped shoes could either button or, if of the latest fashion, lace up.

Since the rural tradition of a heavy breakfast continued when people moved to cities, Laura prepared some kind of hotcake or fruit pie, as well as eggs and meat. Milk was a popular beverage with adults—a habit

European travellers found strange—and John preferred it throughout his life, even when it became identified as solely a child's beverage.

While Laura cooked, John would rise, wash himself, and attend to shaving. Etiquette books regarded facial hair as natural, expressive, and virile, and a fully-shaven face as effeminate. Consequently, men like John, who did not go in for a fancy beard or mutton chop, used the straight-edge lightly and often skipped a day. (For a while he sported a neat mustache, which gave him a handsome appearance.) His underwear was much simpler than Laura's: anklelength drawers with button fly and a cotton shirt. His dark suit was loose-fitting with baggy tube-legged trousers. His shirts were also cut loose, but were topped with stiff paper cuffs and collars. John chose white shirts even though bright colors and bold stripes were becoming popular. When he left the house, he put on a hat—straw in summer, and either a silk or beaver top hat in cooler weather. Again, he characteristically eschewed the sporty bowlers and derbies that were coming into vogue. This neatly tailored, conservative look would suit him all his life.

John's place of work was within walking distance of his home, but because of his frequent travel within or away from Cleveland, he did not regularly appear there for lunch, as many men did. Saloons and restaurants provided fast food for busy male customers, a "Hamburg steak," or boiled eggs and pig's feet, to swallow down for the ten-minute crew, or, for the more leisurely twenty-minute diners, a fifteen-cent plate of beans, meat, potatoes, and coffee. If John did come home for a simple meal, he would similarly bolt his food, another American habit that puzzled Europeans. (Not surprisingly, the universal American physical complaint was "dyspepsia" or indigestion.)

For the evening meal, Laura built upon the staple of meat and potatoes. The meat was beef, chicken, or turkey, but not pork, which was considered "lower class." The potatoes were mashed, scalloped, fried, baked, or the latest style, French-fried. Raw fruit, cheese, and various baked goods were the other evening staples. The only raw vegetable likely to appear would be celery, which Americans nibbled incessantly throughout the courses. Apart from corn, vegetables were not well-liked, perhaps because they were boiled to mush.

John ate moderately, and favored fresh fruit. When he was growing up, a wave of nutrition advisors appeared on the scene, men like Sylvester Graham (known for his then bran-heavy cracker) and Dr. John H. Kellogg (who was about to introduce cold cereals to the market), and domestic writers like Catherine Beecher. The Adventists proselytized their blend of religion with a vegetarian lifestyle. The advice from these various quarters for the most part was sensible, although many overweight, tobacco-using, stressed-out Americans thought them faddists. They urged moderation in eating, consumption of foods now called fiber-laden, daily exercise, fresh air in the home (too contaminated with noxious fumes from coal stove and kerosene lamps), and napping to revive one's energy. By following these practices, which led to his being described as "peculiar" later in life, John perhaps contributed to his near-century lifespan.

What most marked family life for brothers John and William, their wives Laura and Mira, was the separation of time and space. The day began and ended with couples in unison, but the hours in-between were spent in same-sex companionship. Knowledge of one another's worlds was imbalanced. Having intimately viewed their mother's household labor, John and William understood much of their wives' daily activities. But Laura and Mira had known little of their fathers' work, and were it not for her knowledge of bookkeeping, Laura would understand little of John's. Her sharing this essential business skill forged a bond between the two that was unusual for spouses of the day. Biographers who later claimed that Laura took no role in John's business were ignoring their subject's own words. "If I had not the support of [Laura], I know I could not have gone on. I had no ambition to make a fortune . . . I had an ambition to build . . . to participate in the work of making the country great."

Laura's hand may be seen in an audacious move that John made several months following the wedding. Unhappy with partner Maurice Clark, he forced the man sell his share of the firm. The newly named company of Rockefeller and Andrews was soon the largest refinery in Cleveland, with a capacity twice that of its nearest competitor. Aware that the European trade was an essential market, John sent his brother William to set up an office in New York City to run the export end of the business. Standard Oil was about to be born.

To understand the brilliant future of these young brothers and their families, one has to consider the role of timing and historical fate. Entering the commission business at the approach of the Civil War accelerated their experiences and opportunities. Under pressure of the war demand here and that overseas, they quickly learned the complexity of markets and the need for efficient organization. They rode the crest of the powerful wave of the Second Industrial Revolution with cunning and balance.

Yet their quick riches, which they then used to capitalize their oil plan, would not have materialized had they started out in the early 1850s or late 1860s, both periods when the economy sputtered.

If people still read omens in the heavens, they would say these fortunate brothers had been conceived under favorable alignments of the stars. But new ideas were sweeping away old, deeming them superstitions. Writers like Ralph Waldo Emerson had venerated the individual, and urged a life of action and the creation of a distinctly American culture. Such ideas implied that young men could place their futures within their own control, that their self-reliance could slice through the inertia of tradition. At the same time, the rising tide of science propelled God further into a darker part of the universe, leaving Him a shadowy all-powerful Creator no longer interested or willing to intervene in human affairs. If He no longer punished sins, rewarded goodness directly, or predestined a life, then a man could follow his own compass and enjoy the heady confidence of riding through difficulties on his own talents.

Curiously, if Americans less felt the hand of God in their daily lives, they were more ready to gather together in His name. Contrary to nostalgic reconstructions, Americans had never been a highly pious lot. Before the Revolution, the intertwining of church and civil governments granted authority and advantage to church members, hence their dominance in later memory of the time. Following the Revolution, Americans identified an essential feature of themselves as Christian, meaning Protestant, yet when the Rockefeller brothers were boys, only about fifteen percent of the population actually attended church. (Their childhood region would not have been singled out as Burned-Over had the fires of salvation blazed throughout the nation.) By the end of the Civil War, Sunday meeting attendance had swelled to almost fifty percent of the population, who could choose from among an array of old denominations and local sects. "They are willing to have religion, as they are willing to have laws," carped an English commentator, "but they choose to make it for themselves."[6]

The people scheduled God now rather than followed His plan; they reduced His presence in schools, meeting halls, and workplaces to brief ritual. In city skylines, city halls, office buildings, and factories rose above the once-dominant spires of the churches. This spatial and temporal separation represented a social split as well. Piety and morality became the protectorate of those closest to the angels, the women. Men were flawed by passions and lusts, and dependent upon their mothers, sisters, and wives to rein in unhealthy desires.

Science reinforced these distinctions. Charles Darwin's theory not only undermined some biblical truths, but suggested a metaphor for social life as well. God no longer predestined one's success, evolution did, for the fittest passed on their survival qualities to their descendants. Rather than quash initiative, this idea as popularized by Herbert Spencer, instead motivated men to prove their superiority through their achievements. As Social Darwinism developed, it rationalized the growing concentration of wealth in the hands of a few by suggesting that millionaires were the naturally selected agents for society. It naturally followed that society should be grateful to have its best in charge, and those in charge could be gratified knowing they were the best.

If men were by nature made of more vile stuff than women, then they must be better competitors. They would be more willing to do whatever was necessary to win the free-for-all game of market capitalism. Guile, deception, and bribery were not only permitted but encouraged. Such unregulated, ethics-free commerce was present before the appearance of Darwin's book—Cornelius Vanderbilt with his ruthless running-down of small railroad owners being a noted example. But after Darwin, after the easy cheating rampant during the Civil War, American businessmen found no conflict between serving their church as deacons on Sunday and lying to a wholesaler on Monday. Soon these leaders of commerce supplanted images of Washington and Christ as heroic models for youth, down to their being the subjects of boys' trading cards.

For the Rockefeller brothers, the God and Mammon conflict resolved in different ways. William's move to New York placed him among the barons of the Gilded Age, named for its elite's shameless flaunting of luxury and pleasure. There William would befriend some of the more nefarious dealers of the era, and follow their model in his oil business negotiations. Remaining in Cleveland, John retained his commitment to Christian manhood and middle-class modesty, self-consciously creating a virtuous life in his home and in his community while conforming to amoral precepts in his office. Compartmentalizing his acts successfully hid from consciousness his hypocrisy, for neither he nor other God-loving businessmen of his day seemed to recognize the contradiction in their ways.[7]

Nor did the scions of Gilded Age capitalism recognize the deleterious effects of their unfettered activities. On the grand scale, the economy rode precipitous boom-and-bust cycles. Between 1866 and 1897, fourteen years of prosperity stood against seventeen of hard times. During booms, workers labored six days a week, ten to fourteen hours, under often hazardous conditions. During busts, they begged for work that paid barely survivable wages. Mechanization replaced highly skilled cabinet-makers, ironworkers, and shoemakers with "green hands," largely immigrants or women, who with minimal training and lower pay operated the machinery. Clerical workers and salespeople did not have a much easier time nor shorter hours than laborers.

One consequence was an increase in prejudice and discrimination: against freed slaves, against European newcomers (and by implication, against Catholics and Jews), against Chinese in the West, against employed women. Social Darwinism provided a scientific explanation for blaming others—their "natural inferiority." According to its tenets, a Yankee was better than an Irishman who was better than a Greek. The lighter one's skin, the greater one's worth. And a man was always better than a woman. In time, some of the aggrieved looked beyond these immediate hatreds to blame all their problems on the capitalists, but they would be in the minority until the turn of the century. The social fabric was rent with protests and violence on all sides, from Ku Klux Klan to anarchist union organizers. Business came to depend upon government to protect its interests by bullet as well as by legislation.

For the families of John and William Rockefeller, life following the war seemed insulated from these disruptions. They were young and healthy, affluent, and graced by God. They were not prejudicial by nature, quite the contrary. They turned inward, as fledgling families are wont to do, but the isolation would not last long.

4

Cleveland: A Promised Land

"Lo, children are an heritage of the Lord: and the fruit of the womb is His reward . . . Happy is the man that hath his quiver full of them."

—Psalm 127:3.5.

The biblical injunction to bear children found loud secular accompaniment in the nineteenth century. As Josiah Gilbert Holland, the most popular advice essayist, remarked, "The foundation of our national character is laid by the mothers of the nation."[1] In hundreds of articles he propounded the thesis that children were essential to a proper marriage because they enabled women to reach their highest development. That God gave women wombs was proof of their destiny. Holland even claimed that bearing children made women so healthy as to delay the onset of old age—an odd assertion given maternal death rates. Other writers agreed. Some intoned that since men's semen was of finite supply, sex without reproduction was simply immoral, a waste of God-given seed.

Such exhortations were understandable in light of problematic birth control. Early versions of diaphragms and condoms were available, but not widely used. Women traded formulae for douches, and advised on the relative efficacy of red rose leaves, alum, bicarbonate of soda, zinc sulphate, or vinegar. They tried vigorous exercise after intercourse, such as dancing or horseback riding. Yet even the most educated people remained ignorant of contraception, for it was a "delicate subject" physicians felt uncomfortable discussing. Thus normally fertile couples conceived within eighteen months after their weddings.

Accordingly, for John and Laura Rockefeller, a little more than a year passed before she became pregnant. For the middle class, midwives were being displaced by doctors, almost all men who obviously lacked experience in childbearing. Not surprisingly, they disagreed as to the nature of pregnancy. Some argued it was a natural state needing only monitoring; others insisted on many restrictions and the confinement of women in a hospital for a forceps-assisted delivery. Laura preferred the natural approach, and had her first child, as all others, at home. But she engaged a homeopath, Dr. Myra Merrick, to assist her through the pregnancy and the delivery. The professional relationship soon grew into a personal one.

Homeopathy was the most formidable competitor of orthodox medicine. Its originator, Samuel Hahnemann, taught that minute amounts of homeopathic, often herbal-based mixtures, cured better than harsh medical treatments. Homeopathy had gained in repute as orthodox physicians failed to remedy sufferers during the episodes of cholera epidemics that struck communities during the 1800s. In the 1860s, most homeopaths were trained in conventional medicine as well, but discarded its mutilating and "heroic" methods.

If Laura's choice of a homeopath to attend her was not unconventional, selecting a woman was. Dr. Myra Merrick was Cleveland's first female physician, and so successful in her obstetrics practice that orthodox doctors referred difficult cases to her. She ran into prejudice among her own, however, when Cleveland's Homeopathic Medical College decided to no longer train females. Dr. Merrick started her own school, which lasted only a year, for her male colleagues soon capitulated to her call for equality. Laura admired Dr. Merrick's determination, and would support her later establishment in Cleveland of Women's General Hospital, a facility run by female doctors for female patients.

On August 23, 1866, Dr. Merrick arrived at the Rockefeller home to guide the birth of Elizabeth "Bessie" Rockefeller. The baby was born when a new wave of childrearing literature had taken hold, and would benefit from the new ideas. Until early in the 1800s, the Calvinist theory of "infant damnation" or inherent evil ruled. A change occurred during the 1830s and 1840s when advisors pointed to external sources, a child's home environment, and not inborn sinfulness, as the determinant of its misbehavior. Provide a proper Christian rearing, and the child would grow up a proper Christian in action. Reason and affection would nurture the child better than rigid rules and corporal punishment, they urged. The Rockefeller boys grew up more under the old methods, rules and the switch, but that would not do for their offspring.

Bessie's presence was an implicit test of Laura's competence as a nurturer. That is, should Bessie turn out to be fussy or impish or sickly, society would hold Laura at fault. Regrettably, the advice writers conflicted on just how to be the perfect mother. For example, disagreements arose around feeding methods. Nursing bottles had been around since 1800, and physicians debated their use. A columnist for the popular woman's magazine *Godey's Ladies Book* suggested that those who refused to breast-feed were "misled by the charms of the fashionable world." Nevertheless, the bottle industry boomed in the late nineteenth century. On a related matter, experts argued over the use of opiates, then legal and a common component of patent medicines, in treating childhood ailments. How Laura chose to handle Bessie—to breast-feed or not, to give narcotics or not—is unknown.

What *is* clear is that Laura saw children as innocents to be directed toward the good. She was convinced that her patience and gentleness, combined with her force of character, would obviate the need for corporal punishment. As her sister Lute observed, Laura had "a gracious persuasiveness . . . there was persuasion in her touch when she laid her fingers so gently on your arm." Her children would come to know this commanding, gentle touch well.[2]

Laura was also fortunate in that John shared some child care. Lute noted that John would take a crying, ailing infant and walk the halls with it for hours at night if necessary. A child once reminded him of her earliest memory, of how as a toddler "you came up [to my room] and rubbed my back which was making me restless on account of the prickly heat. You came up so quietly and you went down again so gently."[3] Contemporary views of parental duty did not require this assistance on his part. If anything, popular notions asserted a father should ignore the bawler and leave her to her mother, aunts, and grandmothers. Here emerged a most striking feature of John D. Rockefeller's character, his abiding love of children.

Following the Civil War, parental relationships, not spousal ones, defined the family. A childless couple felt itself defective, and wondered why God failed to fulfill them, how they were lacking that He would withhold such riches. In an era where Social Security was only a dream for futurists, children also provided a safety net for their parents' old age. Even though in working outside men had lost many functions in the home, they still maintained a limited role as fathers. For many middle-class men, a "good father" saw to the biological act of procreating, provided comfortable shelter, and met certain religious duties, such as leading morning and evening prayers. Otherwise, during their leisure hours, men were free to associate with other men, often in fraternal orders, political and civic meetings, or taverns. They found solace in fraternity, not in the home.

Despite the pressure to define one's masculinity through work, after business hours certain men were adopting a lifestyle of "domestic masculinity."[4] Rather than spend their evenings with cronies, they sought companionship with their wives, and took on some of the responsibility of raising the children. The men who took this path shared certain qualities. They rejected the old notion of the stern patriarch ruling the family, and supported their wives' interests in outside pursuits, usually social reform activities. They were economically secure, and able to locate the family home away from the vicinity of all-male gathering places. John D. Rockefeller was among these men choosing emotional comfort in the home rather than among male lodge brothers and club men.

Nonetheless, John's model of fatherhood was his often-absent father. What he disdained about Big Bill was his infidelity, not his scarcity. Overall, he held fond memories of the man who had taught him the magic of compound interest and of wheedling a successful deal. Besides instructing his children in commercial skills, Bill had brought evenings of fun and music into the home. John would repeat Bill's patterns with his own offspring. That is, he would vanish for long periods, but when around he was a confidant, advisor, and playful companion who took very seriously his charge to raise children who were morally upright and also individualists.

In 1868, John bought his family a home on Euclid Avenue, "Millionaire's Row." Cleveland's population had doubled since 1860, and those who benefitted from the profits of the war economy created one of the most noted streets of its day. Its splendid broad boulevard with overarching elms was known as "the most beautiful avenue in the west," even "better than Fifth Avenue" in New York. Even the usually sarcastic Mark Twain admitted it to be "one of the finest streets in America."[5]

The newly rich Clevelanders purposely took their inspiration from the great European models—Champs Élysées in Paris, Unter den Linden in Berlin, Regent's Street in London. They believed they were creating estates to pass on to their children and grandchildren, as well as building monumental memorials to their own achievements. (In later years, as commercial development started to encroach, patriarchs put instructions in their wills that the houses be torn down rather than be subdivided into rooming houses or offices. This unhappy eventuality was however a half-century away.)

Residents set their houses far back from the street, behind well-trimmed lawns and finely pruned shrubs. Humorist Artemus Ward jibed that the length of the setback pronounced "the length of the owner's pedigree." An ex-Clevelander, he poked fun at the "sacred highway where the houses present a distangy [distingué] appearance and the owners employ hired girls and are patrons of the arts."[6] Since no fencing was placed between the homes, the properties flowed one to the other, the vista broken only by scattered side streets and one railroad crossing. Cast-iron fencing posed a uniform barrier between the sidewalks and the properties, while allowing the stroller to admire or envy the gardens and statuary behind the filigree.

British visitor Anthony Trollope observed that Euclid Avenue homes were more comfortable than those of comparable Englishmen, but that the English probably spent more money on fine food, wine, and amusements. The Euclid houses were large, from six thousand to fifty thousand square feet, typically designed by an architect rather than the builder. Their facades tended toward the Romanesque, the Gothic, or pastiches, and were not notable from a design standpoint. Inside, however, the homes exuded warmth and good manners. Decor ran the gamut from gaudy to elegant, depending upon the taste of the owner. Popular colors were cobalt blue, plum and purple, crimson, and oxblood red. Carved wood panelling trimmed the walls and furniture; patterns in deep shades of blue, brown, and even gold enhanced the ceilings, leather-covered walls and chairs. However costly the furnishings and decorations, the rooms invited sociability.

The Rockefeller house was less showy than others. It was an Eclectic Manse, as the term implies, a combination of decorative forms. Its facade was of a symmetrical Italianate design on the first two floors, while a French mansard roof topped the third floor. Adding to the pastiche were a classical-columned portico and large window groupings favored by the Victorians. Unpretentious, it had no towers, turrets, or fancy decorative trim, apart from a delicate iron baluster along the roof line. It was much simpler than the house of their friends Charles and Anne Otis, whose facade had a grand long colonnade of double columns; nor did it gleam with gilded and elaborately paneled interiors as found in John and Clara Hay's salons. Often these showier residents travelled to New York to buy the latest in china, furniture, and clothing. Laura saw that their home, which she had redecorated before they moved in, was furnished for comfort, not fashion. Just as soothingly appointed was the servant's ell, for the Rockefellers were paternalistic and considered their help as members of the family, deserving as much private ease as themselves.

Desiring more room for gardens and trees, in time John surprised his neighbors by purchasing the house next door. Rather than tear it down, he donated it to Augusta Mittleberger, head of a girls' school, and underwrote the challenging project of moving the mansion a block away to its new site. For two weeks the behemoth crept atop greased logs along Case Avenue, annoying travellers and amazing onlookers.

Besides its unadorned facade, the Rockefeller house was unusual for its being set on the south side of the street, the "wrong side," where the "bobs" dwelt. Preferred by the social set or "nabobs" was the northside Ridge, because buildings set there topped a hundred-foot elevation, affording an unfettered view of Lake Erie from their back lawns and windows. Thus, the resident capitalists daily found reassurance in the sight of the sail-powered and steam-driven trading ships bringing in raw materials and moving out manufactured goods to the urban East and frontier West.

Behind his house, where the land stretched back a full block, John ordered built a large stone stable to accommodate Midnight, Flash Eye, Truffle, and other Rockefeller trotters. (Some visitors thought the horses' pine-panelled home more elaborate than that of the family.) As in New York City, well-to-do Cleveland men spent free hours in the afternoon racing their thoroughbreds. Influential residents had even routed the public horsecar line off Euclid so the street would be free for driving.

Residents also turned Euclid's most annoying defect into an advantage. Because of poor drainage, during storms the street became flooded, which meant in winter it became an ice pond. On winter days, businessmen went to work early, to have the afternoon free for racing their sleighs down the boulevard. They placed red flags at Ninth and Fortieth streets to warn away all public traffic. Bundled in bison and fur, a charcoal warmer at his feet, the athletic John was a skillful challenger. (His love of ice skating, passed on to his descendants, would find lasting expression in the rink at Rockefeller Center.)

Of course, life on Euclid Avenue was not always so idyllic as it appeared. Thieves sneaked into yards to strip clotheslines, or climbed through large unscreened first-floor windows to carry off a bibelot. Iron fences could not prevent a vandal from tossing bricks to smash garden statuary or windows. Smoke and coal dust from the refineries and iron mills choked the lungs of the capitalists and their families, but they welcomed the pollution as a sign of progress. "The children are well and very grubby from coal smoke," wrote John Hay approvingly to his friend Henry Adams.[7]

To live on Euclid was to join a privileged group, with all the demands an exclusive community requires of its members. "The hoy-poloy visitor to the street, by wiping his feet on the mat at the lower end of the thoroughfare and showing a certificate of good moral character, will be permitted to traverse the sacred precincts free of charge," tittled Artemus Ward.[8] Such "hoy-poloy" had better stay on the sidewalk and walk quickly by to get to his home in the working-class neighborhoods further east.

Nevertheless, the Cleveland elite were not so rigid as the Boston Back Bay or the New York Knickerbockers or the Philadelphia Old Guard, whose wealthy families had held money for several generations. Most elite Easterners were large landowners and mercantilists who prided themselves on their insularity, their good blood (and conveniently forgot if their bloodlines included fur trappers, peasants, and crooks). Family ties and traditions, however artificial and nonegalitarian, formed a bulwark against the loss of fortune to outsiders. Their style rigidified into the cage of manners so ironically described in the novels of one of their own, Edith "Pussy" Jones Wharton. This was the world to which William and Mira Rockefeller refitted themselves.

In contrast, the Cleveland elite were newly rich; therefore, they had to create Society afresh and fashion the customs for future generations. What they shared were circumstances similar to the Rockefellers and Spelmans. That is, they had originated in the villages and farming areas of New England and upstate New York, and valued hard work and piety. Few came from the cosmopolitan upper-class of New York or Philadelphia. The men were mostly industrialists and bankers, not artists, journalists, or professors. Few had attended college, or acquired the cultural interests such education engenders.

Having known little luxury in their youth, they did not avoid comfort and elegance in their lives. In that regard they shed some of their Yankee heritage and mimicked the acquisitiveness of the nouveaux riche. Nonetheless they retained a strong commitment to social responsibility, to serving their community. In effect, tending to the larger welfare of society was proof of their worthiness, and their right to own a mansion, hire servants, and take an afternoon off now and then to race a trotter down the street. John D. Rockefeller stated this belief succinctly: "I believe it every man's duty to get all he honestly can, and to give all he can."[9]

Thus, despite the grandeur of the mansions, Euclid Avenue reconstituted a New England village. One's relatives lived nearby, next door, or on the same block if possible, and one's friends were neighbors or the people across the street. John D., more of a loner, chose his male friends from among fellow Euclid residents, and his business associates also moved to the Avenue. Such camaraderie fostered both commercial ventures among the fathers and marriages among the children. Boys in particular learned that the *best* society was essential to success later in life, as basic as hard work and integrity.

A further link for the men were the downtown private clubs, where they could lunch away from the distracting presence of females, who were thought to "spoil" the life of a busy man. The club was almost equal with the family in building the network of elite connections. John joined the most prestigious, the Union Club, which purported to be "a space where cultivated gentlemen will meet to read and discuss the topics of the day and entertain each other and their friends abroad."[10] Intellectual cultivation took second place to the all-male friendships that formed. The men had not grown up together in one town, so club members substituted for lost playmates and relatives. The conversations ran from the philosophical to the ribald. As men do today, they bantered about sports, politics, the economy, and women—especially women. Humor and wit were particularly valued. Although John D. was a poker face, and seldom spoke out, he was quick with the occasional *bon mot.*

Liquor often lubricated the conversation in the clubs, but John D., a teetotaler, did not partake. Neither did he avoid the friendship of men who drank, although he might pity them for succumbing to the dissipating habit. He taught a simple strategy for avoiding the evils of liquor: just don't take the first drink. Since smoking in public was ungentlemanly, the club was a refuge for chewing, spitting, and inhaling the weed. John's avoidance of tobacco, he advised friends, resulted from his father having once caught him and William smoking in a barn. John was so humiliated that he never tried tobacco again; William, on the other hand, was not so easily intimidated.

John seldom went to the club after work, however. He depended upon it more for business discussions, a congenial and neutral setting for negotiations. For fraternity, the fictive brotherhood, he relied more upon the firm.

Throughout his later recollections of this time, John unconsciously used metaphors of manliness and Americanism to describe his relationships. One of his heroes was Napoleon, admired for his "virility—his humanity . . . because he came direct from the ranks of the people . . . none of the stagnant blood of nobility or royalty in his veins."[11] One key to success in business was to be a "man." Businessmen who failed he described as "children" or "childlike" for their inability to control their impulses. "The man who does not believe in anybody else has a screw loose somewhere. The man who is sane, well-balanced, well-disposed, believes in other men, though some may at times deceive." Such trust develops "strength and manhood."[12] In hiring men, he "sought men of courage, initiative, enterprise, real ability, pluck and foresight [in other words, the Self-Made American], but beyond all . . . whom we could trust."[13]

When convinced of their "manifestation of manliness," John encouraged employees to run their operations according to their own devices and preferences. It was this respect for individuality that inspired loyalty, if not affection for Rockefeller. Character, the basis for manhood, guided his hiring, not an applicant's religion or appearance. When an associate whispered that a potential employee was a Catholic, John responded that all he wanted to know was whether the man was honest and able.[14] Similarly, he was tolerant of peccadilloes such as mild drinking or smoking, so long as the man conformed to higher values. Thus workers from the poorest part of society found themselves rising to top administrative positions if they proved their mettle.

John's view of business was also shaped by religious metaphors, a Moses-like vision. He saw his efforts to bring rationality to the oil business as providing "salvation," pulling "this broken-down industry out of the Slough of Despond." Competitors broke their "covenants," hence, deserved to fail. "What a blessing it was that the idea of co-operation" helped him to do "God's service."[15] Accordingly, he followed the principle of mercy, of expecting that a worker might err now and then, and would be deserving of another chance if he were repentant.

Even an extroverted man with such firm opinions would find making close male friends difficult. But John was so silent as to make people around him uneasy, so detail-oriented as to nose about anywhere in the operations without warning. He knew others found him aloof, yet he did not feel lonely. It was his grace to be treated gingerly and without bonhomie by coworkers, yet not feel aggrieved that he was excluded from their more informal intercourse. One suspects he even found amusement in being considered distant, and manipulated that image to his advantage.

Still, a few men befriended him beyond business talk. One was Henry M. Flagler, who joined the firm as a partner in 1867. Flagler was a war profiteer who later lost his fortune investing in salt. Then, through marriage to the daughter of whiskey tycoon Stephen V. Harkness, Flagler was once again rich. Harkness joined the firm, renamed Rockefeller, Andrews & Flagler, as a silent partner. Besides bringing an influx of money to the fledgling business, Flagler bridged the generation gap between Rockefeller, nine years his junior, and Cleveland monied interests. He filled three indispensible roles, as transportation negotiator, legal expert, and communicator with Rockefeller on new ideas. But just as importantly, he also understood John D.'s taciturnity and brilliance, and was as active in the Congregational Church as his partner was in the Baptist. As the men's bond grew, they shared an office, and Flagler moved his family to Euclid Avenue.

For the Euclid Avenue women, conventions ordered their days as regularly as the men's office clocks. Unlike their counterparts in New York City or Boston, they worked side-by-side with the household help on lighter chores. In later life, news articles about Laura would remark on her small number of servants as a sign of her humility and modesty. Yet from the viewpoint of Cleveland society, her behavior was not unusual. Euclid women were more democratic and less given to pressing class distinctions upon their employees.

Unlike Eastern Society women, the Euclid Avenue neighbors were less formal among themselves. They rejected the notion of "at home" days and of calling cards. Rather, they followed more casual neighboring. Laura could cross the street to visit a friend unannounced, or open the door to find an unexpected, welcome visitor. Gatherings occurred spontaneously in the evenings as well, as friends dropped by for a chat on the porch or even an informal dinner. Also popular was joining with others to attend an "improving" event, a lecture on some uplifting topic such as spiritual salvation and temperance. Families that wished to avoid the "contamination" of theaters gathered for evenings of singing and instrumental playing.

If business and club united men, and domestic culture women, the institution that bound American families together was religion. The Euclid elite allowed only church buildings to disrupt the flow of their urban estates, and soon after the Rockefellers settled on the street, Erie Street Baptist Church moved there as well.

Sunday morning services were for more than holy worship; they were a time to show off fashionable carriages and dress. While for some the churches were little more than social clubs, for most, such as the Rockefellers, they were organizations through which to carry out good works. They collected money for Baptist missions, food and clothing for church-sponsored homes for the poor or aged. John and Laura both taught Sunday School. When not restricted by the final stages of pregnancy, Laura participated in the many ladies' projects organized by Katherine Chisholm: the sewing circle, the mission study classes, and the planning of church picnics and dinners.

Of all the Baptist causes, foreign mission most drew Laura's attention. By now she accepted that "God, who never makes a mistake" had not fulfilled her childhood hope to call her as a missionary. Rather, she accepted that her role was "to help others to go and thus multiply my one little life manyfold."[16] Her commitment was part of a general upsurge of Protestant women's desire to spread Christianity overseas, particularly to Asia. To advance that end, Baptist women discussed forming their own missionary support organization, one separate from the male-controlled American Baptist Missionary Society.

Because Baptists disapproved of theater and dancing, the church provided the main source of artistic experience for its members by sponsoring musicales. Although professional musicians usually played, church members also contributed their talents. Accordingly, John and Laura performed piano duets for their fellow congregants.

In terms of social standing, in Cleveland as elsewhere, the Baptists were less prestigious than the Episcopalians or Presbyterians. By not "moving up" in denomination, the Rockefellers further demonstrated their independence from convention. What mattered ultimately to Euclid residents was not the church one attended, but that one demonstrate Christian, meaning Protestant, conviction. Indeed, Josiah Gilbert Holland made clear that it was white Protestant women who should be reproducing to save the nation from the contamination of too many Catholic or otherwise unseemly foreign influences.

Laura did her part. In 1869, she bore a second daughter, Alice, whose life was short—less than a year. Alice's grave was among the first in Cleveland's famous Lake View Cemetery, for which John would later serve as a trustee.

Laura was soon pregnant again, and gave birth to Alta in April of 1871, and then to Edith in August of 1872. Yet with three daughters under six, she did not restrict herself to the house, but continued her church and charitable activities.

From the start, John and Laura identified themselves as civic-minded Clevelanders and would assert such even after leaving the city. Consequently, they were quick to identify community needs and contribute in some way, however small at first. Eventually they aided over 150 organizations and activities in that Lake Erie city.

One of their first efforts was for the Western Reserve Historical Society, formed in 1867 by prominent men who had the vision to preserve the "history, biography, genealogy, antiquities, and statistics" of the region.[17] Membership was by invitation, and soon the leaders of what was to become Standard Oil were active contributors. John donated ten thousand dollars toward the purchase of a building to house the society. Laura gave her time to the organization so avidly that when pregnant with Edith, John gently reprimanded her "overworking" there.[18]

When John had first moved to Cleveland, he joined the Young Men's Christian Association and made large gifts to it over the years. At that time the YMCA also included women, so early in the marriage Laura joined. In 1868 she was her church's delegate in the formation of the Women's Christian Association, a precursor of the YWCA. One of the key activities of the Cleveland branch was finding suitable boarding places for the rural women and immigrant women seeking employment in the city. Another project was a home for "fallen women," to help them leave the life of prostitution.

Given her frequent pregnancies, Laura did not hold any offices in the YWCA. Yet through exposing her directly to the troubles of urban working women, the YWCA broadened her understanding of poverty and sexual exploitation. Unlike late twentieth-century feminist movements, which were largely centered in the upper middle class, the early YWCA grew rapidly among all the social classes to enlist the factory worker, the shop girl, the teacher, and the wife of the well-to-do businessman. The slogan "Every young woman is her sister's keeper," meant that the leadership and committees strove to be inclusive and democratic, even though such diversity guaranteed conflict. The only requirement for holding an office was Christian commitment, and membership included Jewish women.

By 1871, the YWCA had grown so rapidly that it held its first national conference. Members shared stories of their accomplishments: housing for single working women, job referrals, free lecture series, free classes (Bible study, vocational, artistic), free libraries, musical presentations, day nurseries, distribution of fruit and clothing to Civil War soldiers' homes, assistance in prisons and orphan asylums, night schools for factory boys, retreats for "sinful, sorrowing women." Its 1873 conference reported, "We are helping to solve the problem in social science, as how to bridge the gulf that divides the favored from the less fortunate. . . . We are to vitalize the teachings of our Lord, that 'we are members of one another.' "19

Not all Christian men supported the women's independence, however. Some objected that the programs were not grounded in a particular denomination. Others attacked as morally questionable policies such as opening the reading rooms to young men or holding classes for women in the evening. More commonly, men believed that women lacked the ability to organize and manage, especially with regard to raising income and managing a budget. Of course, in setting up a separate YWCA, the women implicitly announced their independence from the men. When their effectiveness proved the men wrong, resistance in some quarters only increased. Fortunately for Laura, John was not among these critics.

Laura's major community activity was one the YWCA supported early and strongly, the temperance cause. Following the Civil War, middle-class women in various towns made raids on saloons to close them down. Itinerant temperance orators such as Dio Lewis were often responsible for inciting these aggressive episodes among proper ladies. These were isolated events, however, and it was not until late 1873 that an organized crusade emerged. Somehow a cluster of towns in southwestern Ohio simultaneously developed temperance leagues tied to their churches. By February of 1874, reports of the leagues' successes in the newspapers ignited a brush fire of activity throughout the nation that the South excepted. In November of that year, Cleveland hosted the first convention of the national Woman's Christian Temperance Union, or WCTU.

Temperance was not a new cause, but women's assertive participation was a new development. It was their pronouncement to male temperance leaders that women were fed up with slow progress. The men had connected the cause to political parties and election issues; the women, lacking the vote, naturally felt left out of the process. For women like Laura, the movement allowed public expression of deep religious feeling, to answer God's call, as one leader noted, "to meet a sin which is fast undermining and destroying our nation."[20] From her work in the YWCA she was familiar with the possible deleterious effects of the saloon world: impoverished families, wife-beating, prostitution, venereal disease. She was less aware of an unstated goal of the movement, to prevent white Protestant children from adopting the cultural practices of Irish and German Catholic immigrants. As the literature exhorted, one must make the saloons "odious in the eyes of [white Protestant] young men."[21]

Although pregnancy and childrearing kept Laura from being as active as she would have liked, she fully supported the WCTU and was a charter member. When possible, she joined some of the events, as did her parents in Brooklyn, where they now lived. The women were not sedate. They began at a church with a prayer session, then marched out on the streets and swarmed into a saloon, arriving around eleven o'clock, just when workers were apt to make a short midday appearance. They crowded in such numbers that the men could not escape, then compelled their prisoners to listen to the prayers and Gospel singing. They felt particularly successful if a hostile crowd hooted, jeered, and pulled the ribbons from their bonnets. They welcomed arrests, for the jailed could be held up as martyrs.

In addition to protesting, the WCTU women rented empty storefronts and set up canteens. There they served "wholesome food and sarsaparilla" as well as delivered Demon Rum lectures. Placed near immigrant workers' homes, these centers did draw some laborers away from the saloons, as well as attracted their wives to spy upon the elegant ladies. As such, the canteens were forerunners of the more elaborate settlement houses of the future.

In Cleveland as elsewhere, the WCTU's actions did close some saloons. But the real payoff was the organizational skills women gained. Now that they saw the power of their temperance war, they had a model for attacking other problems. If women still lacked a ballot, at least they now had swords.

While Laura tended her infants and social causes, John was often away on business. On January 10, 1870, John and his associates formally organized the Standard Oil Company of Ohio. The name was chosen to suggest a "standard quality of product," to contrast with competitors' less reliable kerosene. John D. controlled one-fourth of the stock, as well as conceived "the Plan," namely to consolidate nearly all of American oil refining into one giant concern.

During the early 1870s, he spent months at a time in New York City on negotiations concerning the South Improvement Company, a scheme created by railroad men in which railroads and refiners would organize cartels and split the markets. Member refiners received rebates on their freight charges, while nonmenber competitors paid full-price for transportation of their barrels. Consequently, members like Standard Oil could charge less for their products, at the expense of shut-out competitors.

Meanwhile, Standard Oil was executing its squeeze play on fellow Cleveland refiners. William Rockefeller characterized the plan as "war or peace," that is, competitors had to sell out to Standard Oil or suffer deadly consequences. Much of the operation was covert, with Rockefeller representatives negotiating under fictitious fronts. John was sanctimonious about his actions. While Standard Oil "were most kindly disposed toward their weaker brethren," he explained, "they could not stop the *car of salvation* in their great enterprise which meant so much to the consuming public the world over. And they proved themselves, while good and sensible businessmen *missionaries of light,* always with the best quality and the lowest price, and servants of all."[22] By bringing order to the oil market, he averred, the company was making life easier for the poor, who were no longer victimized by the price vagaries of disorganization.

Such activities fomented a small yet vocal set of critics who understandably sniped at Standard Oil for years to come. First to chastise were those competitors who had bargained for a large financial settlement and refused Standard Oil stock in the deal. This short-term gain turned into a comparative loss, for those who accepted stock found themselves much better off in the long run. (Indeed, even low-level clerks in Standard Oil who held stock long enough found themselves able to live on streets like Euclid.) One voice was particularly grating, for it was that of youngest brother Frank Rockefeller, who had become an executive at a refinery that refused to be absorbed by Standard Oil and went under as a result. From that point Frank's relations with his two older brothers was strained, and only Eliza's calming hand prevented a total breach among her three sons.

Others would join the din of criticism as years passed, and for less personal reasons. No matter how much John rationalized the actions of his company, he could not convince critics of what he saw as his good intentions. True, it was a time when "business ethics" was not part of the vocabulary, and other capitalists, like the Vanderbilt men, were more venal with their bribery of politicians and vengeance towards competitors. Despite John D. Rockefeller's suggestion of the contrary, being relatively less deceitful than one's colleagues does not place one closer to the angels.

During the winter of 1871–72, John was gone for almost half a year to negotiate with railroad men Commodore Vanderbilt and his son William. His letters then hint at the warmth and affection he showed Laura during their private hours. These messages reveal the tenderness of the man as lover, toward his wife now expecting their third child. He had some reason to feel guilty, for he had seen the pain brought into his mother's life by his father's uncommunicative disappearances. He had already surpassed his father in his ability to support his family in material ways. For John, this meeting of material duty, which would suffice for many of his peers, including his brother William, was not enough. Without affirming so explicitly, he acted as though his manliness was not weakened by creating deep emotional ties with his family members.

A repeated theme in his notes to Laura that winter was of his sadness and loneliness in being separated from her. Following eight days in a row of working late into the night, he apologized for not writing more frequently. "I can understand how *you* must be very lonely and feel myself as I just told Mr. Devereux like a wandering Jew."[23] Two weeks later, he noted wistfully, "I would give *anything* to be quietly at home until Monday next without a soul *outside* knowing it. Oh for a *home* dinner and . . . the quiet & peace of our own table."[24] He particularly regretted having to miss Christmas with the family.

To deflect the blame for his extensive separation from the family, he referred to society's demands upon him as a male. He was providing his family "a home and a protector . . . to a *man* it is worth working for." Other men he dealt with, such as Jay Gould, he described as deceptive and selfish. Consequently, he felt "more than ever thankful for a true and loving wife, why shouldn't a man be stimulated to *efforts?* The world is full of Sham, Flattery and Deception, the *home* is a haven of rest and free-dom."[25] He was proud that he could provide his wife and children with comfort and prosperity, the ability to live well independent of the econ-omy's intermittent plunges.

Indeed, so typical of the age are John's remarks concerning manhood and family that they have an artificial air. Yet, to conclude he was parrot-ing what he thought he should write, that he was insincere, is a mistake. This vision of home as a refuge was an accurate one for John and other men who chose domestic masculinity. He preferred to direct the battle of business from the rear, where he had ready access to the safety of the home, not fight on the front line.

During his business trips to New York, he stayed with William and Mira, who now had two toddlers, a girl, Emma, and a boy, William Jr. Being in the presence of that family added to John's melancholy. "How much I would give for *wings* to reach you tonight. Tell Bessie I would fly down that chimney and that also Emma slept with me last night and didn't she kick."[26] He also frequently visited his in-laws and Lute in Brooklyn. Laura's father was not well that winter, and Lute's "lung problems" con-tinued to prevent her from working.

Yet the most prominent themes in his letters were his love for Laura and his business negotiations. He worried that she was working too hard. He was concerned that she was using up her energy writing him so many long letters. In one note, he remarked, "I dreamed last night of the girl Celestia Spelman and awoke to realize she was my 'Laura.' "[27] He praised her as being the source of "improvement or growth" in himself, the result of her "elevating, & enabling."

When Laura confessed her mutual loneliness, he sent her mother west to provide companionship. But that could not assuage her real concern, that she would have another daughter rather than a son to carry the fam-ily name. In response, John recounted a conversation with a friend who had experienced similar anxiety to have a boy, but was very happy once the girl was born. When Laura in fact gave birth to a third daughter, Edith, he showed no disappointment.

At another point, Laura apparently wrote something to shake his cer-tainty in her, or he may simply have been worried by knowledge of the high rate of divorce that followed the Civil War. Whatever, he felt the need to address the issue straight on. "Don't allow any misgivings—we will together make the most of our experiences and try for all the good and happiness that can come from our united life."[28] This unshakable certitude in the durability of family ties was to become the keystone for strong loyalty and members' tolerance of one another's individuality. The Rockefellers simply refused to consider the possibility of any other path.

In the spring of 1872, the facts of the South Improvement railroad-oil cartel became public, with the name Rockefeller singled out for blame. The problem was not that the railroads gave Standard rebates on their transportation charges, for the practice was common in that time of free-for-all business competition. Critics deplored the "drawbacks," the fact that railroads gave Standard Oil a portion of the transportation charges collected from its refinery competitors. Those producers left out of the South Improvement cartel started the Oil War, and Standard's workforce plummeted to a tenth its usual size. The press vilified Rockefeller, who found himself portrayed alongside railroad magnate William Vanderbilt in editorial cartoons, as symbols of business evil. Where Vanderbilt's stocky frame readily shaped itself to a voracious piglike form, Rockefeller's lankiness lent itself into becoming a snake or a vulture.

During the height of the scandals John repeatedly explained himself to Laura. She should not worry because his other investments outside of oil ensured their continued wealth. She should remember that the game was chess, not checkers, and that his intentions were right. The "Union of American Refineries is worth much labor and patient effort. . . . Let us be temperate in all things."[29] As for the criticism from the press, which Laura advised him to attack straight on, he refused to follow her advice. "We *did* not contemplate swindling the public in *it* [South Improvement] and it is not the business of the public to change our private contracts."[30]

The Oil War failed. As other production areas opened up, gluts developed. Oil became so cheap as to flow uncollected and unused into surrounding streams and fields, ruining the very communities it begot. Standard Oil saw a drop in crude oil prices as an opportunity to buy. That housewives used to paying forty cents for a gallon of kerosene now paid only four scared fortune seekers off to other endeavors, and further affirmed John's faith in the social value of centralizing the industry. By the end of the 1870s Standard Oil would control over ninety percent of the market.

January 29, 1874, was a date that would mark a transformation of unimaginable consequences on each of the family members. As Laura Rockefeller later recounted, "That is the date of the Woman's Temperance Crusade in Ohio, when Mrs. Duncan marched thru' the streets, and talked and sang and prayed in the saloons, with many other ladies as intelligent. I might have joined them, if a sweet baby-boy had not claimed me."[31] The choice of names was obvious, John Jr. Greeting clerks at his office later that day, Senior—as we shall now refer to the patriarch—later described their amazement that their boss literally danced about the rooms. Laura gave thanks that the boy was in perfect health. His three sisters gathered around the crib, as youngsters do, to delight at the tiny toes and fingers.

The heir had been born. Laura need no longer worry through a pregnancy that yet another girl would appear. In fact, she would have no more children. John Jr. would suffice.

The full consequences of this most happy occasion could not be imagined, however. The little girls had a baby brother to spoil and adore. The mother saw before her fulfillment of the most revered relationship in that era, that of mother and son. The father proclaimed his link to posterity, a carrier of the Rockefeller name and cause into another generation. What they could not foresee was the eventual role of the heir, a prince really, whose mere presence produced a magnetic pull on each family member. The parents had sought this new binding tie, and would reap exceptional reward. The girls, however, would eventually find themselves mere commoners cast into the margins of the family. But several decades would pass before this relization, and for now there was only rejoicing.

5

God's Precious Jewels

"That our sons may be as plants grown up in their youth; that our daughters may be as corner stones, polished after the similitude of a palace."

—Psalms 144: 12.

L aura and Senior united in their expectations for their children. Namely, they should be good Christians. As Baptists, this meant daily practice of religious expression and vigilant avoidance of worldly temptations. God, not Mammon, permeated daily life.

Laura fueled this family philosophy. As her sister Lute explained, Laura was "a *religieuse*." God and church came first with her . . . and together she and her husband deepened and expanded their religion to cover and include every phase of life."[1] Both parents saw their children as "precious jewels" loaned by God in trust, and "to be handed back when the call comes."[2]

Mornings began with the family gathering for worship. Each child participated, repeating a simple memorized prayer when very young, reading from Scripture when older. They said grace before each meal. On Friday, the entire family attended prayer meetings at the church. (Punctuality was the Rockefeller watchword, yet Senior was more often than not late for devotions, and was fined accordingly.)[3]

This democratic approach to religious ritual was unusual. In most families of that period, fathers read Scripture and mothers added instructional comment. Children said little beyond joining in united prayers or hymns. The household religious practices reinforced the gender roles, the father's place as prophet and king, the mother's as his willing follower. In contrast, the Rockefeller children experienced religious practice more as a setting for independence and self-expression. As a result, each would eventually follow an individual spiritual path.

Sober and solemn grandmother Eliza, who often stayed with the family, furthered the pious atmosphere. Letters from the Spelman grandparents affirmed the values of temperance and service to others. Grandfather Bill Rockefeller, a man of more profane interests, seldom appeared.

Wealth aided in isolating the children from taboos readily available to other city children: tobacco, card playing, dancing, theater, frivolous amusements, books lacking in moral message. The children did not go to school, but were tutored at home. Cleveland flourished with classical music schools and performing groups, so accomplished musicians came to the house to instruct. Bessie played viola, Alta piano, Edith cello, and John violin. The children had virtually no opportunity to go out alone beyond Euclid Avenue and explore.

Like other protected children, the Rockefeller brood did not feel their lives particularly restricted or narrow. At church and Sunday School they met other families such as their own, and were proud of their Protestant devotion, which was virtually identical with American patriotism in those days. When lessons were completed, they had chores (for which they earned pennies, as their father had when young). They left no record of cruel or abusive tutors. On rainy days they had spacious rooms to romp in, ones where furnishings were not considered more precious than the inhabitants. When father was around, they could count on his starting games and cracking jokes.

Even the childhood diseases so dangerous in that era left little mark. Alta alone suffered; recurrent ear infections caused partial deafness. She compensated so artfully most people were unaware of her condition. Worse for her than the hearing loss were recurrent severe earaches that troubled her throughout her life. Otherwise the children passed through episodes of measles, scarlet fever, and such without apparent harm.

In the mid-1870s, a failed business venture presented a circumstance that would further these idyllic childhoods. With several friends, Senior started the Euclid Avenue Forest Hill Association to establish a public resort offering water cures, a popular form of rejuvenation. In conjunction with this plan, they set up the Lake View & Collamer Railroad, a small urban steam railway, which conveniently had as its terminus the partners' Forest Hill acreage. The railway fared well initially, as it ran through a populous neighborhood. In Forest Hill, construction began on a large, turreted hotel with spacious verandas to accommodate the spa visitors. Then the nation fell into one of its frequent bust cycles, and both resort and railroad went bankrupt.

Laura Rockefeller so liked the property that Senior bought out his Forest Hill partners and saw the hotel completed. His thought was to continue it as a summer resort for his well-heeled friends, as well as provide a second home for his family. (One of John Jr.'s earliest memories was of the black waiters serving food in the dining room.) What Senior did not make clear to his friends was the proprietary nature of the establishment. The result was a family story repeated in more than one household. As a descendant of Henry Chisholm's family recounted, "Grandfather and his family were most cordially invited to Forest Hill for a visit, but hesitated to take the children so far out in the country [four miles southeast, in fact, from Euclid Avenue]. Mr. Rockefeller urged them to come, assuring them there would be plenty of fresh milk for the children, and they went." To Henry Chisholm's surprise, upon leaving he was presented a bill for ten dollars. "Grandfather had not realized they had been at hotel."[4]

The experiment was short-lived. In 1878, Senior ended it when he discovered that the guests expected Laura to play hostess throughout the day. He fired the waiters and announced the place was now exclusively for the family. Nonetheless, many of the previously paying guests continued to visit Forest Hill, for the Rockefellers enjoyed sharing its comfort and healthful environment with others. Senior eventually expanded the property to seven hundred acres crisscrossed with eighteen miles of roadways. For adults, there were tennis courts, bridle paths for riding the thoroughbred horses, a track for racing horses, and trails for hiking and biking. Laura's favorite spot was the boathouse on one of the two artificial lakes, and she also revelled in driving the horses around the property.

To children, Forest Hill was a wonderland. The romantic woods and ravines invited fantasy. The farm, which furnished most of the food, dairy, and meat for the household, offered fascinating sights to the youngsters. Senior ordered construction of play areas and smooth pathways for small-wheeled vehicles. He would call a farm cart, pile the children on the rough boards, and have them driven very slowly about the estate as he chatted with his hangers-on about their lessons. As soon as children were mature enough, he taught them to ride, to swim, to handle a boat, to drive a team, and to ride a velocipede. All readily grew adept at these various skills, and shared their father's enjoyment of the outdoors. When guests were about, he would lead a jaunty cycling expedition, and pedal fast ahead to lose his panting followers in the maze of beech trees.

By then, Senior's sisters had each married Cleveland businessmen and eventually had children. Lucy's husband was Pierson Briggs; Mary Ann's was William Rudd. Yet their families did not associate often with that of their eldest brother. Nor of course did Frank's, for he felt rejected by his brothers and resented their success.

Eliza's influence upon her daughters was obvious. Typically dressed in plain black dress and shawl, Mary Ann Rudd kept a large house in Cleveland without benefit of servants. She observed a minimal social calendar, where she expected visitors to arrive punctually and stay only briefly. She was said to have a deformity, likely a humpback, which added to her solitariness. For the most part her remoteness was a rejection of worldly ways. She gave away much of the family wealth to needy individuals, always insisting her benefactions remain anonymous. In later years, Eliza spent most of her time living with Mary Ann, who most matched her in temperament. Oddly, Mary Ann's husband was much like Senior, fun-loving and sociable. He played the kind of joke Senior would pull, such as giving someone a present of a bag of dirty potatoes, in which were secreted gold coins.

Lucy Briggs was also seldom visible in Cleveland society, though not as remote as her mother and sister. Senior was fonder of her than any of his siblings. She was not healthy, though, and died in 1878 at age forty-two.

The Briggs and Rudd cousins were of course welcome at the Rockefeller house and especially enjoyed the outdoor outings at Forest Hill. But the most frequent companions of Senior's and Laura's children were the offspring of church members and of live-in staff. Among their fondest playmates were John, Charles, Mary, and Kate Strong, whose father Augustus Strong was minister of the First Baptist Church in Cleveland. The most bookish was Charles, who would sit in the crook of a tree and read aloud to his playmates below. John Strong took more after his father, and later followed the call to the ministry. Kate was a winsome, bright child who became like an older sister to John Jr. When not together, the Strong and Rockefeller children kept a steady correspondence, particularly Edith and Charles, John Jr. and Kate.

Laura had a special kitchen, where she taught the girls cooking. A visitor joined them one day to learn "Alta Rockefeller's Bread" recipe. Later, she hired a teacher to come from New York. Even John Jr. and the Strong boys participated in these classes, their favorite dish being "frizzled beef." This was one way John Jr. was directed toward domestic masculinity, and he would see that his own sons were similarly raised. He even learned to mend his clothes or sew a button.

Chores continued at Forest Hill—raking leaves, breaking stone, laying out a vegetable plot, weeding a garden. For example, John Jr. noted receiving two cents for killing flies and ten cents for sharpening pencils. From their earnings, they were to make their contributions to church, Sunday School, and other good causes. Thus from the start they practiced a form of tithing, and learned that giving to others came first.

While the children and friends vacationed at Forest Hill, Laura's days were not totally restful. The house was ungainly, a warren of rooms to tend. Laura made as much a fetish of cleaning house as John did of his account books. Edith would later be known for her efficient organizational skills both in the home and in her civic work, and it is likely Laura's household management was the model. High standards inflict high stress on the manager, however, who must be very vigilant that they are being met.

Complicating Laura's housework was the continual remodelling. Restless by nature, Senior was always implementing ideas for expanding this room, shrinking that one, and adding windows here and there. Ongoing construction complicated her pristine housekeeping. His other constant activity, which affected her less, was landscaping. Perhaps without realizing it, Senior was following the vogue for the Romantic, naturalized landscape. The aesthetic principle was to enhance the dramatic hand of nature by encouraging a stream to ripple here, or by removing some brush to open a vista. Massive mature trees were hauled in and arranged in pleasing compositions. If one had the money, why wait thirty years?

Despite all this planning and botanical technology, the resulting view should not appear manipulated. It was of course trying to improve upon God, for were the landscape truly left to nature it would reforest with native plants, and streams would chatter where and when they pleased. Asserting the removal of artificiality was in itself doctrine of artifice. This control of the earth, this reshaping to the paradisiacal oils hanging in the drawing rooms, was repeated in estates around the nation. On the one hand it announced that the Garden of Eden could return, that it was America's promise. On the other, it proclaimed the zeal for subjugating wild and heathen forces, an expression that would evolve into a broader American imperialism. Men who could move forty-foot trees could move nations.

Several signs appear at Forest Hill that the Rockefeller family was taking on the style of their showier Euclid Avenue neighbors. Laura had more staff than in the city, including two butlers. In spite of her austere demeanor and perfectionism, she gathered a loyal and devoted staff. Unlike some society matrons, she threw no hairbrushes at her maids. Like her husband, she kept her temper. Thus workers who took pride in meticulous service felt appreciated for their skills. Slackers would not last long.

Another hint of growing class consciousness is that in the evening the family dressed for dinner. True, the meals were not fancy, but they were taken in an atmosphere of formality. Senior developed a preference for cold food, and would sit while the family ate until his meal was down to its desired temperature. He also developed a fondness for bread and milk, which led to myths concerning his having a poor stomach. In fact, the choice was further expression of his asceticism and belief in the current food faddists.

Despite touches of upper-class demeanor, the family remained essentially Protestant middle class. Fashion meant so little to Laura that she was seen about in Cleveland with patches on her dresses. The children's clothes, while well-made and expensive, lacked showy decoration. (She once stunned a visitor by remarking that all any young lady needed in her wardrobe was two dresses.) Rather than buy a cycle for each child, one was purchased so that they learned to share.

Truly upper-class form required the children disappear after dinner, but such was not the case for the Rockefellers. Instead, all gathered in the parlor to play Senior's favorite game, Numerica. A popular game of the day, it consisted of a board of small colored squares with numerals and required skill in calculation. As the children grew older, he posed complex arithmetic problems for them to solve:

> Bought 78 A., 135 P., 7 sq. yd., 5 sq. ft., 9 sq. in. of land at $80 an acre. I sold 2/5 of it to A at $120 per acre, 2/3 to B at $100 per sq. rd., and the residue to C at $0.05 per sq. ft. What was my whole gain?[5]

Other favorite games were Blindman's Bluff and Musical Authors. The family also sang hymns, preferring the joyous ones. The games and evening worship over, Senior often retired, because he had to rise early to tear his horses through Cleveland to the Standard Block downtown.

On Sundays, the family loaded their carriage with cold food for luncheon, and headed for church. Senior liked to toll the bell signalling the start of services. During a lull he would pull out a stack of envelopes, write down the names of older or dependent church members, include some bills, and pass them to an elder to distribute afterwards. Sometimes he would shake hands with someone and stuff an envelope in their pocket at the same time. When one woman he had helped refused, and explained she was going to live with her brother, he made her take the money anyway and told her to bank it. When another church member was invalided, he saw that a man was sent regularly to get her, drive her, and carry her up the stairs to their home for company. In this manner his children learned a pattern of personal giving that had been passed to Senior from Eliza.

Besides attending services, everyone went to Sunday School. Senior and Laura had their own classes to teach, and underwrote many of the expenses. They also hosted annual picnics for the teachers at Forest Hill, even long after they had moved from Cleveland. Senior was also a trustee who implemented his belief that pinching pennies led to saving dollars. At the service's final "Amen," he immediately cut all the lights except the one needed for the exit.

Following church, the family spent the afternoon at the Euclid house. Often a minister or visiting preacher was invited to spend the day. The regime was strictly Sabbatarian: no unnecessary work, no games or play, no study, no letter writing. One read Sunday School magazines, gospel stories, or books with moral themes. In conversation one referred only to uplifting topics, such as temperance.

Late in the afternoon, the family returned to Forest Hill. There Laura gathered the children around her after tea for a ritual she called "Home Talks." She prepared these as carefully as her Sunday School classes. The notes for one reveal her use of spiritual precepts in guiding one's life.[6] The guiding passage was Matthew 7.7.8, "Ask and it shall be given to you; seek, and you shall find . . ." To this she connected a verse reference to a gospel story:

> Two men went up to the temple one day,
> The one to brag, the other to pray.

Rhymes aided the children's memorization and recall of the theme, that of approaching prayer with open heart. One must be "under the guidance of the Holy Spirit. There must be entire commital to the Spirit before he can take possession of the being, and anoint the lips for true prayer." The mental state was important. "It is not enough to pray for a blessing; one must be in the expectant attitudes, waiting and watching with assured hope for [God's] fulfillment." Prayer is always answered, she advised, albeit not as one might wish. God has a "plan for your life" which each child "must learn . . . in that communion which is the soul's condition when God's purposes and will are made known to it."

Significant here is how Laura used the Bible to set a direction, not to impose arbitrary rules of behavior. It was up to each child, through private communication with God, to discover his or her duty in life. (Senior agreed, and when home he did not press the children with orders or expectations about their direction in life.) Each child was to uncover the "besetting sin" that was currently tempting, and come upon means for conquering the weakness. Following the Home Talk and discussion of its precepts, each child met individually with Laura to discuss the week's previous behavior, confess sins, pray with her for forgiveness, and obtain guidance from her.

Laura's constant refrain was "Is it right, is it duty?" She taught the children to obey not out of fear of punishment, but out of rising to meet a moral standard. "Our attitude was due entirely to Mother, who . . . instilled a personal consciousness of right and wrong, training our wills and getting us to *want* to do the things we ought to do."[7] Their obedience then was not fear-driven, externally enforced, but incorporated within their self-concepts. Their most resistant child, Edith, reflected later in life, "Mother's love for children and her belief that to mould them was building for the future was an inspiration."[8]

So completely did they absorb certain lessons that they kept childhood pledges even after they no longer held them to heart. All the youngsters vowed never to use tobacco, strong drink, or profanity. As adults, when they had friends who smoked or drank, they moderated their attitudes, though not their own behavior.

Of the four children, John Jr. took the family lessons most avidly. He considered his mother a saint, and easily donned the cloak of piety she wove for him. As the sole boy in a household of women (which often included Aunt Lute and Grandmother Eliza), he found his conformity ensured constant approval and attention. Much more of his allowance went to church donations or "a poor girl" than to candy. The feminine coddling did not foment rebellion. Rather, his sweet nature flourished in the hothouse atmosphere, making it easy for his sisters to join in his praise. Sibling rivalry would not visit the family until later.

As long as possible, the children were kept innocent concerning the source and size of the family wealth. They watched their father fill out a modest amount on the church pledge card, unaware that he was giving much greater sums without their knowing. Senior did not discuss Standard Oil or other business matters in their presence. They did not know where their father's office was, much less ever visit him there. Through simple practices at home they were learning that money resulted from labor, and the purpose of money was to help others. Accordingly, the children were directly exposed to their parents' philanthropy. It is worth examining in detail one of their first large charitable donations because its execution reveals much about their basic values about giving.

On June 18, 1882, the Rockefellers attended the Wilson Street Baptist Church in Cleveland at the invitation of its pastor, George Olcott King. Reverend King's wife had been a lifelong friend of Sophia Packard and Harriet Giles, the onetime teachers at Oread Academy that the Rockefellers had met on their honeymoon. Both women had come to town specifically for an invitation to meet with Senior and Laura and to solicit a donation from them for their latest educational venture.

In 1877, Sophia Packard helped form a woman's auxiliary of the American Baptist Home Mission Society, the WABHMS. This splintering off from the male-dominated parent body was a trend occurring throughout voluntary groups in America. The women gained control over their contributions to mission causes by an appeal the men would not dispute: that women were more moral, hence should oversee the needs of other women. Females, they argued, could better evangelize other women, redeem prostitutes to take more legitimate work, ameliorate the effects of poverty, and educate other women. Although the WABHMS was not totally independent of the ABHMS board, it gave Baptist women a voice they had lacked in the past.

The first objective of WABHMS was to address the needs of black women and girls in the South. The cause was urgent.

During the early nineteenth century, while public education was spreading for whites, it was outlawed for slaves. "Why we were no more than dogs!" recalled one ex-slave. "If they caught us with a piece of paper in our pockets, they'd whip us."[9] Common punishments included cutting off the forefinger of the literate slave, and putting to death the teacher. One consequence of this repression was an underground network through which literate slaves taught others to read. Charity Bowery recalled, "On Sundays I have seen the negroes up in the country going away under large oaks, and in secret places, sitting in the woods with spelling books."[10] The other was to inspire the great majority of slaves, who remained illiterate, to identify education with liberation. "There is one sin that slavery committed against me that I will never forgive," expressed one ex-slave. "It robbed me of my education."[11] Consequently, when the Confederacy surrendered, the black community was quick to demand universal education. They welcomed assistance from the Radical Republican politicians, the Freedman's Bureau, and northern missionary workers, all of which supported this goal, but much of their educational system was self-created and self-managed.

Sabbath Schools attached to black congregations were the first to provide formal learning, and out of these were spun full-time private schools. Then the federal and state governments capitulated and offered classes as well. "Every little negro in the county is now going to school and the public pays for it," groused one planter. "This is a hell of [a] fix but we can't help it."[12] The notion of a whole race of recently subjugated people, from toddlers to elderly, arising with demands to go to school terrified the vanquished Southern leaders, who found ways to "help it." Through legal maneuverings, intimidation, and eventually violence, public education for blacks grew spotty and inadequate.

In 1868, Samuel Chapman Armstrong founded the Hampton Normal and Agricultral Instutite, whose philosophy undermined the interests of the freedmen. A self-proclaimed "friend of the Negro race," Armstrong, the son of a Hawaiian missionary, saw the "darkies" as similar to the Polynesian "savages." He urged blacks not to vote or seek office because they were too culturally and morally deficient to run a civilized society. They were "little better than . . . brutes because their moral nature is dormant."[13]

Armstrong argued that blacks should be trained for the jobs the South needed if the region were to return to economic viability. In other words, they must become cheap and contented labor for the whites to make peace with them. Thus Hampton required small shop and farm experience of students, an ethic of hard toil, the "dignity of labor," and practical knowledge within a system of Christian morals. Dull plodders, not sharp debaters, received the highest praise. Most important were punctuality, neatness, order, obedience, and suppression of emotion. Those who took the course to become teachers need not have a high school diploma, as aspiring white teachers did, and received only two years of training, in contrast to four for whites. Supporters of what became the Hampton Idea mocked the value of sharecroppers learning about Beethoven and the Greeks.

Although the Hampton Idea appealed to white Southerners and some northern industrialists, it did not persuade the missionary vanguard. Henry Morehouse of the ABHMS was typical. He believed that blacks must be led by their own gifted intelligentsia. While learning trades was useful, he asserted, it should be subordinate to the development of culture and wisdom. If the most talented white men were taught the value of the Classics, then so deserved black men. The experience of slavery, not something inherent in race, was the source of behavior that conflicted with white Christian standards. Missionary philanthropists like Morehouse were not radical in the modern sense; they did not urge desegregation, nor the redistribution of property. Yet they were radical in the context of the postbellum South for assuming that blacks had the ability to advance and to take their equal place in politics and law.

Amid this heated debate, females were overlooked. Of the five million freed slaves, three million were female, and one million were females under the age of twenty-one. During a long journey through that South, Sophia Packard quickly identified their special need. She and Harriet Giles returned with a deep conviction to serve in Georgia, which had the largest black population, yet had not a single school offering advanced education for women. Packard explained the resulting inspiration: "Even in the still nights watches a voice seemed to say: Go South and help these women and girls who have never had a chance."[14] They sold their own belongings (even their beloved piano) to travel farther and raise money for this proposal. Thus their appearance at the Rockefeller door.

Packard and Giles formed an easy harmony with the women in the Rockefeller household. Laura, Lute, and their mother were all committed to education, temperance, and serving the "freed people." The shared roots with Oread helped; so congenial were these five women that long-time friendships resulted. Of course Senior controlled the funds. In deciding whether to grant benefices, he applied the same method he used in hiring his managers, that of examining the character and potential of the applicants. He easily concluded that the women had the moral standards and talent for their plan. But before making a large grant, he donated in small amounts until he could be assured of the "stickative qualities" of the endeavor. Since his strategy was to support organizations that were vigorous, and not fatally dependent on one major funding source, he preferred matching or conditional gifts. Thus over the next half year he sent small checks to meet particular needs of the young institution.

In late 1882, Packard and Giles set up classes for the Female Seminary of Atlanta in the basement of Friendship Church, and had 220 pupils by the end of the year. With the help of Morehouse, they acquired nine acres and four barracks buildings of a deserted Army camp nearby. Morehouse wanted the school to be subsumed as "The Girls' Department" of the Atlanta Baptist Seminary. He argued that the Society had helped the women obtain their mortgage on the assumption the men's school would locate on the site as well. Packard persisted and won full title, along with full responsibility for funding the school.

By now convinced of the women's abilities, Rockefeller pledged $2,500 toward the $6,500 mortgage, on the stipulation that they show proof of raising the total. (In fact, he gave more in the end to prevent the firing of a teacher.) This gift was so significant that the women invited the family to the school and asked to rename it "Rockefeller College, or if you choose not to give it that name, perhaps your wife's maiden name."[15]

On April 11, 1884, the family travelled to Atlanta for a celebration of the school's formal incorporation. Upon taking the podium, Senior advised the now 450 students, "Confidence is a plant of slow growth. It is in your heart to make the school one that people will believe in." He concluded that "those who have invested here have made the best investment of their money that could be made."[16] Then a trustee announced that the school would now be called Spelman Seminary in honor of Lucy and Harvey Buel Spelman. Each of the Spelman women—Lucy Henry, Lute, and Laura—took turns speaking more personally about their father, their admiration for Packard and Giles, and their faith. Upon returning home, the family set up a full scholarship, including expenses for clothing and sundries.

Over the next ten years, Senior donated almost $100,000 to Spelman. The grants went toward the purchase of more land; the first brick building on campus, Rockefeller Hall; a heating plant and laundry facility; another classroom building, Giles Hall; and personal grants to the founders. Packard and Giles started receiving larger amounts from Rockefeller after they told him of getting a grant from the Slater Fund to support the Industrial Department. The Industrial Department actually taught cooking, sewing, general housework, and laundry work—in other words, prepared maids and cooks for Southern households—as well as offered needlework, typesetting, and penmanship—skills for other low-paying jobs. Consequently, Spelman leaned toward the Hampton model, educating few women initially as teachers and nurses. Packard and Giles, who had taught white women a program including Latin, Greek, and ethics, omitted these offerings from Spelman's early curriculum. In praising and supporting the school's offerings, the Rockefellers reinforced the Hampton Idea with its economic subordination of blacks.

It was the turn of the century before Spelman had two thousand volumes in its library. It was even later before it would develop into a notable liberal arts college for black women. And when it did, a Rockefeller family member present at the 1884 convocation, ten-year-old John Jr., would be ahead of his time in supporting its transition to academic excellence.

Starting in the winter of 1878, the family left Forest Hill not for Euclid Avenue, but for New York City, where Senior spent so much time in Standard Oil's offices at 26 Broadway. After that, New York was their main and legal residence, with only summer interludes at Forest Hill. Nevertheless, the Rockefellers considered themselves residents of Cleveland, primarily because they felt more at home at its Euclid Baptist Church than Fifth Avenue Baptist in New York.

In 1881, Harvey Spelman died, so Lute and her mother joined Laura and Senior's household permanently. For several years the family spent its winters in a New York hotel, but in 1884 Senior purchased 4 West Fifty-fourth Street. The previous owner had been Arabella Worsham, a widow who had recently married railroad magnate Collis P. Huntington. During her seven years in the house, Arabella had enlarged the four-story brownstone and redecorated according to the designs of English architect Charles L. Eastlake. In revolt against the highly ornamented curves of Victorian fabric patterns and furniture carvings, Eastlake based his designs on straight lines, flat surfaces, and small symmetrical elements. The Rockefellers bought the house with all of Arabella's furnishings, down to fire tongs and servants' bath mats.

The basement held a billard room, kitchen, servants' dining room, and Turkish bath. The first floor held the public spaces: a parlor, dining room, conservatory, and that oddity of the day, a Moorish room set wtih ottomans, cushions, and tentlike ceiling drapings. The third and fourth floor each held five bedrooms for other family members, and one bath to share. Seven other rooms on the top floor included additional bedrooms, mainly for servants, and various storage rooms.

The second floor was Senior and Laura's private domain. Here were a large library and their sleeping quarters. Their bedroom and dressing room are now preserved as an exhibit at the Museum of the City of New York. From their large canopy bed, the couple looked up at a ceiling with plaster painted in intricate, repeated motifs. The dressing tables of ebony veneer and floral marquetry, the red damask armchairs, and heavy draperies added further richness to this carefully planned scheme in which every element, even heating registers, were made to fit into the whole. The adjoining dressing room was as elaborate. Woodwork and furniture were rosewood and satinwood with mother-of-pearl inlay. Design elements included a frieze of cupids on the walls and an inlay motif on the door frames of hand mirrors and combs. The blue-and-white color scheme echoed the atmosphere of elegant luxury found throughout the house.

Considered ornate at the time of its construction a quarter-century earlier, the townhouse was considered plain and modest by the 1880s. Knickerbocker New York had always decried ostentation, preferring brownstones such as 4 West Fifty-fourth. Typical interiors, however, were smothering with their heavy drapes over curtains, small rugs atop large carpets, dark woodwork, genre art from Europe mixed with patriotic portraits, and Victorian geegaws. Alva Vanderbilt had recently challenged that lack of aesthetic vision when she worked with Richard Morris Hunt to place a luminous French limestone château nearby on the corner at 660 Fifth Avenue. This section of the city, until recently considered "in the country," was now mushrooming with massive stone accretions of Italian Rennaissance, French Gothic, and Beaux Arts. (Unfortunately, few of these new mansions exhibited the taste of Hunt and Vanderbilt.)

In addition to this monumental dare, Alva broke down the barriers of the Knickerbocker "Four Hundred," ruled by Caroline Astor. To celebrate her new home, Alva held a costume ball that was to go down in social history for its opulence and impact on New York society. Through Alva's clever plotting, Caroline Astor was forced virtually to beg for an invitation. Now it was not only the Vanderbilts who found a welcome, for Alva brought along other families made wealthy as a result of recent industrialization. Among them was that of William Rockefeller, who attended the ball with Mira.

William even moved his family across the street from Alva, to 689 Fifth Avenue. That he aligned with the somewhat outrageous Alva, who hung a luscious Bouguereau nude in her bedroom, shows how quickly life in New York had undone for him Eliza's strict upbringing. He was socializing with people who "sinned"—danced, attended theater and opera, drank spirits, gambled, and, in the case of married men like Willie K. Vanderbilt, kept ladies on the side.

Although Laura and Senior would find little to approve in Alva Vanderbilt's crowd, they were not the sort to distance themselves from William and Mira as a result. The couples remained close despite their differences, and the children of each benefitted as a result of this expanded family connection. With William living an easy stroll nearby, frequent visits passed between members of the two households. But William's children were growing up in an atmosphere where the secular had pushed out the sacred, and they lived less ordered lives than their cousins. Nonetheless, Laura and Senior näively believed they could protect their own children from the "corrupting" influences of New York. The home schooling, music instruction, and daily religious practices continued as in Ohio. What they failed to consider was that the girls need only walk around the corner to Fifth Avenue and they would see opulent mansions with liveried servants. One of the daughters in particular would succumb to this extravagant style.

✻   ✻   ✻

In late 1883, while visiting Cleveland, a friend asked why Alta, Edith, and John Jr. had not been baptized. Realizing she should provide some impetus for the children to decide on this move, she brought them together in the parlor to pray over the matter. "We found it very helpful and delightful—the nearest to Jesus, perhaps, one gets this side of the pearly gates."[17] Laura was pleased not only that they were all agreeable to be baptized together, but that their Christian witness inspired other adolescents in their church to follow. She failed to see that one child, Edith, was not heartfelt.

Soon afterward, Senior set up accounts of Standard Oil stock for each of the four children equally. Yet at the same time he established a practice that would set the children into an unequal relationship. Ten-year-old John Jr. became responsible for keeping various accounts, from family fines to the number of hours each child practiced music daily. He was gradually given management of other family issues, such as buying tickets for trips, arranging stopovers, and handling tips. Thus the youngest child, being a boy, was granted authority, however implicit, over his elder sisters.

His relationship with Alta and Edith were to be most affected. Bessie was away at Rye Female Academy, one of the best-known schools of its kind in the country. Her cousin Emma, William's eldest daughter, was also a schoolmate. Some years would pass, though, before the implications of John Jr.'s rise in status above the girls would be noticeable to them. For the most part Alta and Edith were pals with their brother, the trio forming a mutual admiration society.

The three enjoyed teasing one another. In February of 1884, John Jr. had his first puppylove crush, on Grace Sanders, a minister's daughter. As he noted in his diary, one day Alta told Grace that he was "going wild" over her, and Grace blushed, then laughed. John Jr. told Alta that "if [Grace] went to the Temperance meeting with me she would make it pretty hot for me." Edith also goaded Grace, who replied she would pull John Jr.'s ears rather than respond to him. Yet a few days later while he was walking from a meeting with a buddy, Grace, a few steps ahead, kept glancing back at him. He knew she wanted him to "walk with her. But I did not because I was a fool."[18] A few days later Grace invited John Jr. and his sisters to tea, and eventually she became a close friend of Edith's.

As if John Jr. were not surrounded by enough admiring females older than himself, he sought out others. Typical was Kate Strong, who had joined Bessie at Rye. Kate fawned on the youth, finding him earnest and likeable. John Jr. sought her out for advice as he did his parents and their adult friends, and wanted her approval for his beliefs.

While Alta and Edith were being tutored at home, John Jr. went to the New York School of Languages, which despite its name offered a conventional course of study in basic skills and subjects. An essay written then captures the range of his attitudes towards technology, women, alcohol, race differences, peace, and the ameliorating effects of education:

> I think that, in a hundred years, balloons will be made so large and strong, that people will travel in them instead of in cars and steamboats; and that they will go twice as fast. Women will have a right to vote, and may be presidents. There will be no manufacture of liquors as a drink, throughout the United States, and consequently fewer jails and policemen.
>
> Earthquakes will be frequent and destructive. The western part of the United States will be as densely populated as the eastern. Wars will be no more. Foreigners will be educated before they can vote. Indians will become civilized and intelligent. The center of the earth will be explored, also the North and South poles. Engines will be driven by electricity.
>
> It is to be hoped and expected that the people of our country will be wiser and better and therefore happier than now.[19]

John Jr.'s optimism and faith in societal improvement would remain unshaken.

Another essay depicts how much he was oriented to the world of market capitalism, while ignorant of its operations. There an imaginary country boy challenges a city boy as to the value of his education, for example, the usefulness of French lessons. The country boy asserts he has learned trades, so that if his father suddenly died, he would be able to farm and to support himself. The city boy responds that were his father to die, he was sure men in his father's office would help him out!

This story hints at another feature of family life for the Rockefellers, its connection to staff at Standard Oil. By now, certain employees at the company offices on 26 Broadway were responsible for handling the personal needs of the family. Laura used Standard staff for such private needs as purchasing corsets, while the children used it for all kinds of arrangements, including ordering magazine subscriptions and making appointments with the barber. The children were sent their allowances from the office, and every month wrote a thank-you note to the company representative in charge of the transfer. As a result, in exchange for certain conveniences the children lost some autonomy by the time they became adults. John Jr. in particular thought it normal that nonrelatives be involved in family matters, but he was to be least personally affected by this intervention.

John Jr.'s workbooks from this time further illustrate a more subtle transference of capitalist values. The front contents of his 1884 diary, for example, had information seldom seen in today's equivalents. Several pages explained the values of foreign coins, as well as included distance and population charts, information useful not only to a traveller but to a business person involved in international trade. One page gave a glossary of common business terms, ones familiar today but new to the vocabulary then. Most interesting is a table on interest:

ONE DOLLAR LOANED 100 YEARS
at compound interest, would amount to the following sums:

I percent	$2.75
3 "	19.25
6 "	340.00 . . .
24 "	2,551,709,440.00

In addition to such instruction, his *Spencerian System of Penmanship* practice books had him repeatedly copy moral and ethical sayings:

"Pure living leads unto peace."
"Intemperance leads to ruin."
"If the power to do hard work is not talent, it is the best possible substitute for it." (James A. Garfield)
"Unite gentleness to firmness."
"He who conquers self is the greatest victor."

Nowhere in John Jr.'s private writings is there any sign that he questioned or rebelled against such injunctions.

Though bright, John Jr. was not a quick learner. Like his father, he earned his high grades as much by tenacity as by natural ken. His neatly prepared workbooks and essays reveal a patient, careful mind. His entries into his account books resembled his father's—notations made regularly, regardless of one's mood or whim, and to the precise last penny. He was comfortable with order, hence found the many clearly defined demands made of him agreeable to follow. Yet, like many with compulsive streaks, he was never satisfied with his efforts or his results.

Less is known about his sisters' schooling. Edith later mentioned having learned three languages by the age of ten. The same people who tutored the girls had taught John before he attended a regular school, and he was well-prepared. Oddly, although Laura had thought bookkeeping an important skill when she was a girl, she did not have her daughters instructed in its techniques. Only John gained the basics in the recording and understanding of the flow of money, while the girls at best kept lists of expenses.

Apart from their classes, the youngsters lived highly scheduled lives that allowed no exposure to competing viewpoints. On Wednesday nights the family attended prayer meetings, on Friday nights, temperance meetings. Saturdays the children took French classes together. During the week music teachers—top professionals, of course—came to teach Alta the piano, Edith the cello, and John the violin. On a typical day Alta and John practiced at least two hours, while Edith usually doubled that, and on some days practiced as long as six. Part of this time was spent practicing trios, such as the Beethoven First, for public musicales. Each week the children had to compose an essay and read it aloud to the family on Sunday.

Baptist ministers frequented the dinner table, and naturally added to the emphasis on hard work and service to others. (One of these was Edward Judson, son of Adoniram Judson, who had settled in New York and remarried following his missionary work in Burma.) Reformers came as well, such as Frances Willard, who had vitalized the Women's Christian Temperance Union and broadened its scope to include the needs of working girls, prostitutes, poor children, immigrants, and others. As opposed to most Fifth Avenue mansions around the corner where children were banished from dinner and adult conversation, in the Rockefeller household they were always included. Consequently, they were more familiar than their peers with current social problems and the call to solve them.

In addition to giving money to charity, the children acted more directly in the service of their beliefs. One day John Jr. and Edith each bought a set of paperdolls, which they played with for several days; they then took them to a hospital and gave them to children. John Jr. was the most fervent in his Christian belief, and at age twelve was composing compelling sermons for his Sunday School. One told the story of a starving Indian who on successive days of praying for food offered his blanket, hatchet, and gun to the Great Spirit. Each day nothing happened. Desperate, he offered himself, and a deer appeared. "What have we given to Christ?" asked John.

Despite their full schedules, the youngsters found time each day to join with their cousins Emma, William, and Percy Rockefeller. They threw snowballs, played games such as dominoes or Go Bang, watched magic lantern shows, took long walks, went horseback riding in Central Park, skated in winter, and played tennis in fall and spring. In his diary, John Jr. often mentioned "horseplay" with Edith and Alta. Sometimes Laura had to tell them to go to their rooms. (Emma, William, and Percy felt sorry for their cousins' stern upbringing.) Reading the accounts of their delight over innocent play and games, the modern reader has difficulty remembering the trio are already adolescents. While they lived a cocoonlike existence, they had leisure to develop fully before bursting out into a more dangerous world.

In 1884, the family took the first of several annual travels together. The trip began with the ceremony at Spelman Seminary, then continued on private railcar to New Orleans, across to Tucson, over to Los Angeles, up to San Francisco, eastward over the Rockies. In his typical penny-counting style, Senior had Alta, Edith, and John Jr. share hotel rooms, though each had a separate bed. That they did so without incident is further proof of their camaraderie.

During the summer of 1885, seventy-five-year-old Bill Rockefeller appeared at Forest Hill, gave John a gun, and taught him and Bessie to shoot. During his stay, he charmed his grandchildren as he had his own offspring years earlier. Eliza was another matter, however, for she delayed coming from her Cleveland home due to a "stitch in her side."[20] Eventually she could not hold back, and appeared for at least one day while he was at Forest Hill. Clearly Eliza was no longer admiring the moon and imagining Bill were somewhere else gazing upon it. Perhaps by this time she knew that he was living out West with another woman.

In 1886 the family boarded a private railcar for a trip to Yellowstone. Accompanying them were Aunt Lucy, Rev. Judson, and the Biggars. Dr. Biggar was the family physician, a Cleveland homeopath, and one of Senior's closest friends. The railcar had six sections, including an observation room, state room, and kitchen. Soon after the train pulled out, the family had tea and sang gospel hymns. In Chicago, they stopped to explore businesses such as the grain exchange, as well as parks and the houses on Prairie Avenue. As the train wound through the Midwest, the children continued their demanding study schedules. Rev. Judson held an hourlong Bible lesson each morning. Afterwards the children practiced their instruments and read between meals. In Minneapolis, Senior and

Biggar attended a tent revival meeting. Some evenings more informal entertainment occurred, such as the night they "sang funny songs, and Mrs. Biggar dressed up [in blackface] and acted old Uncle Joe."[21] Following a week of horseback riding and hiking in Yellowstone, the group travelled to Tacoma and through the Willamette Valley of Oregon before returning home.

Bessie was now attending Vassar College up the Hudson near Poughkeepsie. Old family friend Dr. Augustus Strong had left his Cleveland congregation to head Rochester Theological Seminary, a leading Baptist divinity school. He was also chair of the trustees of Vassar. Another old Cleveland friend now teaching at Yale, Dr. William Rainey Harper, came to Vassar on Sundays to lecture on Bible subjects. Consequently Senior went to Poughkeepsie most weekends to visit Bessie and talk with his friends concerning Baptist matters. Another man who joined these discussions was Frederick T. Gates, executive secretary of the American Baptist Education Association.

Vassar was to gain materially in later years from Bessie's attendance, as Rockefeller would fund Strong dormitory, Davison House, and Rockefeller recitation hall. But it was another school that would most benefit from the gathering of the men in the falls at Vassar, and in the summers at Forest Hill. Concerned that the country needed a great American university under Baptist aegis, though one not rigidly sectarian, the men debated and eventually decided to build one in the Midwest. The result would be the University of Chicago. Rockefeller became its main donor, giving more than forty-five million dollars over the course of his lifetime to the building of the campus.

Another of Eliza Rockefeller's children was less interested in noble causes. It took Alva Vanderbilt to pry money from William for anything other than his personal enjoyment. Alva's scheme was the result of a social snub. Singer Lilli Lehman later recalled, "As, on a particular evening, one of the millionairesses did not receive the [Academy of Music] box in which she intended to shine because another had anticipated her, the husband of the former took prompt action and caused the Metropolitan Opera House to rise."[22] More precisely, Alva provoked her insouciant husband and several other similarly snubbed friends into funding a new building that would hold more boxes. William Rockefeller joined the new board, donated to the cause, and helped Alva reach into the pockets of other capitalists. (Although Senior and Laura now allowed themselves to attend symphony concerts, they would not bend their scruples enough to join William in his Golden Horseshoe box at the Met.) This was one of William's few major donations in his lifetime, and when the Met suffered a disastrous fire in 1893, he refused to give to the rebuilding.

The influence of Alva was soon apparent in another of William Rockefeller's activities. In 1886 he purchased 179 acres fronting the Hudson River for three-quarters of a mile near Tarrytown. After seeing its previous owner's stone castle torn down, he brought to the site Scottish stone masons, Swiss wood carvers, Japanese horticulturists, and American artisans to create what he planned to be the most magnificent residence in the area. The castellated Elizabethan manor had walls three-and-a-half feet thick, all grounded on bedrock. The drawing room was almost forty feet long, with rosewood panelling and silk tapestry on the walls. The second floor held five master bedroom suites, the third floor six more bedrooms. All the bedrooms had fireplaces. The servants' wing held fifteen bedrooms, two laundries, and sundry workrooms. There was a coach stable, an ice house with a capacity of four hundred tons to store meat and vegetables, a barn to hold forty animals, seventeen greenhouses, a hennery, a mushroom cellar, a river house, a boathouse, and an electric generating plant. With over a hundred acres of forest in addition to the farm area, the estate required a hundred people to operate. Dubbed Rockwood Hall by William, it was called the Rat Trap by Senior.

William's land purchase inspired Senior to look for a similar place that his family could use. In 1893 he would choose an area of rolling, forested hills in the Pocantico River area. The principal house, a farmer's dwelling really, sat atop Kykuit (Dutch for lookout) Hill. It was a commodious, unpretentious wooden structure with broad piazzas and a verandah from which the family could survey the broad band of Hudson River and the Palisades in the distance. Its furniture was the usual hodgepodge. As John Jr. would later note, while the homes he grew up in were not aesthetically pleasing, he would have no quarrel with the Pocantico landscape.

On June 21, 1887, England celebrated the Jubilee of Queen Victoria. To share in this historical event, Senior took his entire family, along with the Biggars and the family of Dr. Augustus Strong, to London. There they rented a room along the procession route to glimpse an unobstructed view of the queen in her splendid golden carriage. The rest of the trip was little different from today's tourism, with stops at the museums, cathedrals, and historic buildings. Notably, in a London gallery it was a painting of the crucified Christ that most appealed to John Jr.; accordingly visits to orphanages and church services most satisfied him.

John Jr. jotted little in his diary about his family during this voyage, and hardly ever mentioned his father. Possibly Senior was off on business part of the time, for it was always one sister or another who was accompanying John Jr. about. But the most important person was evident. As a characteristic entry explains, "I went to mama's room & teased her most of the afternoon away."[23]

While in London, Laura attended an address given by Isabella Bird Bishop, a noted world traveller who had spent four-and-a-half years in Asia. Bishop's presentation suggested to Laura "the desperate needs of the heathen world." She was stunned to hear that there were "eight hundred millions on our earth who never heard the name of Jesus. Of these, thirty-five millions pass every year in a mournal procession into Christianless graves."[24] She concluded the "whole continent of Asia is corrupt," not only for its absence of Christianity, but for its "infinite degradation" of women. Her belief in raising the "civilization" of those living in the lands across the Pacific would be passed on to John Jr.

This was the last trip all the siblings and parents took together. Bessie was soon to become engaged to her childhood playmate, the bookish Charles Strong. Alta and Edith were preparing to go to boarding school and were preoccupied with the concerns of approaching womanhood. John's education was more demanding now that he had college entrance examinations looming ahead. Laura was ill, showing signs of an unidentified chronic weakness. Approaching his fiftieth year, Senior was losing interest in business, and thinking about a new career.

During the late 1880s, Senior and Laura must have looked with much contentment over their brood. The children were well-behaved, self-disciplined, pious, thoughtful of others—the good Christians they had been raised to be. They had been baptized, taught Sunday School, and taken the temperance pledge. Unlike their cousin Emma, the daughters were not frivolous or preoccupied with Society; unlike his cousins Percy and William Jr., the son had not supplanted the saving of souls with going to parties and dances. It is good that the parents had these moments of contentment, for the children were about to test their love.

Angelic Invalids

> *"We looked for peace, but no good came; and for a time of health, and behold trouble!"*
>
> —Jeremiah 8:15.

D isease is not merely biological; it has a social vector. One culture's food preferences, for example, can stimulate the likelihood of stomach cancer, while another's can spur the onset of cirrhosis. Epidemics are specific to time and place. Cholera waves struck American cities in the 1800s, and were not vanquished until politicians finally agreed upon the need for municipal sanitation. More curious are the disorders of an age that have a less-apparent physiological source—no bacilli, virus, or other organic threat. Following the Civil War, two such "diseases" appeared, and both struck at members of John Rockefeller's family.

The first to suffer, in the fall of 1887, was thirteen-year-old John Jr. He had a nervous collapse so severe that he went to Forest Hill to recuperate. Looking back on this period, he described himself as "shy, ill-adjusted, and not very robust," a different self-portrayal from that expressed in his earlier cheerful, outgoing diary entries.[1] Perhaps those early jottings were self-deluding. Perhaps he felt so strong a need to be the "perfect young man" that he could not even admit his discontent on paper. After all, no matter how much a youth might love music, and John Jr. did, he must have chafed some days over having to practice his violin for an hour or two before breakfast. Add to that a drive to excel in all endeavors, and exhaustion is inevitable.

John Jr.'s collapse marked the first onset of a nervous disorder that would recur. Some might attribute his ailment to his constrained upbringing, or argue that he was expressing an unconscious rebellion against strictures he claimed to accept. Others might point to a genetic predisposition that would have emerged regardless of his parents' childrearing practices. These are modern interpretations and difficult to verify given available evidence. Furthermore, the views of his day, now considered archaic, make more sense.

Back then his illness would have been called "neurasthenia" and attributed to overwork of the mind. It was epidemic, doctors explained, because a class of men now spent their days performing only sedentary mental labor. Where the physical laborer eventually felt muscle-weary, hence knew to rest, the brain worker perceived no such warning. The contrary could occur. "The longer I worked the clearer and easier my mental process seemed to be . . ." explained one patient.[2] Exercise was the cure, because "during active exertion of the body the brain cannot be employed intensely, and therefore has secured to it a state of repose which even sleep is not always competent to survive." With its working farm, Forest Hill furnished ample curative physical work for John.

Laura accompanied her son. Now in her mid-forties, she was facing menopause and the stigma it held. Since doctors defined women as being governed wholly by the "two little glands," the ovaries, either "an excess or a deficiency of the proper influence of these organs over the other parts of the system may be productive of disease."[3] Menstruation was thought to carry off the seeds of illness, so with its cessation would follow a host of ailments. To stay healthy, the wise woman "ought to commence her prudent cares as early as the 40th year or sooner . . . withdraw from the excitements and fatigues of the gay world."[4] This retreat included a prohibition on sexual intercourse, which after menopause was believed to be of "morbid impulse."[5]

The atmosphere was not totally negative. Women themselves admitted a sense of relief over no longer being of childbearing age. Women's reformers such as Eliza Farnham wrote of this "secret joy of advancing age." Consequently, many women faced menopause with ambivalence. If they were particularly given to follow male authorities, as Laura was, they were more susceptible to watching for signs of debility. What medical experts did not yet recognize was that menopause often coincides with the onset of chronic illness, which in Laura's case was high blood pressure that would lead to heart trouble.

At Forest Hill, John Jr. followed the usual prescription for neurasthenia in men, namely, physical exercise to compensate for overuse of the brain. He chopped wood, worked about the grounds, rode horses, hiked and, in warmer weather, swam. His saw his tutor several times a week instead of daily. He continued his daily prayers and meals with his mother, who used her time to read or chat with friends from church she invited for tea. One visitor admired how John Jr. would skate behind a wooden chair, pushing Laura around the frozen lake.

As a result of this isolating sojourn, John Jr. and his mother deepened their dependence upon each other. While their intense intimacy seems excessive today, it would have been thought admirable by their friends. Following the American Revolution over a hundred years earlier, the notion of Republican Motherhood emerged. Namely, though denied the vote, women could participate in the polity by raising their sons, the future voters and leaders, to be virtuous citizens. By late in the nineteenth century, Victorian sentimentality had laden the mother-son relationship with a highblown religious dimension as well. As the minister of a New York Baptist Church illustrated:

> Dear John [Jr.], it makes me glad indeed, to see you love your mother as you do, and as long as you live, how ever old you may get to be, and in how ever many enterprises you may engage, you will never regret any affection or reverence or obedience shown her . . . For a little while you are to be more to each other than ever before. What a pleasure and companionship that memory will be![6]

Other older men intoned similar advice to the boy over the years. What is remarkable is that John Jr. and his mother were able to achieve this difficult ideal without seeming to incur a neurotic dependency. When time was right, she let him go.

Others were not always happy with the situation of course. Even Senior felt excluded that the woman he too called "Mama" was isolated with their son. Given responsibility for seeing to maintenance work on the property, John Jr. wrote his father about his plans for various tasks, ostensibly to get his approval before proceeding. As Senior replied to one request, "Concur in your decision about painting the storm doors. You and Mother will surely have your own way in all these affairs, what's the use my saying a word. You are monarch of all you survey."[7] Explaining his regrets that an appearance before a Congressional committee would prevent him from coming for Thanksgiving, Senior observed, "You say you are not lonely. That is not the case with me."[8]

Meanwhile, Alta and Edith resided in New York City with Aunt Lute and their two grandmothers. Living under the probing eyes of three strict, moralistic women rankled the sisters at times. When John Jr. wrote about his enjoying the society of a young woman, Alta advised him to mark such parts of his letters "only for Edith and Alta" or "strictly private," because "Lute and the Grandmothers . . . think that everything that comes from you must be for them to hear; but they did not hear that letter, although they made a great fuss about it."[9] Now and then their father would appear, and the girls happily accompanied him to concerts and prayer meetings. As usual, he brought light and humor into the dark, heavy atmosphere created by the older women. When Aunt Lute lifted her skirts and walked primly down the staircase, Senior lifted his coattails and minced behind her.

Cooped up as they were, Alta and Edith overlooked their usual differences. Alta was contentedly conventional, comfortable to be led, to obey. Of all the children, she felt closest to Senior, and was always looking for signs of his particular attention. (Regarding a birthday she wrote her brother, "Tell father I was so pleased to learn that *he* had selected my watch.")[10] Alta lacked her father's analytical bent and vigorous constitution. She lacked her mother's confidence and sure convictions. If she resembled anyone in the family, it was most likely her Aunt Lute, the woman in the background ready to serve. Alta took pride in her traditionalism, and throughout her life referred to her conservative ways as proof of her superiority over Edith.

Edith was the most like her father in disposition, if not in interests. She was the most intelligent of the four children, a natural scholar, at ease with abstract thought. She absorbed languages easily. Hers was not just a theoretical mind, however, for she had her father's astuteness concerning human nature and social organization. On the other hand, she was certainly the one passionate member of the family, as expressed by long hours with legs wrapped about the resonating buzz of her cello. From her earliest days in Sunday School, she experienced doubts about her faith. "I never heard a Baptist minister say anything that convinced me he was Divinely inspired."[11] She bore her doubts privately, however, and hoped with maturity she would better understand her family's religious devotion, but it was not to be.

During 1888 the sisters were aswirl in the preparations for Bessie's wedding, for which they would be bridesmaids. No matter how much emphasis was placed upon their studies, their future was clearly marked: to marry and continue the line of Christian family life. Perhaps for that reason Laura and Senior saw that their eldest daughter be given an elegant, if not lavish event. The expenses went more for the comfort of the guests than for show. A private railcar from Poughkeepsie brought the majority of the guests, Bessie's classmates, and teachers from Vassar. They may also have provided transportation for the many Cleveland guests, for in a rare show of family cooperation, even the alienated Frank Rockefeller attended.

On March 22, 1889, Bessie, twenty-three, married childhood friend Charles Strong, twenty-seven, during an evening service in the front drawing room on Fifty-fourth Street. About the mantels and staircases were white lilacs, lillies of the valley, and American Beauty roses. Two flower girls carried fragrant freesias and Pilgrim roses. In their white lace over moire gowns, Alta and Edith were dressed richly for perhaps the first time in their lives. Bessie, resplendent in embroidered satin, descended the main staircase on the arm of her father. The nuptial couple stood before a large floral shell of orchids, Baroness Rothschild roses, and ivy.

Laura kept precise accounts of the expenses, which included Bessie's necklace of forty-eight pearls ($8,000), three scarf pins for the ushers ($10.50 each), and a ring for the maid of honor ($4). Delmonicos catered the meal for six hundred. One of the larger expenses was a donation to the minister's church, five hundred dollars, even though it was not used for the ceremony. Overall, the event was very modest for the Four Hundred ("brilliant though quiet" noted the *New York Times*), but members of that clique, the William Rockefellers excepted, were not invited. Nonetheless, that Bessie was so bedecked in the finest jewels is a further mark of the family's movement away from its middle-class roots.

Bessie was the most retiring of the three daughters.[12] Scarcely any women attended let alone graduated from college then, so she was well-suited to be the wife of an intellectual. Charles was a graduate in philosophy from Harvard, where he had studied under William James. He had taught at Cornell, and following the wedding joined the psychology department at Clark University, then one of the most innovative in the country. However, he was not to last there long, and his spotty academic career was perhaps the result of a dour and difficult personality. Unfortunately, virtually no information remains to inform us about Bessie's relationship with this egocentric man.

A week before Bessie's wedding, Eliza Rockefeller, who had been staying at her son William's house on Fifth Avenue, took to her bed. Then, in the words of her sons, "she had a slight stroke of paralysis . . . [and] could not speak to us . . . but was conscious until the last, very peaceful and resigned. She knew us all and did all her strength would permit to show her affection, appreciation, and Christian resignation."[13] The families accompanied her body to Cleveland, where they held a private service in the Euclid Avenue home. They saw her buried next to her infant granddaughter Alice in Lake View Cemetery. Her husband was not present.

Big Bill appeared before his children for the last time a year later, when he brought a brother still farming in the Owego area to see New York City for the first time. John Jr. wrote Bessie, "[Grandfather] is just eighty years old, but as jolly and entertaining as can be."[14] To the end, he remained vigorous and charismatic as on that day Eliza Davison spied him coming up the steps.

Following Eliza's burial and Bessie's wedding, the remaining family went on a tour of Europe. John Jr. was attracted to the landscapes and churches, but Edith was tempted by the extraordinary paintings, furniture, and jewels displayed in museums and homes. What her parents failed to see was that she might be enticed not just to admire, but to possess.

That fall, John Jr. attended the Browning School, actually a school made to order by several families. His classmates included cousin Percy, friends Howard and Everett Colby, and two newcomers to town, Harold and Stanley McCormick. The McCormick boys were the sons of Nettie McCormick, widow of the farm machinery tycoon. Her appearance was pleasing and unthreatening; she was a tiny woman whose chubby cheeks added youthfulness. Her partial deafness invited people to draw close to converse. In truth, she was a firebrand who ruled her family and, upon her husband's death, his company. (As an aged lady she would continue to appear at the factory to question the hardness of wood used in crating, or the procedure some workmen were implementing.) She was as avid a philanthropist and missionary supporter as the Rockefellers (albeit Presbyterian), and greatly admired them. Having heard that Laura had arranged for John Browning to tutor a small group of boys, Nettie moved from Chicago so her sons could join the class.

The handsome McCormick brothers easily fit in with the social gatherings of all the adolescents at the Rockefeller house. Left fatherless while still youngsters, they had been spoiled by their mother yet carefully led along the path of Christian piety. Unfortunately, neither Cyrus nor Nettie McCormick were as gifted at parenting as Senior and Laura. Cyrus had been a distant, unloving father whose few interactions with his children often consisted of angry shouts in a squeaky high pitch. Nettie vacillated between smothering concern and forgetfulness. Raised to think one is put on earth to serve and suffer, she lacked a sense of humor, and enforced her moral precepts with minute precision. Having lost one child to scarlet fever, she hovered over the remaining ones with constant surveillance, ever ready to administer her latest diagnosis and prescription. What she produced of course is hypochondriacs. One week Nettie would meddle in her children's activities from wakeup until bedtime, hug and baby them constantly, then the next suddenly ignore them, forget her promises, or simply be gone. Worst, as one child recalled, their mother had "a real disregard for the rights of—I would say almost anyone, but especially any child who would be present."[15]

In another important regard the McCormick children differed from the Rockefellers—their parents' puritanical sexual beliefs. Unlike Laura, Nettie forbade any discussion of sex, except to intimate certain activities, such as masturbation, were sinful. At the same time, her intrusion into her children's lives had an erotic overtone. The first sign of the onset of daughter Virginia's mental illness was her passionate goodnight kisses to her mother. Left unsupervised, one governess sexually molested Stanley, and perhaps Harold as well.[16] In later years, Nettie faked heart disease to keep her son Stanley close by, and did all she could to prevent his marrying. Apart from eldest son Cyrus, all of Nettie's offspring would have emotional difficulties.

To outsiders, however, the McCormick children seemed normal and well-balanced. To the extent that they were so, their older sister Anita was responsible. She used whatever influence she could to undo Nettie's harmful practices, and give the boys what their mother could not: "a kind heart." (For example, Anita questioned her mother's requirement that the governess sleep in the same bedroom as the brothers.) Besides being well-mannered, both were handsome, slender, dark-haired lads with intelligent deep-set eyes. Harold, the younger brother, was more outgoing and funloving than the moody Stanley. "They had to run and find me in the morning and catch me for school," Harold recalled.[17] Rather than study, he preferred playing tennis or skating on the ice rink Senior ordered to be placed in the garden every winter.

While John Jr. attended Browning, Edith and Alta went away to Rye Academy. Even though they had to speak in French at the dinner table and the food was not very good, they liked being at a boarding school with other girls their age. Laura's disciplinary hand reached through the mail, however. In a letter to her brother, Alta fretted, "This morning Mother's letter came and I think you can imagine whether we were glad to get it or not. I suppose we have done nothing but break the rules, however we shall learn in time I hope." Alta also asserted her seniority over Edith, who balked, but then became "submissive again and does not make a fuss if I ask her to do something."[18]

For the most part, the sisters got along. Alta was becoming interested in boys, and at times found Edith in the way. She grew jealous of Edith, who was prettier and more vivacious. During a winter break in 1891, the sisters went to the Philharmonic, where they were joined by Harold and Stanley McCormick. As usual, Alta complained to her brother. "Edith was very tired and feared that she might have an attack of cramps, but someway she forgot her bad feelings and managed to talk with Harold most of the evening. I tell her that I cannot have anything to do with such an inconsistent girl."[19] Another time Alta whined that Edith was supposed to be writing a letter to their mother, but was having a good time downstairs with Harold, so Alta would have to write the letter instead.

That Alta would mention Edith's menstrual problems to their younger brother hints at the candor existing among the siblings, for such reference was highly unusual between the sexes. Their mother was most likely the source of this openness. As a result of her work with the WCTU and YWCA, both of which addressed the issues of prostitution and venereal disease, Laura grew more liberal in her thinking and frank in her training. That she bore no children following John suggests she used birth control. Although illegal, early forms of diaphragms were readily available to women of means. (It is also possible, though, that she had simply refused intercourse, another common method of the day to limit family size.)

Free from the constraints of home, at Rye Academy the sisters displayed the same playfulness their mother and aunt had shown as schoolgirls at Oread. In one letter, Alta described an adventure when they had been given permission to buy birthday flowers. Several other girls who lacked permission wanted to go as well, so all waited until the housemother had taken off for her town chores. "After she was out of sight we started at full speed and soon reached the bakery, but to our dismay the charlotte-russe was all out. However, we satisfied our disappointment . . . with fruit and chocolate cake, kisses and chocolate eclairs," giving the extras to "the first poor child we met." They next went to a soda shop, where for the first time they tried a lemon fizz, which they found undrinkable. "And we all nearly died laughing, for when the man's back was turned one after the other poured as much as she could into the spittoon." At one point they caught a glimpse of the housemother down the street, and had to hide. Then they encountered a delivery boy they feared would tattle on them, but they bribed him with candy.[20] Alta was nineteen, Edith eighteen when this daring adventure occurred.

Edith and Alta were unaware that their brother was not fully trustworthy, that he might be tattling on them. "Although I was the youngest my parents turned to me for advice on many questions, including my sisters, particularly their love affairs, and because I was close to my sisters I was able to understand their point of view, which in turn I could translate to my parents."[21] Unfortunately, he did not always understand their point of view, and this misperception would cause heartaches later on all sides.

During part of the winter of 1891 John Jr. had another nervous collapse and went to Forest Hill for the regimen of exercise and solitude. This second depression may have been brought on by a frightful tragedy. In 1888, at age fourteen, John Jr.'s approaching manhood was signified by his being allowed to wear long pants. About the same time he grew infatuated with a girl of his own age. A pretty brunette with porcelain skin, Bessie Dashiell set tremors up his back when he sat behind her in church. "I felt very miserable to think I would not see her till Tuesday anyway, and perhaps not then."[22] He wandered about the neighborhood in hope of glimpsing her. Fortunately, her brother Lefferts Dashiell and her cousin Everett Colby were John's best friends, who provided him a pretense to see her often under properly chaperoned circumstances. She soon took to his shy, gentle manner. One day they even posed for a photograph together, as though they were engaged.

They were of course too young to consider marriage, but a worse impediment came between them. In the summer of 1890 Bessie went with her family on a trip to Alaska, so John Jr. did not see her for several months. While there, she injured her hand and an apparent infection set in. When the family returned to New York, the problem was discovered to be sarcoma, and even amputation of Bessie's forearm did not stop the spread of the disease. John Jr.'s experience of sitting by her bedside and watching her suffering made an indelible mark. At age seventeen he was finally exposed to the cruelty of fate. On January 21, 1891, lovely Bessie died.

At first he approached her death intellectually. He sought out her doctor and other cancer specialists to better understand the course and treatment of the disease. He sensed Bessie's death might have been needless had more been understood about cancer. Her final anguish became the source of his lifelong fascination with illness and public health, as well as his certainty that scientific research must play a larger role in American medicine.

Late in life, Senior remarked of his son, "It was his mother who developed him."[23] This was not totally true, for while often separated from the boy, Senior sent notes of constant support. He was especially reassuring during this time that John Jr. was mourning alone at Forest Hill.

"The girls must not be too jealous because I write you so often and not them. It is on account of your being the active member of the hay farm [the children's latest venture]."[24] In another, he wrote how "I long to be with you . . . to transplant trees . . . at the sugar making."[25] These sympathetic notes must have meant a lot to John Jr., because his father in person was not demonstrative. The affection between the two would always be caged by a formality that onlookers found curious.

Bereavement further hampered John Jr.'s college preparatory work. During this time at Forest Hill, he studied Virgil, Ovid, and other classics as required by the Yale entrance examination. When he failed a section of the test, he decided to spend another year of study at Browning. His best friends had decided to go to Brown University, and John wondered if he should go there instead. In making his decision he consulted with Dr. William Rainey Harper, then president of the University of Chicago, and Rev. W. H. P. Faunce of the Fifth Avenue Baptist Church. Harper admitted that Yale had a wider reputation and was attended by "more men of better family," yet recommended Brown for its exceptional president, Benjamin Andrews. Faunce used a more convincing argument, noting that Yale had a "fast set" that would be uncongenial to John, and that Providence was more healthful than New Haven.

John Jr. was not the only Rockefeller child to experience emotional turmoil during these years. In the spring of 1893, Edith was sent to the Hospital for Orthopedic and Nervous Diseases in Philadelphia. Its founder, Dr. Silas Weir Mitchell, was the most prominent physician in America for the treatment of nervous disorders, and specialized in women patients. Mitchell's cure was world-renowned and much-copied. In Europe, the center for the growing science of psychiatry, he was considered a major contributor to therapy. His contemporaries would find it hard to believe his reputation would not achieve immortality, that a young Austrian Jew named Sigmund Freud was going to overwhelm the theory of nervous disorders and delete the names of other contributors from history.

Mitchell was a noted, inventive neurologist at the time of the Civil War, and achieved fame for insisting that battle fatigue, shell shock, and hysteria were genuine disorders, not the malingering of a cowardly soldier. Provided a hospital for studying these cases, he devised techniques for diagnosing and treating varieties of battle neuroses. One of the most successful cures, he discovered, was simply rest, isolation, and good nutrition. The nerves would not settle until the body was rejuvenated.

Following the war he became fascinated with a mental disorder that became epidemic in late nineteenth-century America, hysteria. The afflicted were most often young females from middle-class or wealthy families who enjoyed a life of material comfort and "good, right-minded" parents. First written about in an 1859 medical journal, they were called *sitophobes.* In Mitchell's words,

> The woman grows pale and thin, eats little, or if she eats does not profit by it. Everything wearies her,—to sew, to write, to read, to walk,—and by and by the sofa or the bed is her only comfort.... Then comes the mischievous role of bromides, opium, chloral, and brandy. If the case did not begin with uterine troubles [dysmenorrhea], they soon appear.... [O]ften the result is to cultivate self-love and selfishness.[26]

By the 1870s, new terms were used, *anorexia hysteria* or *anorexia nervosa.*[27] Desperate families called in a variety of healers, whose use of plaster jackets, braces, water cures, and even gynecological surgery often only exacerbated the invalidism. Mitchell used a simpler strategy, one that worked.

When Edith and her family arrived at the hospital, they met with Mitchell, whose probling eyes and assured demeanor inspired quick confidence. Mitchell explained that his treatment required the separation of patient and family for an extended period. He cogently recognized that the sufferer provoked "the self-sacrificing love and over-careful sympathy of a mother, a sister, or some other devoted relative" whose solicitude reinforced passivity. As a result, these caretakers suffered exhaustion and needed the separation as much as the patient. The family must have felt great relief upon their return home to know that Edith was in capable hands.

Mitchell's cure was deceptively simple. To rest her jangled nerves, Edith spent her day in bed, allowed to do nothing—not read, not sew, not converse with a sympathetic ear. To prevent further weakening, daily Swedish massage and electrical stimulation of her muscles was recommended. (Through careful record keeping, Mitchell had found that low-grade fevers common to these cases disappeared following massage.) To build up her strength, her meals were small enough not to overwhelm her, yet nutritious. The day likely started with coffee, followed by well-balanced meals and snacks supplemented by malt drinks, iron tonics, and aloe pills. (In special cases, morphine, chloral, and strychnine, common medications then, were applied, but whether Edith received them is unknown.) With improved nutrition, menstruation reappeared.

Mitchell visited daily to provide Edith's only extended interaction with another person. He called these conversations "moral medication," psychotherapy really, a form he conceived several years before Freud would claim the invention. In response to Edith's discussion of her past experiences and current feelings, he "urged and scolded, and teased and bribed, and decoyed along the road to health."

Mitchell's psychotherapy, with its use of ingenuity and paradox, resembles that developed much later by Milton Erickson. When one outpatient claimed paralysis and refused to move from her bed, he put her in a carriage, rode her a few miles from home, told her to get out and walk back. She did, and was cured, although she never spoke to Mitchell again. When he believed another patient was strong enough to get out of bed, and she refused, he threatened to crawl in bed with her. She scorned him, so he started to unbutton his clothes. Once he reached his fly, she leapt up angrily and went on with the rest of her treatment.[28]

Some historians have interpreted Mitchell's approach as governed by Victorian patriarchy and male chauvinism, a power play over women in other words.[29] They overlook that while his method was explicitly authoritarian (and what therapy is not?), it resembled that used with his battle-fatigued Civil War soldiers. His cure required not only the counsel of the male physician, but the accompanying skill of the female nurses and masseuses. Furthermore, Mitchell's writings show much sympathy toward the plight of what others saw to be simply spoiled girls and wives. Granted, a few cases he called Degenerates. These were "pests . . . annoying examples of despotic selfishness." Yet many of these, he reminded, were misbehaving as a result of inheriting a weak nervous system. In most cases, he averred, the women were genuinely ill, Angelic Invalids, exhausted by overwork or a sudden change in circumstance, such as an unhappy love affair or loss.

Even today clinicians dispute the cause of anorexia, whether it is primarily biomedical, cultural, or psychological in origin. In Edith's case, all appear operative. The genetic or biomedical argument is supported by the fact that periodically throughout her life, Edith suffered spells of nervous malaise. A cultural source was the common Gilded-Age response to the emotional volatility common to onset of puberty. Physicians warned mothers to intervene with their daughters' moodiness and brooding. The claims were that with the ovaries now active, a girl who mistreated her body could end up with consumption, inability to carry a child full term, or sterility. Christian-based folklore attributed menstruation to God's curse on the daughters of Eve. This exagerration of the "dangers" of puberty encouraged family members and doctors to perceive a normal physiological process as something abnormal, requiring careful supervision.

Apparent in Edith's case, too, was her adherence to the changing ideal of beauty. Where earlier in the century a plump woman was evidence of a family's financial success, the reverse was now true. Terms like "jumbo," "porky," and "butterball" entered the vocabulary, and girls were warned to pass from the plumpness of childhood so as not to become "overripe pears" in adulthood.[30] In his dissection of social class, Thorstin Veblen explained to readers at the time how the thin, frail woman became the mark of prosperity precisely because she was unfit for work. Women of means were the first in America to diet as a way to control their self-presentation. Weight became equated with working-class status, hence vulgarity. Neither Laura nor Aunt Lute impressed such ideas on the girls, for Alta, the most conforming, retained her slight plumpness. But walking about Fifth Avenue, Edith would see the sylphlike forms of Vanderbilt cousins Gertrude and Consuelo, the "princesses" of her age group, and their skinny friends.

With maturation, family strictures regarding a woman's place in the world became more problematic for Edith. There was no place in Standard Oil for a multilingual, philosophy-reading, cello virtuoso in skirts. Even if she went to college, as Bessie had, she foresaw only two choices in life, to marry or to be a dependent spinster like Aunt Lute. It never occurred to her that in college she might find what other independent women of her social class were discovering, the possibility of a career in education, social welfare, or medicine. Through increasing her dependency on her family, invalidism postponed adulthood with its unattractive promise.

It may seem ironic that women disabled by a life of leisure were cured during a period of forced rest, but that was the case. During Mitchell's moral medication, for perhaps the first time in their lives, his female patients had a respectable male of authority listening to them, taking them seriously. Indeed, his shock tactics presumed they were fully competent and capable, even sexual creatures. When Laura and Senior were finally allowed to visit Edith, they were pleased to find her improving and let her remain with him.

During the summer of 1893, on Mitchell's advice Edith went to a mountain rest home in upper New York. That September another Rockefeller child went to Dr. Mitchell's. Now Bessie was suffering anxiety and weakness. Unrecognized was that her fatigue and frailty were the possible result of a heart ailment.[31] Edith returned to Philadelphia in November, where the two sisters remained in treatment together until the spring of 1894.

Alta, the only fully healthy child at this time, was having troubles of another sort. She had lost Charles Strong to Bessie, and Harold McCormick, now at Princeton, was clearly going to seek Edith's hand when the time was right. During the early 1890s Alta grew fond of a man of whom the family disapproved. Having completed her studies at Rye Academy, she lived at home. There she took on her ailing mother's household responsibilities, which included seeing to the care of Grandma Spelman and Aunt Lute as well. She much missed the companionship of her brother.

Along with children's problems, unexpected publicity provoked long sleepless nights where Senior and Laura discussed their troubles in the dark of their bedroom. As Standard Oil prospered, it became the scapegoat for populists and radicals of the day, the exemplar of all that was wrong with trust-dominated capitalism. More precisely, John D. Rockefeller became the scapegoat. From a young age the children learned to be alert on the streets to avoid harassment or possible kidnapping. Senior regularly received abusive mail, even death threats. These attacks were hardest on John Jr., who as the only son felt a growing need to vindicate his father's reputation.

One peak in this outcry occurred in 1888, when Senator Frank Arnold called an investigation of trusts. Called to answer questions about Standard Oil, Senior riled people with his frequent claims of "not recalling" and his denying ever injuring competitors. Even newspapers normally supportive of him wrote in opposition. As the New York *Herald* taunted, "[John D. Rockefeller] proved conclusively that [Standard Oil] is the greatest philanthropy of the age, a sort of missionary society engaged in spreading the evangelical light of kerosene oil over the dark place in a naughty world. . . . The only thing this company lacks is a chaplain."[32]

What Senior did reveal for the first time was Standard's secret trust agreement of 1882. Journalists uncovered with further alarm that not only oil, but sugar, milk, meat, furniture, glass, rubber, and other commodities investigated had been similarly organized in recent years for the profit of a few. They explained how trust agreements allowed small numbers of men to control numerous interrelated corporations without public scrutiny or accountability. They showed how in half a dozen years Standard had doubled in value, and its dividends to its few owners exceeded fifty million dollars. At the same time, trust-controlled commodities like sugar or glass forced greatly increased prices upon consumers. The Senatorial committee's final report did not condemn Rockefeller and Standard Oil, but that was irrelevant to the public. "Antitrust" became the new cause for members of both political parties.

Furthermore, on March 2, 1890, the Supreme Court of Ohio supported a suit brought against Standard Oil by the state attorney general. Holding that the company had achieved much good, the justices nonetheless affirmed that it did so in violation of common law, for "it is not wise to trust human cupidity where it has the opportunity to aggrandize itself at the expense of others."[33] Cognizant that more lawsuits were on the docket in other states, and that the U.S. Supreme Court would not reverse the decision, in 1892 the trustees and certificate holders of Standard Oil voted to dissolve the trust.

Standard Oil changed only in name. Through a legal sleight of hand, the eight trustees ended up with proportional shares in each of the separate companies once belonging to the trust. Thus, they observed the letter of the Supreme Court decision without actually dispersing the concentration of power. This solution seemed safe from further political attack, particularly following the election in 1896 of Republican William McKinley, who rode to victory on the support of bankers and corporate owners. McKinley's major advisor was Senior's old schoolmate Mark Hanna, who argued that monopolies were not bad. That same election brought in a new attorney general to Ohio, Frank S. Monnett, an ambitious Progressive who took Standard Oil to court, alleging it was in contempt of the 1892 Supreme Court decision. Although never able to prove his case, the protracted hearings kept the company on the front pages. Subpoenaed as a witness, Senior was so taciturn during the interrogation that one headline quipped "Rockefeller Imitates a Clam." A company employee admitted that great quantities of books and records had been burned.

Whether prodded by the Ohio prosecution or not, Senior and his associates realized they needed a more fundamental reorganization. New Jersey law provided the solution. Shrewdly, that state's politicians enacted legislation that allowed the establishment of holding companies, that is, corporations which held stock in other ones. The reporting procedures were lax as well. By the end of the decade Standard Oil of New Jersey was born, fully-grown, and New Jersey would grow fat from its franchise taxes on it and other companies.[34]

In addition to external legal problems, Rockefeller had felt himself beleaguered within his own company. During the 1880s, his geologists warned that the company's major oil source, the fields in Pennsylvania, were giving out. Many of his colleagues, men he had chosen for their capable daily managerial abilities, lacked his vision. Rockefeller fought hard to get his cautious board of directors to expand Standard from refining and manufacturing to production. They long resisted before agreeing to buy up leases in potential fields elsewhere, such as Ohio. As a result of Rockefeller's foresight, by 1891 Standard was producing a quarter of the nation's output of crude oil, and built the world's largest refinery, in Indiana. He had proved to others in business the value of what would later be called "vertical integration." (Despite its grasping and chicanery, Standard was not a complete monopoly, for competitors variously held on to ten to twenty percent of its markets.)

To those early competitors who had suffered the "good sweatings," that is, had been forced to sell out their business to Standard, John D. was a monster. His seeming arrogance, his rationalizing all his actions as moral and the "best for the country," rubbed wounds raw. That he was basically right, that he had turned a wild, chaotic industry into an efficient, orderly business that brought stability to the economy and low costs to consumers failed to soothe his victims. Others, notably workers suffering under the unregulated labor system, lashed out at Standard as a representative of the concentrated power that took all the profits while they broke their backs. (Standard proved it treated its workers more humanely than other employers, but what was "humane" to owners was sometimes "abuse" to workers.)

More than once Senior took public blame for his brother William's schemes. William had masterfully captured the European oil market for Standard, and managed to hold on to the bulk of it even after the Russians discovered lush oilfields near Baku in Central Asia. In his avarice, however, he had befriended James Stillman, the president of National City Bank, also known on Wall Street as "the man in the iron mask." Stillman was a twisted, cruel man. (One day, for no apparent reason he threw out his wife and mother of five small children, and insisted her name never be mentioned in his presence.) William joined Stillman in questionable deals separate from his work for Standard Oil, which, after they were uncovered, were attributed to John D. Nevertheless, Senior held silent in face of the falsely based attacks, as his mother had done when rumors attacked her husband's honor. Critics took his stubborn silence as proof of guilt, and no matter how much Laura begged him otherwise, he would not speak out on his own or the company's behalf.

Apart from its impact on Senior, the collaboration between William Rockefeller and James Stillman would extend beyond business. With each having children of similar age, the possibility of joining the families through marriage was attractive. Stillman's effects upon the Rockefeller family would thus pervade beyond his lifetime.

By the early 1890s, unlike his mischievous brother William, Senior lost interest in the "war" of business. Partly he felt restless upon achieving success; partly he was weary from the roar of criticism. What most satisfied, he noticed, were the discussions concerning the University of Chicago, the giving rather than the gaining of dollars. Since childhood he had been unusually charitable, but with notoriety came hordes of suppliants who tracked him on the streets and even followed him into the sanctuary of church. Some months these pleas numbered many hundreds, further evidence of the rise in human suffering related to the inequitable boom-and-bust economy.

Doubtless some of the increase in requests was due to critics of inequality in the pulpits. As workers sought recourse for their poor wages and working conditions, liberal Protestant congregations started to take on social justice as a cause. Popularizers such as Congregationalist minister William Gladden urged an *Applied Christianity*, where employers returned to Christ's precepts in managing their businesses. With the depression of 1893, these writings proliferated. *If Christ Came to Chicago*, imagined a British journalist, how would he respond to the ugly sight of a city with 200,000 unemployed men and two hundred millionaires?

The ideas of the Social Gospel, as it came to be called, undermined the theory of a free market, a society where the best would eventually succeed, the weak fail. Instead, it suggested that unrestrained American capitalism had failed by ignoring the human suffering. (If all are equal under God, then to brush off the poor is inexcusable.) Church members now had a clear responsibility to go beyond the saving of souls to duplicating Christ's model of justice toward the poor and downtrodden.

Few of these ideas were new to Senior, who with Laura had built the family tradition upon a foundation of generosity. Even before the popularization of the Social Gospel, both the YWCA and the WCTU had practiced many of its principles. The Social Gospel offered guidance to those more moderate Americans who saw the need for reform, but were unwilling to follow the Socialists or even the WCTU.

Another force behind what would become the Progressive movement was an atheist, steel magnate Andrew Carnegie. In his influential 1889 essay "Wealth," Carnegie argued that Society must not only accept, but welcome the concentration of business in the hands of a few.[35] Capitalism's law of competition was best because it ensured the survival of the fittest part of the race, albeit at some cost to less successful individuals. In return, however, it was incumbent upon the Gilded Age aristocrats to channel their money into remedies for the ills of the cities and factories. The successful man, he averred, would not leave a treasure house for his descendant's dissipation.

Thus Carnegie managed to find what seemed an impossible fit between the Social Darwinists, who proclaimed the inevitability of a harsh and unjust society, and the cries of reformers, who implied humans could improve their lot. The capitalist was to be the mediator, the "trustee and agent for his poorer brethren, bringing to their service his superior wisdom, experience, and ability to administer . . . better than they would or could do for themselves." On the one hand, this Gospel of Wealth, as critics came to call it, was an implicit attack upon the growing influence of union organizers and socialists. On the other, in an era when government assiduously avoided involvement in social problems, it encouraged some men of wealth to underwrite research and social services on a level impossible to achieve any other way.

With so many social currents supporting Senior's change in priorities, he remained in a dilemma. A favorite needlework design of the day explains the counterforce: "Work is prayer." Labor was a blessing in which all men should partake. Thus, in placing charity before business and other wordly accumulation, Senior must withdraw from the key expression of manhood. Now he, too, became ill with various neurasthenic symptoms, hence had an "excuse" to reduce the pressures of the office.[36] The manifestations lasted for almost a decade and were severe. The most troublesome ailment was alopecia, a stress-induced condition that resulted in the permanent loss of virtually all his hair.

The first act in his transition to virtually full-time philanthropy was to designate a wise manager to sift through the almsmen's causes and dispense his gifts prudently. He found his servant in Frederick T. Gates. Impressed by Gates's good sense in the University of Chicago dealings, in 1893 Senior offered him the position of philanthropic administrator. A gifted and wise administrator, Gates investigated each case thoroughly, sifted out frauds and incompetents, and made suggestions on the distributions of benefits. He shared Senior's belief that amounts should be modest until the recipients proved their worth, and that larger donations be accompanied by such conditions as the raising of matching funds, so that the organization not be dependent upon Rockefeller for survival. Gates brought bureaucratic methods to giving, and would eventually have a slew of his own assistants to execute the fact-finding.

With Gates handling the administration, Senior was free to be as visionary in philanthropy as he had been in oil. Together, the men delineated an approach to philanthropy distinct from Carnegie. For one, Senior eschewed Carnegie's tendency toward self-advertisement—he would have no equivalent of the Carnegie Library that appeared in towns across the country. He also conceived that wealth could remain in the family, that philanthropy should be the primary aim of his and later Rockefeller generations. (Less conscious was the implication that continued generosity required continued attention to family wealth.)

Concerning the direction of funding, Gates and Rockefeller preferred attack of root causes to relief of symptoms. Find the cure for a disease rather than build a clinic. Help the best minds in medicine, sociology, and education develop and test solutions that local communities can implement. Implicit was a belief that problems could be dissected and analyzed by appropriate experts, just as a pathologist cuts and probes to locate the bacterium or tumor. Indeed, Gates eventually came to see the sole cause of all human misery as disease. Get people healthy and they will be productive workers, hence poverty and its accompanying ills will vanish.

With this emphasis upon social betterment, artistic needs became secondary. Although music was an essential part of Senior's "balanced life," he seldom gave to performing groups. Nor were Gates and Rockefeller unconventional when it came to race and gender. They supported Negro causes, but ranked work-related training over liberal education. Gates in particular did not approve of organizations run by women. In these regards, the two men held to the paternalism of the day, confident that as white Protestant men they had a special talent and duty to oversee others of lesser status. This prejudice would cause a permanent breach between Senior and one of his daughters.

The winter of 1892–93 had been one of the worst in years. The warmth and blooms of spring were mocked by a money panic that threw the country into its worst depression ever. During that troubled summer, the Rockefellers joined half their fellow Americans who sought diversion and hope at the Columbian Exposition in Chicago. No World's Fair before or since so captured the ethos of the population. As historian and visitor Henry Adams explained in his inimitable way, "Education ran riot in Chicago, at least for retarded minds which had never faced in concrete form so many matters of which they were ignorant. . . . Chicago asked in

1893 for the first time the question whether the American people knew where they were driving. . . . Chicago was the first expression of American thought as a unity."[37]

For Senior and his family, and most of the 27 million visitors, that unity amounted to a vindication of the American dream. There was first of all, the spectacle of Chicago itself, the queen and guttersnipe of cities, "Porkopolis" to Easterners. The sky blackened from its industry, the river flowed so sluggily and with such a foul smell from its sewage that engineers were working to reverse its course to try to cleanse it. The people were polyglot, immigrants having long ago outnumbered the original Yankee settlers. Brothel and honkeytonk sat near mansion and theater. Yet this city of windy and corrupt politicians had risen from the ashes of its great fire to create a celestial playground known as the White City at the end of a dirt road. It would later be transmuted by L. Frank Baum into the Emerald City of Oz.

The two hundred buildings on over six hundred acres formed an American cornucopia of past achievements and emerging accomplishment. To prove that biggest was best, there was the world's largest building, the Manufacturers and Liberal Arts exhibit, which could seat 300,000 people. The world's first ferris wheel rotated over two thousand people riding its seventy-two cars. Inside places like Electricity Hall and the Transportation Building, visitors had a glimpse of the future: fiberglass, the zipper, long-distance telephone, an electric cookstove, a monorail. If the oil-rich Rockefellers were troubled by the mass display of electric lighting and technology, they could take hope in the first American automobile, built by the Duryea brothers. Just when Standard's major product, illuminant oil, was losing its market, this new invention with its guzzling appetite for petroleum arrived on the scene.

Hints of advertising and mass consumption echoed Standard's early venture in this area. Name brands were introduced to products once sold generically: Chase & Sanborn Coffee, Quaker Oats, Pabst Beer (which later inserted "Blue Ribbon" for the award it won there), and Aunt Jemima (in person). States competed to show off their products: a Liberty Bell made of oranges, a life-sized knight of prunes, a building constructed from ears of corn. Surely here was proof of the fulfillment of the new Eden, or for the more scientifically inclined, the survival of the fittest.

Social Darwinism and Manifest Destiny shared the spotlight. For the first time in exhibition history, women had their own building, but only after Chicago's social queen, Bertha Honoré Palmer, forced the issue. And by making women's achievements separate from men's, the implication was that they were less than equal. Excluded from even menial jobs, afforded a restroom only in the Haiti exhibit, African-Americans were ignored in the national self-adulation. One consequence was Ida Wells's decision to publish her discerning pamphlet on "The Reason Why the Colored American is Not in the World's Columbian Exposition," namely, simple racism. In such accord, exhibits concerning "folkloric" white countries (German, Hungarian, Irish) were placed closest to the White city, while those portraying South Pacific, African, and Asian cultures were positioned toward the margins of the grounds. A sign at the Dahomey display reassured viewers that the native inhabitants were not cannibals. South Sea Islanders were depicted "before" and "after" Christian missionaries introduced "civilization." Few questioned this propaganda proclaiming the benefit of introducing American progress and morals to "lesser" people. Perusing such displays, Laura and Senior must have felt well-rewarded for their years of supporting Baptist mission work overseas.

Yet, the fair was more egalitarian in another regard, its Parliament of Religions. Here proponents of faiths from around the world spoke on their beliefs, and some were so effective as to counter the denigrating imagery shown in other parts of the fair. The openmindedness did not please all—the Archbishop of Canterbury refused to allow the Church of England to participate because the display implied Christanity was not the only true religion. It could well be here that John Jr. found inspiration for his own growing ecumenicism, his recognition that "other sheep have I that are not of this fold."[38]

Despite the grandiosity and jingoistic chest-beating, the exposition touched even the most cynical participants with its visual splendor. However commercialized, however tacky with its hootchy-kooch dancers and sword-swallowers, the White City exemplified some of the best of American architecture and art. The enchanting landscapes of Frederick Law Olmsted perfectly set off the magnificent neoclassic buildings of such architects as Richard Morris Hunt and Stanford White. At night from gondolas on the lagoon, visitors watched the spotlights focus on the Saint Gaudens sculpture of Diana, then slide across the waters to cast an iridescent glow over the immense greenhouse dome. "In that lovely hour, soft and gentle as was ever a summer's night, the toil and trouble of men, the fear that was gripping in men's hearts in the [panicked] market, fell away from me, and in its place came Faith," wrote one.[39] And another commented, "It was America saying: Look. Someday . . . we'll have finished with all our grime and disorder and haste. Someday we'll have time for a world of beauty and leisure—far ahead."[40] Here were no better expressions of Senior's faith and John Jr.'s hope.

But what of the daughters? Edith and Bessie, languishing on sick beds, never saw the luminous vision of the White City. For Alta, it provided a memory of wondrous entertainment, and a reaffirmation of her traditional belief in the secondary role of women.

7

Come Into My Garden

"A bundle of myrrh is my well beloved unto me; he shall lie all night be-twixt my breasts."

—Song of Solomon I:I3.

Laura's heart went out to all of her children during their troubles of the early 1890s. What hurt her the most, though, was her separation from her son, who went off to Brown University in September of 1894. For the next four years, frequent letters expressed the loving and longing of each for the other. By early adulthood, John Jr. displayed a temperament much closer to his mother than his father. He was deeply compassionate, but his caring was somewhat abstract and intellectualized, grounded in Biblical precept. He would be quick to help those in need, but was less capable of expressing tenderness in the process, as Senior could. He mimicked his mother's lack of humor. Though witty in her youth, Laura's later chastening manner likely emerged as she committed herself to a Christian life. It was as though she had equated service and piety with seriousness, and interpreted loving others as one's self to mean the avoidance of any mirth or teasing. In contrast, Senior wove wordplay, tricks, and games throughout his daily encounters, as though to remind himself that the things of this world were not so serious! In these and other regards, John Jr. and his mother were soul mates, who saw in one another a reflection of close-held values.

Thus, although from the wealthiest family in the country, John Jr. exhibited little of the brawny manhood in vogue with his peers. He was vigorous and willing to face challenges, but not of the hale-and-be-hearty fraternal sort with their emphasis upon athletics and reenactment of "primitive" rituals. Even religious magazines touted Muscular Christianity, a hardy Jesus who made "the snarling pack of his enemies . . . slink away."[1] John Jr.'s classmates misunderstood his shyness, and found him formal, overly serious, and desperately earnest. He pledged Alpha Delta

Phi, but was accepted only after much debate. He would rather practice the violin than sit around and josh with other fellows. He neither smoked nor drank nor danced nor played sports. "Here comes Johnny Rock, reeking with virtue and without one redeeming vice," said onlookers.[2]

His penury drew much comment. He was seen once trying to unglue two two-cent stamps. When a theology student working his way through college delivered the laundry he had done for $1.97, John Jr.'s friends were surprised he asked for the three cents change. They could not get him to follow the practice of tipping. He kept his accounts to the penny, typically went Dutch, and seldom treated.

He became a fisher of men, and set up regular Bible study classes held at the Providence Boys' Club and in his dormitory room. There he held forth on such topics as courage, taking up the cross, following God's ideals—the components of Christian Manhood. "The path of duty is not one of our own choosing; it is the course marked out for us by God."[3] His piety attracted like-minded men, but Brown did not have many of this kind. Most of his classmates were self-confident and fun-loving, and earned grades of "Gentlemen's Cs." Protestant Christianity was less a creed than a mark of status.

Yet however much others expressed dislike or indifference to John Jr., they did respect him. He was so unpretentious, so sincere in his position, that they admired his sticking to his convictions. Also, he lacked malice, and was so agreeable and well-mannered that only louts heckled him. It helped, too, that word spread regarding his private aid to needy students. Others saw how he not only preached a demanding ideal, he conformed to it. His freshman account book included a formula: "Friendship=Congeniality, Unlikeness, Generosity, Personal Worth." Judging men by their character, and not by their family status or finances, John Jr. slowly gathered around him a set of devoted friends. That some were very secular in outlook was secondary—after all, his Christ did not limit his associates to the pure of heart and the believers.

Brown further liberalized John Jr.'s worldview. He wrote his mother of attending worship services at different Protestant denominations. He told his Bible students that following a particular sect did not make one a Christian. "The essense of Christianity is rather in the individual's attitude toward Christ."[4] Interestingly, Laura did not dissuade him from exploring beyond the Baptist Church. But then she need not worry about the waywardness of a son who wrote following a visit, "With so firm an anchorage, it seems as though I could not drift far from the path of duty. . . . With God's help, dear mother, I will never bring disgrace upon the home and the parents who have done so much for me."[5]

During his freshman year, John Jr. often wrote his mother the equivalent of what used to be Sunday evening accounts of confession. He admitted to doing poorly in Latin, but decided he would rather hire a tutor than use a "trot" or translation to cheat on homework. He apologized for travelling home on a Sunday, but explained it was the only way he could have enough time with her over vacation. As Laura preferred, he chose Glee Club over the Banjo and Mandolin Society. When she disapproved of his joining the Operetta Society, he followed her counsel. He wrote how he was not worthy of "his Mother's Love," her many gifts, including a blotter, cuff studs, handkerchiefs, the twenty-four volumes of George Eliot.

During his sophomore year, John Jr. became a full-fledged member of Alpha, and capitulated to his fraternity brothers' pressure to learn ballroom dancing. While Providence socity was less flamboyant than that of Gilded Age New York, it was as ritualized. Unaccustomed to anything but church socials and sedate parties at home, John Jr. felt out of place, even guilty, in gossipy, opulent settings. Certain his mother would disapprove, he walked nervously around the edges of tea dances, choosing wall flowers for partners. Shy women were grateful for this handsome young man with no pretenses. As he gained confidence, he entered in his account book bouquets sent to several young women in Providence, particularly a Miss Addeman, who played with him in a string quartet.

Interestingly, neither mother nor son wrote much about other family members. Once in a while Laura reported on the recuperation of Edith and Bessie, or of Senior's health. John Jr. returned polite gratitude that they were doing well. Otherwise it was as though mother and son had only each other. On his twenty-first birthday, John Jr. heard from her, "You have now stepped over the threshhold of youth into manhood, but you will ever be your mother's *boy*. You have always been her comfort, her helper, her sweetheart, her joy, her pride, one of God's best gifts."[6]

Whether her daughters ever received such fulsome praise is not known, for her letters to them have vanished. Yet her attention to her son is so effusive that partiality was likely. One has to wonder whether Laura's preference for John Jr. provoked some of the sisters' difficulties through their passage to adulthood. What resentments could not be expressed, even to one another? While growing up, how could they confess envy or jealousy during Sunday night confessionals with their mother?

Supposing there was no secret ill-will or sense of lesser appreciation, there remains the problem of a mother who is "too nice." Laura easily conformed to the arduous path of Victorian Christian womanhood and Baptist morality. Though her family was much wealthier than those Fifth

Avenue women, she eschewed their glamorous lifestyle. She resisted temptations of the flesh: gluttony, alcohol, illicit sexual pleasures. She kept a straight course guided by daily Bible readings and prayers.

It is very hard to be the child of a saint, and it was more so for the Rockefeller daughters because a woman's role was changing. Their mother had come of age when the nation was in an evangelical fervor, while they grew up when the secular and material came to the fore, when what one wore or owned was more important than one's moral actions. There was no equivalent of Christian manhood that served their brother so well. Other well-to-do young women came out in debuts, attended fancy dress balls, vacationed in Newport and Saratoga, travelled to Paris for annual fittings at the House of Worth, and celebrated "the season" in London. Were a wealthy daughter to rebel, she could go into the arts, social welfare, or professions on her own money. (The women artists of the age included more heiresses than would normally occur.)

The Rockefeller daughters were permitted neither the debutante's way nor that of the New Woman, educated and independent. They were among the wealthiest young women in the world in the abstract only, for they had few resources of their own and hardly any options. The youngest, Edith, was more attracted to the new ways, and as the most talented of all the children, felt the most constrained.

While at college, John Jr. continued his endearing devotion to his sisters. He frequently sent flowers to Edith and Bessie at the Mitchell hospital, and visited them in Philadelphia. By the spring of 1894, Edith was staying at Laurel-in-the-Pines in Lakewood, New Jersey, where she had a comfortable suite and opportunity for such health-building activities as carriage driving. That summer, all three sisters relaxed at a resort in the Adirondacks. Laura and Senior rejoiced that their daughters were all finally well.

John Jr. also invited Alta to accompany him to Brown football games and parties. (One classmate overheard Alta quip that her brother should have been the girl in the family, and the girls his brothers!) Alta's unsuitable beau, one Mr. Ashworth, also attended Brown. John Jr. did not like the man and assumed the role of protector. At a party he approached Ashworth and advised that "all but the most formal acquaintance must cease between himself and Alta for years at least. I told him it would be extremely hard to live up to this in N.Y. and he said that if he could not, he would go away."[7] Plans were made for Alta to join cousin Emma and other members of William Rockefeller's family in Europe for the summer. Presumably, such maneuvering was to inhibit Alta's undesirable courtship.

But Alta could not get over her lost love, and her sorrow expanded when Edith and Harold announced their engagement. When John Jr. expressed his sympathy over her heartbreak, Alta was most grateful. "Do what I will I cannot change it. . . . Sad hearts can love as well as glad hearts and you are more to me now brother than you ever were before."[8] She seemed unaware of the part he played in tampering with her romance.

John Jr. had planned a summer 1894 cycling tour around England with friend Dick Richardson. Before leaving, he wrote his mother, "We will not judge others, 'as for me and my house, we will serve the Lord.' Far too many American Christians are ashamed to own their master on foreign shores. A consistent living always and everywhere is the most powerful advocate of our religion."[9] His lofty convictions against frivolity were proven when Dick convinced John Jr. to attend the theater. After viewing performances of *The Two Gentlemen of Verona, A Midsummer Night's Dream,* and *Charley's Aunt,* John Jr. concluded that "I soon tired of it . . . much of it would simply bore me."[10]

With Alta and John Jr. overseas, Senior and Laura could attend more to Bessie and Edith. Bessie's husband Charles again was having employment problems. In 1892, through family connections he gained a post with the University of Chicago. Somehow that situation did not work out, and by 1895 he was looking for other employment in New York. Senior may have been behind the move, as he was concerned that Charles was not supporting Bessie well. At Senior's behest, Charles considered going into business, and even explored joining a start-up long distance telephone company. A man preoccupied with the Nature of Mind was not a good prospect for commerce, and Charles eventually found a position at Columbia University, again possibly through family influence.

And however much Laura and Senior admired Nettie McCormick's piety and missionary spirit, they did not completely approve of her son Harold as a mate for Edith. He was the only guest to ever smoke in their presence, and had never taken an abstinence pledge. When Senior asked Harold to take one, he responded in a forthright way that earned the elder man's admiration for his honesty. Harold explained that he once had discussed the pledge with his mother, herself a temperance supporter, who had nevertheless advised that it would be unwise. She explained that Harold would manage better without making the promise because he had the willpower to say "no" to anything. He did not like being restricted, and preferred to be motivated by self-pride rather than self-coercion.

Thus he assured his future father-in-law that he was determined to follow a course "worthy of my [deceased] father and the girl I love . . . to make me a man of unquestioned honor, integrity, and habits, and finally to make me a man fitted to stand at the head of a home, of supreme happiness."[11]

Harold was otherwise such a likeable young man that his future in-laws would not let his intransigence regarding tobacco and temperance withhold support for the marriage. His talent for drawing people together, his warmth and humor, all augured well for success as a future executive with the McCormick International machinery company. His easygoing, amiable ways seemed the perfect support for the more highstrung Edith. In any case, the two young people were deeply in love, and brought happiness into any room that they entered.

In 1895, the New York Four Hundred buzzed about another's approaching wedding, that of Alva Vanderbilt's daughter, the swanlike beauty Consuelo, to the Duke of Marlborough. Earlier in the year Alva had shocked Society by declaring her intention to divorce her husband on grounds of adultery. Wealthy wives were supposed to ignore such peccadilloes, and instead present a facade of morality. Alva not only challenged that custom, but was rumored to have taken a lover of her own, Harry Belmont, a man some years younger. Rumors spread that Alva had secluded Consuelo from the man she really loved in order to force a marriage to the Duke, a land-rich, money-poor British aristocrat.[12] The public and press decried such buying of titles, or Gilded Prostitution.

Consuelo's wedding guests included the William Rockefellers, who sided with Alva despite her status as a social pariah. The ceremony at St. Bartholomew's Episcopal Church included music played by the symphony orchestra under the baton of Walter Damrosch. Thousands of spectators lined the street to glimpse the carriages, as though watching a major parade.

Coming from a wealthier family than the Vanderbilts, Edith had a major hand in the design of all aspects of her wedding and demanded an expensive yet tasteful display. It was as if she wished in viewer's minds to erase the memory of Consuelo's extravaganza. Fifth Avenue Baptist was small, with no central aisle for the bridal cortege. Edith had several front pews removed, and a platform resembling a proscenium stage erected and decorated with masses of palm and pink chrysanthemums. The seven bridesmaids, who included her cousin Emma, and the maid of honor, Alta, were to enter from this platform, then march to the back of the church where Edith would join them, and circle back the opposite aisle to return to the platform. That way the twelve hundred invited guests (ten times those invited to Bessie's wedding) could all admire up close the resplendent gowns.

The attendants' dresses were pink and white, and in place of bouquets, they were to carry sable muffs, gifts from Edith. The bride chose an ivory satin gown of princess style, with antique lace trim, and a veil topped by a diamond tiara given to her by Harold. She also planned to wear a string of pearls that cost her father fifteen thousand dollars.

On the eve of the wedding, November 25, the Rockefeller household found its members rushing about, writing hundreds of notes, consulting with florists, meeting with the minister. The plans had to be changed. "No Ceremony in Church . . . Illness Causes Change of Plans" headlined the *Times* the next morning. Harold had been in bed with a cold for several days, and his doctor feared he was on the verge of pneumonia. Consequently, the wedding took place by his bedside in his suite at the Buckingham Hotel, with only family, bridal attendants, and ushers observing. Harold managed to dress in his black frock coat and gray trousers, and stand by the bed, but had to lean upon his brother Stanley during the ceremony. Afterwards, Edith refused to leave her new husband's side to attend the reception at 4 West Fifty-Fourth, but her parents prevailed upon her to let Harry rest. As her mother-in-law Nettie McCormick described the event to friends, "Edith was most courageous, feeling keenly not having Harold at her side . . . she stood there calm, and sweet, and dignified until all the guests had been received."[13] When the bride returned to her husband's bedside that evening, she was relieved to find his fever had broken.

There followed a lengthy honeymoon in Europe, where they saw, in Harold's words, "the sights very much as Mark Twain did when he journeyed up a mountain through the lens of a telescope."[14] The couple settled in Council Bluffs, Iowa, where Harold went to learn more about the family business. He wanted to start at a branch, rather than move immediately into a high-level slot at the Chicago main office. With his usual wit, Harold explained the experience to an old college chum:

> The harvesting machine business is very interesting, but I presume it can be likened to a railroad business, concerning which a person said that all those who were in the business wanted out of it, and all those who were out of the business wanted to be engaged in the railroad business. By the way, the harvesting machine business is an ancient "Trust," and has always adapted its product to the needs of the consumer, or consumee.[15]

Actually, Harold enjoyed life on the road, meeting other travelling salesmen, and learning about the company from the viewpoint of its customers. The slow, steady retreat of his hairline upset him much more
than any turmoil on the job.

In March of 1897, Edith gave birth to a son, John "Jack" Rockefeller
McCormick. The difficult delivery so debilitated her that Laura, Nettie,
and various friends alternated visits because Harold was away most of the
time on business. Laura was pleased to see that Edith seemed more mature and matronly. Senior was not well enough to go to Iowa, and in a
very shaky hand wrote his wife, "How thankful we all ought to be that
everything seems so favorable. . . . We miss you very much."[16]

Senior increasingly divided his time among New York, Pocantico, and
Lakeport, where he was often accompanied by Bessie and Charles. Bessie
was now pregnant and ailing. After her difficult birth to Margaret, in June
of 1897, the doctor stayed on for three days until the crisis passed.
Bessie's problems were increasingly emotional as well as physical. The
most striking symptom was a fear of impoverishment, which resulted in a
neurotic preoccupation with saving and an obsessive penny-pinching. It
was totally illogical, because she had her own trust and Senior was generous about contributing to her household. Laura wrote John Jr. that she
hoped "love and care for the child will take her [Bessie] out of herself."[17]

Bessie's neurosis was an extreme expression of the family culture of
frugality. An analogy may be drawn to Edith's earlier anorexia. Rather
than seek control through the irrational restriction of food, Bessie sought
to prevent the loss of money. Counting pennies was a reversion to childhood practice, an escape to the past, presumably a more halcyon time for
her. What was happening in her relationship with Charles that she acted
so desperately? The historical record is blank. Not even the extensive correspondence between Laura and her son hints at the situation. Whatever
was going on was only for family members' ears.

During his final two years at Brown, John Jr. grew more comfortable socially. He continued to press about the evil of drink and upset some fraternity brothers when he attempted to eliminate certain "unwholesome"
hazing practices. Yet he was elected junior class president, and did not
prevent kegs of beer from appearing on the deck of the boat for the annual class social. With a roommate's encouragement, he again attended
plays and decided they were not necessarily frivolous after all. He admitted his avid pleasure in ballroom dancing to his mother. "You can say a

very selfish life I am leading. . . . But you know college days will never come back again."[18]

The summer following his junior year, John Jr. and Alta, who had been seeing Mr. Ashworth again, journeyed about Germany, Russia, and Sweden. John Jr.'s precise account noted:

> Away 59 days
> On the water 41 nights
> Cars 6 nights
> Stationery beds 12 nights
> Travelled over 15,000 miles

The people and their cultural practices held little interest for him. His cursory travel notes emphasized rather the extraordinary splendor of the Russian churches, museums, and palaces, as well as the breathtaking landscape of the fjords. "Beautiful" and "unspeakably glorious" were favorite adjectives. He may have meant these rapturous expressions as well for a young woman present on part of the cruise.

Abby Aldrich was the daughter of Nelson Aldrich, Republican United States Senator from Rhode Island, and one of the most powerful politicians of his day. His rise had been self-made, starting as a clerk at age seventeen, volunteering for the Union army when war struck, and then rising rapidly through Providence financial firms. He married Abby Pearce, whose family line went back to the Mayflower. She had been raised by wealthy relatives as though their own daughter, and chose Nelson from a crop of much wealthier suitors. Their courtship was marked by his passionate, introspective letters composed as he travelled about the country for his employers. A proud man, however, he did not want to live on her ample inheritance, and waited until he had ensured his own financial success before marrying her.

Conjugal life proved disenchanting to both. Abby Pearce was to be pregnant eleven times, and see three offspring die before age five. Ambitious and constantly on the move, Nelson Aldrich left his wife to cope alone with her troubled pregnancies, demanding toddlers, and drafty homes. Following the death of their first child, Nelson Jr., he deserted her to wander about Europe for six months, forcing her to experience the Continent vicariously through his letters. Abby was proud of her husband and encouraged his ambitions, but her delicate beauty soon wore haggard as she bore the consequences.

Nelson adored his fourth child and eldest daughter, named Abby as well, and brought her along on his travels once she was old enough. In

1878, when she was fourteen, he was elected to the House of Representatives. By then, her mother was frequently indisposed and surrounded by ailing children in Providence. (Abby's sister Lucy, who was to become her closest sibling, grew deaf, probably as a result of scarlet fever.) Meanwhile, in Washington Nelson indulged a patrician lifestyle, by assembling collections of fine furniture, Indian artifacts, rare books, and paintings. He passed his aesthetic enthusiasms onto his children, who enjoyed arguing over a work of art as much as a game of Whist. Rejecting the summer colony of Newport, he developed an estate in Warwick, on the western shore of Narragansett Bay. This conveyed a message that while of high society, the Aldriches rejected its most gaudy and self-indulgent contingent. Though well-appointed, Warwick offered unbuttoned hospitality, where young people's voices prevailed.

If Nelson and Abby Aldrich failed as a couple, they excelled as parents. Both avoided the stern Victorian model in favor of unlimited affection and encouragement. The siblings felt little rivalry, and throughout life remained close friends. Nelson expected his daughters to be well-educated, self-confident, and of broad vision. While they grew up as Gilded Age heiresses, learning needlepoint and the arcane language of calling cards, they were not raised to be docile wives, unseen household managers for successful men.

Firmly identified with business, Nelson Aldrich had grown rich through favors from such corporate interests as the Sugar Trust. No key meeting of Washington Republicans occurred without his input or influence. Abby shared his energy, curiosity, warmth, and spirit, and was much more comfortable with his cosmopolitan ways than her mother was. Consequently, once old enough, Abby usually took her mother's place as hostess at parties and political gatherings. As a result, she absorbed the methods of power-brokering that would serve her well in later life.

A year prior to the chance encounter on the ship, John Jr. had met Abby at a dance organized by one of his string quartet players. He noticed her around Providence, where they often attended the same plays and balls. She was not what many would call pretty. Her pale amber eyes softened a face dominated by a square jaw, prominent chin, and distinctive nose. Her lips were too thin for such strong features. What attracted observers was her warm, lighthearted, spontaneous manner and easy smile that put the most self-conscious person at ease. She was tall, with a voluptuous body that in corsets matched the hourglass ideal of the day. Her excellent carriage drew attention to the highly feminine style of dress she preferred, one with light, billowy fabrics with lace, intricate tucking, and fine decorative detail.

Much of Abby's days were passed volunteering at a home for aged colored women, the Providence Art Club, a day nursery, the YMCA, and an exchange for women's work. When convenient, she joined her father in Washington, where women felt freer than anywhere else in the country to live a full life. Nelson Aldrich admired and respected forthright women, and thus encouraged Abby's interest in politics, the arts, and social reform. Her innate sensuality combined with her intelligence and wit led many men to compete as her escort. (One suspects Edith, possibly Alta, would have enjoyed the freedom Abby had.)

Aboard the *S.S. Columbia*, John Jr. had no competition for the popular Miss Aldrich's attention. The similarities between them stirred his interest; the differences tantalized. She shared his commitment to service and learning, but was freer and more liberal in the way she led her life. Her example suggested that one could contribute to society and enjoy life, too. The wonder is that she was equally attracted to this somewhat priggish young man. She coyly pulled ginger snaps out of his coat pocket, a brazen action for a time when well-bred women blushed over an accidental brushing of an arm or a leg against a suitor. Physical attraction was evident, but there was more. "She was self-possessed without being cold, feminine and independent at the same time. She was manipulative, indeed she was, in the sense that women always are, in order to survive," observed a niece.[19] Abby had a powerful maternal drive, and John Jr. was a man molded in his relationship with a powerful mother.

Abby was not ready for a serious romance, however, and upon returning to Brown for his senior year, John Jr. found himself one of many admirers. He sent her flowers weekly, accompanied her regularly to vespers, a stroll about Hope and Benevolent streets, or to the theater. Yet she was just as likely to have spent time earlier that day with another suitor. Persistence won out. By the New Year of 1897 she was narrowing her field, and listed John Jr. more frequently in her day book, the others less.

That February John Jr. asked his parents to sponsor a dance he wished to give "in return for the kindess I have received" from classmates and people in Providence. His strong-willed mother opposed the idea. As she explained to Senior, "I would so much like to change the character of it somewhat, and please John Jr. as well, and perhaps better." Her preference was for opera singer Mme. Nordica and a string sextet, with possibly a "little dancing" *if* John Jr. insisted.[20] John Jr. did insist, and asked Abby to join him in the receiving line. Laura, pleading a headache, remained in her hotel room, while Senior took the young lovers to dinner before the fête.

Although John Jr.'s devotion to his mother did not waver, he understood the importance of asserting his independence from the family. On the night of the senior class dance, he received a telegram from home, but put it aside until the ball was over. He feared it was a message of trouble, perhaps involving Bessie's pregnancy, and did not want such to interfere with this special night with Abby. To his relief, the message announced Bessie's successful delivery of her daughter Margaret.

Later that May, Laura invited Abby to lunch with the family in New York. Abby also accompanied the Rockefellers to the Rhode Island governer's reception following John Jr.'s graduation from Brown. Laura took a liking to this thoughtful, warm young woman with so many charitable interests.

Following his graduation, John Jr. spent several days at the lavish Aldrich estate in Warwick, Rhode Island. Such a visit was usually limited to engaged couples, but Abby was not one for strict convention. Abby allowed John Jr. to embrace her, a forwardness that stayed in his memory for many years.

At the end of June, John Jr. left for another bicycle tour abroad with Dick Richardson. Upon returning home, he started to work at his father's offices at 26 Broadway. Despite Standard's immense profits, these were shabby rooms crammed with rolltop desks and overstuffed chairs, where managers and clerks crowded together without privacy. Senior offered little direction, so his son floundered. What projects Senior did assign were often personal, such as arranging a granite monument for the family burial plot in Cleveland, repairs at various houses, and matters concerning horses. A fastidious worker, slow to make decisions, John Jr. sent countless letters on such particulars as the wallpaper for a sitting room. He might require letters be retyped a half-dozen times to accommodate his successive emendations. He could spend a half-hour on the wording of a telegram to reduce its length to the minimal charge. Had Abby the opportunity to watch her suitor at work, she would have foreseen how very different their temperaments were.

It was Frederick Gates, now Senior's major domo, who introduced John Jr. to business and philanthropy. If Gates's energetic, outspoken manner intimidated the young man, his patience and uncanny business sense won his admiration. In addition to managing the philanthropies, Gates now advised on the many Rockefeller investments in land development, mining, timber, steel, paper mills, railroads, and various manufacturing ventures. By inviting John Jr. to sit in at conferences and to accompany him on trips, Gates provided a thorough apprenticeship in the family financial management. John Jr. also assisted on decisions concerning charity requests, composed the letters that would accompany Senior's gifts, and joined philanthropic committees in his father's place. He even executed his father's wishes in church matters, such as the hiring of a new minister for the Cleveland congregation.

He was not happy. His father's large shadow left him feeling unequal to the tasks. His mother had sculpted his strong conscience, which now demanded the impossible. Rather than enjoy the freedom of an appointed permanent position, he felt he was not earning his way. He saw Abby now and then, but he knew she was seeing others. He missed his college roommates, the dances, and football games.

Alta remained at home and was his most frequent companion. Now in her late twenties, and prevented from marrying the man of her choice, Alta could be sulky and envious of her siblings. She thought Abby was too fast, too likely to lead John Jr. astray. For example, though raised a Congregationalist, Abby did not attend church faithfully, and was not tied to a particular denomination. Alta also increasingly criticized Edith, who defied the family's disapproval of ostentation. To Alta, that rebellion was an insult to their saintly parents, grandmothers, and Aunt Lute.

Yet Alta was the first child to align publicly with a Progressive cause, that of assisting immigrants. During one summer in Cleveland she learned about a day nursery and kindergarten started by Italians in the Murray Hill district. She easily drew Senior into the project, and he sometimes accompanied her up steep, dusty Mayfield Road to the center. Some of the neighborhood men worked at Forest Hill, where their diligence earned Senior's admiration. Consequently, when activities at the center thrived, Senior rewarded the community's efforts by funding a new, larger building and underwriting its maintenance. At the dedication ceremony in 1900, the community christened their new center Alta House in appreciation for her and her father's participation.

Now closer than ever, Alta and John Jr. arranged a financial partnership. Their father lent them money at six percent interest for John Jr. to invest. For over a year, he bought and sold purchases of shares in Western Union, sugar, railroads, and others. He learned to sell short, to take chances. He gained more than he lost, though not by a large amount. Then he met David Lamar, later known as the "Wolf of Wall Street," who convinced him to invest in the highly speculative U.S. Leather Company. Lamar encouraged John Jr.'s purchases to drive up the value of the stock, so he could then sell his own shares at an inflated price. Once Lamar had taken his winnings, the stock collapsed, losing Alta and John Jr. about a million dollars.

Greatly humiliated, he informed his father of the mistake. Trusting that experience was the best teacher, Senior's response was simply, "All right, John. Don't worry. I will see you through."[21] John Jr. wrote in appreciation, "Most fathers would have up-braided and stormed, and that, too, justly . . . I would rather have had my right hand cut off than to cause you this anxiety."[22] Following that debacle, he continued to invest in the market, but not on speculative issues.

In light of the family fortune, the loss was insignificant. By 1893, in addition to Standard Oil, John D. Rockefeller had accumulated sixty-seven major investments in railroads, mining, manufacturing, and banks. His income was over $10 million a year. As leonine Frederick Gates roared at Senior, "Your fortune is rolling up, rolling up like an avalanche! You must distribute it faster than it grows! If not, it will crush you and your children and your children's children!" To distract his worry about how to help the family spend even more of its money, one evening Gates picked up Sir William Osler's *Principles and Practices of Medicine*, the most authoritative text of its kind. What stunned Gates was Osler's admission that the best medical practice could cure few diseases, that nature ultimately made the final decision. Gates advised Senior of the great need for medicine "to become a science," that it needed "qualified men enabled to give themselves to uninterrupted study and investigation, on ample salary, entirely independent of practice."[23]

Senior needed persuasion, and John Jr. became Gates's salesman. Provoked by memories of Bessie Dashiell's final suffering, he systematically wrote and spoke with leaders at the major medical colleges, and gathered the mass of details needed to convince Senior of the plan. It would eventuate in 1902 with the first laboratories of the Rockefeller Institute, an independent medical research center in New York. Once in operation, it produced significant medical discoveries early on. Less obvious until decades later was how the Institute and related Rockefeller philanthropies legitimized a narrow biological model of medicine. Thus Senior, who used only homeopaths, unwittingly contributed to the exclusion from American medicine of healers who understood the social and psychological aspects of health and illness.

Now in his late fifties, and retired from Standard Oil, Senior had time for new enjoyments. One was his Pocantico estate, where he and Laura lived in an "old house where the fine views invite the soul and where we can live simply and quietly."[24] Throughout the 1890s he added parcels, piece by piece, to those around Kykuit Hill, until he held over 1,600 acres. Those purchases allowed him to indulge what he called landscape gardening on a grand scale. As he walked the woods and ravines, he imagined how the views would change were he to lay a path here, transplant a tree there. He experimented until he could move trees seventy feet higher or more.

Laura was most content at Pocantico, for it reminded her of Forest Hill, too far away to visit often. When not restricted by her heart ailment, she hiked and drove horses. A charming landscape brought her more pleasure than a carefully decorated parlor. In that regard she was as much a Romantic as her husband.

Given the grandiosity of Senior's vision, his associates thought he was balmy at times. "I am thinking of moving that hillock. Offhand, I would say there are just about six hundred fifty thousand cubic feet of dirt there."[25] He built a stone wall to hide the railroad that ran through the property. He spent entire days placing stakes and flags to mark the roads and planting locations. He gloried in the hard work outdoors as much as he savored the final results, which, as visitors who walk his trails about Pocantico find today, were most pleasing.

A vigorous man, even past sixty Senior continued to ride a bicycle and skate. His favorite fun though was the latest vogue, golf. The first American golf club, the six-hole St. Andrews, had been built in 1888 in Yonkers, not too far from Pocantico. Several years later, while visiting the recuperating Edith in Lakewood, New Jersey, Senior tried the game at its course and caught the fever. He had nine holes laid at Forest Hill, where he secretly took lessons from famed professional Joe Mitchell, and later put a four-hole course down at Pocantico. He had a photographer to record his strokes so he could analyze them. He hired a boy to yell, "Hold your head down!" as he set up. He fastened his foot with a wire croquet wicket when he learned that restraint improved his drives.

Senior became so indentified with golf that doggerels featured his enthusiasm:

> Eight years of health with golf to burn
> While saving the cost of a funeral urn
> Are some of the dividends John [D Rockefeller] did earn.[26]

He was a role model for the Physical Culturists of the day, those urging Americans to the tennis courts and greens, the amateur boxing rings and calisthenic classes.

Golf appealed to Laura as well, but initially she hid her interest from her husband. Instead, unbeknownst to him she also hired Mitchell to coach her. One day she approached John on the first tee. When he saw her clubs, he began to explain the game to her. As she went up and hit a long, straight drive, he stood flabbergasted—until she laughed and revealed her joke on him. Senior gave her an electric brougham to travel about the course with her friends. (These electric runabouts became a common mode of transportation on the Rockefeller estates—an ironic choice for a family enriched by the rise of gas-powered automobiles.)

For the most part Senior golfed with his closest friends, who included his homeopath, Doctor Biggar, and several ministers. If a light snow had fallen, he would have it cleared from the fairways. In the worst part of winter, he would travel to warmer climes to keep up his game. His devotion to the game was such that when the Lakewood Golf Club was placed on the market, he bought it for his personal use. This purchase brought double pleasure, for he had his own large course in an area less affected by winter, and he had many more new acres to landscape.

Thus Laura became one of the world's first golf widows. Aside from pure enjoyment, Senior used the game to gauge a man's character before inviting him to participate in a philanthropic venture. Any supplicant had better play honestly!

In 1899, John Jr. and Alta joined their parents and a variety of friends on a hectic journey to California and Alaska. For Alta, now twenty-eight, it marked a further sign of her status as a spinster. Despite being his first vacation since joining the firm, it was not restful for John Jr. More therapeutic was his next trip in early 1900. The Aldriches invited him to accompany them aboard President McKinley's yacht on a trip to Cuba, recently "saved for democracy" by the Americans. Before accepting, he asked his mother's advice. Laura recommended the experience as a good way to become better acquainted with Abby and make up his mind about proposing to her. Although the trip went smoothly, the couple remained uncommitted concerning their future together.

After returning home, John Jr. continually prayed for guidance, but heard no answer. That summer he and Alta accompanied his parents and several other young friends on a trip through Europe that included the Oberammergau Passion Play. His diary noted outings on a tandem bicycle with a Miss Platt, one of the other guests.

Upon his return, John Jr. still vacillated about asking Abby to marry him. "Marriage either makes or breaks a life, and I felt I couldn't afford to make a mistake, for my sake, much more for her."[27] They resolved the impasse by following a test featured in romantic fiction of the day; they would separate for six months to judge their love.

Though desperately confused, John Jr. refrained from sharing his distress with his parents. When they approached him concerning his obvious pain, he said he would never trouble them as Alta had over her difficult romance. After visiting their parents, Edith pleaded with her brother to open up. "[T]hey seemed so lonely. . . . There is a great longing which they both have to have you confide. . . . It is because I love you and because your happiness means a great deal to me that I write."[28] But Edith now lived in Chicago, saw little of her brother, and had no influence over him. It is even possible she was unaware of the source of his melancholy.

John Jr. remained alone in his misery, which must have increased when Alta told him *her* good news. She had met a Chicago lawyer, E. Parmalee Prentice, the general counsel for the Illinois Steel Company. Harold McCormick, who was a friend of Parmalee's, introduced the two when Alta had been in Chicago for a visit. When they met, Parmalee was thirty-six and still living with his mother. His family line, though nowhere as rich as the Rockefellers, was of patrician New England, of the same lofty elite as the Boston Cabots and Lodges. Accordingly, Parmalee had attended Amherst and Harvard Law, and considered a major role in his life that of perpetuating Brahmin superiority.

Aunt Lute was the one who saw the possibility of a match and invited him to dinner one evening when others in the family were out of town. In that atmosphere, Parmalee foresaw that the somewhat deaf, compliant Alta was a woman worth leaving mother for. He proved his mettle by approaching Senior after church one day to ask for Alta's hand. After offering four references for her father to check, he approached Alta with tears in his eyes, certain that he would be accepted.

Alta wrote her brother to ask for his blessing, "Yes, Parmalee is good and noble and true, and in this way he is like you."[29] She was correct. In addition to being a man of rectitude, Parmalee was an aloof perfectionist. Regrettably, he would soon outgrow his youthful tears to become a rigid autocrat. Nonetheless, he agreed to leave the Midwest, and his career there, for a job in New York. Alta did not want to be far away from her parents, and Parmalee saw the advantage of living near Senior.

While Alta prepared her trousseau, Edith was establishing herself as the social queen of Chicago. One of the few beliefs Nettie McCormick did not share with the Rockefellers was a rejection of luxury. Her three-story brownstone mansion, which her late husband had built in 1879, was surpassed by only one other, that of the very society-oriented Potter and Bertha Honoré Palmer. Although Nettie denounced glamorous homes, her own was a veritable palace, stuffed with the finest European tapestries, carved furnishings, rare rugs, crystal and gold chandeliers, oil masterpieces, and historic art objects. Unlike the party-giving Mrs. Palmer, Nettie used the sumptuous setting as a center for her work in the spread of Christianity and Christian education. Visitors would approach the tiny figure and lean forward to speak into her ear trumpet. (One of her favorites was the son of missionaries in China, a young man named Henry Luce.) Nettie was very fond of Edith and may have encouraged her interest in sumptuous design.

Thus Harold and Edith purchased a three-story graystone mansion at 1000 Lake Shore Drive, the neighborhood known as the Gold Coast. Its Romanesque portals and windows, Norman turrets, and massive porte-cochère exuded command and permanence. Exquisite filigree wrought-iron fencing and gillwork gates softened the fortresslike appearance. Newspapers reported that Senior had purchased the property for the couple, but Nettie was more likely the donor. Edith loved decorating the salons with costly paintings and art objects similar to those that she had read about, and possibly glimpsed, in the homes of the New York Four Hundred. They would eventually hold gilded chairs that had once belonged to Napoleon, a rug once owned by Peter the Great, and the gold dinner service once on the table of princess Pauline Borghese. A prolific reader of scholarly works, Edith also started a collection of rare books and manuscripts.

Unlike her mother or mother-in-law, Edith was eager to entertain. Her arrival on the social scene in 1900 was propitious, for Mrs. Palmer, who ruled Chicago's equivalent Four Hundred, was failing, and would be the last of "gracious, charming, genuinely hospitable older women" to oversee the elite.[30] Youth was claiming its day, and Edith, coming from the wealthiest family in the country, easily exacted the crown. It did not matter that she was not from Chicago, that she was neither much of a club person nor an athlete. She was rather plain, with an odd figure, and too temperamental for many people. Nonetheless, Edith would establish her position in society on the basis of her intelligence, taste, and energy, as expressed in stylish house and entertainments, and especially in her contributions to the cultural life of the city.

Still, Edith was a Rockefeller, and exhibited family qualities Chicago socialites sometimes found strange, traits they may have tolerated less in the daughter of a minor grain baron. To those who did not know her well, she appeared aloof and reserved. She was known for having an "imperial complex." She applied the family perfectionism not to account books—for she had no sense of budgets—but to manners and household procedures. She held the social code with its minuscule, often irrational directives as firmly as the Ten Commandments. For a man to wear the wrong cravat was a worse blot on his character than his cruel treatment of another. She ran her large household staff like a bureaucracy; the chain of command held that she spoke only to her secretary or head butler. (Her employees actually appreciated this impersonal management, for it assumed they were professionals.) She had the Rockefeller love of punctuality and scheduling. Her staff knew when she would take her daily walk, that Monday's menu was filet mignon with mushrooms.

These peculiarities were minor in comparison with her greatest social fault, her refusal to serve alcohol in her home. As Edith explained, on her wedding day her father had summoned her to the library for the purpose of swearing her to a promise. She approached the room anxiously, and turned over in her mind many unappealing possibilities. When she learned his wish, that she never take nor serve alcohol, "Unthinkingly, I said, 'Why, of course, father,' and immediately set off in a peal of laughter over the solemnity of what seemed such a trivial request." Interestingly, Harold agreed to go along, even though he knew "red-blooded Chicagoans . . . simply must have their cocktails, their wine, their highballs and cordials." He did not explain this practice to her though, until after their first social gathering, which Edith found curiously dispirited compared to other parties they had attended. Although she was tempted to weaken, "after a while the thrill of finding other means of keeping the spirits of my guests lively helped me to keep my pledge."[31]

Despite her Rockefeller fastidiousness and formality, Edith had endearing qualities which she reserved for her intimates. Her gift for mimicry set friends into laughter, and her dramatic rendition of gossipy stories held their admiration. She was exceptionally well-read and conversant in many fields. Reading was "more important to me than eating . . . I must feed my mind more than my body."[32] Consequently, she held strong opinions, ones based upon study and reflection. This intellectual acumen was unusual for social matrons of her day, few of whom possessed advanced education or took learning seriously. She was quick to respond to a story of a person in need, and always insisted that the beneficiary not know the source of the assistance. She gave of herself emotionally as well; she astutely intuited when another needed reassurance and sympathy. Clearly, Edith would have strong advocates and strong detractors; few would remain neutral about her complex personality and sometimes bizarre manner.

Like so many women of her class, Edith pursued Progressive causes. Among her first civic acts was on behalf of juvenile probation officers. In

1899, Chicago created its first juvenile court system, and authorized the appointment of such officers, but neglected to fund them. Edith came forward and embarrassed the politicians by providing the money.

She and Harold now had two sons. Harold Fowler, known by his middle name, had been born the year after Jack. Her oldest boy had a strong personality, characterized by persistent curiosity and a high degree of inner discipline. Grandmother Nettie "loved that golden hair; that spirited little figure, springing over his toy wagons with a leap and a bound."[33] He would sit in someone's lap for hours looking at pictures or reading a story, and comment with perception. During the winter of 1900, Edith took her sons to Tarrytown for a visit with their Rockefeller grandparents. While there, the two toddlers fell ill with scarlet fever, and Senior offered a New York specialist a half million dollars to save their lives. Despite the best medical care, soon after New Year's Day Jack died. When she was unable to attend her parents' fiftieth wedding anniversary several years later, Edith thanked them again for "the great love and untiring effort which you put forth to save dear Jack's life. Absolutely forgetful of self and showing a love much like the Christ love."[34]

Years later reports falsely claimed that Edith fell into a terrible grief following the death, but it was actually Harold who collapsed beyond functioning. The other fraudulent story often printed was that she heard of Jack's death from her butler while hosting a banquet. "Edith nodded, and continued eating with her guests," goes the tale.[35] But Edith was not in Chicago when Jack died; she was at her parents' home by the bedsides of her suffering sons. Edith was like all the women in her family, restrained, but she was never heartless. She grieved privately, and worried about Harold's health.

Jack's death altered Alta's wedding plans, which had already been postponed once the previous year. In 1900, she consulted a hearing specialist in Vienna, who urged her to stay longer for a full course of treatment. Now, give her nephew's tragedy, she surrendered her arrangements for a large, elaborate church ceremony. On January 17, 1901 she exchanged vows with Parmalee in the rose-laden main hall of her father's house on Fifty-fourth Street. Following the reception, she and Parmalee went to honeymoon in Pocantico, then travelled to Forest Hill. They settled in a house within the Rockefeller compound, at 5 West Fifty-third Street. It was a gift from her father, who instructed John Jr. to handle the details of outfitting the place, which he did, down to the last broom.

Most days Alta made the short walk around the block to her parents' home to help Aunt Lute run the house and care for Laura, who was often ill-disposed. She molded herself contentedly to Parmalee, a man like her parents, with all the answers. A year later she was pregnant with her first child, a son, who appropriately would be named John Rockefeller Spelman Prentice, but acquired the nickname Fritz.

During the late 1890s the William Rockefeller cousins had been courting and marrying as well. Their few surviving letters hint at how much more secular their upbringing had been than that of their cousins. Unlike Laura, Mira dressed her well-fed body in the latest fashions. Unlike Senior, William was neither a devoted nor a warm father. Growing up on Fifth Avenue, the children absorbed more secular values than religious ones. When Mira wrote daughter Emma from Paris, she described the people she met and her clothing purchases. She shared gossip that Laura and Senior would never allow in their house. "I fear Mrs. S———— and Mr. S———— have separated as I hear she will be absent for two or three years. . . . [I]t looks as if Mr. S———— did not intend to do anything for his daughter. I think he is a *crank* and feel the fault cannot be only one side."[36] Mira's advice also lacked Laura's Biblical homilies with their reminder of higher values. For example, when Emma was on her way to Europe, Mira reminded her, "Do not buy anything but the best. Get less but be sure and purchase good things."[37] Then there was the curious message, "I think I have a very good maid. She certainly pleases your father, she has quite won his heart with her energetic rubbing of his feet."[38]

William and Mira were not above tittering about Senior and his overly serious household. Following a wedding ceremony both families attended, William observed "the friends of No 4" so frustrated by a long reception line that "the ladies of the party went home in disgust leaving poor J.D. in the crowd on the sidewalk, with his hat in his hand perspiring like an ox mopping his brow with a silk handkerchief."[39] They seemed almost delighted to share how a neighbor was carping over how Senior imported snow to create a skating rink in the winter.

In 1895, Emma became engaged to Dr. David McAlpin of Bellevue Hospital. The McAlpins were an old New York commercial family, currently completing in Herald Square the largest hotel in the world, the McAlpin of course. Their major income was from tobacco products, and they were among the nation's top manufacturers. Consequently, Emma had gotten herself a "catch." Upon applauding Emma's choice, her mother wrote how "you are not a brilliant individual any more than your mother; but I feel any man you choose is to be sincerely congratulated."[40]

Then she attended to the more important matter, the purchase of a trousseau, down to the sizes and numbers of tablecloths and napkins. Her father teased how he warned the future groom that Emma was a self-indulged, obstinate, and self-willed young woman. (He told the truth, and both he and Emma knew it!) On the other hand, her Aunt Laura remarked how McAlpin was "a young man of deep religious character, of fine musical taste, one who has done . . . something to help the world."[41] Laura's conception was perhaps more projection than a valid assessment.

Emma married McAlpin in December of 1895 at Rockwood Hall. The normally understated *Times* spilled purple prose in describing the lavish event, which it judged "one of the most elaborate that has ever taken place." William ordered private railcars to bring the fortunate four hundred guests to the estate, where carriages met them for the short trip to the house. The ceremony took place in the Music Room, under a massive Gothic floral canopy. He had the veranda glassed in for the forty-piece classical orchestra. John Jr. was among the seven ushers.

The month before, Emma's brother William Goodsell Rockfeller married James Stillman's daughter Elsie. This service had taken place in a tropical garden constructed within St. Bartholomew's Episcopal Church, which Society favored over all other congregations. Reporters drew special note of the sumptuous gifts, which included a solid silver vase from President Grover Cleveland, and a diamond necklace and tiara from William and Mira. Laura and Senior sent a painting. Following the honeymoon, William G. and Elsie moved into a fully-furnished house provided by her father.

A story spread that the marriage was the result of purposeful planning by the crafty fathers as a way of ensuring their dynasties. Younger daughter Isabel was Stillman's favorite, with whom he most often consulted about his business. Consequently, when it came to making a tie with the William Rockefellers, it was she, not elder Elsie, who was invited by the fathers and told to pick a son. Isabel was said to choose Percy because he was tall, good-looking and better-humored than his older brother. This left Elsie with squat, less dependable William G. Whether true or not, in April of 1901, following his graduation from Yale, Percy Rockefeller married Isabel Stillman in yet another extravagant display.

Elsie and Isabel, who had been told nothing of their mother's name after her banishment, had been raised by housekeepers. In the mornings they had to line up with their siblings by the door to see their father off to work. Only once did the two sisters hear from their mother, in the form of pairs of matching earrings mailed anonymously from Europe. Given this tyrannical upbringing, they hoped for a very different life as

Rockefeller wives. William's sons had grown up with yachting, summering in Newport, hunting at the family estate on Jekyl Island, Georgia, and mixing with the Four Hundred during the New York winter social season. They had attended Yale with the likes of the Vanderbilt sons. They had done the European tours, met royalty, and aspired to live royally.

An unexpected quandary spoiled the sisters' expectations: James Stillman and William Rockefeller competed for dominance over the couples. After James Stillman gave his daughters imposing mansions in New York City, William Rockefeller took a vast tract of land he owned in Greenwich, gave half to each couple, and had even grander mansions built. The fathers raised the stakes on one another with subsequent purchases of art works, tapestries, and expensive furnishings.

The fathers even jousted in the naming of the grandchildren. Elsie's first two sons were named William Avery and Godfrey in honor of the Rockefeller line. Upon delivery of her third son, James Stillman swept into the birthing room and announced it would be named after himself. Several weeks later, when Isabel gave birth to her first child, a daughter, James Stillman announced the child would also be called Isabel, in honor of a sister who had died young.

In 1901 a Stillman wedding took place that would have surprising consequences for Senior two decades later. James Stillman, Jr. married a member of the sporty "Tuxedo set," Anne "Fifi" Potter. Fifi was a stunning, vivacious redhead of less than perfect credentials. The Potter line was connected with the eminent banking firm of Brown Brothers. Its only eccentric member was Episcopalian bishop Codman Potter. Determined to save the souls of drinkers, he opened a saloon decorated with thoroughbred horses rather than buxom ladies in tights. Despite the bishop, the Potters were admired for being staid, snobbish, and conservative. Fifi's father was thus most acceptable to high society.

The problem was Fifi's mother, Cora Urquhart, a luscious Titian-haired beauty from a fallen patrician Southern family. During her first fight with her husband, which occurred on her wedding night, she threw her ring out the train window. In New York she easily insinuated herself among the Four Hundred and became famous for her performance in that clique's amateur theatricals. In 1886, she deserted her husband, taking Fifi, her only child, to Europe to go on the stage professionally. As she explained to her husband, "I am an artist now. . . . We are not now living in the dark ages, when wives were slaves. P.S. I hate your family."[42]

Until her father finally gained custody, Fifi joined her mother barnstorming in England and the States. In Cora's American debut as Cleopatra, she tore off the silk fleshing of her bodice and virtually bared her breast to place the asp. In England, she easily entered the highest levels of Edwardian Society and became a mistress of the Prince of Wales. Young Fifi adopted her mother's impulsive, dramatic, and daring manner.

In 1899, during a party on the yacht of Standard Oil millionaire Oliver Payne, James Stillman, Jr. came upon redheaded Fifi lounging on his coat as though it were a throw rug. He was instantly smitten. Finding the young woman a totally inappropriate choice, his father cut the courtship short by sending his namesake son to Wyoming. For the first time in his life, James Jr. stood up for himself and rushed to Mexico, where Fifi was staying with her father. He proposed; she refused. When Fifi returned to New York, she accepted the dinner invitation of a prominent social matron. Upon arriving, she found herself maneuvered to be alone with the family's randy son, who made advances appropriate to his reputation. Fifi fled, contacted James Jr., and accepted his previous proposal.

Realizing he had met his match, James Stillman gave in, and presented Fifi a rope of magnificent pearls as a wedding gift. Fifi's dress for the occasion hinted at her future behavior. Not only was her veil draped in a new and startling way, but she carried in her hands neither bouquet nor prayer book, but a white ostrich fan. It must have brought trepidation to Senior and Laura to hear of James Stillman's later present to this couple. He purchased 340 acres adjoining their lands in Pocantico Hills and financed the construction of a thirty-five-room Swiss chalet there. Given this propinquity, Fifi would one day join John D.'s line in a most curious and sensational manner.

William and Mira's last child, Ethel Geraldine, would not marry until 1907, but she, too, would connect the family to a notable dynasty. Her husband was Marcellus Dodge, heir to Remington Arms, the leading manufacturer of guns, rifles, and ammunition. Though only twenty-six, he had already inherited the family wealth, and was worth over $60 million. They were a handsome pair the newspapers dubbed "the richest couple in the world." With this marriage added to the list, the next generation of Rockefellers seemed to represent the best of the American pseudoaristocracy.

8

"Being Married Is Perfect."

"A gracious woman retaineth honour: and strong men retain riches."
—Proverbs 11:16.

In August of 1901, when Abby's voluntary six-month separation from John Jr. had ended, she was losing her patience. She must have wondered if his indecisiveness in this matter was a trait that would infect all his actions. On the one hand, she was used to being around men quick to draw conclusions and act upon them; on the other, she loved her irresolute suitor and was not ready to withdraw from the relationship.

To resolve his quandary, as usual, John Jr. asked his mother what to do. Laura laughed and told him to propose. Even his mother's directive was not enough to reassure him. Seeking approval from an even higher source, he prayed to petition for an answer. A few days later during meditation, a clear and unmistakable voice told him to go to Rhode Island. Without stating his reason for coming, he immediately telegraphed Abby at Warwick for permission to visit her. When she agreed, he went first to Newport, where Nelson Aldrich was vacationing on his yacht. There John Jr. assured his future father-in-law of his ability to support Abby. When Aldrich said all that mattered was for the young man to make her happy, John Jr. rushed up to Warwick to meet Abby. Afterwards, though, one can imagine Aldrich's relief for his daughter and glee that she was marrying an heir to immense wealth.

John Jr. arrived in the evening, and asked Abby to walk with him about the moonlit grounds. When he finally managed the question, Abby could not disguise her weariness over his previous vacillation. "Do you *really* love me?" she demanded. Suddenly he realized he had dallied too much, that he could well have lost her had he waited any longer. Several days later he wrote his mother, "I can't believe that it is really true that all this sacred joy, this holy trust is mine . . . instead of leaving you, for I shall never leave you, I am bringing another daughter to you who will add a hundred fold to your happiness."[1] Abby wrote Laura, "There never was a man like John, so true, so tender, so manly. I am supremely proud of him."[2]

Once news spread of the engagement, however, the journalists took advantage of this private joy to attack the fathers. It was as though there were a race to prove just who was more repugnant: John D. with his Standard Oil machinations or Senator Aldrich, who grew rich from providing political favors to great capitalist trusts and combines. The couple, however, was spared this calumny, and praised for their good works. Their fathers might be voracious and evil, implied the editorials, but the offspring had chosen the righteousness of Progressivism. It was an accurate assessment of the new direction in the family.

Abby and John Jr. preferred a small, modest wedding at the local church in Warwick. John Jr. was uncomfortable at large affairs, and Abby, though more adept in social gatherings, disliked pomp and spectacle. Senator Aldrich, a man who had risen from grocery clerk to his current eminence in government, wanted a lavish event to compare favorably with recent East Coast society nuptials. He set dozens of workers to prepare the Warwick Estate. He chose the grand ballroom of the Tea House for the ceremony, and its surrounding garden for the reception. The laborers had little time, for the date set was Wednesday, October 9, little more than a month away.

The large Rockefeller party travelled to Providence in a private railcar chartered by Senior, and settled in the Narragansett Hotel. Alta, Bessie, Percy, William G., and their spouses attended along with Senior, Laura, Aunt Lute, William, Mira, and even James Stillman, Sr. Edith and Harold were in Switzerland, where he was seeking psychiatric treatment for the extended depression following son Jack's death.

The next morning, when John Jr. entered the ballroom, he scarcely noticed the elaborate weaving of vines, the brilliant sprays of American Beauty roses, the pungent sweet odor of the cattleya. All he saw was "the beauty and loveliness" of his bride approaching on the arm of her father.[3] Abby wore an ivory satin gown draped to emphasize the curves of her ample figure. Her only jewelry was a pearl choker worn over the high lace collar. Fortunately for impatient John Jr., the ceremony lasted only seven minutes. Then the couple and the thirty-five witnesses went from the Tea House to the flower-laden garden marquee, where five hundred guests awaited to celebrate and toast the couple with fine vintage wines, not water. Senator Aldrich was not a temperance man, and would not exclude alcohol for the sake of his new in-laws. One of Senior's teetotalling friends remarked ignorantly on the excellence of the "ginger ale," which was of course champagne.

One odd element of the ceremony was the absence of the groom's mother. Laura had to learn about the event from her husband and sister. "We went from Cleveland, but I was sick and could not witness the ceremony. So disappointing to all of us," she noted in her diary. Upon reaching Providence, she had a severe attack of colitis, and took to her bed. To attribute this absence as psychological, a rejection of Abby for example, would be to overlook the simpler explanation. For a decade she had been subject to episodes of asthma, colitis, and bouts of temporary paralysis. Following her latest attack, her doctor put her on a diet that eliminated fruits, vegetables, and sweets in favor of milk, cream, eggs, butter, fish, and meat. Although doctors did not know it then, this recommendation would aggravate her disorder, and worse, quicken the development of her arteriosclerosis and stress her kidneys.[4] She would have done better following the vegetarian dietary precepts of Dr. John Kellogg, but he was rejected by orthodox physicians as faddist.

Laura's letters never referred to her suffering. She accepted it without self-pity as her lot. Life was now almost totally centered on her religion; her disabilities did not interfere with what was most important to her. If bedridden, she could still read Scripture and pray. Friends could gather round and discuss the temperance fight, which was now reinvigorated by the Anti-Saloon League and its Prohibition cry. Her Sunday School classes continued because Alta stepped in to substitute when necessary. Her beloved sister Lute, so unhealthy in youth, was now the sturdy one, the nurse and constant companion. Increasingly isolated from the world, Laura expressed no regrets or frustration over her limitations. Her faith never failed her.

Having been raised to follow proprieties whatever the inconvenience, Abby and John Jr. each wrote a letter to Laura the morning after the wedding. They had spent the honeymoon night in a suite at the Plaza in New York. Several days later they went to the farmhouse at Pocantico for a month's rest. While there, they opened the four hundred and fifteen wedding presents. (One wonders what they did with the many duplicate silver teasets and candlesticks from Tilden-Thurber in Providence!) Abby welcomed the isolation of Kykuit Hill. The appeal of the natural world was one of the most important satisfactions she shared with her husband. That fall the landscape around Pocantico was vibrant with the golds, russets, and scarlets of the leaves. The morning mists lingering upon the swan-laden lakes offered an idealized image of nature, one without predator and prey.

"Being married is simply perfect," John Jr. informed his mother.[5] Yet marriage failed to satiate his hunger for Abby's attention. Used to the adoration of his female relatives, he expected the same level of attention from her. He would be permanently blind to the possibility that Abby could extend her warmth and compassion to others without diminishing her love for him. When he felt need of her, she was to put all else aside. A more passive woman would have suffocated under John Jr.'s demands, which took the form of petulance as he aged.

While she loved John Jr. no less than he did her, Abby did not have his grasping, insistent nature. She was wise enough to understand his dependence, which might have been part of his attraction. Abby had watched her father neglect his wife; John Jr. would never be that sort of man. Her father had also shaped Abby's independence and self-confidence. Having filled her mother's place as hostess in Washington, she was at ease taking charge. When John Jr. gave her one thousand dollars as a wedding present for her personal pleasure, he was surprised that she gave it away to the Providence YWCA. When he told her to keep careful account books, she responded "I won't!"[6] When he tried to force some of his Baptist demands upon her Congregationalist liberality, she refused to go to church every week. (She did agree however to refuse invitations for Sunday social events.)

At first they settled with his parents at 4 West Fifty-fourth Street while their home, just across at Number Thirteen, was being renovated. When a Brown chum of John Jr.'s asked Abby what they intended to do with the "great big echoing mansion" they were furnishing, she replied, "Why, fill it up with children."[7] Whether John Jr. wanted her to or not, she would.

Before the children came, Abby took the time to assert her authority in the household. John Jr.'s obsession with order and predictability must have required great patience. He brooked no surprises, while she celebrated spontaneity. She tolerated some of this orderliness—his punctuality for meals, his continuing with his church meetings, his preference for the religious dinner guests he had known at his parents' table. Nonetheless, she did not hold back her feelings. She was quick with outspoken, often whimsical opinions about such callers as a self-important minister and his long-winded wife. As soon as all visitors had departed, she would order some hot chocolate, John Jr.'s favorite drink, and practice the latest dance steps with him. Another favorite relaxation was reading aloud. She savored their moments alone as much as he did—after all, she had been the apple of her father's eye.

Abby could also extract her fee for John Jr.'s demands by insisting he cater to her idiosyncrasies. She was a stylish dresser, who could spend a half-hour before a mirror trying this brooch or that hat to create the desired statement. Asking John Jr.'s advice, she would tease, "You haven't half looked at it. Put down those stupid papers and pay attention to your wife."[8] She was passionate about hats, and preferred ones that drew attention to herself. When members of a board were "a bit startled at first" by the "odd fruit" on her chapeau, she explained it was "meant to suggest a Harvest Home Supper."[9] She hated to eat in restaurants, for she was suspicious of their sanitation. She loved silly fun, like donkey rides. Through her, John Jr. could vicariously enjoy the caprice he would not allow himself.

Abby had a harder time adjusting to his extending his patriarchy into what was traditionally the wife's domain. Having been given so many family responsibilities when he was a teenager, her husband expected to have a strong voice over the running of his own household. He was stingy, and she had little income of her own to counter his miserliness. Abby was hardly profligate, for she had the New Englander's bent for repairing a tear rather than replacing a curtain. Such sensible moderation was not good enough for a man used to arguing with his college classmates over a three-cent tip.

Fortunately, Abby was a politician's daughter, and skilled in maneuvering outcomes in her favor. By honoring John Jr.'s deepest insecurities, for instance, through protecting him at social events, she gained his unending appreciation. After growing up in so many cluttered and uninteresting rooms, he was grateful for her exquisite taste. In time she convinced him of the value of spending money for art works, antiques, fine fabrics, and decorators' fees to shape a beautiful living space. The results were sumptuous yet restrained. Alva Vanderbilt would have approved.

When it came to church, she did not follow the Rockefeller path and take over a Sunday School class. Being a Congregationalist, Abby was more attuned to the idea of the church as part of the community, not a refuge from its troubles. Consequently, she persuaded women in the Bible School class she attended at Fifth Avenue Baptist Church to start a regular forum at which neighborhood immigrants could speak about their cultures, their experiences in their new country, and their dreams. Thus, Hungarians, Irish, Italians, and Czechs introduced their foods, their music, and the stories of their daily struggles in the tenements and factories. (Whenever they displayed a folk dance, Abby was quick to join in and learn.) The purpose was not to proselytize the immigrants, but to acquaint the more snobbish, insular members of the congregation with the reality of the city. Eventually this activity formalized into the Good Fellowship Council, which led congregants to act on a variety of Progressive causes, including child welfare, safety, adequate housing, and sanitation in the neighborhood.

Abby's perspective, called "internationalism" then, was one John Jr. shared. Through his Bible study he had concluded that Christ taught inclusion and tolerance. With Abby he shared a disdain for racial bigotry, this at a time when the newspapers fostered black Sambo imagery, the Yellow Peril, and Shylock Jews. (Political cartoons sometimes depicted Senior as a spidery, avaricious Oriental.) Social Darwinism had somehow failed to make its imprint upon the Rockefeller and Aldrich minds. As will be seen, they were not so radical as to believe in desegregation, but then hardly anyone was in those days.

John Jr. once said of his relationship to his father, "I was in a unique position. I could talk with Father at the strategic moment. It might be in a relaxed mood after dinner, or while we were driving together. Consequently I could often get his approval of ideas which others couldn't have secured because the moment wasn't right."[10] Abby used similar tactics to influence her husband, as she had watched her father do with others. The results were monumental. Had John Jr. married a more pious and submissive woman, it is doubtful he would have achieved his level of greatness. Through those intimate late evening conversations, Abby guided him to find the course that would assure he achieved his full potential. At the same time she aided his securing a sense of self clearly separate from his father. She understood that business held little fascination for her husband, and helped him assuage the heavy guilt he felt over wanting to devote his talents elsewhere.

In recent years he had been his father's representative corresponding with Spelman College about new buildings, expansion of its real estate, and scholarships. (Laura and Aunt Lute continued their relationship with the school as well, a more personal one which included writing individual letters to graduates each year.) In his characteristic attention to detail, John Jr. recommended the school acquire quadruple-plated rather than triple-plated silver for the dining hall, for it would hold up better. During the spring before his wedding, John Jr. had taken the "millionaires' special," a train of fifty prominent men and women invited to visit some outstanding Negro schools in the South. At Spelman, he charmed the students with a speech about service to others. In turn, they impressed him so much that he decided to send the school checks from his own account as well as that of his father. At this point Spelman was strengthening its academic focus, and John Jr.'s contributions helped underwrite this new direction.

John Jr. returned from the South with a missionary zeal to improve the lot of impoverished blacks. He expended his vision when a Southern college president advised, "You must lift up the 'poor white' and the Negro together if you would ever approach success."[11] Following his honeymoon, he met with a small group of like-minded men, including Frederick Gates, the family philanthropic advisor, and Dr. Wallace Buttrick of the Baptist Home Mission Society. Together they shaped his intentions into a new philanthropic foundation, the General Education Board. Abby was the only woman present at meetings, and certainly added her forceful voice. She had been accustomed to sitting in with her father and his associates, and encouraged by him to state her mind. She expected the same inclusion from her husband.

The GEB's purpose was to promote "education within the United States without distinction of race, sex or creed." Senior pledged a million dollars, and Senator Aldrich nurtured the necessary federal incorporation process through the Congress.

The GEB was remarkable for its time. The Southern states so poorly supported education then that only Kentucky had a compulsory school attendance law, and most of the students of all races attended squalid one-room cabins. Consequently, one of the GEB's first tasks was to change Southern public opinion toward support of high school education for poor whites and blacks. To upgrade the quality of black higher education, it introduced curricula holding to the same standards of excellence found in white Northern colleges. It funded agricultural experimentation and demonstration projects in the region. It established standards for graduate and professional education throughout the nation, particularly in medical training. Its success can be partly laid to its following the managerial precepts Senior had developed at Standard Oil: Find the best people and give them freedom to do what they believe is best. These people also were skilled at Standard's technique of working in the background to effect change.

Of course, the GEB strategy did not challenge segregation. Despite their willingness to contribute to black education, some GEB supporters were white supremacists. Most of the Southern elite, whose children were educated at private academies, were not people to be challenged with impunity. Yet in being gradualists, John Jr. and his advisors were more liberal than many of their peers, who clung to the "scientific" proof of racial superiority proclaimed by Social Darwinism. To the GEB board, one did what one could, pressed gently but unrelentingly against the forces of racial subjugation.

☆　　☆　　☆

One would think with the children all married and grandchildren appearing with regularity that Laura's and Senior's lives would be more trouble-free. Instead, they found their lives much more complicated than they expected would be the case in the "golden days" of life.

An accident on the night of September 1902 presaged the sequence of challenges that were to follow for several years. Parmalee and Alta, six months' pregnant, were staying in a suite of rooms on the second floor of Senior's home in Pocantico, an old wooden farmhouse. Somehow a fire started, and although it moved slowly, the water pressure at the top of the hill was too low to prevent the steady spread. Parmalee, Alta, and the servants repeatedly reentered the smoke-filled structure to gather belongings and carry them out to the lawn. They saved all the property on the first floor, along with most of the Prentice belongings. Despite these efforts, some honeymoon items belonging to Abby and John Jr., who used the suite at times, were lost, along with all the letters she and John Jr. had written to one another before the marriage.

The next day Abby and John Jr. took the train to Pocantico, where they supervised the move of what had been salvaged to another farmhouse on the property, the Kent House. Laura and Senior were in Cleveland and were due to arrive by the end of the month. Consequently, Abby and John Jr. spent their days travelling back and forth from New York, where they purchased furniture, linens, and household goods (to the last broom, no doubt.) Both contracted severe colds from the stress, and when done, Abby went off to Warwick to recuperate in the playful companionship of her sisters. "I am glad you miss me," she wrote John Jr., "But tomorrow night sweetheart I shall be where I like best to be."[12]

Several months later, Abby was pregnant. She delivered an eight-and-a-half-pound baby girl born on November 8, 1903. Named for her mother, Abby, known always as "Babs," was dubbed "Richest of All Babies" by the press. She was not so fortunate in being the only daughter and oldest child in a family that would grow to include five striking brothers.

Senior's next troubles were more public, the result of intentional harm. During the nineties, the new ten-cent magazines such as *McClure's* or *Cosmopolitan* adopted the sensational style of daily newspapers like Joseph Pulitzer's *New York World.* The labor movement, socialist party activism, and the popularization of the new field of sociology all fed exposés on the evils of business and politics. As the personification of Standard Oil, Senior came under the most vicious attack of all. Frank Norris, Upton

Sinclair, and Jack London were among noted yellow journalists, but the greatest exposé of all was written by a woman born midst the petroleum fields of Pennsylvania, Ida Tarbell.

Ida's father Franklin had been among the Western Pennsylvania independent producers squeezed by Standard during the oil wars of the 1870s. Eccentrically independent and untrusting, he was not the best of businessmen—had he been, Rockefeller might have nabbed him to join Standard, as he had other competitors' managers. Still, Franklin Tarbell had genuine grievances against the Cleveland leviathan, and convinced Ida that Rockefeller alone was the cause of all the family's troubles. "There was born in me a hatred of privilege—privilege of any sort."[13] Ida survived her grubstake upbringing to make her way through Allegheny College, live in Paris several years, and to perfect her writing craft. Now a well-known writer of books on Napoleon and Lincoln, Tarbell had tried to retell her experiences of the Pithole oil boom. Her efforts, all fictional, were unsuccessful. After reading an exposé of the Sugar Trust (which implicated Senator Aldrich as its protector in Congress), she convinced Samuel McClure to sponsor an investigation of Standard Oil for his magazine.

Tarbell was a thorough and meticulous researcher who demanded documentary evidence for every point; McClure was similarly scrupulous as an editor. Consequently, "The History of the Standard Oil Company," which began its serial debut in November 1902, was a lucid, pounding indictment. Boosting its credibility was Tarbell's willingness now and then to cast a story in Standard's favor, if it were clearly due. For the most part, though, she fed the antitrust frenzy by verifying what many had suspected for years: the pattern of deceit, secrecy, and unregulated concentration of power that characterized Gilded Age business practice with its "commercial Machiavellianism."

Ironically, a major source of Tarbell's information was Standard Oil itself. Henry Rogers, a company partner who had once been a wildcat independent like her father, read advertisements about Tarbell's forthcoming series and decided it would be better to cooperate than to resist her. He asked mutual friend Mark Twain to arrange a meeting. As a result, for two years Tarbell frequented Standard's offices at 26 Broadway to examine company documents and to question Rogers, who sometimes evaded her. Unable to get an interview with Rockefeller, she spoke with his onetime partner Henry Flagler, now the great developer of Miami and Palm Beach. An irascible man, Flagler began by complaining about Rockefeller's readiness to steal from any pocket. Although he shifted his tone to praise John D.'s Christian ways, and generally defended the company, Tarbell felt vindicated. Then Frank Rockefeller, so resentful of his older brothers that he had moved the bodies of his two children from the family plot, sought out Tarbell, but he was so venomous she almost felt sorry for John D.

"When you get through with 'Johnnie' I don't think there will be much left of him except something resembling one of his own grease spots," a friend applauded.[14] In the series, Tarbell accused Rockefeller of being behind the South Improvement Company, of cheating a widow, of driving competitors out of business through the most nefarious means. (Years later, a reevaluation of her charges would keep historian Allan Nevins busy for decades.) On the front page of his many papers, whenever possible William Randolph Hearst smacked his lips over the latest Rockefeller story. OIL KINGS DIVIDE $20,000,000 MORE was a typical headline. Tarbell and Hearst competed to locate Big Bill Rockefeller, and were gleeful to dig up the rape charge of a half-century earlier. They could not find him, however, and even today it is unclear when Big Bill died and where he is buried. All that is certain is that in his final years he owned a ranch in North Dakota, and possibly a cottage as well in Freeport, Illinois.[15]

Determined to have a look at Senior herself, Tarbell went to Cleveland and attended a service at the Euclid Avenue Baptist Church. From an artist's sketch of him she had concluded, "This is the oldest man in the world—a living mummy . . . a blank eye . . . the lips quite lost . . . like an old monk in the inquisition. . . . "[16] In person, she observed him "searching the aisles, craning again to see behind him. . . . Fear, fear of the oft-repeated threats of the multitude of sufferers from the wheels of the cars of progress he has rolled across the country. . . . "[17] She was sufficiently evenhanded to include stories of his personal generosity and modesty, and to itemize his charitable gifts, which amounted then to almost forty million dollars. But she portrayed the giver as a hypocrite, whose charity could not begin to compensate for the harm his business had caused. What if, she imagined, "thirty-five years ago, he had turned his great ability of bringing order with justice into the industry in which he was the leader, instead of bringing order with injustice."[18] (Indeed, what if he or Vanderbilt or Carnegie or Pullman had?)

Despite his making jests about Tarbell in private, Senior was angry. He thought the articles unfair, but he could see no value in replying publicly to her and her imitators. He was particularly unforgiving of her sneaking into his church, which she characterized as a dark, uninviting place. She managed what none of his competitors had ever been able to do—scar him permanently. Thereafter, he attended more to reputation, and obsessed over the possible consequences of a family member's behavior when placed in the public spotlight.

Even more wounded by Tarbell's razor was John Jr. While growing up he had been kept ignorant of the history of Standard Oil, yet could not avoid hearing the attacks upon his father, whose name he bore. This latest series of slashes, coming when he was learning the business, forced him into a posture of permanent defensiveness. He would bear the sword of righteousness for his aging parents. Rather than go directly into the fray and skirmish in public to avenge the family name, he chose a different tactic. He would insist on impeccable behavior from himself, his wife and children, his sisters and their families.

The most painful rebuffs came from religious groups. The Congregational Board of Foreign Missions had recently thought of a way to tap into Rockefeller largesse, which was doing so much for the Baptists. Lute Spelman was still a Congregationalist, so through her they sent their plea to Laura, who approached Senior. He was not interested. John Jr. and Gates revived the idea, and following two years of negotiations they convinced Senior to send $100,000. Unfortunately, the gift arrived coincident with the Tarbell series. To avoid embarrassment for their seeking Senior out, the mission board left its denomination with the impression that the money had come from him spontaneously. A group of ministers filed a protest, and asked that the gift be returned, as "tainted money," based on "the most relentless rapacity known to modern commercial history." Soon after, when Yale University and the General Education Board accepted large grants from Senior, the *New York Sun* quipped, "Gifts of ten millions deodorize themselves." Uproar midst the pulpits and the papers continued for years that Senior was merely trying to buy a clean reputation.

At the height of this clamor, Gates finally convinced Senior that to remain silent was to give the impression of guilt. He urged the Standard Oil board to take advantage of a new profession, public relations, to present themselves in the best light. As a result, Senior became more accessible to friendly journalists ready to "correct" Tarbell's views. He presented himself as the wise old man, full of pithy wisdom on success and charity. "How the World's Richest Man Spends Christmas" and "The Human Side of John D. Rockefeller, Esq." brought him down to human scale. He defended Standard as the innovator that brought efficiency and order to the economy. He preached his philosophy of giving. In 1909, he published a compendium of his ideas, *Reminiscences of Men and Events.* Yet so long as Standard Oil reigned invincible, public opinion was with the muckrakers.

✻   ✻   ✻

In the midst of the public rancor, in April of 1903, Laura had a severe stroke. Physicians advised her she would have to live quietly for at least two years before full recovery. "This I accept and shall gain daily feeling thankful that it is no worse."[19] She did improve, though never to full vigor. She continued to rely upon nutritional therapy, such as two eggs a day. "Dieting is becoming a great remedy, and I always believed in it."[20]

Alta came by daily at lunchtime to cheer her mother up, which cannot have been easy given the continual crises afflicting various family members. In May of 1904, the Strong family moved to France. In recent years, Bessie's terror of falling into poverty continued unabated. She reduced the servants' supplies, made over and dyed her gowns, and told friends she could not afford to entertain them. Charles had to change her orders behind her back to see that the pantry was sufficiently stocked. Yet Senior had given her a house in Lakewood, and at the end of 1903 her net worth was about $400,000 (several million in today's currency). Now Senior was helping pay for her treatment for nervous disease with a Dr. Bourcart of Cannes. Eventually the couple settled in the town of Compeigne in the Chateau des Avenues, a property of the Duc de l'Aigle.

That winter, John Jr. took Abby and Babs to France, where they stayed in Cannes so he, too, could consult the specialists there. He had suffered another nervous collapse, and found he needed much more than one month to recuperate. Consequently, his family remained through the winter while he rested and gradually built himself up through strenuous exercise.

Many pressures precipitated John Jr.'s illness, including worry over his mother's infirmity and the shrill notoriety attaching to his father. Yet Babs' birth may have been more significant, for the child was his first rival for Abby's attention. It did not help when Abby took Babs away for long periods to Warwick to visit with her family. John Jr. implicitly viewed love as currency. That is, he assumed Abby had only so much to spend, so that any affection she gave to their children somehow took away from what he deserved. The jealousy was unconscious—John Jr. wrote adoringly of Babs over the years. Yet his children grew up "realizing that we had to compete with Father for her [Abby's] time and attention. . . . His needs seemed insatiable."[21] As soon as John Jr. felt able, he arranged to leave Babs with a nurse while he took Abby on a long automobile trip through parts of Italy and France.

Marriage to Abby had not diminished John Jr.'s family responsibilities towards his sisters, and he continued these duties scrupulously, too much so perhaps. Besides taking over responsibility for the renovations and outfitting of Bessie's and Alta's houses, John Jr. represented them to their father with regard to finances. As long as Senior was alive, he and John Jr. had an ongoing correspondence concerning the women and their money. In the early years, the son deferred to Senior's decisions, but as time passed he gained more authority and as a result undercut his sisters' autonomy as well as their pocketbooks. What at first seemed a convenience to the sisters would become an imposition. Resentment toward their brother was slow to root, but once taken hold, would crowd out childhood affections.

As a result of Senior's gifts, by the turn of the century the children all had accounts worth several hundred thousand dollars and the amounts were approximately the same. John Jr. earned a small salary compared to his peers, ten thousand a year at first, which increased very little. Consequently, working for Senior did not make him wealthier than his sisters. Edith was the best off, having married into the McCormick line, and doing so did not reduce the monetary gifts from her father. Bessie and Alta married men without much wealth, yet Senior wanted both to continue in the style of living he had provided. To insure his wishes, he gave allowances to his sons-in-law, thirty thousand dollars annually at first, as well as separate gifts to his daughters.

In 1904, John Jr. audited Alta's finances and concluded she and Parmalee were spending at a rate of twice their income. He did not convey to his father his dislike of Parmalee, nor did he criticize Alta's spending habits. Rather, John Jr. reminded Senior that Parmalee was a proud man who did not want to receive any money from others. In order to save Parmalee's face, the men arrived at a solution whereby Senior would make up the difference between Parmalee's position at the law firm Abby's brother ran and the $30,000 allowance. Thus, at the end of 1904 Senior paid his son-in-law $12,116 above $4,000 in gifts he had given during the year. Now and then Parmalee earned more than $30,000, but most years he earned less. In 1911, for example, Parmalee's wages were so small that his father-in-law sent $26,000. Furthermore, Senior regularly picked up the Prentice household expenses (heating, gas, and maintenance on their house), the annual trips to European spas for Alta's ear treatments, doctor bills, some servants' wages, and upkeep of their summer home.

Alta began a correspondence with her father that can be characterized as the Begging Series. For a decade her notes showed virtually no concern for other family members, including her parents themselves, but rather bluntly pleaded her latest case for financial assistance:

> Ten years ago when we came into this house you were good
> enough to pay for all the lace curtains. These curtains are now

worn out and I have bought new ones. Those for the first floor and those for the second-floor front I have not replaced, putting curtains as nearly like the old ones as possible. This makes 16 pairs of curtains costing a total of $453.50. If these curtains last for ten years, I feel that we shall get our money's worth out of them. Would you feel inclined to help me out by buying the curtains. If so, I shall be greatly pleased. If not, of course it will be all right.[22]

It always was all right because he always paid. Eventually she owned 5 West Fifty-third, which was expanded to incorporate 7 West as well, and lived during warm months on a farm in the Berkshires near Williamstown. As her landholdings grew, along with her children (who eventually numbered three—John, Spelman, and Madeline), so did Senior's checks increase in size and frequency.

At times Alta used sibling rivalry to boost her cause. "Edith took pleasure in showing me her new furniture. . . . It all seemed very extravagant, especially the costly real lace placed under the glass tops of her dressing table and writing table. For her sitting room table she paid $2,500."[23] She suggested that Senior urge Edith and Harold to move to Williamstown where they could live simply, though she doubted Edith could stand more austere ways. Alta did not understand that Edith's purchases were those of a connoisseur, that she was building a significant collection of antique lace, along with prescient selections of furniture, Oriental art, and rare books. She studied carefully and participated in the purchases, which she saw as part of her eventual cultural legacy to the museums of Chicago. While Senior certainly never appreciated Edith's intent, he nonetheless refused to play to Alta's hand and reinforce the rivalry.

Alta had another reason to feel envious, although she likely never learned of it. Senior gave Harold an allowance of fifty thousand dollars a year, even though he did not need it. Harold understood that Senior needed to give money away, that it was his expression of love. On Laura's birthday, for example, Senior regularly sent five hundred dollars to Laura and each of the children in celebration. He could think of ingenious presents as well, such as having a band appear at Kykuit to play Laura's favorite tunes. Yet he knew money meant the recipient could get what she really wanted, even go against his own preferences, as Edith did. Parmalee's pride meant Alta had to go a-begging, something she knew Edith never had to do.

To be fair to Parmalee, it must have rankled to have his brother-in-law consulted on his private matters. When the Williamstown house the Prentices had rented for some years came on the market, John Jr. examined the property for Senior. Alta asked for help from her father because she did not want Parmalee to have to sell all his stock to buy the place. John Jr. complimented the couple's "disposition to be economical" and recommended the purchase. He advised Senior not to accede to Alta's plan, "which means practically giving it to him [Parmalee]," but instead give the house and land to Alta alone. By the time Senior was ready to buy the property, he learned Parmalee had already completed the transaction on his own. Alta explained it was only right that Parmalee be sole owner of the summer place, for she was sole owner of the New York townhouse.

On the other hand, Parmalee did little to ingratiate himself with his in-laws. His letters were formal, pretentious expressions of his very conservative political views. The requisite thank-you notes, so grounded in Rockefeller family ritual, were missing. He had chosen to join the family, then resented its reach into his life. While ritualistic about manners in his own household, he neglected their function as an expression of caring for others. The Rockefeller politesse flowed from Christian virtue. Parmalee's "good form," when he expressed it, seemed intent to establish superior status.

Harold's relationship with his male in-laws was more relaxed and frank. It helped that he had been a schoolmate of John Jr.'s and a long-time friend of the family. Unlike Parmalee, he did not have to leave his home community nor give up his career. He was financially independent from the Rockefellers. Lacking a father, he welcomed Senior's strong paternal instincts and settled in their embrace. Yet even without some of these mitigating factors, Harold would have been the favorite son-in-law, for he was simply beguiling.

In 1902, Harold joined his mother and brothers in negotiations that led to the formation of the International Harvester Company. The dealings were complicated by the competing demands of the five farm machinery firms that were being bought out to form the new corporation. During that hot summer, Senior and son John Jr. prticipated in the deal as well, agreeing to buy IH stock and lend money to the McCormicks. Consequently, Nettie and her sons readily overpowered the owners of the other firms joining the merger. Oldest brother Cyrus became president of the company; Harold, one of its vice presidents; and Stanley, a member of the board of directors. Thus the Rockefellers helped their in-laws dominate the farm machinery market.

Earlier that year, Edith became pregnant again, and gave birth in September to a daughter, Muriel. A year later, she bore Editha, who was so sickly that the baby was placed in a facility for twenty-four-hour nursing care. Despite the medical attention, the baby died at the age of nine months. During this time Edith had kept an automobile ready during all social events to speed her to the infant's bedside when needed. (She bore her last child, Mathilde, in April of 1905.)

To public view, Harold and Edith were blessed with riches, talent, friends, and supportive families. He was a successful business leader who savored his work; she was a popular hostess now making her way into philanthropy. Despite this bountiful life, both were afflicted by emotional disabilities. Some today would diagnose Edith as manic-depressive, for she had episodes of grandiosity and impulsive activity interspersed with ones of dark, aching melancholy and torpor. On the other hand, one can identify external events that would unsettle even a stable temperament. Over an eight-year period, Edith had borne five children only to watch two sicken and die. During this time, she suffered from tuberculosis of the kidney, which went undiagnosed for several years. (Following Mathilde's birth, Harold and Edith left the baby with Laura and Senior, and against their advice went to Europe for six months to seek a cure. Harold later called himself "The most foolish fellow" for pressing a hard automobile tour upon Edith, who returned in worse condition than when they had left.) While Senior's medical advisors were determining the diagnosis of tuberculosis, toddler Muriel fell ill and almost died of appendicitis. By the end of 1906, both Edith and her daughter were returning to health. Harold praised his wife for her patience through her long illness, which was not cured for good until well into 1907, following long stays at Palm Beach and Forest Hill.

Edith bore these trials alone much of the time, for when her husband was not away on business trips, he was preoccupied with his clubs and hobbies. "I am [on the road] trying to lead a bachelor's life with good grace, which is far from attractive to me," opined Harold, but he was deceiving himself.[24] Harold was just as spoiled a son as John Jr., but his self-centeredness resulted not in demands upon his wife so much as in thoughtlessly neglecting her to pursue his own pleasures. He admired Edith's vitality and activism, and unlike John Jr. with Abby, encouraged her independence. In contrast to his mercurial and disorganized mother Nettie, Edith was so composed and capable that he possibly failed to see how he was not meeting her intimate needs. Very likely, in these early years of the marriage Edith was not cognizant of them herself, for Harold would cancel plans or appointments whenever her illness recurred. Consequently, when well, she sought security in the company of her children, in the exciting ideas of philosophy and mythology, and in adding to her collection of works of art.

The particulars of Harold's ailment are less clear. Hypochondria could have been involved, for Harold kept his pockets filled with pills and worried about not having rubbers when it rained. Yet the Fowler-McCormick line had a tendency to mental illness, which would be passed on to his daughter Muriel. His older sister Mary Virginia had been so unstable that Nettie eventually bought her an estate in Santa Barbara where she could live her life secluded under professional care. Following graduation from Princeton, his brother Stanley grew too anxiety-ridden to function well. More inclined toward art than business, he was never able to resist the pressures of the family to make the company his primary commitment. His mother interfered with his relationships with women, and his sister Anita continued to baby him. His brothers were thus hopeful when he married Katherine Dexter, one of the first woman graduates in science from the Massachusetts Institute of Technology. Eventually, in 1906 he suffered a nervous breakdown so severe that he never recovered. Devoted to Stanley, Katherine used her money and her background in biology to work with scientists searching for a cause for schizophrenia.[25] Anita despised her sister-in-law Katherine, and for years fought with her, through legal means when necessary, to control Stanley's therapy.

On the other hand, Harold functioned well in business, and to others seemed content, often cheerful; yet privately he often felt a melancholy that seemed irrational in light of his many successes. His response was to become even busier through involvements on charity boards and activities at the social clubs to which he belonged. Every Thursday he gathered with Princeton alumni, and additional weekly meetings for committees of the Merchants Club. He was an early devotee of automobiles, then considered a curious fad that would never supplant horses. He was one of the first persons in Chicago to own and fly a plane, as well as produce air shows to interest others in aviation. He was so good at tennis that he would likely have won the national amateur championship in 1905 had Edith not suddenly fallen ill.

Harold was a garrulous correspondent, whose letters disclose much more about his personality than Edith's notes, which were brief and conventional in expression. He had boundless enthusiasm, whatever his current endeavor. He wrote enchanting letters to Senior, his "Dear Father." His creativity sprang from method. When stating a position, he would list reasons against as well as for it, and as a result constantly tested his assumptions. His references to Edith were worshipful, an expression of his commitment to her and at the same time a hint that Senior underestimated his youngest daughter. Yet upon reading dozens of these charming missives, one senses blind spots in Harold's understanding, an excessive optimism, an idealization of individuals, and an ignorance of the full consequences of his actions, however noble. Like so many men of his privileged class, including John Jr., Harold was simply oblivious to much of the world around him. This fault would cause these brothers-in-law, both kind and virtuous men, at times to misunderstand and mistreat their wives.

Despite frequent physical separations and their disabling moods, Edith and Harold wove their mutual interests into a formidable partnership in philanthropy. One of their first joint activities was founding a memorial to their son, the John McCormick Institution of Infectious Diseases. They did more than provide the money; they consulted together in all aspects of the planning. For example, when the architect's plans were drawn up, Edith offered a detailed critique of both the design ("the tower looks like a school house") and the functional arrangements (reassign "the first floor entirely for laboratory purposes").[26] They endowed the *Journal for Infectious Diseases,* the only publication of its kind then. As a result of one of their grants to the institute, researchers at Johns Hopkins University were able to identify the bacterium which causes scarlet fever. Further work developed a treatment that led to the decline of the disease as a child killer and disabler.

Edith's role was not behind-the-scenes, either. In fact, in later years it was she, not Harold, who would be applauded in editorials as the impetus for the medical center and their later collaborations. (This is a rare historical instance of the female partner being given major credit for a couple's joint ventures.) Chicago clearly came to admire aloof, eccentric Edith more than her charming, equally capable husband. Harold never showed pique over her place in the spotlight, for he thought she deserved it.

Harold was unusual among upper-class men in forging a companionable marriage with Edith and in supporting her diverse, sometimes odd interests. His mother had shaped this predilection, for unlike most widows Nettie had taken over the family business. As a philanthropist, she had been similarly assertive and commanding. Edith exhibited many of the same independent qualities as her mother-in-law, and she had her own money to contribute to her ventures with Harold. The situation was very different from that of John Jr. and his wife Abby, who had little of her own funds, or of Parmalee and his wife Alta, who lacked her own sense of importance.

During the summer of 1906, Laura was recovered enough to travel to Europe with Senior, Dr. Biggar, Aunt Lute, Alta, John Jr., a nurse, and Senior's secretary Charles Heydt. Someone quipped that all they needed to complete the party was a clergyman and an undertaker. John Jr. took down notes on the palaces of Charles the Bald, observing for example how the architecture gave insight into medieval life. This exposure would inspire a renewed interest in that historical era, and years later culminate in one of his greatest art contributions to the city of New York. Abby must have been relieved to see her husband focus his mind on things other than Rockefeller family matters and philanthropy.

Laura was joyful to be with her oldest daughter after several years' absence. Senior fell into his favorite role as grandfather and went cycling with nine-year-old Margaret Strong, a shy brunette with religious leanings.

Everyone was pleased to see that Bessie, now forty, appeared healthier and more stable. In celebration, upon returning home Senior ordered that shares of stock be given to family members.

The joy was shortlived. A series of telegrams in November sketch the tragedy:

November 12: ANOTHER ATTACK PARALYSIS. HEART WEAK. CHARLES.

November 14: BESSIE PASSED AWAY AT TWO O'CLOCK THIS MORNING WITHOUT SUFFERING. [CHARLES]

November 14: WE ALL SEND LOVE. ALL IS WELL WITH DEAR BESSIE. COMMAND US FOR ANY SERVICE. FATHER.

Charles and Margaret arrived in the States with the body on November 20, and the family laid Bessie to rest on the crest of a steep slope in Sleepy Hollow Cemetery in Tarrytown.

The job of arranging the plot, the headstone, and the landscaping fell as usual upon John Jr. The stone was modest, with only Bessie's name and dates. For the plantings, he hired the Olmsted brothers, designers more used to commissions for hundreds of acres. In his characteristic manner, he examined every detail of the plan, oversaw its execution, and stopped by the grave regularly to check the results. The rhododendrons, he complained, seemed spindly.

After spending the winter with his in-laws, Charles took his daughter back to Europe. Bessie's estate at the end of 1906 was worth over $200,000, which along with other gifts from Senior over the years provided a comfortable income. Their life was peripatetic at first, with hotels serving as their temporary homes in various cities. Charles eventually settled Margaret in St. Felix School in Sothwold, England, and furnished an apartment in Paris where they could have a permanent base during her vacations. Charles isolated himself from the family from that time on, sent Margaret to various private schools, and refused invitations for her or himself to return to the States for visits. Consequently, Margaret had an unconventional upbringing for a Rockefeller, not being immersed in the family rituals and values.

During his travels, Charles befriended such philosophers as Bertrand Russell and George Santayana. Eventually he settled in Italy, where he continued to pursue the theories of his mentor William James, and spent his days upon a study of the mind. Over the years he wrote such monographs as "Why the Mind Has a Body," "The Wisdom of the Beasts," "A Theory of Knowledge," and "A Creed for Sceptics." No evidence exists whether his in-laws approved of his scholarship. What concerned them most was that he sequestered Margaret and raised her under the questionable influence of the Europeans. A Rockefeller was, they reminded him, first of all an American.

9
Earthly Trials

"Sorrow is better than laughter; for by the sadness of the countenance the heart is made better."

—Ecclesiastes 7:3

Laura's good health the summer before Bessie died was temporary. During 1907, she was so weak she did not attend church for ten months. Nonetheless, as always she moved her residence with the seasons. In the winter, she stayed at the New York townhouse; Senior would leave in January for a month or two in Florida to golf. When spring was in full bloom, she moved to Forest Hill, where she enjoyed her Cleveland friends, and on better days played golf with them. John Jr. visted often; Edith typically came for a month; grandchildren came and went. Now and then she went to the Lakewood or Pocantico houses for brief visits. So despite her semi-invalidism, and the long absences of Senior on golfing trips or other activities, she was never lonely.

In 1908, Laura had special reason to celebrate, a new home. Following the fire at Pocantico in 1902, Senior had immediately started plans to replace it. Both Abby and John Jr. dreaded the likelihood that the replacement would be a tasteless mishmash like the Forest Hill house. She had watched her father create his estate in Warwick to reflect both his high status and his appreciation of beauty, and she pressed similar preferences upon her young husband. He was further convinced that Senior's new home be noble and elegant as a slap at Ida Tarbell, who had mocked Senior for his "cult of the unpretentious" and his vanity over his penny-pinching.

To change Senior's intentions, the couple solicited a design from Chester Aldrich, a distant relative of Abby's. Senior would not be won over, however, until 1905. He not only accepted the design, but appointed John Jr. and Abby to supervise the construction and interior design. They determined to create a home where visitors would sense

Senior's love of simplicity as expressed through a setting of exquisite taste. Consequently, the exterior would be constructed of weathered stones from the surrounding hillsides, while the interior would follow the principles of Ogden Codman's and Edith Wharton's *The Decoration of Houses,* a radical rejection of Victorian bombast and clutter. Abby subscribed to design periodicals, and consulted with family members, especially her brother William, who was studing architecture at the Ecoles des Beaux-Arts in Paris.

In the summer of 1908, completion of the building was imminent. Abby had taken the children to their Bar Harbor retreat while John Jr. stayed behind to oversee the completion of the job, from electric fixtures to wallpaper, from servants' furniture to golf room. The absence of designer Ogden Codman, who was in France, increased John Jr.'s anxiety. Abby was smart to stay away; mail was the best way to handle her husband's impatience. She did return just before his parents' arrival to help John "try on" the place—sleep in various rooms, organize the staff, and arrange final details.

According to Laura's journal, the house was "beautiful and convenient within and without."[1] A favorite feature was a large pipe organ that she played with her sister in the evenings. Yet in truth she was unhappy with the house, whose guest rooms seemed too small, and whose bathroom plumbing bellowed in the public rooms below. Senior was displeased with the squeaking elevator and leaky flues. But worst of all was the expense, for the half-million projected cost escalated to over a million, with more work to be done both on the building and on the grounds. Only Abby's garden plantings, then at peak bloom, escaped criticism.

Following two more years of discussions, Senior decided to tear the house apart and asked architects Delano and Aldrich to radically redesign it. A mansard roof was added to make more space in the fourth-floor servants' quarters. The master bedrooms and guest rooms were expanded, the east end of the house ended. A stone loggia replaced the wooden veranda. Topping the roof was an enormous American eagle perched on a globe, a shield with the letter "R" in its talons. The final result, a blend with a NeoGreco pediment, a French roof, Romanesque arches, and Georgian symmetry, was marvelously successful both aesthetically and functionally. Codman's decor of Chippendale, Hepplewhite, and Sheraton created light, inviting but formal interiors compatible with the owners' decorum.

Senior hiked the surrounding hilltop and ordered more fully mature trees, many from other parts of the property, so that from the beginning the scale of landscape matched the stone mass of the mansion. West of the house was a large enclosed garden with a stone teahouse, pools, fountains, and a linden-bordered walkway. To the south were a Neoclassical grotto, terraces and pools. To decorate the terrace, two-hundred-year-old orange trees were brought over from a chateau in France. To the north was a circular rose garden surrounding a maze of flower beds planted for spring and fall, the seasons the house was most in use. Complementing these European-style gardens was a Japanese garden, formed in a miniature ravine over which were set bridges and stones to invite crossing back and forth. A traditional Japanese teahouse sat on a bank by an artificial lake.[2] Finally, the swimming pool was the largest and central in a series of connected pools paved with black and white pebbles and rimmed with scallop shells. Latticed summer cottages alongside were flanked by sweet-smelling jasmine trees and elms.

The new Pocantico greatly satisfied Laura, and it became a favorite place for her to see her grandchildren. With the constant company of her sister Lute, she could not have been lonely. One wonders whether the girlhood wit still remained, if their conversations sparkled in a way others would never hear.

During 1908, Harold suffered so persistent and dark a depression that he went to Switzerland for treatment at the Burgholzi Psychiatric Hospital in Zurich. His doctor was thirty-three-year-old Carl Jung, whose papers on word association had attracted the admiration of Sigmund Freud and other influential specialists. The Burgholzi, the best-known and most prestigious mental hospital in Europe, was the training center for many American clinicians, who were more open to the new field of psychoanalysis than their European peers. It was probably for this reason that Burgholzi attracted Harold, for Jung was not well-known yet among lay people.

Unlike his colleagues, Jung did not draw strict lines to exclude his patients from friendship. He would naturally be drawn to Harold as more than a case study, and not just because the middle-aged executive was rich (although that helped). Jung had many qualities compatible with an American temperament. A tall, powerful man with blond hair and with the strong hands of a workman, he was filled with such high energy that he wished he could treat his patients while on walks out of doors. Raised in the Swiss countryside, he lacked urban reserve and felt comfortable with people of all classes. In social settings, his humorous banter put others at ease, and he often stirred up party games and dancing. Jung's interest in the occult, mythology, and symbolism also matched him better with Americans, whose history had a long flirtation with astrology, faith healing, and spiritualism. Indeed, unlike his mentor Freud, Jung admired American culture. Over the years he welcomed other wealthy American patients and enjoyed his speaking tours in their homeland. He was comfortable using English and took it as no insult that his American patients would not learn German.

Despite his cosmopolitanism, Jung was quintessentially Swiss, particularly in his proclivity to use money as a measure of one's success. While still a student he married Emma Rauschenbach, whose independent wealth eventually allowed him both independence from Burgholzi and the comforts of a pampered lifestyle. Yet he was also known for charging minimal fees in his practice, so his attraction to Harold and other rich Americans was not solely pecuniary. In fact, Jung did for Harold what he would not do for others. In 1910, just before the meetings of the International Psychoanalytic Association, of which he was president, he made a hurried trip to Chicago. Doing so meant spending three weeks (two in transit) during a time when Freud was expecting him to help on the organizational work of the Association.

Harold's illness was apparently complicated by his relationship with another woman.[3] In 1909, Jung wrote Freud how he had just taken on "a friend of Roosevelt and Taft" (further evidence of his American idolatry) who was suffering from the same sort of conflict Jung himself had just resolved.[4] The reference was to Jung's recent imbroglio with Sabina Spielrein, a medical student and patient of his. Jung seduced Spielrein, who grew despondent over his refusal to leave his wife, and may have started rumors as a result. Eventually she wrote to Freud of her mistreatment by Jung. Both analysts eventually came to the conclusion that Spielrein was the manipulator, not victim, in the matter, although the evidence now points otherwise. Consequently, Jung may have used a similar rationalization in comforting Harold with regard to his troublesome mistress, that is, that Harold was the victim.

Neither analyst nor analysand was cured of their adultery. Soon Jung took on another dark-haired, dark-eyed woman as his mistress. Toni Wolff, another patient, found herself enthralled in a complicated relationship. Jung insisted she be included with his family at significant events, attend Sunday dinners, and be referred to as "Aunt Toni" by his children. He needed two women, he explained to friends: Emma, the domestic creator, wife, and mother; Toni, the eros-winged muse for his imagination. Despite the ongoing embarrassment and humiliation his demands brought to both women, they accommodated to the point of accepting his request they analyze each other.[5] Having developed this two-woman situation into a general theory of femininity, Jung could hardly inhibit similar wayward impulses in patients like Harold McCormick.

Edith must have known of her husband's mistresses—all Chicago society knew. Harold, the perpetual Peter Pan, failed to see anything wrong in his behavior. He had done what was expected of him: graduated from Princeton, married a Rockefeller, and made a successful career in the family business. Writing to his sister of one amour, he explained, "I have never had many *real* friends and here is one. I made real sacrifices. Why not Edith now? And let me have this happiness? I would harm no one."[6]

Edith could reply that she, too, had few real friends, yet this was no excuse for her to find comfort in another man. Always self-contained, Edith was ready to comfort others' troubles, while not reveal her own in turn. Unable to confide, even in writing to those closest to her, we can only surmise how she felt. Her behavior remained conventional, that is, she did what prominent socialites were supposed to do in such instances: pretend that nothing was going on. She had her children, her collecting, and her philanthropies to place in the public eye to counter the tittling in the gossip columns.

Her newest endeavor was the Art Institute of Chicago. Since the 1860s, artists had joined with businessmen and civic boosters to fund this combination of art school, gallery, and design center. Women had been left out of much of the activity, either as artists on display or as fundraisers. In 1909 the Institute initiated the Friends of American Art, an auxiliary to guarantee annual funding for the purchase of works by American artists. Edith and her sister-in-law Anita McCormick Blaine became charter subscribers. Despite this support from key women in the community, the Institute board continued to exclude women from its various executive committees, nor could they help plan exhibits. They could give money, but have no say in its disposition.

It may have been the Art Institute's exclusiveness that persuaded Edith to devote the bulk of her money and managerial skills to opera. Conveniently, Harold was just as interested as she was, which meant he would happily take time out from tractor-selling, flying, clubbing, and bedding others to join with Edith to found a major company.

For several decades Chicago's opera productions had been imported, through various impresarios, or New York's Metropolitan Opera Company stopping on tour. The large immigrant populations provided a ready public for the works of Verdi, Wagner, Puccini, and Massenet. They formed a knowledgeable, enthusiastic, and appreciative audience. (When young Enrico Caruso made his debut in 1905, the audience forced him against his wishes to repeat the sextet from *Lucia de Lammermoor.*) Although many of these travelling shows were of high quality, Chicagoans wanted the pride of owning their own company, one with a predictable season. During a luncheon in 1909, John Shaffer, publisher of the Chicago *Evening Post,* raised the possibility with Harold and Charles Dawes, a leading financier. The three quickly signed up forty-seven other subscribers to found the Chicago Grand Opera Company. Harold was made president of the board, but Chicagoans soon acknowledged it was Edith "who really had the greater zeal."[7]

The fallout from a cultural war in New York aided the company's rapid growth. In recent years former cigar maker Oscar Hammerstein, who had built the Manhattan Opera House, had been trying to drive the Metropolitan out of business. The press backed Hammerstein; the Vanderbilts, Astors, and Morgans endorsed the Metropolitan. The blue-bloods won. By early 1910, the Metropolitan bought out Hammerstein's warehouse of sets, costumes, and the scores to the French operas he featured. In turn, it sold most of the Hammerstein inventory, which it did not need, to the new Chicago company, and some New Yorkers supplied further underwriting. The new organization further benefitted by hiring experienced staff from both Hammerstein's defunct group and the Metropolitan.

On November 3, 1910, the company made its debut with a performance of *Aida.* Beforehand, a parade of carriages and automobiles stopped at 1000 Lakeshore Drive to deposit guests for the traditional McCormick pre-opera dinner. Although jewelry was temporarily out of fashion, Edith wore long diamond pendants that dangled from her ears well down the neck. However, she agreed with the other women in not wearing a tiara. During dinner, Edith kept a clock by her place setting, and directed the service of the courses according to a rigid schedule. One did not dawdle at Edith's table unless one was not hungry. But then, one never arrived late for the opera performance either, as happened to guests dining at other houses. For Edith, the music came first, and when the curtain rose, performers could see her in the center box, sitting in her stiff upright posture, and fully focused on the stage action.

One of Hammerstein's most popular sopranos, Mary Garden, was to dominate the Chicago opera scene for the next twenty years. Brainy and charming, she was known as the "Sarah Bernhardt of the operatic stage." She made up for a less than perfect vocal technique with her magnetic presence on stage and her sensational self-promotion offstage. During a performance of *Thaïs,* she covered her inability to handle certain high notes by raising her arm and rattling her jangly metal bracelets. After delighting Chicago with two French operas, she premiered her notorious *Salome* with its Dance of the Seven Veils on November 25. "It wasn't a hoochi-koochi dance at all," she explained. "Everything was glorious and nude and suggestive, but not coarse." As though running about the stage dropping diaphanous pink veils were not enough, when brought the head of John the Baptist, she kissed it passionately. The audience was stupefied. The police chief later complained, "It was disgusting. Miss Garden wallowed like a cat in a bed of catnip."[8]

Like much of the country then, Chicago was prone to the outcries of self-appointed censors, in this case the Law and Order League, which in recent weeks had been visiting the many legitimate theater houses and forcing changes in productions. They were so intimidating that reporters who knew better wrote columns about "the orgies" on the opera stage and no socialite could be found who admitted having been present. That Chicago had more "peep" shows than any other city in the country did not matter, for bawdiness had its place, the red light district. "If there is any more twaddle about immorality," advised Garden in a delicious threat, "I shall leave Chicago and go to Philadelphia . . . where art is appreciated."[9] (She found it in Milwaukee, where the company performed *Salome* without uproar.)

Eventually the opera board cancelled *Salome*'s third performance. Rumor was that Edith was behind the order, but more likely the management deferred to pressure to avoid further jeopardizing its season. (When told of the fiasco, Oscar Hammerstein laughed and suggested Garden wear flannels in future productions.) Garden deflected this early criticism by appearing soon after in a well-sung *Thais* and, with Enrico Caruso, in *The Girl of the Golden West*. The first season closed a success, with critics agreeing that artistically the company offered fresh renditions, and the business manager was pleased to report a deficit of only ten thousand dollars.

From the beginning, the Chicago board dreamed of producing the first great American opera, and thought they had discovered it in Victor Herbert's *Natoma*. Edith was committed to the concept of opera in English, but she knew it would take time for worthy translations of librettos to be done. Underwriting such projects became another of her obsessions, and she sponsored over two dozen translations during her lifetime. Unfortunately *Natoma* was sung by French singers who could not pronounce English well, and it was not a good opera either.

She also wanted the company to produce original works. Its first venture here was *The Jewels of the Madonna* by a young composer, Ermanno Wolf-Ferrari. This production became a staple of the company for many years. His one-act *The Secret of Suzanne* similarly delighted everyone except some older doyennes and the president of the local Anti-Cigarette League, for Suzanne's secret was her nicotine habit. (Young, independent-minded women were adopting smoking as a sign of their rejection of their mothers' Victorian restrictions.)

The morality attacks had another unseen consequence. Senior and John Jr. must have been aware of the outcries attached to certain productions. Neither appreciated opera. Though both loved instrumental music and attended concerts, they were not notable donors to musical organizations. (Cleveland found this out when it sought their support for its symphony.) The *Salome* scandal would only reinforce their belief that performers did not deserve donations; Edith was never able to change their mind on the subject.

By the close of its third season, the Chicago Grand Opera had successfully toured Philadelphia and cities throughout the west, and continued to make a small profit. At this point, Harold bought out all the stock owned by New Yorkers; thus he and Edith clearly held the strongest influence on the direction of the company. Dramatic soprano Rosa Raisa signed up and became as popular as Garden. The public continued to respond well to new works and new ideas in presentation. Unfortunately, for many reasons the fourth season ended in a deficit of a quarter of a million dollars. A number of key backers withdrew their further support, so the company fell into bankruptcy and cancelled its next season. During the reorganization, Harold "bought" the company's scenery, costumes, and props for seventy-five thousand dollars, but it was really a gift. He and Edith formed a new company, the Chicago Opera Association, which was now completely under their domination. But by the time this company opened its premiere season, Edith's seat in the central box would be empty.

In 1911, Edith published an essay, "Four Family Divisions," whose philosophy mirrored the contradiction and change women were now voicing more loudly through suffrage campaigns and union activity.[10] A marriage should consist of "good comradeship," where the wife follows whatever her heart says is "true, just, well-balanced." Yet, if necessary, she should temporarily give up a plan of her own to help her husband's career. She should not lead in the marriage, for as her husband rises in society, her own opportunities will grow. However, if she is very efficient in running her home, she will have hours free for what matters to her personally. As for child-rearing, "after teaching that cleanliness comes next to godliness, teach obedience, orderliness," and do not spoil the child, but inculcate self-reliance. Do not put aside a movie matinee or lecture if the children are otherwise well. Finally, the healthy woman must develop a sphere of her own. When doing a necessary chore such as "sewing, have a book open on the table nearby." Demand "days out."

What may seem inconsistent and smacking of female submissiveness to today's readers would not have been so then. Though not a radical expression of feminism, Edith's treatise was in the mainstream. Her position aptly captured women on the cusp of redefining their place. Even the most extreme suffragists accepted the Victorian belief that women and men were akin to separate species. What they questioned was the corollary that each served separate spheres. Suffragists argued that women needed to be more active in the world precisely because they had special talents and abilities that men did not have. Edith urged Victorian values of child-rearing, but released the mother from being homebound. Even her remarks concerning marriage reminded that each partner occasionally had to give more or less over time, that it was not the woman's role to pull up the slack every time.

It may not be coincidental that several months later at the last minute, and without explanation, Edith cancelled a dinner for two hundred guests. Now she was the one to collapse into depression. The months leading up to then, unknown to Chicago society, she had gone to a rest home in the New York mountains. Although she later explained to the press that her impoliteness was due to having to help her mother with an emergency in Pocantico, the truth was otherwise. She had remained in Chicago, where she isolated herself and spent many hours each day sitting in the open air. Harold wrote encouraging notes to Senior about her progress, but it was Harold's nature to view all situations as hopeful.

Now thirty-nine, Edith turned inward at the very time her youngest child, Mathilde, was ready for full-time schooling. She had no one in her family with whom to share her unhappiness. Her invalided mother was too preoccupied with the heavenly realm to appreciate her children's daily troubles. Her father and brother disapproved of her love of luxury and support of musicians. Her sister Alta was simultaneously envious and condescending.

Worse, Edith had two strong women competing for her time with Harold—not his mistresses, but his mother Nettie and sister Anita. Nettie hovered about her thirty-nine-year-old son with continued reminders about his "fragile" health. Unlike his siblings, Harold accepted Nettie's overprotectiveness, and at the same time defied her through such risky activities as aeroplane races. Anita filled the void of early widowhood by dominating her kin whenever possible. She manipulated her mother when

William "Big Bill" Avery Rockefeller was a charming travelling salesman with a wandering eye. *(Courtesy of the Rockefeller Archive Center)*

Pious Eliza Davison Rockefeller forgave her husband's errant ways. *(Courtesy of the Rockefeller Archive Center)*

During the 1920s, Rockefeller visited his childhood home in Moravia, New York. *(Courtesy of the Rockefeller Archive Center)*

Despite his long absences, Bill provided well for his family. From left to right: John, Mary Ann, Lucy, Franklin, and William. *(Courtesy of the Rockefeller Archive Center)*

Laura "Cettie" Spelman supported abolition, women's rights, and temperance. *(Courtesy of the Rockefeller Archive Center)*

John and Laura's children were taught to tithe and lead a moral Christian life. From left to right: Alta, Bessie, Edith, and John Jr. *(Courtesy of the Rockefeller Archive Center)*

In his early fifties, John D. Rockefeller quit business for philanthropy. *(Courtesy of the Rockefeller Archive Center)*

Neighbors thought John and Laura's home on Euclid Avenue rather modest. *(Courtesy of the Rockefeller Archive Center)*

Originally built as a hotel, Forest Hill became the family's favorite Ohio home. *(Courtesy of the Rockefeller Archive Center)*

Laura's favorite spot in Forest Hill was the artificial lake John D. designed. *(Courtesy of the Rockefeller Archive Center)*

4 West Fifty-fourth Street contrasted greatly from the opulent mansions on nearby Fifth Avenue. *(Courtesy of the Rockefeller Archive Center)*

An interior from West Fifty-fourth Street suggests little interest in decor or show. *(Courtesy of the Rockefeller Archive Center)*

This portrait precisely captures the psychological relation between John Jr. and Abby. *(Courtesy of the Rockefeller Archive Center)*

Only daughter Babs rebelled against her parents' ways. In Sea Harbor 1921. From left to right: Laurence, Babs, John III, Abby and David, Winthrop, John Jr., and Nelson. *(Courtesy of the Rockefeller Archive Center)*

The decor of a salon at John Jr. and Abby's nine story townhouse at 10 West Fifty-fourth Street reflects Abby's aesthetic eye. *(Courtesy of the Rockefeller Archive Center)*

Kykuit, with its extraordinary gardens, replaced a burned-down old farmhouse. *(Courtesy of the Rockefeller Archive Center)*

Three generations of John D.'s illustrate the passing on of family tradition. *(Courtesy of the Rockefeller Archive Center)*

William Rockefeller's Rockwood was the most opulent spread along the Hudson. *(Courtesy of the Rockefeller Archive Center)*

William and Mira raised their family according to the practices of Gilded Age high society. John and Abby at the right. *(Courtesy of the Rockefeller Archive Center)*

Emma Rockefeller McAlpin and
daughter Geraldine, who fought her
parents' status preoccupation.
(Courtesy of the Rockefeller Archive Center)

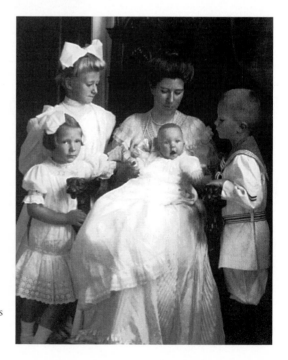

Isabel Stillman Rockefeller,
raised by a heartless father, was
a thoughtless mother. *(Courtesy
of the Rockefeller Archive Center)*

After Laura died, John D. spent his final decades in Ormond, Florida. *(Courtesy of the Rockefeller Archive)*

Alta deeply loved her father, who underestimated her and her sisters. *(Courtesy of the Rockefeller Archive Center)*

Left, Bessie's only child, Margaret Strong, was to inherit John D.'s estate. Here, with husband George de Cuevas. *Right,* Mathilde McCormick's marriage to her Swiss equestrian instructor, Max Oser, scandalized the family. *(Courtesy of the Rockefeller Archive Center)*

Harold McCormick, heir to the farm machinery fortune, and Edith at the time of their marriage. *(Courtesy State Historical Society of Wisconsin, #49141)*

Harold McCormick was a romantic who little understood his children. From left: Muriel, Harold, Fowler, and Mathilde. *(Courtesy of State Historical Society of Wisconsin, #49140)*

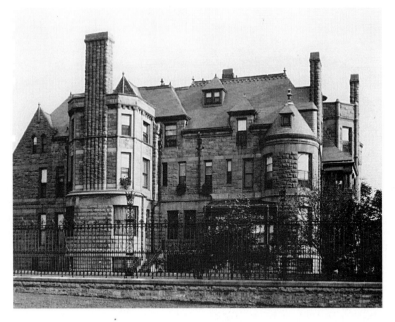

Edith bought up property around the home at 1000 Lake Shore Drive to prevent skyscraper shadows. *(Courtesy of State Historical Society of Wisconsin, #49289)*

Villa Turicum, Edith and Harold's estate overlooking Lake Michigan, was seldom used. *(Courtesy of State Historical Society of Wisconsin, #49288)*

Carl Jung divided women into two classes, the mothers like his wife Emma, and the inspirers of male creativity, like his mistresses. *(Brown Brothers)*

As Mrs. Harold McCormick, Ganna Walska could dress like the prima donna she aspired to be. *(Brown Brothers)*

Even Carl Jung could not reconcile the flamboyant Fifi Stillman with her dour banker husband. Here with daughter Anne in 1926. *(Brown Brothers)*

Bright and vivacious Bobo Sears, daughter of a coal miner, was the first Cinderella Rockefeller. Here with husband Winthrop Rockefeller on their wedding day in 1948. *(Archive Photos)*

Tod warmly encouraged her son Steven's marriage to a household staff member, Anne Marie Rasmussen. *(Archive Photos: Nordisk Pressefoto)*

Blanchette Rockefeller's natural elegance complimented her intelligence and her eye for art. *(Courtesy of the Rockefeller Archive Center)*

Blanchette (left) was a tireless worker for the arts, while Mary, here
with husband Laurence, travelled worldwide on YWCA projects.
(*Archive Photos*)

Happy Rockefeller at the opening of three new restaurants
at Rockefeller Center in 1984. (*Archive Photos: Tom Gates*)

she could, and even maneuvered her into building a new house she did not want. She commandeered Mary Virginia's trust and living arrangements, and bitterly fought for similar control of Stanley. She coddled Harold and resented Edith's influence upon him. Anita brought education to poor children, supported women's trade unionism, and fought for uncontaminated food laws, but poisoned relations with her family.

If only Edith had a wise woman friend to offer consolation, but there was none. To divert her mind from her dark thoughts, she took on a new project. Consulting with architect Charles Platt, she planned a new home to be built on a wooded bluff overlooking Lake Michigan. Harold's brother had an immense estate, Walden, adjoining the property, and perhaps as a salve he offered Edith this gift of her own country mansion. The resulting Lake Forest estate, later named Villa Turicum, was the closest any of the early Rockefellers came to building a home of architectural merit.[11] The delicate, light-filled Renaissance Italianate mansion contrasted with the heavy faux Tudors, Victorians, and castellated rock forts chosen by those who confused bulk with taste. Some of the forty-four rooms were planned specifically to show off tapestries and art works Edith had been collecting. The drawing room was faced with an unusual warm-colored marble and a teak floor. Several rooms featured the carved and painted ceilings common to the palazzo style. A skylit, tiled court with Roman sculpture and fountain was dubbed the Pompeiian Room. The period furnishings from Edith's collections were placed sparely to increase the sense of space and freedom. The gardens were just as carefully planned, incorporating courtyards, fountains, and sculpture true to the era. An elevator took swimmers down a ninety-foot cliff to the beach-level pool house. Villa Turicum became Edith's favorite spot for seclusion, though usually in the daytime and outdoors. As it happened, this wonderful house was seldom used, and in its fifty years its beautiful walls echoed with few voices other than the caretakers'.

Harold's optimism about Edith's health proved ill-founded. Despite spending the summer of 1912 taking a treatment at a spa in Ellenville, New York, she withdrew further. Lurking fears darkened what should have been pleasant moments. Jung agreed to consult on her case. In October, he came stateside to treat both Edith and Harold, who brought him to Pocantico to meet Laura and Senior. The elder Rockefellers were pleased to see an improvement in Edith's appearance, which was unfortunately shortlived.

When Edith invited Jung to visit, she expected he would stay in the states and even prepared a house for him and his family in Chicago. As she explained to him, she had developed phobias around travel, the worst panic occurring on trains. Jung wanted to treat Edith, for he admired her intellect yet found her "the toughest problem he has ever had to deal with."[12] Of course, he had no intention of moving to Chicago, and was aware that forcing Edith to travel to Zurich would in itself be the start of her cure. He recommended that once in Europe she take certain trains that made frequent stops. Her chauffeur should drive a similar route and wait at each station. Were she to feel anxious, she could disembark and continue in the car. Edith finally accepted his challenge and sailed for Zurich on April 1, 1913, accompanied by children Fowler and Muriel. (Harold and Mathilde remained in Chicago until the fall.) Significantly, Edith took the train all the way to Zurich.

Situated at the north end of its namesake lake, Zurich was a charming town in the softer hillside region of Switzerland. The twin towers of the Romanesque Grossmunster cathedral dominated the old quarter, which rose steeply on slopes above the lake. Edith settled into the Hotel Baur au Lac, with its noted gardens and indulgent service. Jung lived on the northern shore in nearby Kusnacht, his house styled after an eighteenth-century patrician mansion. His original plans omitted space for doing therapy at home, so he had converted a linen storage room into a waiting room, and a small study into the consultation chamber.

Edith arrived at the start of the most critical period in Jung's life. His dependency upon Freud had broken when the older man, unforgiving of Jung's criticisms and extensions of his theory, terminated the relationship. Then thirty-eight, Jung withdrew into, as he put it, an "infernal journey" into the the underworld that lasted five years until 1918. He trembled from a recurring fantasy of corpses placed in crematory ovens, then discovered to be alive. His dreams grew more elaborate, with visitations from knights, alchemists, golden-haired girls—figures that later formed the basis for his theory of archetypes. Fearful of growing mad, and rather than deny or sublimate his confusion, he submitted wholly to his unconscious. He played "childish games," building with stones gathered from the lakeside, or painting images of mandalas, circles of symbols. This process revealed a new vision of psychology, one based upon the truth of myths, and their value in personal transformation.

As a result of his turmoil, Jung withdrew from teaching at the University of Zurich and consulting at Burgholzi; he gave up reading professional journals and presenting scientific papers; he neglected his family and friends. What he did not give up was his treatment of certain patients, especially if their struggles paralleled his own.

Jung was attracted to women patients of exceptional intelligence and creativity, and one can trace his theoretical development by reference to these key analysands. He discovered in Edith not a narrow social matron, a dilettante, but an intellectual who studied in a manner similar to European professors. That is, she read in the original language, went to the primary sources, and crossed disciplinary boundaries.[13] As one observer humorously explained, "because she was very careful in the selection of her parents she undoubtedly missed a great academic career."[14] An adept linguist, she even knew Sanskrit. While in Zurich, she hired local professors to tutor her in philosophy. As a result she read the collected works of Kant along with those of such leading commentators as Cohen, Wundt, Chamberlain, Heidegger, and more obscure essayists known only to specialists. Another preference was for Goethe, and eventually she examined over 140 books by or about the writer. In the margins of the texts she made summary comments in German that evinced a patient and understanding mind at work. Her notes incorporated ideas from epistemology, ethics, mysticism, Buddhism, Christianity, Judaism, sociology, archeology, and psychology. Jung exhibited the same wide sweep in his research, hence would find in Edith one capable of accompanying him on diverse pathways in conversation.

Jung originally had been an experimentalist who insisted that psychoanalysis required more evidence than the interpretive assertions of its practitioners. In his break with Freud he conceived of dreams and wakeful reveries as "facts." He read ancient occult texts and came to believe in paranormal phenomena. He did not so much reject scientific method as expand his approach to incorporate artisitic and humanistic techniques. In so doing, he moved far beyond what Freud considered appropriate in the interpretation of dreams. Edith also questioned pure empiricism and the superiority of scientific rationality. Science informed on the physical environment, she acknowledged, but left out ethics and conscience, theology and epistemology. Religious similes and images permeated her book notations, as well as the themes of her art collection in Chicago. Thus Edith was ready to accept as truth the meaning of symbols in daydreams, coincidences, and spontaneous writing or artwork.

During the time of her analysis, Jung demanded relentless self-examination and confrontation with the most unseemly parts of oneself. In a series of letters to Senior Harold tried to reveal the path of Edith's delving into the "impenetrable darkness" and the subsequent fatigue brought on by analysis. A cogent and lucid writer, he would ultimately fail, for no analogy existed in Senior's own life. The best he could offer was that it was "more of a *study*, much more, than any thing connected with medicine, or hygiene . . . she very largely makes her own mental recipes."[15] Furthermore, Harold observed that Senior had a character that would not benefit from analysis, because he was intuitively at one with himself, knew who he was and acted accordingly.

Senior was not one to remark on his children behind their back. Consequently, it is often difficult to know what he was really thinking about this couple's behavior. His usual comment was one of acceptance. When Nettie McCormick expressed her anxiety that Harold's family return to the States, Senior calmed her. "They seem deeply interested in and profoundly impressed with these studies. Let us hope that these will return a rich fruitage, and before it is too late for us to enjoy the benefits of the same with them."[16] Still, he and Laura must have been puzzled by the couple's enthusiasm for the Swiss doctor and his mysterious methods.

In May of 1912, Abby added son Winthrop to Babs, John 3rd, Nelson, and Laurance. "You must get very well now [in recovering from the delivery]," John wrote from a fishing camp. "Five little people need you now, besides a man who needs you more than ever, and who wants a great deal more of you than he has been having."[17]

And the five little people must be raised as he had been. The day started with prayers at 7:50 and breakfast in the formal dining room. Interestingly, he exempted Abby from this duty, so she might appear or not. The horror of waste shaped a variety of rules. "We were told not to leave food on our plates, not to allow electric lights to remain burning."[18] They kept account books where they had to list their spending of their allowances to the penny. John Jr. calculated the allowances to ensure that the children would need to work as well to earn the full amount they needed. The Rockefeller children caught flies and trapped mice and weeded gardens for a few pence, just as their father and grandfather had done. The clock chimes ruled the starting of meals, the hours in study. Sabbatarian observances ordered Sunday activities. He even organized a quartet, with himself and John 3rd on violin, Babs and Laurance on piano. (Nelson was given cello lessons, but had a way of putting his instrument out of commission to avoid playing.)

It was the sort of upbringing a wasteful culture calls repressive, and could be if delivered in too rigid a tone. But the children had Abby, who met with them each week to help them sort out their ledgers and memorize their Bible verses. She taught them the games her husband had loved as a child, Numerica and Musical Authors, and cajoled him into joining spontaneous play. Abby compensated for those traits of Senior (simple fun) and Laura (easy conversation) that John Jr. had known as a child, yet could not find in himself to offer his own offspring. The result was a well-balanced method of child-rearing, and at an unspoken level the two must have realized this, for neither attempted to stifle the style of the other. This does not mean that their children viewed both equitably, however.

A telling contrast is the Prentice household, where Parmalee's rule was rigid and final. His son Spelman always laughed at his cousins in Uncle John's household for complaining about their father's austere style. "I told Win [Winthrop], you guys don't know what forbidding is."[19] The Prentice children dressed for dinner in formal clothes and conversed in Latin, Parmalee's avocation. They could not bring friends to the house, except on formal invitation. Fainthearted Alta went along and did not offer any counterbalance. It was an atmosphere nurturing rebellion or repression.

On the opposite end was the McCormick household. There structure was provided, if at all, by grandmother Nettie McCormick, who cared for the children for long periods when Edith was ill, Harold away, or the two off together for their yearly trip abroad. Nettie had spoiled her own children, and no evidence exists she treated her grandchildren otherwise. Edith and Harold were caring parents—they corresponded about such details as having a competent lifeguard to watch the children when they went swimming—and at the same time not demonstratively affective. Their frequent absences and preoccupation with their other activities made the children of lower priority in practice, if not intent. As the only son, being groomed to take a leadership role in the business, Fowler suffered the least, while his younger sisters Muriel and Mathilde went adrift.

"Home" for John Jr. and Abby most of the year was two places. One was the rental on 13 West Fifty-fourth, an unpretentious home well-suited to a growing brood, but too small. Consequently, plans were in process for a new house to go up on 10 West Fifty-fourth. John Jr.'s preferences prevailed. Forty feet wide and nine stories high, the final version included a gymnasium, squash court, rooftop playground, infirmary, suites for the children and their caretakers, an entire floor for staff, and two elevators. The dominant tone in the public rooms was formality, expressed through the English Chippendale and Louis XV furniture, a great marbled reception area, and Persian tapestries lining the main stone staircase. In the private rooms, John Jr. was satisfied with reproductions and modern furnishings.

The other home was Abeyton Lodge in Pocantico. It began a Dutch-style farmhouse, which grew with the family into a comfortable ramble, furnished with cheerful chintz and cretonne hardy enough to take the wear-and-tear of the children. The heart of the house was Abby's second-floor sitting room, where her husband and their youngsters competed for her attention. The children had miles of pathways for strolling, riding, and bicycling, along with the tennis court and swimming pool beside Kykuit.

Eventually a third home joined the others, a summer retreat at Seal Harbor on Mount Desert Island in Maine. Following a series of rentals, the family acquired the Eyrie, a sixty-five-room "cottage" on a bluff, with sixteen acres separating it from neighbors. Over the years Abby collaborated with her favorite architect, Duncan Candler, to modify the house into a half-timbered Tudor of over a hundred rooms. These she filled with the antiques she loved—John Jr. being satisfied with reproductions—and the art treasures she sought out over the years.

Seal Harbor was a mixed colony of wealthy patricians, such as Philadelphia Main Liners, along with Ivy League scientists and intellectuals. Members of the second richest family in the country, the Fords, also vacationed there. The genteel shabbiness characteristic of such hideaways—scruffy golf course, lumpy tennis courts, modest dock and storage shacks, worn upholstery in the parlors—disguised the concentration of wealth present. Invigorating contests ruled the day, with sailing presenting the greatest challenge, for it had a life-threatening element. As Abby's grandnephew later explained about similar Maine vacations, where his father started each morning with a dip in the chilly sea, "Arcadia is always the site of Old Money's ordeal by nature . . . Arcadia makes Eden's riches look like hell."[20]

Abby preferred nature's challenge, especially sailing, while John Jr. could not leave his work behind. Following a morning with correspondence, telegrams, and reports, he expected her to devote part of the afternoon to more sedate pursuits, a hike or carriage drive about the trails, a stop for tea along the way. An accomplished horeseman, he never acquired Harold McCormick's preference for fast automobiles and "aeroplanes." More naturalist than athlete, he preferred the slow pace so he could stop and smell the sap of a tree or identify a new wild flower. One of the first of his many contributions to the parks of the country was the purchase of lands to expand what would turn into Arcadia National Park. The result was to preserve large tracts of land, particularly the inland granite summits, from being developed into resort hotels. In this way the well-to-do conserved the landscape and protected their privacy as well.

On a more private level of giving, John Jr. persuaded Edsel Ford to join him in building a club for their families and friends. To his mind it was "a unique and attractive family center for parents and children alike . . . because never has liquor in any form been provided." (He and Senior were large contributors to the Anti-Saloon League, which was campaigning for the National Prohibition Amendment.)[21] Few of the member families, however, were likely to exclude liquor completely from their home, as John Jr. and Abby did.

One of the most important functions of exclusive communities such as Seal Harbor was to restrict children's opportunities. Newport's great attraction was not just its beauty and its offering an excellent yachting terminus, but also the small size of its peninsula that permitted only so many of the right type to move in. Just as private schools and social clubs restricted a child's companions, and hence potential marriage partners, so must a summer resort be acceptable. Seal Harbor was more democratic than Newport in its inclusion of well-bred but impecunious academics and professionals, and in that regard fit the Rockefeller ethos better. Still, family members had little association with those not of the blood, so to speak. John might come across a middle-class couple while hiking a trail, and have a most congenial conversation about the bird life, yet a dinner invitation would not ensue. The barrier had less to do with class than with in-group behavior. The rich behave like any ethnic community, except it is wealth rather than national heritage that unites its members to create particular customs and rituals.

Obviously, John Jr.'s family was not living on his salary, which was less than the allowance Senior provided his sons-in-law. Senior had always tried to equalize the amounts he gave to his children. In 1904, he gave John Jr. five thousand dollars toward a European trip, the same amount he provided Alta for her annual visits to the Carlsbad ear specialist.[22] In 1909, he gave real estate on the west side of Chicago as an investment to Edith, and then balanced it with a gift of land in Manhattan to John Jr. Gradually the pattern changed, and John Jr. was the major beneficiary, from the deed to valuable properties in Cleveland, 88,400 shares of American Linseed common and 101,800 preferred, comparable amounts of Texas securities, Colorado fuel bonds, and of course, Standard Oil. Apart from the oil stock, many of these securities were not paying dividends, however, and often brought what was for him the added burden of serving on a board of directors. Still, while John Jr.'s annual income did not increase greatly as a result of these gifts, his potential income did.

Aware of the inequities, years later Senior had letters prepared to be given to his other descendants upon his death:

> The gifts which I have made to John during my lifetime and in my will have been prompted by my desire to have my fortune used, as he has used it and as I know that he will continue to use it, for the benefit of mankind. Through my earlier gifts he as-

sumed in the prime of his life the duty of administering the large sums which I knew could be safely entrusted to him.[23]

John Jr.'s response was always one of surprise and deep modesty over any benefice, which he recognized as being granted for philanthropic work. The gifts reinforced his sense of responsibility:

> I count it one of the highest privileges of my life to have been permitted to have a part with you in working out some of the great and far reaching plan for human betterment . . . and shall earnestly strive not to lower the high standard of wise and efficient giving which you have all your life been building up.[24]

Remarkable as it was that John Jr. more than met his father's wishes, he passed the philosophy successfully on to his children. This was no easy task given their occasional resentment of his strictness. No doubt Abby's softer reinforcement of her husband's credo eased its acceptance among her youngsters.

Unnoticed in all this noble public endeavor were the private consequences for Alta and Edith. John Jr. questioned Edith's style of living, her brilliantly decorated townhouse and the artful Villa Turicum, yet overlooked that he and Senior were also amassing a collection of enormous, well-outfitted homes. Alta was begging for replacement curtains while John was planning one of the largest private residences in New York City. He thought Edith extravagant for her interest in art. In a rare expression of sarcasm, he once wrote his mother, "Edith's efforts at economy are most laudable. When one thinks of them in connection with the price of some $20,000 . . . for a portrait of herself and the children it suggests the thought of this particular economy is a whim rather than the evidence of a steadfast principle."[25] Yet upon discovering a fascination in rare Chinese porcelains, he sought to borrow a million dollars from his father. "Is it unwise for me to gratify a desire for beautiful things, which will be a constant joy to my friends and to my children as they grow to appreciate them . . . ?"[26] Apparently it was all right for John Jr. to enjoy "beautiful things," but not Edith. Possibly, too, he was envious that she had the McCormick fortune at her service, where he was still dependent upon their father.

In their Berkshire home, known as Mount Hope Farm, Alta and Parmalee had found a common cause, that of scientific agriculture, but neither John Jr. nor Senior much acknowledged the value of their efforts. A practical scholar, Parmalee found his training in law with its driving analysis transferred to his interest in farming. While conservative in other matters, in agriculture he questioned common practice and used the land as a working laboratory to test his ideas. Among his more noted contributions was to prove that performance, not ancestry, should determine selection into a dairy herd. This discovery undercut the purebred proponents, and led to a method of breeding based upon a cow's butterfat content and daily production, and the bull's likelihood of passing good milking qualities to his offspring. It is odd that a father and son who had similar curiosity and success in other endeavors would be blind to Parmalee's achievements and good intentions.

When it came to more direct philanthropy, Alta seemed tight-fisted, but this is because she gave to individuals and local causes rather than to national ones. Most of their friends were faculty members at Williams College. Aware of their meagre income, she and Parmalee both tried to interest Senior in the cause of college professors, whom, they noted, earned less than most household servants. Nonetheless, they were unsuccessful in getting him to fund small scholarships or support summer lecture programs to aid the scholars' families. To do so would be to violate his main principle in giving, he reminded, to find the base causes of social and medical problems, rather than underwrite ameliorative projects.

Still, Alta was much less bountiful than Edith, who found fulfillment in organizational work and understood the power of large donations. One cannot help but wonder what impact Edith may have had on some Rockefeller enterprises had she been allowed to participate. Senior and John Jr. were not consciously sexist, in the sense of believing women were not capable or competent outside the home. Both agreed with many claims of the New Woman, that females get a full education, including college and professional school, that they participate in sports and athletic activity, that they speak their mind. These ideas are most evident in their treatment of and letters to young women in the third generation, the daughters of Edith, Alta, and John Jr. As John Jr. moved into philanthropy, he valued women experts and supported them. Although no comments exist concerning either man's views toward women's suffrage, most likely both supported the cause.

Nonetheless, their actions toward Alta and Edith were less supportive than they were of other women. What loomed was not so much the gender, but the familial tie. Both men believed patriarchy to be the proper family order, so that female offspring were ultimately to conform to the social matron role expected in wealthy circles. Alta deviated by marrying a lawyer more interested in ideas and agriculture than making money, and distancing herself from New York or Cleveland social causes. Edith acted the social matron role too exuberantly, and worse, wanted to be involved in big decisions.

Thus, while Senior and his son admired women of talent and ability, even their female kin, they followed the convention of excluding Edith or Alta from activities labeled "Rockefeller." (Even at the Chicago opera Edith had to exert her influence without a title, but there at least her authority was unquestioned.) Gaining more insight into this relationship as a result of her work with Jung, Edith stated her cause bluntly to Senior:

> We would all like to help in your philanthropies. It is beautiful and enveloping work and John is privileged in a way which Alta and I as yet have not had the opportunity of being. I am sure that as women we are serious minded and earnest and deeply interested in mankind and that we would only be too glad to shoulder our inherited responsibilities if we were permitted to.[27]

Her plea was ignored.

Worse, John Jr. and Senior defined worthy philanthropy as that in which they were involved, the Rockefeller Institute for medical research, the General Education Board, conservation causes, and so on. Since the women were not beside them, through no fault of their own, they were by definition not contributing to "the benefit of mankind." And what the daughters did support was interpreted as a poor expenditure. Edith would not be stopped. Nor would Alta, who several times broke out of her timidity and refused to contribute to certain causes John pressed upon her. When Senior did show admiration, which was rare, he referred to Alta for her "sweet kindness" to individuals.

As Laura's health declined, she sought to make larger donations to her favorite causes. In early 1909, pneumonia caused her to lose twenty pounds as well as clumps of hair. Shingles and attacks of sciatica followed. She spent months in bed, mostly in Forest Hill, and attended Thanksgiving dinner in a "rolling chair." When she finally returned to Pocantico for Christmas, Harold McCormick and John Jr. carried her up the steps.

It may seem odd that Senior was away through many of her sick spells. For example, in early 1910 he went to William Rockefeller's estate in Georgia for two months. No evidence exists that these lengthy separations were other than the natural expression of respect for one another's needs. Laura encouraged his fascination for golf, and found compensation in the continual companionship of one or another family member. When Laura was in New York, Alta and John Jr. were nearby; when she was in Forest Hill, Edith visited for weeks at a time, often bringing a child. Senior frequently invited a grandchild to join him on his winter trips South. He was particularly fond of Mathilde McCormick, and developed correspondences with the Prentice children, who were not allowed to join him during the school year.

However faithful the children and grandchildren in visiting Laura, they necessarily appeared only sporadically. Laura had taken her maternal role seriously, and did not interfere in her adult offspring's lives. Nonetheless, she felt deep loss as she shambled about the rooms of her large silent houses. She would enter a room and reminisce to a servant about John Jr. on his rocking chair, or another child at play. Once she was so rapt in these recollections that she delayed Senior's request to join him in New York. Each day the staff tried to rally her to leave for the city, and each day she put them off with more stories of her children's youth. It was clear to them that John Jr. was her favorite, and Alta second.

The staff were devoted despite her exactitude, which increased with age. Laura dismayed a visiting nurse on her first day by asking her to remove a shawl from the middle of a high stack without disturbing the others. She was not fun to work for, as Senior could be, yet her strength, forbearance, and kindness through these pain-ridden days won their admiration.

With her private accounts surpassing one million dollars, and perhaps anticipating the end, Laura sought advice from John Jr. concerning several contributions. Up to that point her gifts seemed small in comparison to her income. For example, in 1909 she gave several hundred dollars each to the Brooklyn Home for Aged Colored People and the Euclid Avenue Baptist Church. Her largest donation was $7,500 for mission work in India. In 1912, she decided to give $100,000 each to Euclid Avenue Baptist Church, the Women's Baptist Foreign Missionary Society, and the Women's Baptist Home Missionary Society, along with smaller grants to Plymouth Congregational Church in Cleveland and to homes for aged ministers. Others' intervention produced a very different result.

First, after sharing her plans with her son, he wrote to family advisor and attorney Starr Murphy, and questioned her desire to provide Euclid Avenue Baptist with a permanent endowment. There should, John Jr. argued, be a reversionary clause returning the money to her heirs in case the congregation ceased to exist one day. Also, if she were to proceed with this donation, then he wished to reduce his own personal annual gift to the church of $12,500.[28]

Then, Frederick Gates, who was still a major advisor on family philan-thropy, communicated his concerns to John Jr. Although Gates was a brilliant, creative administrator, he had strong opinions about women and the church. Consequently, his counsel was skewed by his personal bias. Although he found it "very sweet and beautiful" of Laura to make such gifts, he questioned her wisdom. For one, endowment of churches "do not promote but do retard the cause of Christ" because "our children will [not] be more zealous and self-sacrificing than we are." With regard to the WBFMS, he suggested a different recipient. "Although myself a mere man, I would about as soon see $100,000 go to this Women's Soci-ety as endowment as to see it go undesignated to our regular [American Baptist] Foreign Mission Society." The ABFMS was of course run by men. Concerning the WBHMS, he argued the organization had spent on "unnecessary luxuries, a training society in Chicago which personally I never have approved." Once again, he recommended that Laura's gift go to the national ABHMS because he was against organizations "built up exclusively on sex." His postscript, which was the real point of the letter, was to ask why Laura would not just turn her money over to the recently formed Rockefeller Foundation.

A year later the matter remained unresolved. Gates had convinced Laura to give her money toward particular projects of the ABFMS, and had a staff member prepare a detailed report of those she should assist. Out of six mission hospitals and schools examined, one passed Gates's test. Laura ended up giving $1,500 toward hospital equipment for a dis-pensary in the Philippines. What happened to her other plans for distri-bution is unrecorded, apart from 1914, where notes show she gave modest gifts for projects sponsored by the national Baptist groups, not the Women's Baptist organizations.

Though Laura's son and his advisors had taken over the paddles of her canoe here, she had not lost her early passion for women's rights. Of a day in May 1913 she wrote, "Suffrage Parade. 40,000 in line including 3,000 men. It was a wonderful and suggestive sight." One suspects she would have donned the white dress to join the marchers were she not so feeble. One wonders if there lurked a disappointment she had not been more outspoken with her own son about woman's independence.

10

The Call of the Carpenter

"Thou has given me the necks of mine enemies; that I might destroy them that hate me."

Psalms 18: 40

*A*bby Rockefeller understood that her husband required a noble substitute to escape the yoke of business. "I came out of college something of an idealist and I was immediately thrust into the tough give-and-take of the business world," recalled John Jr. "I wasn't ready for it."[1] Gradually he learned of Standard Oil practices that sickened him, such as executive John Archibold's backdoor distribution of campaign funds to key political leaders like Mark Hanna. By 1910 he had extricated himself from most business activity. He had resigned from virtually all his company directorships, and spent his days attending to the family philanthropies.

He may have been driven as much by the need to prove the Rockefellers true to Christian principles as to escape from the competitive life of commerce. The social gospel movement that had put muscles and a manlier beard on portrayals of Jesus also made him a righteous activist. As one theologian explained, "His ideal is the civil ideal. Its goal is heaven descending from God out of heaven. Therefore the Carpenter-Christ is the fit leader of the multitudes."[2] Thus, socially responsible men should meet with others in Bible study groups and prayer luncheons, and be unashamed to announce to other businessmen their faith. Men must give up the program of the past, industrial expansion, in favor of "a vaster program than our fathers ever dreamed, because our vision of what constitutes a religious life is a greater vision than our fathers ever had."[3]

For many men of John Jr.'s generation, the social gospel was a way of reacting to the deleterious consequences of their fathers' material expansion. Christ the Carpenter allowed them to pursue careers in reform politics and social welfare, to volunteer for the innumerable progressive organizations, to introduce new values into old professions. However, this valuation of human needs over economic ones was traditionally Christian woman's sphere, so men like John Jr. needed assurance that they were no less masculine for choosing this alternate path. The concept of Christ the Carpenter allowed men to substitute individualism and competition with cooperation and altruism, and still feel manly, not effeminate. Unusual for John Jr. was that his father had already undergone a similar transformation at midlife in the 1890s, when the first social gospel writings became popular. So in choosing this direction, he was not like peers who rebelled against their fathers' materialistic beliefs.

While he shared with Senior a belief in giving out of Christian conscience, John Jr. served also out of fervent belief in Progressive reform. The roots of his education at Brown University came to fruition. During his years there, the school was dominated by economists and social scientists who questioned free-market capitalism and Social Darwinism, who rejected simply "holding trust in God and the so-called natural laws of growth."[4] Though not antibusiness, these instructors held that because combines and trusts provided efficiencies, society should demand in return a wide distribution of their benefits. Citizens should monitor business, and urge government to create sensible regulations and controls, including price- or profit-fixing, when needed. Reading such noted studies as Charles Booth's report on poverty in London's East End, John Jr. became further familiarized with the human suffering caused by inequality. During his senior year, he took a course centering upon Karl Marx's *Das Kapital.* Most important was his exposure to Practical Ethics, where the lecturer warned students about the alarming increases in measures of social disorder, and concluded the problems had not moral roots, but social and economic ones. "Where are the young men and women of means and leisure who will duly study the social problems of our time and help to their solution?" intoned the professor.[5]

John Jr. was moved by the call of civic service and reform, but had little opportunity to reveal his sincere commitment to the public weal until 1910. The circumstance was created by corrupt Tammany Hall politicians who hoped to quell the latest outcry against prostitution. Urban reformers were using the issue of "white slavery" as a rallying point in their attempts to take over New York's city hall. In selecting John Jr. to be foreman of a special grand jury on the problem, Tammany politicians thought they were coopting an ineffectual member of the monied class. What they did not discern were his bulldog persistence and perfectionism. What they expected to be a superficial survey turned into a richly documented description of the problem which brought with it indictments against fifty-four individuals. The judge who had appointed John Jr. at first refused to accept the presentment, and eventually did so only as a result of public outcry. Although the mayor did nothing to implement the findings and most of the indictments resulted in acquittals, John Jr. became a local hero among average citizens for his attack on civic corruption.

Displeased with the lack of official response, John Jr. joined with Jewish philanthropists Jacob Schiff and Paul Warburg to sponsor additional research on prostitution. (Working with Jews was itself unusual for a member of the Protestant elite, and further sign of his growing liberalism.) One study explained why young Jewish immigrants fell prey to the temptations of pimps, while another examined new methods of rehabilitating prostitutes. This informal committee led John Jr. in 1913 to incorporate the Bureau of Social Hygiene, the first organization to make serious studies of narcotics traffic, venereal disease, penology, and police systems, as well as prostitution. John Jr. underwrote the program and administered it in its early days. Its first project was Abraham Flexner's landmark analysis of *Prostitution in Europe.* He then sponsored population studies, this at a time when birth control proponents were being jailed. (Laura may have had an influence here, for she donated money to the YWCA to fund classes in sex education for college women.)

Despite the well-deserved praise John Jr. earned in local New York papers, for the most part the name "Rockefeller" continued to draw national censure and criticism. On May 15, 1911, critics of Standard Oil celebrated the culmination of years of lawsuits involving the great trust, for the Supreme Court decided that the oil behemoth had violated the first two sections of the Sherman Antitrust Act and must divest itself of its subsidiaries within six months. Rather than be injured by the judgment, the stockholders became richer, for they received a proportionate share in each of the thirty-four companies that resulted. Since demand for gasoline was increasing, the value of these separate firms rapidly appreciated. Essentially, by holding onto their shares for a brief period of time, the investors doubled their money. Fortunately for American medical and social researchers, this meant Senior had twice as much money to give away.

The medical project that would have the greatest immediate effect on both the sick and the healthy was already underway. Following the Civil War, the stereotype of "poor Southern white trash" formed through jokes and songs about the seeming laziness of this group. In 1902, the wits and editorial cartoonists had a new slant to their stories, "Germ of Laziness Found." At a medical convention that year Dr. Charles Stiles proposed that uncinariasis, or hookworm, was the cause of the lethargy. "These fellows are suffering so terribly from uncinariasis that they wait for the apples to fall off their trees, and then ask somebody to pass the fruit along," quipped one editorial.[6] The matter was much more serious, for hookworm disease was widespread in rural regions, often misdiagnosed as chronic anemia and attributed to dirt-eating. Sufferers were stunted, with joints swollen, stomachs protruding, frame emaciated, skin greenish-yellow, eyes deadened. So widespread was the condition that the Southern economy was affected, and a class of people there unfairly labelled as useless.

For the next few years Stiles journeyed throughout the region and gathered proof of his hypothesis. Nonetheless, he was unable to move government officials to tackle the problem. In 1908, satirists mocked his savior: "Kid Rockefeller versus Battling Hookworm . . . winner take all . . . Rockefeller's going after him blood raw." Some in the South responded with malice upon hearing that Rockefeller money was going to back Stiles, "another dam Yankee bent upon holding the South up to ridicule." In a gracious rebuttal, Senior explained how he spent part of each year in the South and admired its warm-hearted people. The Rockefeller Sanitary Commission for the Eradication of Hookworm Disease sent carefully selected advisors to infected counties to test the residents and treat the afflicted. The cure was rapid, resulting in seemingly overnight changes in entire school populations and communities. By 1914, 900,000 people had been examined, with almost forty percent showing infection. By 1927, seven million people would be treated, and the disease was essentially eradicated in the South.

While Senior seldom appeared now in editorials as the epitome of greed, in 1914 an oversight resulted in John Jr. bearing the direct brunt of revived anti-Rockefeller feelings. Somehow in resigning from various boards of directors, he had overlooked the Colorado Fuel and Iron Company (CFI). In 1902, Senior had bought forty percent of the stock, but the company proved a poor performer. In 1907, to improve the management, he installed as chairman Frederick Gates's uncle, L. M. Bowers, who had worked well for Senior in the past running the Great Lakes iron ore shipping fleet. Unfortunately, Bowers and his new colleagues were virulently antilabor and paternalistic in the extreme. Their immigrant mine workers lived in company towns, and were paid wages in company scrip that might not cover the inflated prices in the company store. In September

1913 labor organizers spurred nine thousand workers to strike for wage increases, an eight-hour day, safety enforcement, the right to live where they pleased, and other causes. Violence escalated, provoking the governor of Colorado to call out the national guard. Killings occurred on both sides.

Concerned about this and similar labor-managment conflicts, a committee of the U.S. House of Representatives called on John Jr. to visit Colorado on a fact-finding mission and to find a solution. Trusting the competence of CFI's management, he sidestepped appearing. Bowers claimed that ninety percent of the workers were against the union, and John Jr. believed him. (As a child, he was familiar with anarchist labor threats against his father, and once noted in his diary how a march of mill strikers were "a wicked looking lot."[7]) Raised by a Hamiltonian father who distrusted the masses, Abby, too, had little sympathy for union organizing. Perhaps because both were so sure of their convictions, John Jr. neglected his usual approach to decisions: consulting with experts and asking for others' views. How could he discredit men he had known for years, men with good records in their previous posts? As if his recalcitrance were not enough, he gave inflammatory testimony to the committee that he would regret the rest of his life. Asked why he was willing to let the deaths occur rather than go visit CFI, he replied that the only resolution was unionization, which he refused to allow. "And you will do that if it costs all your property and kills all your employees," inquired a legislator. "It [the open shop] is a great principle," John Jr. heartlessly replied.[8]

Soon after, on April 20, 1914, during an all-day battle, the Colorado National Guard burned a miners' encampment to the ground. Most horrific was the discovery that two women and eleven children seeking refuge in a cellar were suffocated when the tent above it was set afire.

The public reaction to the "Ludlow Massacre" sent volleys of pickets, death threats, and charges of murder in the direction of John Jr. Socialist Upton Sinclair led black arm-banded pickets to 26 Broadway and Pocantico. When a bomb exploded in a New York tenement, killing four and injuring seven, police concluded it was being constructed to plant at 10 West Fifty-fourth Street. These threats on his life and family stunned John Jr. into realizing his irresponsibility, his failure as a CFI board member to maintain independence from management. He turned to Ivy Lee, the "father of public relations," a man who set high standards of honesty in dealing with the press. "Tell the truth," he advised John Jr., who first had to learn what the truth was. Consequently, Lee visited Colorado and reported back that indeed Bowers had been misrepresenting the situation.

Even after replacing Bowers, however, John Jr. could not get CFI management to settle grievances. The strike ended that December only because the miners' relief funds were exhausted.

Abby and John Jr. were further fortunate in the recent arrival of William Lyon MacKenzie King to the recently formed Rockefeller Foundation. A noted Canadian labor expert, King spent several months educating the couple during discussions over dinner, on walks in Pocantico, and during country drives. His experience convinced both to take a more liberal perspective on employee-management relations. Abby recognized her husband's excitement with these new ideas, and encouraged him to leave more of the details of running their households to her. In doing so, she explained, he could "throw the full force of your thought and time into the big, vital questions that come before you."[9] She admired King's acumen, and his recommendation that the couple be less secretive and more open in their activities. She and her husband suddenly understood they had some responsibility for the labor conditions at the corporations that provided their income.

King also introduced the couple to labor leaders, including Mary Harris "Mother" Jones, the tough, unrelenting saint of the movement. At her request, John Jr. promised to visit the mining camps. Abby wanted to go, but on June 12, 1915 had given birth to her last child, David.

Thus, in the fall of 1915, dressed in bib overalls and miner's hats, John Jr. and his labor advisor, MacKenzie King, toured the coal mines, visited the homes of miners, and even attended a dance. Hired to create a plan for resolving the miners' grievances, King composed a document both offering numerous concessions to workers and building labor representation into future arbitration. In the process, he convinced John Jr. to soften his antipathy towards unions, if not fully support them. As a result, on his return to Congress, John Jr. reported that he now saw it "proper . . . for labor to associate itself into organized groups for the advancement of its legitimate interests, as for capital to combine for the same effect."[10]

Abby was able to see the mining area on a later visit with her husband in 1918, to attend a memorial service recalling the victims of the Ludlow Massacre. Contrary to CFI warnings of likely violence, the miners welcomed the couple. Abby met with the women, and worked on her knitting while she asked about their concerns, and shared her own activities in the Red Cross. She gave spontaneous parties for the children and danced with the men. With obvious pride, her husband wrote Senior how much good Abby's presence was for its influence on the CFI officials, employees, and families. "The masses" reconceived in their minds as individuals deserving respect.

John Jr.'s shift in attitude inspired others in American corporate leadership to reconsider their views. By the 1920s, editors were praising his progressive leadership in labor-management relations, and cartoons depicted him as a rich man on the workers' side. While labor leaders may have preferred a more liberal stance on John Jr.'s part, he gave a convenient "respectable" voice for them at a time when the remnants of the radical Wobblies and anarchists were being persecuted. For if a *Rockefeller* acknowledged the needs of workers, then their time was ripe!

When the guns of August 1914 burst forth in Europe, few could have imagined the slaughter to follow. Most Americans, like the belligerents, believed that the war would be brief. And most held tightly to the famous principle Washington stated in his farewell address over a century earlier, that the country should keep out of other nations' entanglements. President Woodrow Wilson urged citizens, many of whom included immigrants from the warring factions, to be impartial in thought and action. The matter seemed the predictable folly of a Europe still struggling with ancient hatreds and aristocratic dynasties. Even after American bodies washed up on British shores following the U-boat sinking of the *Lusitania* in May 1915, the United States resisted involvement in the European bloodbath. "I didn't raise my boy to be a soldier," went the popular song. It took the revelation of the Zimmerman telegram, a secret proposal for Mexico to ally with Germany, before the antiwar fervor subsided and the country declared war in April 1917.

During the early phase of battle, the most immediate impact on well-to-do Americans was the restriction of their annual travel overseas. Harold and Fowler were about to embark on an ocean crossing to join Edith and the girls, but the sailing was cancelled. A flurry of anxious notes passed among Nettie, Senior, Harold, and John Jr. concerning the fate of the three family members in Zurich and how to bring them home.

The commotion did not move Edith, who thrived in the emergency, and refused to leave. Her first letter bounced excitedly with news of the sudden change in their lives. Her chauffeur had joined a French regiment, while the hotel waiters had gone over to Germany and Austria. With servants off to fight, guests ate together in the large table d'hote room. No gasoline was available for cars, and the trains were reserved for troop movements. She explained that the hotel had correctly read the omens and stocked more than six months' food and supplies. Her only problem was that banks were refusing letters of credit. Through a great deal of maneuvering, for he had to avoid alerting the mail censors in France, Harold arranged for an International Harvester employee in Paris to smuggle gold to Edith.

By early October, Harold had worked his way into Switzerland, and reported how well Edith was doing. "She studies astronomy, biology and history, and music. She does not go to see Dr. Jung any more. Physically I think she is fine." He also hinted at the instability that would increase with Muriel's maturity. "[A]lthough she finds it hard to control herself she is gaining fast."[11] Mathilde, who had been sent to boarding school in the mountains to build up her health, was also thriving. Assured that his family was well, Harold left Zurich to deal with the complications the war had brought upon the farm machinery business.

With European fields ravaged by craters and fire, Alta and Parmalee were gratified that their farming experiments increased in public significance. Since becoming involved in agriculture with her husband, Alta grew more secure and less self-preoccupied. Her letters to Senior now included discussions of potato crops, needy college professors, and her anger that a family employee was spreading unkind stories about Aunt Lute. She was satisfied that her vision of service stay within the boundaries of Williamstown, the community she had adopted. She praised her husband for being such a "companion and comrade" to his children (a comment they might have disputed had they read it). As for her marriage, "Parmalee is so beautiful in his thoughts about me. . . . He makes life one glad song."[12]

Parmalee was a rationalist whose ideas may have undone Alta's early piety. Her adult letters were free of religious reference, and suggest that she accepted the basic ethics and morality of Christianity more than the creed. Generosity could be meaningful without a Scriptural base.

The year before the war, Senior had spent the summer in Forest Hill with Laura, taking her out on rides, returning from church to tell her of the service. He foresaw that she was never going to return to full health, and adjusted his schedule accordingly. Given her high protein diet, she endured chronic bowel problems, which increased in severity as the months passed. In addition, she suffered pernicious anemia and congestive heart failure. Then Lute also fell ill, just as all were about to return to New York for the winter. Consequently, the three stayed in Cleveland longer than anticipated.

Senior's protracted stay at Forest Hill caught the notice of the Cuya-hoga County tax office. Claiming that for the year 1913 Senior had been a resident of Ohio, not New York, the tax officials brought suit to collect from him. Senior saw this as an unforgivable insult to someone who had given so much to Cleveland over the years, and whose stay had been for reasons of compassion. The courts eventually decided unreservedly in Se-nior's favor, impelling Laura to telegram her son, "It was a bugle note that was struck for principle yesterday before our country."[13] Despite his vic-tory, Senior never forgave the Ohio bureaucrats, and spent the next sum-mer in Pocantico. He was through with Cleveland.

The children and grandchildren, minus the McCormicks, gathered on September 8, 1914 for a joint celebration of Laura's seventy-fifth birth-day and her golden wedding anniversary. Senior had a brass band play the Mendelssohn wedding march. That winter he kept his absences brief, and took his meals by his frail wife's bedside. "He was the most affectionate and thoughtful man in illness and sorrow," observed John Jr. "No woman could have been more tender."[14]

John Jr. fretted however that his mother was not receiving the best of care under homeopath Dr. Biggar. In recent years his own friends in-cluded the most eminent medical doctors of the day, such as Simon Flexner, men who were either involved in or counselled him on Rocke-feller Institute activities. Consequently, he was familiar with the latest ad-vances in medical diagnosis and treatment, and broke with his parents' partiality to homeopathy. Recently he had an X-ray picture taken of his hand as a demonstration of the procedure, and used it to persuade his parents and Dr. Biggar to make a "radiograph" of Laura's abdomen. He thought this would offer insight as to whether a tumor was the basis for Laura's enlarged liver. To build his case, he brought Alta into the matter because she was so successful in getting her way with their father.

As it happened, John Jr. eventually capitulated, and no X ray was made. He should have expected this outcome. Some years earlier Frederick Gates had spoken out strongly against Dr. Biggar, and was put in his place. Laura and Senior had grown up in an era when medical doctors were often ill-trained and ill-equipped, when homeopathy with its holis-tic approach to cure was often the sensible choice. It had worked for them so far, taking them beyond the average lifespan of the day, and they would not be persuaded that some fancy machine could make a differ-ence. Moreover, invalidism offered Laura a respected role, that of the silent Christian sufferer, a state she accepted with dignity. In retrospect, the couple's obstinacy was perhaps beneficial, for medical treatment would have culminated in surgery and lengthy hospital stays. Instead,

Laura remained at home in familiar surroundings, her discomfort eased by familiar techniques.

Although still bedridden, by early 1915 Laura gained in strength and encouraged Senior to take his annual trip to Florida. Abby and John Jr. joined him. Messages informed them that although Laura had developed a throat infection and some fluid buildup in her lungs, she was in high spirits. She spent her days writing letters and enjoying the company of Harold McCormick, who told her bright, happy stories about Edith and the children. On March 11, 1915 Laura telegrammed her son:

> Harold dines with Alta tonight. . . . Dr. Allen brought some specialist yesterday . . . and reports good improvement all along the line, though it must be slow. Beautiful letter [weather?] for outing, which does me much good. Glad that you and Abby enjoy the place and people. Send both much love.

The next telegram told of her sudden relapse. She had suffered nausea during the night and awoke still unable to eat. Despite the use of oxygen and strychnine, she slipped away, in the words of her nurse, "with a look of the most perfect peace and comfort and happiness lighting her face."[15]

The funeral was a brief service in Kykuit, with only family, servants, and a few friends present. William Rockefeller was himself ailing and unable to attend, but Percy and Emma came with their spouses. Music predominated—a Bach air, Laura's favorite hymns, and a Simonetti aria. Afterwards, the family ordered that the body be allowed to remain in bed until its removal the next day, because they could not bear to see it go. It seemed as if his mother were just sleeping, John Jr. explained, and she should not be disturbed.

Laura was laid temporarily to rest in Sleepy Hollow cemetery in a friend's mausoleum. Four months later, the governor of Ohio fired the tax collectors who had sued Senior. That accomplished, he ordered a horse-drawn hearse to take Laura's orchid-laden bier to the train station. No one accompanied the remains on the journey to Cleveland and Lakeview Cemetery. There, under a sinking sun, with no onlookers present, workmen placed her coffin in a grave at the foot of a huge monolith inscribed simply "Rockefeller." Thus Laura Spelman Rockefeller finished her life's journey in her favorite city, and lay next to the other important woman in her husband's life, his mother Eliza.

Perhaps the best encomium was Edith's, written to her father upon hearing of her mother's death:

She was always like the Spartan mothers. Everything which came to her, she accepted, and she bore her frailty of body with uncomplaining patience. . . . She had faith and trust in those she loved and she never questioned or criticized. She lived right up to her Light—unquestionably and unflinchingly. I know mother's spirit is going on in a beautiful development . . . [16]

Edith related Laura's temperament to the wisdom urged by a Chinese philosopher, to be like water flowing over and around obstacles.

A month later, John Jr. was consoling Abby, whose father died suddenly of a cerebral stroke. They buried Senator Aldrich in the family plot at Swan's Point Cemetery in Providence. In her condolence letter to Abby, Edith observed, "I fancy by nature you are so adaptable. This is a wonderful thing—it simplifies so much." [17] It is good that she was so resilient, for the past months with the Ludlow crisis, the death of her mother-in-law, and that of her father, all during a pregnancy at age forty, required exceptional character to survive unscathed. She did.

For the train trip northward from Florida for his wife's funeral, Senior had used his influence to see that his railcar went directly through train stations without stopping. Afterwards, John Jr. asked for a list of names of all the agents who cooperated, and wrote each an individual note in which the content was unique, not a template thank you. He also sent similarly personal letters to those who helped with the service. This labor, which must have taken him many hours, is indicative of his considerate treatment of strangers. No social secretary for him, nor a pat repetition of a couple of lines.

For the next few years he attended to the complications of his mother's estate. As executor with Senior and Alta, who apparently approved all his decisions, he pressed for a distribution of Laura's legacy in a pattern that reflected his own biases. His determination in this matter suggests some unconscious working out of his conflicted feelings toward his mother. He had adored her, had held her in awe for her sincere piety and good works, and up to his marriage had been emotionally dependent upon her. But she was also the source of his feelings of inadequacy and over-serious nature. More realistic, Abby assured him that one could lead a life of goodness despite imperfection, and rejoice in pleasures as much as opportunities to serve.

Laura's estate was worth $1.3 million. She assigned $100,000 to each child, the same to Margaret Strong, and $50,000 to her sister Lute. The remainder was to go to charity. She left a list that included the Euclid Avenue Baptist Church, Spelman College, the Bureau of Social Hygiene, several Baptist homes, and the major Baptist women's missionary organizations. Unfortunately, her list was only suggestive, and she gave no proportions concerning the distribution of donations. John Jr.'s advisors added that state law forbade more than half her estate going to charity, so the executors had to decide what to do with the surplus. It is curious that a family with access to the best lawyers could have allowed so vague and problematic a will to be composed in the first place.

By now, John Jr. adopted Frederick Gates's suspiciousness concerning charity recipients. He sought to have money given to Spelman College through the GEB, which was Rockefeller-influenced, rather than directly to the school trustees. The lawyers advised him this would not be wise, so Spelman trustees received a quarter of a million dollars. He also wanted to support a proposed treatment center for drug addicts on Riker's Island, something not mentioned at all in Laura's will, and again was advised to withdraw the idea. Fortunately, the aging Gates was no longer a participant in these discussions, so the two women-run Baptist mission organizations received large grants outright. In time, the overseas mission funds strengthened the facilities at women's colleges in India, China, and Japan, as well as provided the main building for the Women's Medical College at Vellore, India. Ultimately, then, Laura's preferences prevailed.

Of her surplus estate, over $340,000, John Jr. and Senior took control and gave the money to the Rockefeller Foundation. This body had a sweeping charge, "To promote the well-being of mankind throughout the world." Its initial programs dealt with international health and the development of medical schools in China, both interests of Senior and John Jr. As a result of his insights following the Ludlow Massacre, John Jr. initiated as well an industrial relations program to study labor issues. To his astonishment, the press understandably interpreted this activity as his use of the philanthropy to get him out of a personal problem. To disprove such conclusions, he withdrew this program and reorganized the foundation to ensure the family would not influence its topics of study. Then he revamped the board of directors to bring on more people lacking affiliation to either the family or Standard Oil. Here John Jr.'s natural modesty served well, for he insisted that others treat his vote as no more influential than others, and was a harmonious member whenever outvoted. As a result, the Rockefeller Foundation expanded its scope, and by the 1920s was poised for greatness.

John Jr. also directed a new foundation set up by his father in 1918, the Laura Spelman Rockefeller Memorial. Senior gave an initial $84 million endowment devoted towards issues involving women and children. At first the memorial was undistinguished, in that it dispensed small charitable donations to programs primarily in New York City. In the early 1920s, however, John Jr. appointed a strong director and gave him the mission to move boldly in supporting social science research. Up to then, social scientists had relied primarily on anecdotal evidence and unsystematic methods lacking in much rigor. As a result of the memorial's forward thrust, the social sciences at key universities enjoyed a renaissance that resulted in major advances in both research techniques and the systematic understanding of society. At the University of Chicago, for example, the sociology department oversaw a series of landmark studies that are still read today for their insights and research innovations. Without the Rockefeller commitment to uncovering root causes, the social sciences may not have advanced so rapidly.

Another way in which John Jr. honored his mother's memory was his ongoing involvement with the Bureau of Social Hygiene. This was really his own private charity that relied upon his annual contributions for operating expenses. The bureau continued research and education in the areas of criminology and sexuality. Among its most significant contributions during this time was supporting the work of Katherine Davis, whose study of *Factors in the Sex Lives of Twenty-two Hundred Women* was to loosen taboos about discussing female sexuality.

During the war, Harold, now forty-four, found new outlets for his prodigious energy. In 1916 he resigned as treasurer of International Harvester. Senior advised against this, but Harold stood firm that his first commitment was to Edith. So he quit the company and joined his family in Zurich, where he also reactivated his analysis with Carl Jung. Eighteen-year-old Fowler decided to quit school for a year, also went into analysis with Jung, and later joined the American Ambulance Service in France. When the United States finally entered the war, Harold worked in a civilian post for the Army, running procurement from Switzerland. What eventually consumed him, however, was a plan for peace, *Via Pacis*, which he prepared with Edith's assistance. Foreseeing that peace could not last without some forethought about the eventual treaty, he laid out a philosophy for reuniting the belligerants. He published the document at his own expense and met with leaders of various countries to press his proposal, but met no success. In the States, the public confused his plan for postwar peace with the unpopular beliefs of the pacifists, who protested American participation in the war. Various misrepresentations of

Harold's plan prevented any grass roots movement necessary to see it through.

Now a lay analyst, Edith met patients for six hours a day, and continued her various studies. She felt great admiration for the Swiss people, who accepted the shortages of coal, flour, sugar, gas and other essentials with equanimity. As a result of her unbounded generosity toward local residents, the Swiss government rewarded her by exempting her car from the severe gas rationing so she and her staff could continue their good works. (Even this situation was misinterpreted by an American journalist who claimed she was taking advantage of her name. Not knowing the full story, Senior chided her apparent thoughtlessness.)

Edith helped others as well, though few of the incidents were made public. When the fifty-nine American sailors of the *Yarrowdale* were released from a prisoner-of-war camp by the Germans, Edith volunteered to take over the care and outfitting of the men in Switzerland. Had she not done so, an emergency fund to help repatriating refugees would have been depleted. Before the men returned to the States, Edith held a tea and musicale for them at the elegant Hotel Baur au Lac, and quickly put them at ease in the imposing surroundings. As a departing gift, she presented them with spending money for the journey home.

More fascinating was her involvement in a cause célèbre. In 1917, the Swiss were distressed to learn that one of their soldiers had been disloyal and allowed a prisoner to escape. The internee was a French flying ace, who, after crashing on Swiss soil, was confined in a military barracks in the evenings in keeping with the country's stated neutrality. One night the Frenchman's guard walked off, allowing the flyer to escape "in a speedy motor car" that took him to Lake Leman, where "the fastest motor boat" delivered him to Evian in France. Years later, it was revealed that the flyer had attended a tea at Edith's earlier that day, and that she had bribed the guard and arranged the escape.[18]

Many details of Edith's life during these years remain sketchy. Certainly her direct financial support bought more time for the reflection Carl Jung needed during his period of transformation. Jung may have not advanced so far in his theorizing, let alone in his personal psychic integration, without it. She also underwrote translations of his writing into English, French, and Russian, which ensured his ideas would be read by those identifying psychoanalysis with Freud, and offer a counter theory to the Viennese eminence.[19]

More is known of a lasting contribution that proved significant for the furthering of Jungian thought. In 1915, Edith recognized that Jung's patients and analyst-trainees would benefit from a place to meet together and share their experiences and knowledge. At her instigation, the Psychological Club took form. Edith's first move was unwise. She bought a luxurious site in the center of the city, where its services, such as its restaurant, were too costly for the typical potential member. Aware of her error, she purchased a more modest house in the Gemeindestrasse, a quieter part of town. The first floor provided a large room for lectures, smaller rooms for library and meeting halls, while the upper floors were rented out as temporary apartments to visiting guests. Edith gave the club 360,000 francs in a stock fund, the income from which was to cover operating expenses. When it failed to do so, she made up the annual deficit.

The Psychological Club opened on February 26, 1916. Its officers included Jung's wife Emma as president, Edith as a member of the board of directors, and Toni Wolff on the lecture committee. These women played important roles in the early years, in seeing to the educational functions of the club. (Emma was much more than a *hausfrau*. Her letters manifest a perceptive mind well-versed in her husband's views. When Harold was uncertain about his understanding of the term "unconscious," he sought her advice, and wrote a long postscript to a letter correcting his earlier statements as a result.) When he was in Zurich, Harold contributed to the club both financially and as an advisor. He was best known, though, as head of the entertainment committee, through which he organized fanciful parties, pool or Ping-Pong tournaments, and other games.

As a consequence of the club's many functions, Jungians—once isolated from one another—strengthened their commitment and developed lifelong professional relationships among themselves. Since Freud now controlled the major psychiatric association, the Psychological Club served as the ground where Jungian ideas were nurtured and eventually dispersed to all parts of the world.

The club even thrived through a temporary absence of its central figure. During 1917, several members quit in protest of Jung's purported intimacies with his female clients. At one heated meeting, Hans Trub, the president that year, criticized Jung for being authoritarian and unwilling to answer questions. In ironic proof of the charge, Jung walked out and did not return for several years. Emma and Toni felt compelled to leave as well, yet the club did not decline.

Toni Wolff in particular grew tormented as the years passed and she submitted to her lover's authority. Harold certainly knew of his mentor's strange intimate arrangements, for he felt honored when Jung invited him to join the threesome on a weeklong hiking holiday. Harold was similarly enthralled by this *"great man,* and a most genuine one, and spiritual."[20] Of course, he never said anything to Senior of Jung's darker side, which so efficiently rationalized his adultery and his abasement of both wife and mistress.

Jung's genius for understanding the human psyche faltered when it came to his theory of the feminine, for his culture, not his creativity shaped his conclusions. Just exactly how his views influenced Harold and Edith's relationship is not known. Part of Harold's problem was sexual inadequacy, which led to his seeking other women for remedy. His impotence with Edith may have been guilt-based, and he appeared to embark on adultery as a release during her long illnesses. How could he not look at Jung's situation as a validation of his own actions?

Edith's only reference to sexuality occurred years later. Observing the fashion of the day for girls to marry older men, she advised, obviously from personal experience, "None of them marry for the manhood—for the elder men have *not* got it as the young man of twenty."[21] By "elder" she was referring to men Harold's age. Edith was not a sensualist. She related to art and music more through her intellect than through her feelings. Nonetheless, she needed Harold's physical love as well as his effusive verbal proclamations. More often than not he was absent, and when around he was more attentive to her mind than her body.

While Jung's notion of femininity may have misled Harold, his work with the couple did increase their understanding of one another. In his most revealing account of the analysis to Senior, Harold applied concepts Jung would not publish until several years later, in his study of "psychological types."[22] According to Jung, Edith was an Introvert or Stoic type, who lives "within himself; he is apt to deny the existence of all not possessed in his mind." Consequently, this type drew a clear line between self and the world. Harold was an Extrovert or Sympathetic type, who "feels, does, acts, lives in and is a part of the world; he gives out constantly; he runs dry." Since neither type is good in the extreme, analysis suggests a path to balance. Edith must develop her *feeling*, while Harold his *thinking*. Each should promote those aspects of the unconscious that support these less-familiar modes.

To clarify, Harold referred to the example of a handshake. Edith would give a cursory shake, which could disguise her strong affection for the recipient, while Harold might even slap the person on the back as well, while having no thoughts associated with his display of attraction. "Now Edith observing me would say to herself, 'my what a tom-boy Harold is, how rough,' and I would say of Edith in a similar way, 'Lord, how cold Edith is—look at her, she doesn't care a bit.'" However, these "mental comments would be repressions," not expressed to one another. Analysis was teaching them to bring their reflections to the surface and share them. "So this work has naturally been of great help to Edith and me in understanding the other."

Edith's descriptions of therapy were brief and vague. She wrote of "Destiny," "the Path," the "beautiful work." She grew more self-assured, and questioned Senior in a way Alta and John Jr. never would. She dismissed her father's dark Christianity with its rejection of too much comfort, its repression of impulse. "To be a free spirit in the 'beautiful hereafter' is as you say the goal of every soul, and may not this freedom begin in this wonderful world—our heavenly home? An independent soul living for the right and the true as seen in the light of God cannot be chained."[23] She challenged his aloofness. Thanking him for a gift—as usual, of money—she implied he was an introvert who needed more balance in his way of acting. "There is warmth and love in your heart when one can get through all the outside barriers which you have thrown up to protect yourself—your own self—from the world. This warmth and love draws me, for is it not living?"[24]

She continued to seek his trust in her with regard to philanthropy. She was living on a sixth or a seventh of her allowance, she explained, and all the rest went to her causes. "As a woman of forty-three I should like to have more money to help with. . . . I am worthy of more confidence on your part."[25] His form of saying "no" to her and Alta was to say nothing, to ignore the request. Edith continued to press him, and asked for stocks she could use for her many charities. "Dear Father, I sometimes wish that you could forget that I am a woman, so that you might give to me some of the advantages which John has in administering."[26] Harold supported her, and reminded Senior that Edith was the child most resembling him in temperament and organizational acumen.

Senior eventually responded directly, by noting that he had given her and Harold over two million dollars over the years. Furthermore, he regretted that her being away so much meant he could "have not been more familiar with your benevolences as I have been with John and Alta in respect to their contributions to good causes. This contact and the more intimate knowledge of all that they are doing in this regard has afforded me much pleasure."[27] This comparison to her siblings was disingenuous, for Senior knew well about Edith's activities. He knew from Harold, Nettie, Edith herself, news clippings provided by the main office at Standard Oil, and Edith's bankers. Nevertheless she sent him a more detailed account of her annual commitments. Senior's counter was to raise her allowance to five thousand monthly, which was not the outcome she wished: a large fund whose income she could control. Meanwhile, he was transferring chunks of his fortune to John with regularity.

Clearly hurt by his continued lack of support in her philanthropic interests, she poignantly noted, "I wish some times that you would let me get nearer to you—your real self, so that your heart would feel the warmth of a simple soul. Perhaps you will let me some day."[28] Edith had healed, had found that balance to her introversion, and in doing so faced the bittersweet reality that her beloved father was not likely to change correspondingly. Now that she was better able to express love, a key recipient of her affections rejected them.

Senior's motives in excluding Edith will never be known. Some may sense indirect hostility, a disguised disapproval for any of a number of her nonconforming attitudes and actions. Perhaps he was only following convention of the day in excluding women from positions of control over large resources. (Even now many women from wealthy families inherit less, have smaller trusts, and watch their assets be controlled by male relatives and financial advisors.) He had been cautious even in coming to trust his only son, who was middle-aged before Senior really gave him control over part of the fortune. Thanks to her analysis with Jung, Edith understood: Senior kept a scrim before himself that all the weight of his letters, account books, and interviews cannot raise for history.

Senior found Alta easier to cherish, which is not to say she may not have shared Edith's resentment toward him at times. She was too timid to ever confront her father the way Edith did, and she did not have Edith's sophisticated insights about family dynamics and personalities. Both her father and her husband had kept her from developing much autonomy or independence. Though she could be hard on her children, she would argue it was only because she was speaking for Parmalee. Being subservient, she used passive aggression to express anger. Why else would she ask her father repeatedly for art works and furnishings from his New York house, and even, in false anticipation of its being sold, the *woodwork?* She was more successful than Edith in getting money from her father because she pleaded ignorance, not competence. "Of course I know nothing about the stock market" was a typical refrain. In truth, she did not, and showed no interest in learning. Her wheedling paid off, but at some cost to her self-esteem.

While Alta perpetuated her dependence on her father, he used John Jr. as his intermediary regarding her requests. Thus, in 1912, when she asked for an increase in Parmalee's allowance, Senior asked John Jr. to provide a detailed account of his own family's 1911 expenses as a base line to compare with Alta and Parmalee's expenses.[29] The bulk of John Jr.'s $61,230.39 income went to servants' wages and maintenance of the homes. An additional $26,751 went to charities (less than Edith gave that year). Following a microscopic comparison of the two families and their situations, he concluded that Alta was "economical and careful in buying and in her living," hence deserving of Senior's confidence. But rather than raise Parmalee's allowance, John Jr. recommended a promise of thirty thousand annually be made for a limited number of years. Senior should agree to give Alta such a sum in securities that, together with her other sources of income, such as birthday monies, she would accrue an annual income of $100,000. He believed this practice would give the couple a "certain feeling of personal responsibility and independence . . . which all of us like." They would now have to pay all their expenses, rather than have Senior pick up many of their bills.

John Jr.'s plan had much to recommend it, except it ignored the fact that Senior was the wealthiest man in the country, and that Alta and Parmalee had a vision of service of their own. Yet one should not infer that John Jr. was grasping for the fortune for himself, not consciously at least, nor was Abby interested in the fortune. Eccentrically humble, if anything he felt each new bundle of stock from his father a challenge, not an opportunity. An analogy to aristocracy is apt. He would one day carry the title, and with it the awesome weight of the family. Thus he agreed with his father that it was only appropriate that the girls receive "an assured income . . . as less burdensome to them than to give them more property." The problem is that the girls had some inkling they were living in a democracy. While it had been cute and convenient for their little brother to handle their money and needs when they were youngsters, it was subtly demeaning to have him intervene now that they were adults, married to men of ability.

Also operating here may have been John Jr.'s animosity towards Parmalee, proof of which exists in an incident following Laura's death. After the funeral service, John Jr. thanked Harold for his staying with his mother her final days, and offered to return the kindness some day. Harold replied most surprisingly.[30] "[B]e more to Parmalee," meaning "be more kind and accepting." Harold described his grief at having observed mutual misunderstandings, lack of sympathy, and poor rapport between his two brothers-in-law. He allowed that Parmalee was a poor businessman and had made many mistakes, but that he deserved John Jr.'s support nonetheless. He even acknowledged Parmalee's "proud, perhaps even haughty spirit," yet reminded that he had "a keen mind, a heart of oak, and a character of pure gold." Most important, he was Alta's hus-band, and she was "almost torn in two" by John Jr.'s refusal to honor her husband. At the very least, John Jr. owed the man respect on the basis of loyalty to family.

John Jr. responded so briefly to Harold's lengthy, passionate peace-keeping that one senses he wanted to bury the matter without serious consideration. He claimed to always have "a very high regard for Par-malee's character and his ability and a very warm feeling for him." That a close association did not work out disappointed him. "Perhaps I have not come to all that I could in the matter," he replied. He did not achieve a personal rapprochement with Parmalee, although he did later use his legal assistance on some very private family matters.[31]

Where would this dislike be rooted? Following his marriage, Parmalee had opened a law practice with one of Abby's brothers. So perhaps an Aldrich brother-in-law or Abby herself were influential in keeping John Jr. distant. Or possibly John Jr. drew his own conclusions from observing Parmalee's behavior on several boards they belonged to in common. Par-malee was more intellectually adept than John Jr. Legal colleagues ad-mired his clear mind and tight argumentation; he would write two books on law, and argued cases before the United States Supreme Court. He was also not a modest man, whose proud manner alone might repulse a man like John Jr. Consequently, although the two families gathered at times for major holidays, such as Thanksgiving, they were not very close. It would take the next generation, the Rockefeller-Prentice cousins, to build stronger ties.

Beyond the private tragedy of the rift between Parmalee and John Jr. was one with larger consequences. With the war, Parmalee focused his consid-erable intelligence upon the problem of hunger. For the remainder of his life he would explore this phenomenon on many levels—philosophical, economic, political, and scientific. It was an issue Senior and John Jr. might have been expected to be involved with, yet they did not extend themselves to Parmalee on this matter. Possibly they failed to understand the seriousness and significance of his work. After all, the eggs sent down from the Prentices' Mount Hope farm looked no different than those picked at Pocantico or Forest Hill. How would they know these eggs had been grown more productively and cheaply under Parmalee's astute direc-tion? Consequently, lacking the force of an agency such as the Rockefeller Foundation behind him, Parmalee did not achieve all he might have. Had he access to farms other than his own, he could have tried many more experiments. The wonder is that he and Alta accomplished so much using their two hundred acres as their laboratory.

In early 1915, Parmalee and Alta invited the local farmers to band together into a league to share solutions to problems exacerbated by the war. Forty signed up immediately, and more soon followed. With potash for fertilizer scarce, potato production suffered, so Parmalee immediately set to find new ways to increase yields. The couple travelled to major livestock shows together, and Alta studied up on animal husbandry. They experimented with corn varieties from South America, and six varieties of oats.

Parmalee's studies were always practical: the identification of methods anyone could use to increase production of potatoes, eggs, milk, and other foodstuffs. When food prices rose in 1917—due to inflation, rising freight costs, and scarcity—he created the Williamstown Food Commission to assist residents in growing their own at much lower cost. The group carried out a census of vacant lots, and gained the use of these for cultivation, along with acreage on the Williams College campus. They ploughed and sprayed the land, sold seed and fertilizer at cost, and leased plots at a pittance. Three hundred families signed up for the project, while others with sufficient land of their own also grew their own food. Parmalee's idea must have been novel in New England, for it caught the attention of newspapers and politicians. "How One Town May Double Its Food Supply," praised the Boston *Transcript.*[32]

Although he never succeeded in convincing the public, Parmalee intended community gardening to continue in peacetime as well. Reflecting the isolationism of the time, he averred that the prosperity of the nation required meeting its essential needs on its own. "The dollar that goes the farthest is the dollar that stays at home." He took this spirit of independence down to the individual level, and praised the original Yankees of New England, who had imported little food to survive, as models to follow. If each person took responsibility for some of his own food, then his comfort level would not be tied totally to the level of his wages, Parmalee explained.

Once the United States joined the war, Parmalee, fifty-four, received a commission as Chief of Ordnance in the Procurement Division of the Army. With him away most of the time, Alta now had full management of the farm. She kept her father informed of her latest Pocherhorns, her twenty-five swarms of bees, her sending as much milk as possible to feed sickly babies. When discussing Senior's first visit to the farm, she warned him it might not be what he expected, that the house was a little rented place, their cows kept in simple sheds. (Actually, the farm was well-appointed, and following the war Alta saw that a rambling, comfortable mansion was built.)

When war first struck in Europe, Senior opened his pockets and emptied them out. Between 1914 and late 1917 his contributions to the Red Cross, the YMCA, other war organizations, and Liberty Bond subscriptions reached $70 million. Noting how between taxes and contributions he had given away one and two-thirds of his income, he added, "How silly it would be to compare that with the personal sacrifices so many men have made."[33] The Rockefeller Foundation independently gave millions of dollars to these agencies as well, and was significant in sustaining the Belgian civilian population. Ivy Lee sent numerous press releases to ensure that these gifts were printed to good result not only to the family name, but to the charities' benefit as well. At appeals made in theaters, churches, and public meetings, the announcement of the huge gifts by John D. Rockefeller provoked thunderous applause and generous donations from the audience. The name so recently reviled became associated with patriotism.

Since Laura's death, Senior had avoided staying in New York. Consequently, he turned his house on Fifty-fourth Street over to the Red Cross, which used the first-floor salons for meetings and activities, and made the upper floor bedrooms into dormitories for the forty or so volunteers. Abby was often in attendance running one or another meeting, along with women friends who stopped in to help with knitting socks and sweaters for the Russian front, sewing flannel pajamas for military hospital patients, and rolling bandages. School teachers, stenographers, store clerks, and socialites worked side-by-side in the drawing rooms and dining rooms of John D. Rockefeller.

Abby's older children participated as well. "We boys were given white uniforms," recalled Winthrop, "and carried the bandages from the places they were being made to the tables where they were being packed. It . . . helped us to understand the serious realities behind the [patriotic] parades."[34] At Pocantico, the children expanded their gardening efforts. Nelson and Laurance took to raising rabbits from a stock obtained from the Rockefeller Institute. In the kitchens, rationed food such as sugar was divided up in separate jars with each family member's name. A young visitor noted that during his long stay the family had not eaten beef once.

John Jr. also gave millions of dollars, and the majority of his time as well. Always the bridge builder, he sought to bring together the seven major religion-based charities, including the Knights of Columbus, the

YMCA, and the Jewish Welfare Board, to collaborate in their recreational and related services to the soldiers. Antagonism and competition among the groups was rife. John Jr.'s favorite, the YMCA, strongly opposed co-operation. One evening he called the key person from the Y on the phone and successfully "argued and pleaded and threatened . . . while the perspiration rolled in rivers down his face."[35] The result was the United War Work Campaign, which President Wilson quickly applauded for its uniting the country without regard to race or religious opinion. John Jr. personally accepted the task of running the greater New York campaign, with its goal of $35 million.

Abby could laugh, "I never know where John is any more, but he is out saving the world somewhere."[36] The war allowed her to reach beyond the family as well, to test her mettle as an administrator. Highest in priority was the War Work Council of the YWCA, which had over two hundred boarding houses around the country for women workers. She observed that similar housing was not available for women who worked near or in government installations, such as Army camps, and in particular the 100,000 women working for the agencies in Washington, D.C. She was also concerned about the "immoral women" or "actresses" who took such jobs to be near the men. "Our [innocent] young women must have protection [from these women]," she observed.

In 1917, she approached Raymond Fosdick, then head of the Commission on Training Camp Activities, concerning the need for housing. After consulting with the Secretary of War, he replied they saw no need to do anything. Familiar with the ways of Washington, Abby went personally and lobbied the Secretary and others until they agreed with her plea, and agreed to coordinate this activity with the YWCA. Toward that end, Abby oversaw a study, "Suggestions for Housing Women War Workers." The recommendations reflected both the attitudes of the day and Rockefeller philosophy concerning assistance. The housing would separate women by age, for the younger women would need some restrictions on their activities, while the older ones would want quieter, more intimate housing. Non-English speaking girls would be housed in small groups with a social worker who would acquaint them with American customs. And, "in every case, colored girls and women should live by themselves, and provision should be made for their social life." The residents would have a say in the management, and also pay board sufficient to cover costs. "Houses should not be philanthropic but cooperative."

Throughout this time, Abby pressed Fosdick further. Since the government was collaborating with the YMCA with regard to war work, why not do a demonstration project with the YW? When he set up an office to oversee women's work issues, she chided him for appointing a man. Would it be so annoying to have a "very strong, able, tactful woman" on his staff? But the war ended before she was able to move the bureaucracy in Washington, and she was nonplussed to discover many local branches of the YWCA were not interested in the war workers' needs either. This was not the end of her campaign, however.

If the women's housing project did not achieve her goals, it did boost her sense of value away from the family. Her husband might be uncomfortable making speeches, but not she. She spoke to any group that would listen about the effects of the war on young women. The men who would be their helpmates were being maimed or killed, she reminded; the women had to abandon motherhood as a hope. Those men who were returning from abroad did so with a liberal view based upon the experience in other cultures; the girls at home deserved to have their horizons accordingly broadened. Six children and a needy husband would never again stop this woman!

11

By Their Fruits Be Known

"Let him give, not grudgingly or of necessity: for God loveth a cheerful giver."

—II Corinthians 9:7

In December 1917, Senior learned that the Forest Hill home had gone up in flames, all property inside with it. The loss seemed incidental now that Laura was dead, the children settled in their own households. In recent winters he had enjoyed resorts in Georgia and Florida for golf, and he grew to prefer the latter. In 1918, he purchased a house in Ormond, Florida that would become his full-time home during his final decades. "The Casements" was a classic gray-shingle cottage, with broad terraces descending to the Halifax River.

Rising early in the morning, the octogenarian might enjoy a walk barefoot in the dewy grass before breakfast. Of course, morning prayers and scripture reading set the tenor of each day. Following a quick meeting over morning mail with his secretary, he went out with friends for nine or twelve holes of golf on the public links. He liked to bicycle between holes, and to drink a malted milk halfway through the course. On cold days he wore a paper vest (a favorite gift of his to others), on hot days a pith helmet. His companions especially enjoyed his quips of dry humor. When one missed a drive and the ball bobbled only a few inches off the tee, Senior teased, "What you need when you play, Cline, is a feather-bed attachment."[1]

About noon he bathed, took a light lunch, and briefly napped. After that he turned to his favorite mental activities: playing the stock market and planning the latest changes to his house and grounds. That done, he often ordered his chauffeur to bring out the Peerless motorcar and drive him about the country backroads to admire the scenery. If someone along the road, a porter or farmer or youngster, caught his eye, he might stop to converse with him, and often invite him along. After so many years of associating with people of prestige and power, he welcomed the opportunity to learn from local workers, students, and other average people living around Ormond.

Dinner started punctually at 7:30. Senior always dressed in formal clothes, and ate little. Because he enjoyed having house guests as well as dinner guests, a dozen or so would not be unusual at the table. Afterwards, he liked to have someone play his pipe organ or move the markers of Numerica with him.

On Sundays he attended the Ormond Union Church, and distributed shiny dimes and advice to the children afterwards. He took on the management of an annual local charity, a bazaar and auction to benefit the poor of the town. Call me "Neighbor John," he asked townsfolk, and they did so without cynicism or mockery.

His preference for simple pleasures remained. Knowing this, Alta often included in her letters clippings of jokes from newspapers. He sent invitations to his grandchildren to visit, and played with the offspring of his staff. When the famous or notable visited, Senior granted them no special treatment. He still pursued his hobby of landscaping large-scale and moving trees about. Before retiring, he read from a popular inspirational volume, *The Optimist's Good Night,* as well as collections of sermons. He remained very much a man of 1840s rural New York sensibilities.

Accustomed to the companionship of women, Senior asked a cousin from Ohio, Fanny Evans, to become his hostess. She proved exceptionally capable at running the household and winning the affection of his family and guests. Even though he thought his sister-in-law Lute prim and overly serious, he invited her as well to stay with him. This kindness saved her from being alone during her final years of poor health. No matter how many male acquaintances were about, he seemed to need a gaggle of interesting women around for conversation, and preferably, to be the only man present, the center of their attention.

During his eighties—indeed, to the end—Senior's mind remained sharp, possibly because he never stopped analyzing complex problems, and kept curious about the latest ideas in science, business, education, and religion. His secretaries marvelled at his ability to retain exact numbers on his various stock holdings throughout their frequent changes. Guests were surprised when he requested they retell a story concerning an event they had long forgotten. When a University of Chicago professor explained the emerging Soviet system in Russia, Senior was so immersed in this new economic model that he spent the entire night awake thinking about its benefits and disadvantages.

Thanks to Ivy Lee and his public relations minions, Senior now accepted a flow of journalists who came to interview him for magazine profiles. He was a "good interview," quick to supply crisp, concise opinions. He now understood the usefulness of the press as a way to spread his philosophy of simple living and frequent giving. Photographers arranged iconographic shots of the kindly, wise, aged patriarch. If a toddler was about to set in his lap, so much the better. Looking at these articles in today's cynical times, one cannot help but wonder about the underside, the unspoken. Was he really so kindly, so good-natured, so democratic? Living in a time when "rich and famous" is coterminous with venality and greed, it is easy to be suspicious about past men of wealth. All the evidence suggests the elderly John D. Rockefeller was as virtuous as he was portrayed in the popular press. (Even in his stock dealings, he recognized how the size of his trades could damage the economy, and chose a moderate path.)

Yet in one regard he was not content, that concerning the family reputation. He still suffered the sting of past criticism. Thus when John Jr. hired journalist William O. Inglis to prepare a biography of Senior, the old man used the opportunity to talk day after day explaining why Ida Tarbell had been wrong in her interpretations of Standard Oil. Using his prodigious recall, he dissected one item after another, cited chapter and verse of counter evidence. His insistent protests reflected a mind unsettled, ashamed really. He kept at this account, he repeatedly informed Inglis, so his son could understand what really happened. Somehow he sensed that John Jr.'s coming of age at the height of the criticism had scarred the young man. In a way, it was a message to his son that he was wrong not to have fought back more in the past, as Laura had always urged.

Examining old wounds must have been cathartic, but even more healing was a trip to the old family sites around Richford, Moravia, and Owego. His brother William joined him and Inglis on this first long automobile trip of his life. These visits elicited pleasant childhood memories from both men, who were happy to find some old playmates, such as a daughter of the LaMonte family, still in the area. The two elderly brothers found this visit so satisfying that they continued to repeat it annually for several years. (In 1924, Senior regretted that the Moravia house, which was being used to house convicts doing road construction, had burned down.)

Now that he had shaped a life independent of family, Senior decided to cut more financial ties with his children. For John Jr., this meant the progressive transfer of most of his father's wealth to him. For the daughters, in 1917 he put twelve thousand shares of Standard stocks, worth almost $4 million, into trust funds. Over the next few years, he added shares, more than doubling the value of the trusts. These were generation-skipping arrangements. Thus Edith and Alta had access to the income, but no control over the principal, which was to pass to their children upon their deaths. Having done so, he informed them he would no longer give annual allowances to them or their spouses. Where John Jr. had control of the gifts from his father, his sisters did not. Consequently, between 1917 and 1922, Senior put in trust for each of the girls approximately $12 million in securities. During that same time he gave John Jr. enough to make his net worth about $500 million.

If Senior thought these benefices would end the begging letters from his daughters, he was mistaken. Alta continued to write for bits of his New York townhouse furnishings, while Edith looked to him to help her with debts arising from her charitable giving. Though extremely wealthy by standards of the time, the daughters had high aspirations, ones that required a larger income. Certainly they knew their brother was being granted opportunities denied them.

While Senior knew Edith borrowed against her trust income to support the Chicago opera, he was unaware of the extent of her philanthropies. In addition to her helping underwrite the opera, the Institute for Infectious Diseases, and the Psychological Club, she took on a new role, that of patron. Artists streamed to Zurich during the war because it was a cosmopolitan city on neutral land, one more easily reached from France and Germany than some other attractive destinations. In time, its bohemian enclave included the innovative director Sir Max Reinhardt, various Dadaist painters, musicians, dancers, and writer James Joyce. Among lesser-knowns a Russian émigré who called himself Lenin joined the bohemians at Cafe Odon. If Edith heard of a needy case or simply liked an artist's work, she would establish an account for that person anonymously through her bank.

One of her first cases was Ermmano Wolf-Ferrari, an opera composer whose work she had premiered in Chicago. He may have come to Zurich specifically on Edith's behest; he was suffering a creative block and she thought Jungian analysis would aid him. Edith became his analyst and supported him financially as well. In time Jung recommended that as part of the treatment Edith cut off her financial aid to the composer. When she did, he had a breakthrough and was grateful for the therapy. (Unfortunately, Wolf-Ferrari's operas written following this time never met the promise of his early works.)

Edith had less success with writer James Joyce, who went through life dogging people for money to pay for his fine dining habits. In 1918 he had completed his play *Exiles* and sought backing to produce it. A friend suggested staging it with an amateur cast that included Edith in the role of Bertha. The hope was that in fawning upon Edith, he could get her to underwrite the show. Edith wisely refused the part, but secretly arranged for her bankers to create an account from which Joyce could draw a thousand francs a month. "It's high time," he remarked to a friend congratulating him on this fellowship.

Wanting to express his appreciation, and perhaps extract even more funds, Joyce eventually forced the bank manager to reveal the name of his unknown angel. He doubtless thought he made a good impression, and indeed all Zurich remarked on the dapper man, impeccably tailored, with well-trimmed mustache and raffish pince-nez. He walked with confidence, for *A Portrait of the Artist as a Young Man* had established him on the forefront of modern writing. His private life, however, was a mess. He had a complicated relationship with his deeply disturbed daughter Lucia, who as an adolescent still slept in her parents' bedroom at times. He had stopped speaking with his wife Nora while he immersed himself in the sexual fantasies that would bloom in his latest manuscript, *Ulysses*. (Nora was amused by her husband's relationship with Edith, and wondered what kind of underwear the heiress wore.) As a result of their meetings, Edith astutely concluded that the writer, however gifted, was badly in need of analysis. When she offered to pay for treatment with Jung, Joyce balked.

Joyce did eventually meet Jung as a result of his daughter's illness. Years later, he took catatonic Lucia to the Burgholzi, where the doctors were unsuccessful in cracking her frozen demeanor. They urged Joyce to move her to the private sanitarium in Kusnacht where Jung consulted. Very quickly the analyst broke Lucia's trance and persuaded her to talk. Joyce was gratified to see her gain in weight and mood. Unfortunately, neither father nor daughter was able to accept Jung's deeper probing. Lucia resisted "a big fat materialistic Swiss man [trying] to get into her soul," the psychologist later explained.[2] Joyce resisted evidence of Lucia's profound illness, and the implication that he enmeshed himself with his daughter's state of mind. As Jung commented to a colleague, "[Lucia] was definitely his '*femme imperatrice*' which explains [Joyce's] reluctance to have her certified. [He was] so solidly identified with her that to have her certified would have been as much as an admission that he himself had a latent psychosis."[3]

In October 1919, Joyce went to pick up his monthly allotment from Edith and was told that after eighteen months his fellowship had been terminated. He begged her to "consider the advisability of the revivability of her aid" without success. She finally wrote him a kindly letter to congratulate him on finding a publisher for his new novel and to "say 'Good-bye.'" Even then Joyce was not deterred, but appeared at Edith's door with some of his *Ulysses* manuscript in hand as a gift. (He asked for it back later when he realized how much money he could get from a collector; Edith graciously complied.)

"It seems that gentility cannot be acquired in a single generation," Joyce quipped to a friend.[4] To another he advised, "Hope you get something out of the McCormick Stiftung. Just mention my name."[5] He may have made a literary attack as well through basing a character in *Ulysses* upon Edith. There, in the "Circe" section, Mrs. Mervyn Talboys, a haughty society woman in riding clothes taunts Leopold Bloom for his obscene desires and threatens to spank him with her riding crop. In time, Joyce blamed not Edith, but first Jung, then later his wife's lover for directing the end to his sinecure. He had no lack of replacements for her patronage, including Harriet Weaver, who had been paying him five hundred francs a month at the same time as Edith, and had to be placated when she discovered she was not Joyce's only benefactress. After leaving Zurich, he cajoled a translator to provide him a flat for free in Paris. From there he reported to friend Ezra Pound, another writer on the make for patronage, of wanting "to get the Duchess of Marlborough [Consuelo Vanderbilt] to apply for the position vacated by Mrs. M[cCormick] but her bloody old father W K Vanderbilt died here in the next street to us the day before yesterday, very inconsiderately, I think."[6] Ungrateful though he was at the time, upon Edith's death many years later Joyce acknowledged "she was very kind to me at a difficult moment and was a woman of considerable distinction."[7]

Joyce never understood why Edith cut him off, and failed to consider the simplest explanation, that she had never intended to be his permanent angel. Her termination fits with the Rockefeller philosophy of giving to people of promise so long as in return they develop means to be self-sufficient. Joyce did not realize that his achieving success, his finding a publisher for *Ulysses*, signified his readiness to be cut loose.

Of course in his narcissism Joyce did not consider that Edith might have problems of her own. For one, Harold was away most of the time now. During the war, Cyrus McCormick repeatedly asked Harold to return to International Harvester and assume the presidency. In mid-1918 Harold moved back to Chicago and at the end of the year gave in to his brother's wishes. Fowler joined his father during his vacation breaks from Princeton, yet much of the time despite his many activities Harold was lonely.

The Chicago opera was at its height then, and Harold kept Edith well-informed of its productions. At its season opener a week after the Armistice, the company inserted the Belgian, Italian, Japanese, French, English, and American national anthems in the midst of a performance of *La Traviata*. This patriotic fervor meant no German operas were presented. Audience members arrived in automobiles now and on time, for they wished to avoid tickets for breaking the ten-mile-an-hour speed limit downtown. Women's hems showed some ankle and calf, and their colorful dresses were more form-revealing. Younger socialites arrived early to show off their jewelry and gowns before cameras that filmed them for avid movie audiences.

Outside the opera, Chicago was rocked by the postwar disorders that shook American idealism. Prices rose while wages remained stagnant. Workers who had kept quiet during the war struck now for five-day work weeks and safer conditions. Immigrants found their social clubs under scrutiny for possible Bolshevik association. African-Americans who had moved north for war jobs, and stayed on afterwards, found themselves victimized in riots. Youth seemed angrier and more self-centered, quicker to attack old customs. These upheavals, like the recent deadly flu epidemic that was devastating the entire planet's population, little touched the various branches of the Rockefellers at first. It would be several years, the onset of the Jazz Age, before the tumult of modernity penetrated the family walls.

Harold McCormick was preoccupied with falling tractor sales and with maintaining the Chicago Grand Opera's high quality. His life suddenly changed, however, as a result of the performing group's tour to New York. There, his appearance in a box seat caught the eye of an audience member, Ganna Walska, an alluring Polish soprano of meager ability who had been trying to break into an American company. Her real talent was in acquiring wealthy husbands. She was married at the time to second husband Joseph Fraenkel, a much-older physician popular among New York society. Fraenkel was ailing, and Walska perhaps anticipated widow's weeds. Hearing of Harold's connection to the Chicago company, she finagled a meeting with him at the Plaza Hotel, where he was staying.[8] There she told him how Chicago's artistic director, Cleofante Campanini, had auditioned her in the past, praised her as a potential Thais or Fedora, but refused her a role until her voice matured. She begged Harold to speak to Campanini on her behalf, and he agreed.

On later business trips to New York, Harold took to visiting Walska, whose husband was now dying. The "sweet letters and telegrams" from this man with the "wonderful boyish blue eyes" helped her through her "sinister Walpurgis Night."[9] Another death besides her husband's eased her path. Campanini suddenly collapsed and succumbed, thus removing the major obstacle between Harold and a contract for Walska at the Chicago Grand Opera. Consequently, he had her signed for the 1920 fall season.

That summer Harold went to a meditation retreat in upper New York. Afterwards, he sailed to Europe on the *Aquitania*, "and perhaps not by chance" admitted Walska, who was also a passenger. On deck, however, she was taken with another man, one with cold expressionless eyes. He was Alexander Smith Cochran, one of the country's wealthiest and most cynically handsome men. He also lacked Harold's major encumbrance, a wife. Two months later Walska married Cochran in Paris, but within days she was soon back in touch with Harold. Cochran was a cruel, mentally unstable man, she decided.

In December, Walska arrived in Chicago to rehearse for her company debut in Leoncavallo's *Zaza*. Rumors of Walska's beauty and diva personality intrigued ticket buyers, who quickly bought out the house. During practices, the artistic director, who was also conducting, became so frustrated over her failure to project her voice over the orchestra that he turned the baton over to his assistant. At the dress rehearsal, that man, too, asked her to sing out more, to which she spat, "Pig, you would ruin my performance."[10] With that she stomped from the stage, fled to her hotel, packed her bags, and departed for Europe. Two weeks later the company director quit, complaining he could no longer put up with the grievous behavior of the stars. Harold consulted with Edith to put Mary Garden in charge, making her the first woman to head a major opera company. Walska returned to her luxurious apartment in Paris to spend some of her husband's wealth.

So far as Senior could tell from Harold, despite frequent separations all within the McCormick branch of the family was congenial. Harold kept assuring his father-in-law that Edith and the girls were well, that he heard from them weekly. Mathilde wrote her grandfather letters of her delight in the Swiss countryside and the daily riding lessons she was taking at a local academy, of her piano study and ballroom dancing. Edith added that Mathilde was first in her class at school. As for herself, her therapy practice was full-time, evidence of Jung's confidence in her abilities. "My patients are coming to me all the time, and I have had some fifty cases now. I hear in a year twelve thousand dreams."[11] She was gratified to watch people come to her hopeless and lost, and as a result of the therapy find joy.

Senior and John Jr. failed to acknowledge her achievement, however. They were less bothered by her supplanting Christianity with psychology than her mounting indebtedness. The trust company overseeing Edith's accounts informed them that she had been borrowing money against her securities to give large donations to the opera company. Her debt by mid-1919 was over a half million dollars. John Jr. wisely advised the trust company to treat her no differently than any regular customer, but Senior asked her to provide more particulars on her spending, as he often asked his other two children to do. Edith explained she had not told him of her dealings earlier on account of the war censors, who could take advantage of privileged information. Yet by November her debt increased to $613,000 at six percent interest, and she had an outstanding income tax bill of $140,000. Senior sent the trust company $100,000 toward reducing the debt.

Edith's thank-you note must have caused some trepidation in her father and brother. She was going into business, she explained, manufacturing a new chemical process for treating wood to strengthen railroad ties, mine supports, telegraph poles, and construction beams. She was sending her partners to Chicago to test the process further and to establish a factory in the States.

Senior shot off notes of disapproval and asked Harold what he thought. In his usual thorough way, Harold traced the history of Edith's venture, which started when some German scientists approached her with their discoveries. In addition to the new wood treatment, they claimed to have discovered a new chemistry for making copper and for turning ordinary cutstones into something resembling diamonds.[12] Although Harold was skeptical at first, he went to Zurich to investigate the men's background and consulted with Jung, who after initial doubt quickly changed his mind in support of the scientists. "Mrs. McCormick has managed the business side in a most admirable way. . . . I [Jung] went with her through it all in silent collaboration."[13] Aware of the idiosyncrasies of experiments, Harold agreed that the researchers should be sent to America to repeat their studies. He praised Edith's conservatism, her refusal to sell her own securities to fund the project. He supported Edith's taking out loans to back the opera company. He explained they had a plan in place to establish it well enough to turn over to other patrons in the near future. Seen in this light, Harold asserted, Edith's debts were temporary and sensible. In conclusion, he made clear that had the business proposal been offered to him instead of Edith, he should have taken it up as well. So much did he feel necessary to defend his wife that he dashed off another letter to emphasize his admiration of Edith's executive abilities.

By March 1920, Edith's loans totalled $812,000. Senior put forty-five thousand more shares of stock into her trust account, and advised her to let the income accumulate for the benefit of her children. In April, Harold advised him that Edith's business was being closed down. The experiments in Chicago failed to replicate the findings of those first done in Europe. Consequently, Edith dissolved the companies and ceased making disbursements. In a later detailed accounting, Edith showed her father how she lost $339,000 in the deal. "I am sorry, but the business looked good and I moved cautiously, never taking a step precipitously, and insisting on tests and extra proofs. . . ."[14] Senior suggested she stay out of all business schemes in the future.

By 1920 Edith knew of Harold's infatuation with Walska. She was friendly with Mary Garden, who visited her in Zurich that summer and may have filled her in on the romance. After Walska married Cochran, Edith notified her father that she would soon be moving back to the States. She sent seventeen-year-old Muriel back with Harold that fall; a few months later she sent fifteen-year-old Mathilde home as well. Accompanying Mathilde on her visits to both her grandmother Nettie McCormick and Senior was an older woman, Julia Mangold, the bookkeeper from her riding academy. That summer, the girls and Harold reunited briefly in Europe with Edith. Nonetheless, Senior must have heard that all was not well among the McCormicks. He pressed upon Edith to leave Zurich and settle back in Chicago with her daughters. He said he would not take "no" for an answer. Edith kept delaying a return.

Edith finally made reservations to sail home in late September 1921. Several weeks before her departure, Cyrus McCormick urged Senior to stop her, "thus giving opportunity for mutual meditation and conference."[15] Senior agreed to intercede, and immediately cabled her to delay her return. Why this sudden change in attitude? Harold wanted a divorce. Edith sailed anyway, with a travelling companion, a much younger man. The family was horrified at the thought of the resulting scandal. Edith must be reined in.

Following the war, despite her devoted motherhood, Abby Rockefeller was like many women of her day who had helped in the relief effort. Instead of returning to a fully domestic life, she chose to remain active outside the home. Her main priority remained adequate housing for working women. In her report to the YWCA, she blamed herself for some of the problems in the wartime boarding homes. Some residences failed to thrive due to weak managers; others never materialized because the local Y branches were not interested in the project. Abby did not think the project should be set aside just because the war was over. Single urban women continued to have difficulty finding affordable rents in respectable areas, and frequently resorted to taking rooms without kitchens, she noted.

More than housing was on Abby's mind. She had become sensitized to other needs of workers, and eventually held more liberal views than her husband. Where he preferred a nonunion model of worker-capitalist cooperation, she saw the value of labor organizing. When she heard of a chorus girls' strike, she contributed funds to their support. From that point, she quietly dispensed donations to various trade union groups and striking workers' funds, even though her husband disapproved.

Abby took her enlightened perspective into the strategy fights at the highest level of the YWCA. In 1920, when the National Board split over the question of aiding industrial workers, she supported a platform known as the Social Ideals of the Churches. In an article explaining her views, she reviewed others' objections to the YWCA being so vocal regarding social justice. Some board members believed that to do so was to be socialistic, thus prone to alienating the support of conservative donors. Some men, notably in unions and the trades, objected to women as competitors for jobs. Younger members feared that were the YWCA to become involved in legislation, then its various services would decrease. Sounding much like her husband, Abby argued for a committed stand:

> Are we [of the YWCA] afraid to stand for better moral laws, such as a uniform divorce law, a law raising the age of consent, better laws for the commitment of prostitutes, all leading to a single standard? Are we afraid of laws that will better the working and living conditions of men, women, and children, or those affecting housing, sanitation, and immigration? . . . [L]et us remember that it is our function to bring together the employer and the employee, the teacher and the pupil, the young and the old, the board member and the girl, the old and new world.[16]

At the 1921 annual YWCA convention, she spoke eloquently that its leadership should be dreaming, thinking of experiments in education, housing, and ways of taking the Christian message to particular people, such as teachers and actresses.

In 1922, Abby brought her own dream to fruition as an example to others. Under her direction, a YWCA hotel was constructed in Washington, D.C. Abby named it in honor of Grace Dodge, a YWCA leader who had mediated bitter conflicts in the organization in the early 1900s, thus ensuring its success both on national and international levels. Situated at the corner of North Capitol and E Streets, the hotel provided four hundred units, many with private baths, and even suites for women with small children. All rooms faced the outside to receive sunlight and fresh air. Every functional need was considered, from cribs to laundries. "If women can go down the corridor in their kimonos knowing they will not meet a man, it will add to their sense of freedom and comfort," she explained to a reporter.[17]

Between 1922 and 1935 Abby provided direction to Mary A. Lindsley, manager of the Grace Dodge. With her usual thoroughness and common sense, she advised on all details of the operation. She visited regularly, took notes, and sent back suggestions. Her letters specified decoration (pongee curtains in the dining rooms, tidies for the backs of light-blue chairs and sofas), food service (chop ice more finely for oyster presentation), advertising (place a notice in Good Housekeeping), cost cutting (eliminate the ventilation system part of the day), and the gift shop (goods look too cluttered to show off well.)

At the time the Grace Dodge Hotel opened, another YWCA hotel, the Phyllis Wheatley Hotel, catered to African-American women. Consequently, in keeping with the segregation of the times, the Grace Dodge Hotel did not accept black women. The question soon arose as to how to treat other non-Caucasian women. Abby discussed the policy with her Y committee and instructed Lindsley "the only women whom we cannot take are the negroes, which means we should extend the privileges of the hotel to the Chinese, Japanese, Indians, and South Americans." Furthermore, even if the Indian women were "so dark they might be mistaken for [Negroes]," it was "absolutely essential" that the hotel not discriminate against them.[18] Another time she chided Lindsley for using the term "Southern darkies" in a letter to a Senator, explaining that "the colored people" were very touchy, and did not like such terms even when meant as an expression of affection.

Abby's inconsistent attitudes reflect the subtle loosening of racism's hold on the mindset of Americans. This was, after all, the decade when the Ku Klux Klan ran its fiery rampages throughout the small towns of the nation, not only against African-Americans, but against Catholics and Jews as well. Even the most radical feminists of the day, the outspoken cadre of the National Women's Party, held to separate-but-equal principles. Yet many thoughtful people like Abby were repelled by the lynchings and the Red Scare attacks on immigrants, and began to erase many earlier racial distinctions from their minds. The once-inferior Poles, Greeks, or Italians were now equal as "whites." With so many European rungs on the ladder eliminated, Asians suddenly moved into positions of near-equality with "whites." Yet, while the number of rungs on the ladder reduced and the distances between them shrank, the descendants of slaves remained, as always, at the bottom.

When it came to her own hotel's labor practices, Abby was more conservative than her usual stated beliefs. For the hotel brochure, she wrote:

> The Grace Dodge Hotel is operated on a no-tipping basis. Its labor policy insures to all employees adequate wages without tips. Local labor—the colored man and woman—is trained occupationally and ethically to give the type of service worthy of a self-respecting citizen.

(Whether the workers preferred this policy—whether they earned more or less under it—is unknown.) Accordingly, she commended Lindsley for not publicly joining the campaign for the minimum wage and the eight-hour day. One had to consider others in the hotel business, she explained, meaning one should not provoke other hotel keepers who did not follow the advanced practices of the Grace Dodge Hotel. On the other hand, Abby did insist that the hotel be managed completely by women, which was in itself unusual.

Abby remained devoted to proving the success of her concept. In 1924, when she fell ill with exhaustion and promised to drop all her committee assignments for a year, she would not drop her administration of the hotel. During visits to Washington she would stay there rather than at the homes of friends.

Despite careful management, the Grace Dodge continued to have a higher vacancy rate than anticipated. In 1928, Abby decided to allow the husbands, brothers, sons, or other male relatives of women guests to stay as well. Even that expansion of clientele did not increase profits. When Abby heard that the men stayed away because the hotel had a woman's name, with much regret in 1929 she changed the name to the Dodge Hotel.

Abby's donations to charity increased considerably following the war as well. Before the war, she typically contributed small amounts, often fifty dollars or less, mostly to individuals in need. She provided dairy foods for a poor woman she heard about or paid for a mother's helper for a working woman. By the mid-1920s, she was giving sizeable gifts, such as nine thousand dollars for organ fittings for the Beneficent Street Congregational Church in Providence and five thousand dollars for various YWCA projects. She paid the salaries of the women Sunday School teachers at Park Street Baptist Church. Her eventual list of organizations would grow to over two hundred, many of which concerned women's needs. If her contributions were small for a woman married into one of the world's wealthiest families, they were a good portion of her own money derived through her Aldrich family income. These gifts pronounced her independence from her husband, who was not always in approval of their recipients.

In late September 1921, when Edith disembarked in Manhattan, Senior and John Jr. could think only of avoiding scandal. As a consequence, their actions placed favorable publicity ahead of Edith's needs. Senior, as always, was the remote, dutiful father. He refused to let Edith visit him because she insisted on bringing her male companion, but he continued to write and counsel her. If he had long ago lost faith in her administrative abilities and disapproved of her particular philanthropies, he nonetheless loved her as his child, hence deserving of his patience, tolerance, and forgiveness. Unfortunately, from this point John Jr. behaved as though she were beyond the pale. For years he had been annoyed by her determination to go her own way, and now he seemed bent on subtle revenge. (Where Abby stood regarding her sister-in-law, whether she was complicit in her husband's reaction, is unclear.) As Senior aged he more often accepted John Jr.'s interpretations of events, so that his son's animosity would finally cleave father and daughter. Senior and Edith would never see each other again.

Edith's young man was Edwin Krenn, a Swiss architect and devotee of Jung. They were not lovers, although the family and the press inferred that they were. Most likely Krenn was homosexual. That would explain why Edith would appear with another man precisely at the time Harold was pressing for divorce: Harold would have known Krenn's leanings. Nonetheless, it was a stupid move, one possibly encouraged by Jung, who was ignorant of how it would play before Americans. Edith considered Krenn her protégé, and wished to help him get established in the States. Since Jung had encouraged her earlier business ventures, it could be he fostered this one as well.

Edith's primary reason for returning was hope of reuniting with Harold. After arriving in Chicago, she refused to get a lawyer or take Harold's divorce demands seriously. The reunion was not to be. Harold was not only implacable, he was vindictive. He warned Senior's advisors that if Edith did not cooperate, he would sue not for desertion but for adultery. An obvious question is whether Edith had in fact committed adultery with anyone in Europe. No evidence supports the accusation, and her behavior later on in life, where she had no romantic involvements with any men, argues further against that likelihood. Harold was desperate to marry Ganna Walska, who was ready to ditch Alexander Cochran. He could have been bluffing; he could have found witnesses in Switzerland to testify to any of Edith's behavior that had a hint of impropriety, such as her entertaining a male friend alone in her hotel room. In any case, he did not want to give Edith anything—alimony, any of the houses, the personal property. All he was willing to do was pay the minimum allowed by law, child support. Edith dug in to resist this humiliating settlement. She wrote her father, "I feel just as you do that the most natural and heartful thing is for Harold and I to be together."[19] She said all Harold cared about was marrying "the actress."

Finally convinced a reconciliation was impossible, Edith deferred to her father's offer of assistance, which included the counsel of both John Jr. and Parmalee. Eventually the three men retained a noted Chicago jurist as Edith's attorney. During the negotiations with Harold's counsel, they grew fearful of the possible notoriety resulting from a contested litigation, and agreed to do what was necessary to reach an out-of-court settlement. Without Edith knowing, they struck an agreement that gave Harold all he wanted and more. "It is important that Mrs. McCormick should not, for the present at least and until we have agreed that it is wise, know that I have written you or that you may know any of these facts," wrote John Jr. to Edith's counsel.[20] As a result, Harold received his divorce very quickly, in late December 1921, and received large sums of money from Edith, who had to purchase both their Chicago townhouse and Villa Turicum from him. In return, the Rockefeller men were gratified that Edith was to be on record as the aggrieved party, suing Harold for desertion. To their relief, the papers announced the divorce matter-of-factly in the back pages.

Harold's actions at the time were strangely out of character. He was never known to be hard, mean, or spiteful—quite the opposite. In business and at home he was always the mediator, the one seeking to resolve disputes. Indeed, following the divorce he continued to write Senior and John Jr. as though he were still a member of the family. That his actions injured Edith and the children, and threatened the Rockefeller name, never seemed to come into mind. He would have his comeuppance though. Drunk with passion over Ganna Walska, he sought out a faddish cure for an embarrassing medical ailment. Months later satirists would write about his operation for "glandular" replacement. The question was, had he used monkey glands, or had he, as it was rumored, paid a healthy college lad to give up his own? This surgery would tag onto news stories about him for the rest of his life, and even mar his obituary.

Harold would also learn that when given a choice, Chicagoans placed their support behind Edith. His affair with Walska was well-known. His social set also likely recognized that Krenn was no "corespondent" in the usual sense of the term. The general public delighted both in Edith's dramatic, idiosyncratic personality and in her thoughtful civic contributions. In 1920 she had donated several hundred acres on the west side of town for a new zoological park, eventually known as Brookfield. (When they learned of this gift, both Senior and John Jr. were displeased that she gave away properties that had been meant as investments.) The scientific study of animals would help in the understanding of humans, she explained. In discussions over the design of the park, she required that the animals be uncaged and placed in natural habitats. Also, upon her return to Chicago, she had made clear her continued commitment to the opera company.

Harold even encountered criticism at International Harvester. Humiliated by the publicity of the courtship with Walska, his brother Cyrus encouraged stockholders to ask for Harold's resignation from the presidency. Harold had never been happy with that post anyway, and was not aggrieved to be forced out.

Only one intimate, his sister Anita Blaine, was sympathetic with Harold's situation—but she always petted him, no matter how bad his behavior. Walska appealed to Anita's natural sympathy for the afflicted. "People . . . imagine that I am foolish, vane, consited personne who imagines that she can sing because she is pretty. . . . [I am] a person who wants to give at cost of terrible suffering and undiscrable misery."[21] Anita assured Walska of her support, and urged the young woman to ignore the publicity, and pray for the strength to learn the "sacred lesson" associated with her troubles.

Following the divorce, Edith blossomed in her inimitable way. She immediately started a practice for Jungian analysis, which attracted socialites from around the country. She accepted invitations to speak in public, something she had not done before. In one curious talk, perhaps misrepresented by the press, she argued that women were a "negative creative force." Her point was that women approach the world differently from men and should not try to play by men's rules. Were women to realize this distinction, they would be more serene. In another speech, she reminded that women were the original creators in early society, the potmakers, grain growers, and healers of the sick. With civilization, they were treated as property and enslaved. Now that modern women had become victors, by gaining the vote, they could once again enjoy a more expansive role in society. As if her admirers did not get the point, she now signed herself *Miss* Edith Rockefeller McCormick.

During this tumultuous postwar period, Senior saw further the difficulty of achieving his goal of one hundred years. His sister Lucy Briggs had died decades before at age forty. His brother Frank passed away in 1917 at age seventy-two. His sister-in-law Mira died suddenly and unexpectedly of heart disease while vacationing at the Jekyl Island estate in 1920. Lute Spelman died that year as well. For a man his age, such reminders of death were commonplace. Yet his religious faith instilled a belief in resurrection and in reunion with his deceased family and friends, so he exhibited few signs of deep grief.

The most personal loss, though, was of his brother William in June 1922. Just the week before, he and Senior had journeyed together for their annual visit to their childhood haunts. Despite covering seven hundred miles in four days, the eighty-one-year-old William felt vigorous enough to return immediately to his office at 26 Broadway, where several board meetings were scheduled. He went to the office again on Saturday, but upon leaving was caught unprepared in a sudden downpour. A few days later he came down with a cold, which his doctor feared was incipient pneumonia. Senior came by in the evenings to keep his brother company. By Thursday, William's condition was so critical he was placed under oxygen. Nonetheless, he rallied repeatedly, and Senior was not present when his brother and business partner unexpectedly died two days later. William was buried with his wife in the newly completed quarter-million-dollar mausoleum in Sleepy Hollow Cemetery in Tarrytown.

William's obituary reflected how different his life had become from that of his older brother. Unlike Senior, he had continued his business interests to the last. To disguise his lack of philanthropy, the *New York Times* tactfully remarked "few of his benefactions ever became public."[22] His only contribution in his lifetime had been one million dollars to a war relief drive. His will made no bequests to charity, but gave virtually all of his estate, estimated between $150 and $200 million, to his four children. Characteristic of his class, a son received the bulk of the estate, three-fourths worth outright, while the other children split the last quarter share in the form of trusts. Unusual was the passing over of his first-born son William G., forty-two, in favor of Percy, thirty-four, as recipient of the majority of the estate. Typical of other Rockefeller generation-skipping trusts, Percy's siblings could enjoy the income only, with the principal at their death to pass on to their children.

Only a few months later William G. caught a cold while attending a football game at Yale, and died soon after of pneumonia. The *Times* obituary writer had to stretch his sentences to fill out his spotty career, which had many fewer directorships and involvements in charity than would have been expected of a Rockefeller male. The paper did not discuss how William G.'s body rested for days in the Madison Avenue mansion while the family tried to locate his wife Elsie, who was travelling in Europe.

When he was a young man, the inner circle at Standard Oil had originally picked William G. to be the crown prince of his generation. Robust, quick-minded, gregarious like his father, he seemed better suited than his more sickly, detail-oriented cousin John Jr. But early on William G. preferred cocktails and racehorses to stock reports. With John Jr. turning more to philanthropy, Percy became the most prominent businessman among the male cousins. Using the influence of his father-in-law James Stillman, he became a director of National City Bank. Through his father's many interests in railroads, he joined the boards of over a dozen lines. More entrepreneurial than his brother or male cousins, he extended his interests to nitrates, copper, matches, industrial alcohol, and steel. By the 1920s, Percy Rockefeller was known to be a shrewd player of the stock market as well.

Percy worked hermetically in offices at 25 Broadway, and seldom ventured out to meet friends at restaurants or clubs. He had some of his noted Uncle John's ways of working. He was patient and tenacious, willing to work hard and long toward a goal. He would not be rushed. He also had a reputation for keeping his word and following his principles. As a result, by the time he inherited his father's fortune, he had accumulated one of his own.

Percy's enthusiasm for making money was perhaps a compensation for an unsatisfactory marriage. His wife Isabel had inherited her father's cold, cruel temperament. She could not control her husband as she had been controlled throughout childhood, for Percy could easily refuse to stay in her demanding presence. She ignored her five children, except for the youngest, sickly Gladys, whom she smothered with her constant yet detached presence. (In his eighties, son Avery still burst into tears recalling his mother's disregard of him and his siblings.) She went off to Europe for months at a time. Were it not for her sister Elsie, who took over such duties as planning debuts and weddings, Isabel's children would have been even more neglected. (Elsie was only too happy to add her nieces and nephews to her brood as a way of avoiding her drunken husband William G.)[23]

To the outside world, the Percy Rockefellers represented all that the American Dream promised: healthy good looks, lives on glamorous estates pampered by servants, nights spent in gaiety and friendship. The Rockefeller name added panache. However admirable the charities of Senior and Junior, their family line lacked flair and glitter. What good was giving all that money away if you did not also enjoy it?

12

As Plants Grown Up

"But now they that are younger than I have me in derision . . ."

—Job 30:1

Alta's eldest son was the first of Senior's grandchildren to behave in a way that would have been unheard of before the war. John Rockefeller Prentice, who went by Fritz, had always been a spirited lad, quick to object to his parents' methodical family life. He resisted the rules, the exclusions, the demands that childhood be akin to boot camp. Alta and Parmalee had not spoiled him or his siblings. He had grown up amid the families of Williams College professors and had been encouraged toward a life of the mind. (Only later in life would Fritz come to appreciate the companionship of foreign-born tutors, of conversing in Latin at dinner.) He had regular chores in the hilly pastures and fields of Mount Hope—serious tasks, not a little garden to weed.

While his parents were strict, they were also rich, largely through the graces of Senior. Every spring until the war, Parmalee and Alta spent six weeks or more in Europe so she could have her annual ear treatments at the Carlsbad spa. Though Alta implied to her father that their home was austere, she exaggerated. It might not be John Jr. and Abby's hundred-room summer home in Maine, but it was not so unadorned as she implied. The interior included art works and furnishings she had wrangled from her father. In warm weather she held musicales, inviting the intellectuals and farmers of Williamstown to attend. Alta also used any excuse to invite numerous children over for a party, where she lavished a bounty of entertainment and souvenirs upon the happy guests. Fritz and his siblings grew up in an unusually cosmopolitan environment for a farming family.

When America joined the fighting overseas, like so many mothers Alta pressed her children into war service. They wrote on stationery with patriotic symbols. They raised money for the Red Cross and planted potatoes for the community gardens. Madeline sewed clothes and dolls for

Belgian children. They helped their mother with the luncheons she gave on Sundays for the members of the Williams battalion.

During this time, Fritz left to board at Taft School, where he added Greek to his languages, and took piano and dance lessons. Alta was pleased to see him behave more kindly toward the family during his vacations at home. Fritz wrote earnest letters to his grandfather concerning all his plans. In response to one, Senior provided a capsule of his life philosophy: Give to others, do not work too hard, and keep a healthy body. As a Rockefeller, Fritz had a special calling:

> I want you and all the other grandchildren to develop the ability to fight life's battles and to take care of yourself independently of your families, and then with what can be furnished to you from the experiences of those of your ancestors, and your observations of the good training of your parents, I hope you will all be fitted for the large responsibilities which will be entrusted to you from the estate, provided you show yourself equal to the assumption of such responsibilities.[1]

Had Fritz been close to his cousin Fowler, he would have seen how Senior kept his promises. The oldest male grandchild, blessed with the best qualities of two talented family lines, Fowler easily matured to meet all Senior's challenges and expectations while maintaining his individuality. Consequently, when Fowler reached twenty-one, Senior began to transfer relatively small amounts of stock to the promising and prudent young man. He also granted his grandson a higher rate of interest then available in banks on some of his investment money. As a result, by 1921 Fowler's net worth was almost $700,000. This meant that at twenty-three the earnings provided an income equal to that of successful professional men. Sensible and philosophical, exposed at an early age to Jungian mythology, Fowler handled his riches without illusion.

When Fritz got into trouble his last year at Taft, Alta consulted about her son with Senior, who suggested a military school. Did he know anyone he could influence to get Fritz into West Point? she replied. Apparently not—in fall of 1919 Fritz attended Yale. There he wallowed in the freedom; he gambled, piled up debts, and was tossed out of school. "Please do not come and get me," Fritz advised his parents. "We will not come and get you, and furthermore we do not expect you to come home," they coldly returned.[2] The battle lines had been drawn.

Senior was at first sympathetic to his daughter's plight. "Hold steady.

Do not yield anything . . . [May] all this through which he is passing prove a blessing in disguise."[3] This was the wrong advice to offer Alta and Parmalee, who assumed he meant to support them in any punitive action toward their son. Their response was to rewrite their wills to disinherit their oldest child. From Yale Fritz moved to Boston, where he did well as a sales agent for a hardware firm. Flush with his newfound independence and success, he sent word home that he intended to pay all his debts and correct his past mistakes.

Fritz's apology was not enough for his parents. Claiming he had not yet learned his lesson, they urged Senior not to send the youth a birthday check. Parmalee demanded that his son must fully repent. Senior grew frustrated over what seemed to him harsh treatment of Fritz, and sent him the money anyway. He urged them to soften their stance, by noting that the situation required "great wisdom and patience and much of the parental love . . . if he is possessed of the frailties of the human, he is but one of us, and we are responsible for his failings, and God have mercy on us all."[4] Alta was furious that he would recommend tenderness along with firmness. In a long defense, she enumerated Fritz's faults: his stubbornness, his mutinous ways, his past disobedience. She and Parmalee insisted that "discipline will teach this most profitable and necessary lesson."[5] Yet in curious self-contradiction, she quoted from Fritz's letters in which he expressed his appreciation for all his parents had given him. He was obviously longing to return home, even to his "keepers."

Alta's next attack upon her son was through her trust. A committee member had died, and she asked to be appointed as the replacement. She argued before her father that she had been "sane and sound" in managing her affairs, and had a right to share in control of the investments. Both Parmalee and Harold, who also served on the trust committee, backed her at first, but eventually saw that Senior's advisor Bertrand Cutler took the vacancy. Alta's motive to have a say in the trust was less for her own recognition than to punish Fritz. When this attempt failed, she tried another maneuver. She informed Senior that New York law allowed her to revoke the trust, and she could thus prevent Fritz from his rightful inheritance after all. She was wrong. Senior's advisors proved that as written the trust was irrevocable by her.

In January 1922, after two years without any contact with Fritz, Parmalee wrote his son a long letter recounting the errors of the youth's ways, and appended a barely visible olive branch. In response, the prodigal agreed to return to Taft School in hopes that a good record there would convince Yale to let him return. His parents still forbade him from coming home, though, and Alta urged her father to place his usual $2,500 birthday check to Fritz in trust. She argued that he had only a few hundred dollars in debts left, and would spend the remainder unwisely. At this point Senior reconsidered the wisdom of giving money to any of his descendants. He wondered about "the danger of giving money into the hands of inexperienced children . . . in this age of wastefulness and harmfulness . . ."[6] Because of Fritz's waywardness, Senior's other young grandchildren would no longer receive these celebration gifts, money of their own to control.

Throughout this period Senior fenced with Alta concerning her own money and investments. Her problems were typical to her class, who before 1914 paid hardly any income tax, and since then found their investments, trust incomes, and death estates in the purview of seemingly greedy federal agents. Consequently, money management became much more complicated, even more so for females like Edith and Alta, who lacked the training in finance that their brother had received. For example, in 1920, upset over a drop in the value of Standard Oil stock, Alta decided to sell her holdings. Senior advised her that this was unwise, for she would have an enormous taxable gain. More important, those advising her could "not appreciate and be interested in [the matter] as we are, *as a family*."[7] Her action would demoralize the market, he explained, and by implication reflect badly on the family's reputation.

Alta found perplexing other financial offers her father made to her. When she regretted not having taken advantage of an opportunity to sell options for Standard Oil stock at $80,000, he made up for it by giving her $400,000. This practice on Senior's part, of assuaging Alta's discomfort with additional gifts of money, continued despite his displeasure with her strictness toward Fritz.[8] Eventually, with the assistance of John Jr. and his aides, he finally allowed Alta to sell off small lots of Standard Oil over a year, and purchase $5 million in Liberty Bonds giving 3½ percent interest. (It was a move she could smile on ten years hence, during the Depression, but not during World War II when the oil stock soared.)

It was late 1923 before Fritz was allowed to return home, although Alta remained disgruntled and distrustful. He was too prideful, she kept insisting (without realizing he had been raised by a very proud father). "A person who really repents of wrongdoing is not ashamed of repentance, [which] is the foundation of good character and is necessary for trust."[9] Without her knowing, Senior wrote Fritz among the most remarkable letters of his later years. Unlike his usual terse notes, he composed a gentle and thoughtful sermon for his prodigal grandson, who had recently recounted his mistakes to him. He began:

Grandfather would not have forgotten you—be assured of that—nor the thorny path you have been walking. Nor does grandfather require any photograph as a reminder of you. You are his grandson, and he is ever and always deeply concerned for your welfare; hard as your experience has been, he has suffered in it with you, and in the fond hope that it would prove to be a blessing in disguise. And he is so hoping.

It is indeed a great boon for a boy to be obliged to build his own foundation. I had a rich inheritance in foundation building from both my father and mother, and I reverence them, and often long to see them even though it is so many years since they passed away. They probably had the average imperfections of human beings, and with the average opportunity in life, but . . . I cherish their memory more and more with gratitude for all they did for me—and the things they did at the time did not always please me, but I can see now the wisdom of their rigid requirements.[10]

He went on to describe the dullness of his early years as a book-keeper, the value in discipline and self-control gained by that experience. He warned Fritz, though, not to work overtime, for he believed a proper counterbalance of leisure cultivated the calm temperament that had seen him through the difficulties of running Standard Oil. He discussed the "great boon" of attending church, for its opportunity to associate with "people in the most humble of circumstances." He urged knowing "good and true people" without regard for their wealth or position. He sympathized with "the bitter cup" Fritz had tasted, and commended his persistence and achievement with the hardware company.

Waiving its regulations, Yale accepted Fritz for another try. There he quickly rose to the top of his class and became very popular. Because of his exemplary academic performance, the school granted him a scholarship. Then a journalist revealed Fritz's relationship with Senior, so Yale revoked its award. To make up the loss, Senior sent Fritz a similar amount of money, along with much praise. Fritz went on to become a lawyer and even adopted his father's avocation of animal husbandry. He would later become a leader in the American Breeders Association.

The public splintering of the Rockefeller-McCormick family had not ended. In February 1922, much to Senior and John Jr.'s dismay, an announcement story hit the papers that was beyond their reach to squelch.

Harold had gone out of town, leaving sixteen-year-old Mathilde and Julia Mangold, the bookkeeper from the riding academy, alone in his new house. After he departed Mathilde called the Chicago papers, and led the reporters into the parlor for tea. There, she announced she was going to marry her Swiss riding instructor, Max Oser. The reporters raced out to see who could beat placing the story in headlines first: One of America's wealthiest heiresses had chosen the hand of a middle-class man thirty years her senior. They knew Senior would never approve, for recently he had come out publicly against American women marrying foreigners. When the reporters caught up with Harold the next day, he confirmed prior knowledge of the engagement, but noted his daughter would have to gain also the consent of her mother and grandfather Rockefeller. From that point even the discreet *New York Times* pursued the unfolding drama with a tabloid flair, offering rumor and half-truth.

Telegrams from the family flowed to Senior's door. Harold informed him that the engagement had been on for some months, and that he had planned to notify him before Mathilde made the public announcement. Fowler wrote that he regretted his sister's act, but did not think the situation was beyond repair. Muriel reported to her grandfather that both she and Fowler felt terrible about their sister's behavior, and asked him to do what could be done to "stop this nonsense now before it's too late."[11] Edith asserted she had known nothing of the plan, that she believed Julia Mangold and Oser had conspired to win over Mathilde's affections. (In time, reporters would learn that Mangold was related to Oser.) She believed her daughter to be too inexperienced and strong-willed to listen to anyone else's reasonable counsel. Fowler then suggested that Mathilde was looking for a father-figure, and that Oser loved "something besides Mathilde's personality."[12]

Edith wrote to Mathilde, who refused to see her. "I miss seeing you very much," she pleaded. "What your problems are which keep you from coming to me as one human being to another, you must know. What can it harm to talk to one's mother . . . it does not mean that we have to follow [her advice] and certainly we do not unless we find understanding in the words spoken."[13] Unfortunately, Edith's appeals were not the sort to sway an adolescent. She suggested that in marrying an older man Mathilde's children might be prone to insanity, as happened to two of Nettie McCormick's offspring. Furthermore, older men "lacked the manhood" of men of twenty. Even so, Edith would not cut off her daughter. One afternoon she passed by Mathilde while walking up the aisle of a theater, whereon she extended her hand and attempted a cordial conversation. Mathilde rebuffed her mother.

Throughout subsequent months, Harold and Edith offered Senior contrasting views of the situation. Harold supported Mathilde because, he concluded, "it was a deep and vital life matter" for her.[14] Although he hired people to examine Oser's past, he was sympathetic to the man from the start. Given that Oser was middle-aged, Harold fully anticipated that reports would show that the man had previous love affairs. Furthermore, he advised Senior, he was not going to ask Jung's thoughts on the matter because he expected the psychologist to be against the marriage. Oblivious, Harold wrote as though Senior agreed with him. Perhaps in supporting Mathilde's passionate and impulsive behavior, he saw further rationalization for his own involvement with Ganna Walska.

Edith did not realize that she had a competitor in the McCormick family, one who would use the situation for her own self-satisfaction. Harold's sister Anita, who had lost her only child to the 1918 flu epidemic, saw an opportunity to fulfill her frustrated nurturant drive. In a letter of welcome to Max Oser, she explained, "there are deep places that we should go into all together . . . M[athilde] has no mother near her and although I cannot be all of that, I can be some of it—and I love her dearly."[15] Anita had seen little of her niece over the years, so this claim of affection was duplicitous. Nonetheless, Anita's doting must have been most welcome to a troubled adolescent used to a rather capricious mother.

Edith's views toward the engagement were more thoughtful and insightful, and were shared by other McCormicks, notably Cyrus and Nettie. She knew that Oser had earlier tried to romance Margaret Strong; she correctly perceived Julia Mangold's role in the matter as Oser's spy and accomplice; she recognized Mathilde's need for a father-figure to replace Harold, who had been absent so much of her youth. Edith, too, had her lawyers investigate Oser's past. Word came back that he owed the previous year's taxes. Furthermore, he was telling friends of his plans to purchase a large estate and farm it—something he could do only with outside money. As for his previous intimacies, no sign of scandal emerged. Yet even though Oser had a perfect reputation, Edith reminded Senior, "Swiss men are such tyrants to their wives, and so ordinary and coarse—even the well-bred ones."[16] Swiss men would do anything for money, and the laws allowed them full control. (Was she thinking of Jung here?) Several months later, Oser reportedly told Edith's representative that if she ever returned to Switzerland he would sue her for slander: "I can *make her pay.*" Edith responded that were Mathilde to marry Oser, she would cut her daughter off from all support.

Meanwhile, Mathilde left Chicago with Julia Mangold to relax at Hot

Springs in Arkansas and escape the press. She could also evade the possibility of a surprise visit from her mother. Senior decided that if anyone could influence the rebel, it would be her brother Fowler, who followed her to the resort for this purpose. When he asked his sister at least to postpone her plans, she refused. Her intention was to go from Hot Springs to Florida to obtain her grandfather's approval. In the end, Senior refused to see her and told her not to show up at his door.

Newspapers turned Mathilde's engagement into a melodrama. One said that not since Greece went to war to recover Helen of Troy had obstacles like those built by Senior and Edith blocked Cupid's way!

Continually stymied, Edith hoped the law would prevent the marriage. In Switzerland, an underage girl needed both parents' consent to marry. Unfortunately for Edith, Harold pulled an ace. Without warning he went to probate court to have himself appointed Mathilde's guardian, which meant his signature alone sufficed. When Edith learned of this action, she appealed to the court to amend the decision to restrain Harold from having sole consent for the marriage. Somehow, outside the courtroom, Harold convinced Edith he would not give permission without her approval as well. After she reported this handshake agreement to the judge, he let the full guardianship Harold requested stand. Why Edith trusted Harold at this point is puzzling. Soon afterward, Harold and Mathilde travelled separately to Europe and joined up in France.

In August 1922, Harold interviewed Max Oser for the first time, and informed Senior he admired the man's character in all regards. Mathilde went shopping for her trousseau with Ganna Walska, who was now divorced. (Her separation from Cochran had been a sensational one; at one point she barricaded herself for several weeks in their Paris home.) On August 13, Harold cabled Senior that he had just married "Mrs. Cochran," and followed it up with a long letter extolling his unbounded joy in taking the path he just "had to follow."

In October, Harold described to Senior a visit with Max, Mathilde, and chaperone Mangold at a Swiss mountain retreat. "Lovely fellowship; eating chestnuts by the bright fire; watching kittens play; talking to a faithful dog and roaming around, constitute part of the life." Max showed love and deference to Mathilde, but was "indeed the master of the situation, as it should be."[17] Harold asked them not to marry until the following April, and the couple agreed to his stipulation. The couple impressed Harold with their economy, and stated they had agreed upon separate property rights. Yet after their marriage, this agreement meant that Harold's normal annual allowance to his children of twenty-five thousand dollars was split in half in Mathilde's case, with half going to her husband. Harold also bought the sizeable farm Max Oser long had his eyes on.

Mathilde's choice of mate was a common social phenomenon in the early 1920s, that of wealthy daughters choosing to marry déclassé men. They defied their families by marrying chauffeurs, gardeners, and those of questionable foreign title. Worse still, they married more than once. Among the many well-known cases was Alice Drexel, who found herself impoverished and abandoned with her newborn baby in a French hospital by a fortune-hunting aviator. He was later discovered to have stolen the jewelry of Mrs. John D. Spreckles, Jr., for whom he had deserted Alice. (Alice later atoned her mistake by marrying into the Philadelphia Biddles.) On the other hand, fun-loving sons of Gilded Age barons were marrying chorus girls, waitresses, and speakeasy sorts, as Regi Vanderbilt did when he wed the stunning Gloria Morgan. In a speech with clear implications to her daughter's case, Edith announced that women marrying beneath their status were violating "the clan" of class. Such women would end up enslaved, she warned. Unfortunately for Mathilde, Edith's prediction was correct.

To add to Edith's troubles, her daughter Muriel also turned against her, although not so publicly. Upon returning to the States, she continued taking her voice and acting lessons. When her mother moved back to Chicago from Zurich, Muriel kept on cordial terms with her at first. She accompanied Edith to the opera, taking the seat that was once Harold's. Muriel and Fowler both lived with Harold, whom she called "Doodsie," in his childhood home on Rush Street. Harold encouraged her theater interests and probably paid for her classes. Like so many young socialites, she served on various charity boards, and especially enjoyed arranging the entertainments at fêtes. She pursued starting a civic theater in Chicago, though never fulfilled the plan.

In April 1922 Muriel had her stage debut in *Le Pasant*. This was apparently a vanity production of the Modern French Theatre. Muriel designed the sets and costumes and acted the male lead, Zanetta, in the original French. Although Muriel affirmed that the stage was her life, she had a serious vocal impediment to making a career of acting in the States: She had grown up speaking Swiss-German and had a strong accent, this at a time when anything German was greatly disapproved. In subsequent months the papers reported rumors of a million-dollar movie contract offer, which made more sense given that the movies then were still silent. Muriel replied her heart was set on opera. She moved into an attic studio with a friend, with whom she started a small boutique, The Band Box.

From that point Muriel began to cut herself off from her family. Her first target was Senior. Following the receipt of a birthday check from him, she returned it, saying it pained her that he would express his "loving feeling in such a materialistical [sic] manner."[18] He responded that he had always given such checks to her parents while she was growing up, and she was old enough now to get them directly. She was also angry that he had repeatedly denied her requests to visit him. When he explained he thought it best in light of all the publicity surrounding Mathilde, she rejoined that she was *"innocent"* of all that, and would never again ask to see him. Of course, Muriel was unfamiliar with the defamation her grandfather had suffered in the past, and could not appreciate his fear of drawing any untoward attention to himself, especially now that he was in his halcyon eighties. That Senior would refuse to allow any of the McCormick grandchildren around him at this time hints at how deep the wounds remained from earlier public criticisms. He knew it would be a heavy price to lose any of these grandchildren's affections, yet he took the chance anyway, for self-protection.

Muriel rejected Senior's money, but not that of her father, who decided to settle upon her the same amount he was giving to Mathilde, twenty-five thousand dollars a year. The catalyst for turning on her mother may have been money, for Harold initiated a lawsuit to prevent Edith from receiving certain trust income he thought should be reinvested for the children's future sake. Doing this brought him further in favor with Muriel. Also, Harold scheduled her to sing with the Chicago opera when Ganna Walska at last made her debut on its stage.

Sometime in the mid-1920s Muriel came under the influence of her godparents, George and Marian McKinlock. A spiritualist had convinced Muriel that their son George, Jr., who had died in France during the war, was her soulmate, that she had been "married" to him. Marian McKinlock held no love for Edith, and told others, probably speciously, that she had adopted Muriel as a favor to John D., who wanted the young woman under better influences. Muriel moved in with the McKinlocks, and often accompanied them to the grave in Lake Forest where their son's ashes rest.

Then Muriel had a nervous breakdown, the first of several to occur during her life, and lived for a time with the McKinlocks in Palm Beach. Muriel rebounded well enough to attend the Eastman School of Music in Rochester, but she seemed unable to discipline herself to a career any more than she could commit herself to her short-lived boutique. She became a favorite prey of the traffic police looking for speeders, and of partygoers searching for someone to pick up the check.

✤ ✤ ✤

Only Fowler remained on good terms with both his parents, yet even he, too, caused his grandfather worry. Senior read in the papers one day that Fowler was involved with Anne "Fifi" Stillman, who still lived on her estate adjoining Pocantico.

Fifi was twenty years older than Fowler, yet in middle age remained striking. She was tall and beautifully proportioned, with red springy hair and enormous dark brown eyes. Her histrionic personality was well-known around Pocantico. Cooperating with her was, in the words of one employee, a Herculean task. Where the Rockefellers kept the same staff for years, Fifi made clean sweeps without warning, replacing an all-British crew with an all-Oriental, which would soon be fired for another set. One evening the Ku Klux Klan, which was active in nearby Yonkers, burned a fiery cross outside her windows. Fifi fired everyone, inside and out. When angry, her eyes burned dark, she would run her hands through her hair, and mature men quickly scattered from her sight.

Fifi was also a tease, who was not above wearing flimsy outfits in front of her workmen, yet expected them to behave like sticks of furniture. Those who stared got her boot, sometimes. The problem for her staff was that she was also simply playful, and they were never sure which mood she was in. Once a new worker went to the kitchen to help her move some furniture. When he returned to eat lunch with the others, he was smiling broadly. "Boy, that's some cook they got up there now—that new cook." What cook? they asked. "I really had a lot of fun with her. I mean that big redheaded dame."[19] Another worker answered her call to find her dressed in fencing attire, flexing the saber blade this way and that. Worried he would end up "skewered like a Thanksgiving turkey," he pulled back. Pleased she had scared him, she laughed and dropped the sword.

What compensated for Fifi's mercurial moods was her energy and intelligence. She was the rare wealthy woman who had mastered all household and maintenance skills. She cooked, scrubbed floors, and pruned shrubs as expertly as her staff, often better. Her mastery was more than practical. She studied as well, so as a gardener she knew the botanical names of every plant and their particular growing needs.

In addition to the main house, a series of thatched cottages dotted her estate. Fifi kept a full stock of clothing at each, so that she could move from one to the other on impulse. She also controlled a pack of fierce dogs she would send after any youngsters crossing her property by mistake. Fifi was further unusual for being an avid sport, who spent part of each year in Canada, where she regaled in the frontier life of long canoe trips and hunting. The Stillman lodge lacked modern facilities, and required of Fifi the hard physical labor Eliza Davison had known a century earlier.

Under normal circumstances Senior would have been shocked by a possible liaison between Fifi and his grandson. The news even more distressed him because Fifi and her husband were on the front pages regarding several sensational lawsuits. Fowler assured Senior of his innocence. Fifi Stillman's son Bud had been Fowler's roommate at Princeton, he reminded his grandfather, and it was Bud he was visiting during his frequent trips to the Stillman home in Pocantico.

The first legal charge had come in July 1920 from James Stillman Jr., who wanted to divorce Fifi on the grounds that her latest child, two-year-old Guy, was not his. The real father, he swore, was Fred Beauvais, an Indian guide they hired when living at their lodge in Canada. He therefore sought to disinherit Guy, to prevent the toddler from ever inheriting the trust his father James Stillman had set up for his grandchildren. When asked to give testimony from Montreal, Beauvais said that all the charges involving him were false. By the end of the hearings, which protracted over two years, out of twenty-four witnesses testifying on Fifi's private activities, all but one refuted her husband. Worse for James Stillman, Jr., his own sister, Isabel Rockefeller, testified that her brother was living with Fifi in New York during the period of Guy's conception.

Fifi had first learned of her husband's complaint when she received papers for the suit in her *Olympic* stateroom, just before sailing to Europe. She was so distraught that during the Atlantic crossing she almost committed suicide one evening, but an elderly missionary happened by and consoled her. She went to Zurich to consult with Carl Jung, whom she would have learned of through Fowler, and returned with full heart and courage to fight her husband. The battle would be terrific, she knew, for she was up against the awesome financial and social power of, in her words, "the bolsheviki of Wall Street." That power pressured two sets of lawyers to quit her case before she found an attorney who would see it through.

While this trial was underway, arguments began in another courtroom concerning the paternity of Jay Ward Leeds, infant son of Mrs. Florence Leeds, a former chorus girl. A reporter revealed that "Mr. Leeds" was the alias James Stillman, Jr. used when visiting his mistress when he visited the Long Island home he had maintained for her. Now Fifi, who had no prior knowledge of her husband's second family, countersued her husband by naming Mrs. Leeds as corespondent.

James Jr. felt so cornered that he started a new scandal by displaying purported love letters from Fifi to Beauvais. Again Beauvais and Fifi denied any prior relationship, and the letters proved to be of dubious origin. His frustration mounting, James Jr. cut off his allowance to Florence Leeds. In turn, Fifi befriended her rival and told her to "fight like a tiger" on her own child's behalf. She even offered to take Florence's son into her home. Fifi's refusal to accept any out-of-court settlement won even the Wall Street crowd over to her side. James Jr.'s friends cut him socially, and his clubs ostracized him. He was even forced out of the presidency of National City Bank, which his father had started.

By late 1925, James Jr. had lost all his appeals, so that he was both refused a divorce *and* identified as the legal father of Guy. When he pursued with Fifi the possibility of an uncontested divorce, she refused to cooperate. In early 1926, James Jr. suggested to Fifi that they end their separation. She agreed, and accepted his reconciliation gift of a $100,000 necklace. They went abroad to consult with Carl Jung and returned with a proclamation of fidelity. "Once you have loved and lived together and had children, I do not believe it is possible to break off the marriage tie by divorce," Fifi announced.[20] She explained Jung helped her to discover the male side of her self, her "anamus [sic]."

Each corespondent from their earlier lawsuits left the scene. Florence Leeds went to England, where she married one John Rouseau Metcalfe and settled with him in France. Canadian guide Beauvais started a garage and filling station in one of his tribe's settlements.

Exactly where the truth lies in all this will never be known. In five years leading up to her husband's lawsuit, Fifi was indeed often in Canada. Furthermore, Fifi saw Fred Beauvais in Pocantico as well as Canada, for she brought him to her New York home to teach outdoor lore to her children.

During the scandal, newspapers printed pictures of infant Guy beside Fred Beauvais and James Jr., and invited readers to choose the likely father, but they omitted a third possibility. Wherever Fifi lived in recent years—Canada, New York City, Pocantico—Fowler was often present. "I would not marry the finest man in the world," Fifi told reporters who dogged her about Fowler's companionship.[21]

Edith shared her father's concern about Fowler. "There is always a pitfall for a rich young man in a much older, designing, and fascinating woman."[22] Her fears abated some when he took a job in New York as a stock broker. He also accompanied Carl Jung on several journeys to see tribal cultures, including the Indians of the Southwest. By the late 1920s, he was working for International Harvester, where he was to prove himself a deft executive.

Fowler had lied to his mother and grandfather. He was not out of the

Stillman circle, and following an amicable divorce, Fifi married him in
1931. The Social Register deleted his name from its books for marrying
the much-older divorced woman. By then he was thirty-one, and the mis-
match was not so sensational.

As has been intimated in the cases of Fritz and Fowler, youngsters coming to maturity following the war had more autonomy than their parents
had enjoyed. Young women went about unchaperoned, drove automobiles, and smoked. They shed their earlier stiff undergarments, donned
silk stockings, and revealed their calves. The nature of courtship changed.
"Good times" moved from the parlor to the movies and other places of
public amusement. Despite prohibition, alcohol was available to the well-
to-do in luxurious speakeasies that paid large bribes to the police. (The
Rockefeller compound in New York was right in the center of the city's
classiest speakeasy district, which may be another reason Senior stayed
away.) A young man no longer "called" at a girl's home; she wore a hat,
expecting him to take her out. A new word, "date," appeared in the vocabulary.

Dating, like prostitution, required that men have money to have access
to women. In the days of calling, to court effectively a man need only
show up at a house at the appropriate time and follow all the rituals. This
was particularly convenient to young heirs, who could save their often
small allowances for other pleasures. It also meant that sons of architects,
college professors, or other professionals of modest means could compete with the sons of capitalists. By the 1920s, men controlled courtship,
in that they invited women into a man's world and paid the costs. Yet they
complained about having to buy feminine companionship, and came to
expect that women owed them something in return, namely her sexual favors. Movies and magazine advertisements reinforced the notion that
women use their physical and erotic expression to charm men. A new
contest was on.

Babs Rockefeller jumped into the fray wholeheartedly.

Of all Senior's children, John Jr. and Abby were the most attentive and
thoughtful parents. In spite of their many outside activities, they were less
preoccupied or neglectful than the McCormicks. Although they had
strong ideas about raising children, they were not so authoritarian as the
Prentices. They examined the particular needs of each of their six children, and did not impose identical demands as a result.

This was the era of "modern mothering," when medical experts and
child specialists referred to science as a basis for raising children. (Rocke-

feller philanthropy had fed this trend through its grants to social scientists and psychologists.) In other words, out with the Bible and in with Holt's *Feeding and Care of Infants.*

Abby's notes for talks she gave on mothering hint at this new ideology. One must extend "external vigilance" concerning health. Educate the child about its body, be frank, explain why it is sick. Use a thermometer often. Concerning sex education, be direct and scientific, as explained in the modern sex guide of the day, Morley's *Song of Life.* Abby's letters reveal her preoccupation with the bodily states of her brood, her husband, and herself. Her focus seems overblown to modern readers, given that the ailments were generally respiratory problems. Her concern was valid though, for antibiotics did not exist and the various drugs to relieve respiratory symptoms were yet to be available. A sinus infection meant weeks of rest to prevent bacterial spread and more serious disease. Now and then she reported the death of someone in good health who was felled following a trip to the dentist or a cold that progressed to pneumonia.

Modern psychology also encouraged a more individualized approach to parenting. Thus Abby preached that because each child is an individual, a parent must recognize that a method that worked felicitously on one child would not necessarily work for another. Consequently, she scanned each child for his or her particular inclinations and temperaments, and sought to encourage their talents. This was quite different from John Jr.'s experiences, where he and his sisters, apart from gender differences, were raised to be good Christians and responsible citizens. Of course he continued to exert these pressures on his offspring, notably through daily prayers, account books, and such, but Abby introduced more variety into their lives. Nonetheless, she had very high standards of excellence. Whatever direction in life her children chose, they had better be among the best at it.

Beyond her scientifically based directives, Abby urged a principle less discussed in the literature: tolerance. Very few apart from the Quakers practiced this charge, she observed. A child needed to learn that someone who dressed in a different way, who ate unusual foods, who spoke a strange language presented "a privilege to be sought rather than something to be shunned." The battle for good will began at home and at school, she asserted, as in a letter to sons John, Nelson, and Laurance:

> I want to make an appeal to your sense of fair play and to beseech you to begin your lives as young men by giving the other fellow, be he Jew or Negro or whatever race, a fair chance and a

square deal. It is to the disgrace of America that horrible lynch-ings and race riots frequently occur in our midst. The social ostracism of the Jew is less brutal, and yet it often causes cruel injustice.[23]

This refusal to be exclusive or ethnocentric was a stance John Jr. whole-heartedly supported, as he had grown up with it himself.

From the many letters and leavings of John Jr. and Abby, it is clear they discussed and carefully thought through their parenting. They agreed on most principles, and examined how best to implement them. One way they practiced their values was by sending the four youngest boys to Lincoln, a coeducational, nonsegregated experimental school. Lincoln began with a grant from the Rockefeller Foundation to Columbia University in 1917 to carry out the ideas of John Dewey. Students created the rules, chose their course of study, and in the lower levels had no grades or tests. Girls took shop, and boys learned to cook and sew. Laurance said it best: "We loved the Lincoln School. It was a blessing, so normaling [sic], no status connected to it, nothing at all like a fashionable prep school. . . . That was where I learned to participate, to make my way with all kinds of people."[24] Lincoln was especially supportive of Nelson, who had dyslexia, an unknown learning disorder then, for the curriculum allowed him to learn by listening and speaking out. John 3rd stayed at Browning with its tiny classes because his parents worried his shyness and timidity would be better overcome there.

As is common even today, both parents were more stern with their eldest children. Although Abby was strict about the house rules, John Jr. in particular thought he must be the tough police, judge, and jury. His bluster suggests an unease around parenting. He was best when alone with one or another youngster, and only then seemed free to relax and show spontaneity. Consequently, both Babs and John 3rd had greater insecurities than the younger children. They expressed their self-doubts in very different ways, with Babs choosing a path that made her harder to manage.

Being the only daughter, Babs had some privileges her brothers lacked. She did not have to share her toys, and had her own four-room fully-furnished play cottage in Pocantico. She did not get into the intense sibling disputes that occurred, as when mischievous Nelson prodded introspective Laurance into playing tricks on pudgy Winthrop. But it must have been frustrating to go from being the center of attention to the side show for five brothers who were being groomed for their places as Rockefeller men.

Of all the children, Babs was least suited to a regimented upbringing. She hated the morning prayers, "fannies wagging," she recalled, and rising at 7:00 A.M. on Sundays to go to church. She avoided doing chores for extra pin money. "I can always get a dollar from Grandpa," she told her brothers, and could. When the war came, she saw no point in her keeping a Victory garden.

John Jr. held a special affection for Babs, which increased as she matured to share many of his interests in music and theater. He was especially attentive to her, but through thoughtlessness could suddenly ruin a special moment. He might take her to buy a present, then so agonize over the choice that the purchase was painful to her. Once he took her with him to see her grandfather in Florida, then spoiled the trip when he reprimanded her too sternly for forgetting to pack a comb. She knew he loved her, but she could only fear him or, in softer moments, pity his inability to have fun.

Seeing so much of himself in Babs, John Jr. drove her hard to be exceptional in all her endeavors. He would bring out his old report cards to show how he had done better in a subject and press her for reasons she was doing less well. Unlike Senior, who never lectured his children, John Jr. could not hold back his strong opinions, which could turn into sarcasm. His criticism left Babs shy and high strung. She rebelled the only way possible, by doing poorly at Brearly and Miss Chapin's, both schools good at easing the problems peculiar to rich girls. Though an upper-class school, Brearly gave its students a classical education identical to that of elite boys. Consequently, many of its graduates, such as Gertrude Vanderbilt, had acquired the independence to forge a life other than that of social matron. Babs would not be one of these Brearly notables. When the time came for her to attend college, she refused.

Unlike her brothers, Babs found little comfort in her mother, whose social causes, women's committees, and insistence upon homey family gatherings held little attraction. Once when her mother was entertaining at Pocantico, Babs arrived unexpectedly and stormed through the gathering toward the stairs that led to her room. When her mother stopped and quietly asked her to circulate among the guests, she announced firmly, "I will not!" Of course, Babs's outspoken behavior was characteristic of her generation of young women, many of whom repeated similar scenes to the shock of their Victorian-age mothers.

Abby was not fully aware of Babs's differences from her. For example, Babs hated Abby's favorite home, the Eyrie in Maine, yet Abby believed otherwise and wrote how much her daughter seemed to enjoy being there.

Babs much preferred the company of Abby's sister Lucy, a frank, adventuresome spinster with few pretenses. Lucy was often in Europe or Asia searching out art works and fashions for herself and Abby. (Once, while traveling on a train in China, Lucy was kidnaped at gunpoint by bandits. Her account of the forced march through the rugged landscape, dressed only in a pink silk nightgown and robe, is a classic example of steely New England courage and wit.)[25] Abby wisely encouraged her sister's involvement with Babs.

With physical maturity, which came early, Babs discovered she was attractive to men. She grew up to become a willowy, athletic blond, more attractive than her mother. Born with the Rockefeller stamina, she could dance for hours or play tennis, twenty or forty games a day. If her father thought the swains kept her out too late, Abby would remind him of her own experiences as a popular young woman. Yet her strong will was too much when it came to drinking and smoking. She refused to give up cigarettes even after she fell asleep with one lit and set fire to her bed.

In a wise move, in 1920 Babs's parents sent her on a world tour with her Aunt Lucy. "Tell Babs that Seal Harbor is prostrate with grief over her departure," wrote a male companion to Abby.[26] In her letters to her sister, Abby expressed as much love for Babs and understanding of her needs as toward her five sons, yet somehow Babs did not perceive this caring from her mother. Perhaps she was embarrassed by her mother's fussy dressing, her fancy hats, worn even in informal settings. Perhaps, too, she felt in competition less with her brothers than with Abby's outside interests, which were taking her away from the family more often. The tutelage and undivided attention of fearless Aunt Lucy was fortunate compensation.

In 1921, John Jr., Abby, and Babs crossed the Pacific on the *Empress of China* to attend the official opening of the Peking Union Medical College, supported by the Rockefeller Foundation. On the Pacific crossing, he relaxed with his daughter, danced with her nightly, and bribed her to stop smoking. She agreed, and at the end of her journey she received a fleet roadster, in which she loved to tear down the winding country roads. A year later, however, she wrote her father, who was recuperating from uncontrollable headaches in Dr. Kellogg's Battle Creek Sanitarium, "I've smoked, thereby losing my car. Mama told me to take it up to Tarrytown tomorrow and put it away."[27] That she would confess her failing shows the reach of her parents' conscience.

In December 1922, Babs made her New York society debut, one that was quite different from that of Percy Rockefeller's daughter Isabel Jr. In 1920, Isabel's presentation to society was planned with all the strategy of a military campaign. In addition to glittering parties sponsored by the family, Isabel went to London to invade that society and be presented at the Court of Saint James. Hers was the first lavish debut in Rockefeller family history, and hinted at changes in family values, at least for William's line. Although Abby accepted the ritual, for she had gone through it herself, she arranged for Babs a simple, informal affair at home featuring a performance by the noted violinist Mischa Elman. Babs was not drawn to fancy society events, and must have liked being freed from starring in a major production. "There has been such a riot of gaiety in the house as almost makes my hair stand on end," John Jr. remarked.[28]

Though she went out on all-night dates, Babs seemed to settle down. She took university classes in French, American history, and political economy. On a family vacation to Europe, she paid attention to the art and battlefields. In fact, she was living fast, enjoying the forbidden boot-leg liquor and jazz clubs of Harlem. The truth struck her parents hard when they read the headlines in the papers of May 13, 1924: A sharp reporter exposed that Babs had gone to traffic court twice for speeding, yet each time had her case dismissed. Without telling her parents, she had used her close friend and law student David Milton to act as her attorney. The papers made so much of "one law for the rich and one law for the poor" that the mayor ordered an investigation, and several people lost their jobs as a result.

At this point, Babs realized that as a Rockefeller she earned special public scrutiny. Ashamed of her behavior, Babs withdrew from her friends, smoked heavily, and hardly ate. John Jr. forgave her, but she was unable to sense his sincerity. In despair over her daughter's despondency, Abby took her to Paris. There Babs recovered in the round of parties and dances forced upon her. The arrival of Aunt Lucy for a tour of museums and fittings at Worth further buoyed her spirit. Apparently Babs had out-grown her rebellion.

After returning from Europe, Babs became engaged and was married on April 24, 1925, in a ceremony praised for its "simple grace and humble bearing." The groom was her childhood pal and now lawyer, David Milton. His prematurely gray hair matched his quiet, unobtrusive, soft-spoken, steady manner. "Our rich girls are getting sense," approved the newspapers in reporting the couple's plan to live on David's twenty-three-thousand-dollar annual salary (over ten times that of the day's average worker). Abby secretly worried that this attraction of opposites could not last, but threw herself into the plans nonetheless.

Abby understood the attraction between the two, yet questioned its longevity. David Milton was a tall, athletic, handsome sort, who owned a

Stutz roadster and loved speeding around the Pocantico winding roadways. Estate workers would hear the couple's approach in his car well before it appeared on the drive. Because Abby and John Jr. insisted upon
chaperoned gatherings for their offspring, courting was surreptitious,
therefore more delectable. Forced to explore intimacies in the woods, the
lovers were not alone. As one observer noted, "those of us who worked
on the ground crews drew the full benefit. They didn't deliberately carry
on their romance under our noses, but like most people they were able to
ignore our presence, marking off laborers as so many sticks of furniture."[29] Despite the strong physical attraction and sharing of excitement,
David and Babs had very different temperaments and interests. For example, he gloried in farm work of any kind, whereas Babs was more cosmopolitan. If Abby ever tried to reason with Babs to wait, she was
unsuccessful.

On the day of the wedding, thousands stood along West Fifty-fourth
to glimpse the arrival of the several-dozen guests, mostly relatives and servants. Eighty-six-year-old Senior arrived in a touring car, posed for cam-
eramen in his silk hat, and went in to enjoy the family reunion. All his
children and grandchildren were present except the McCormicks. Although invited, Edith did not appear. Fowler was off in Africa with Carl
Jung, and Mathilde remained in Switzerland. Thus, only Muriel represented her family line.

Perhaps recalling the floral splendor of her own wedding, Abby had
the public rooms of the house arrayed with masses of scented flowers,
large rubber trees and palms, wall sculptures of apple, cherry, and quince
blossoms, and fuchsia trees. To observe the rites, guests went up to the
front salon on the second floor. There all the furniture had been removed, forcing the guests to stand on either side of an aisle of roses leading up to the white silk altar. More flowers along the walls and Chinese
porcelain vases were the only decoration. Since it was an afternoon event,
Abby had the large windows draped so that the only lights were from the
overhead crystal chandeliers. Babs accepted the traditional dress, her lace
train alone costing one hundred dollars a yard.

For the wedding to take place at home may have been Babs's wish, for
she had long ago become resentful of religion (and after this point would
seldom attend church). She could not resist one public act of rebellion
during the ten-minute service. She required that the minister leave out the
words "obey and serve" her groom, and she omitted "to obey" from her
pledge to him. She was less making a feminist statement than announcing
her freedom from having to heed anyone anymore. Babs looked forward

to having her own household and living a quiet life, raising children. With "Milton" as her last name, she was free of the burdens attached to being a "Rockefeller."

John Jr. was equally relieved to see his own daughter off with the son of a longtime family friend, a young man obviously devoted to Babs. After the twelve hundred reception guests had left, John Jr. walked outside with a beaming smile and graciously escorted strangers in to see the decorations in the ceremonial rooms. When an elderly black woman refused his invitation, he insisted she take his arm and personally helped her across the street and about the rooms. This spontaneous kindness of John Jr. to strangers was typical. Tragically his notions of proper fatherhood kept him from often showing such warmth to his own children.

As the third-generation cousins reached marriageable age, it was Percy's eldest daughter Isabel Jr. whom the press described as the Rockefeller princess. Tall, slender, and with lovely carriage, she wore the chemise dresses of the day like a fashion model. Tabloids gave her double spreads. Four times she showed up at home with diamonds blazing on her engagement finger, and four times she refused to set a date with her frustrated fiancés. As much as she savored the deb life, she longed to attend Vassar College to study science. When her parents refused, she enrolled for courses at Columbia Teachers College and befriended a noted bacteriologist who encouraged her interest in a research career.

In a prescient move, Isabel Jr. finally settled upon a lifelong chum, Frederic Walker Lincoln II. The son of the head of H. W. Peabody, a prominent import-export firm, Freddy had grown up in Greenwich under domineering parents. When he enlisted for World War I without advising them first, they used their political influence to have him pulled from his regiment just as it was going overseas. Later, when he was about to enter his final semester at Princeton, his father suddenly ordered him home to take over the firm. For several years he watched closely as Isabel Jr. accepted one beau, then another, while he served as her ever constant chum. His steady devotion quieted her mercurial impulses.

LOVE IS WORTH MORE THAN MILLIONS approved the headlines when the engagement of Isabel Jr. and Freddy was announced. The ceremony, which took place in September 1925, received the press coverage of a British royal wedding. Before the event, papers described the extravagant plans: the private railcars for guests, the four thousand acceptances, the munificent flower arrangements, and the delicate rare-point lace on the gowns. Sixteen ushers saw the crowd to their seats. Aunt Elsie Rockefeller handled the arrangements, for Isabel Jr.'s mother refused to change her plans for an extended visit to Europe, and returned home only just before the ceremony. Both Senior, now eighty-six, and John Jr. were present in the second pew, along with Alta's family. Following the ceremony, a cluster of street boys waiting outside ran up to Senior for the newly minted dimes he gave out. Although he had none in his pockets that day, he shook the youths' hands and chatted with them. At the reception he repeated how pleased he was that his niece had chosen for her wedding the seventieth anniversary of the day he had started his first job.

Isabel Jr. thought her mother could never again wound her so badly as when she had neglected her wedding preparations, but she was wrong. Despite being told she could never conceive, she became pregnant on the honeymoon. The following spring, she fell seriously ill with measles and the baby, a son, was born prematurely. Upon hearing its cry, Isabel Jr. begged to hold the infant, but her mother, who was present at the birth, refused. Because he worried for his ailing wife's life, Freddy did not counter his mother-in-law. Fortunately, the child responded well, and the doctors expected the best. Yet without consulting the physicians, Isabel Jr.'s mother ordered an ambulance to take the baby to a hospital. The day was unusually cold and windy for April, and the child died, perhaps because of the poor conditions of the move. After the burial, Isabel Jr.'s mother refused a headstone or marker on the grave. A date, after all, could lead malicious gossips to create a scandal that did not exist. (As if to add to the shock, the bill for the delivery was ten thousand dollars, equivalent to well over ten times that today. The doctors did not realize that the couple lived only on Freddy's small salary.)

To work through her grief, Isabel Jr. returned to school to study science and found a job in a bacteriology laboratory. To her surprise, she soon became pregnant and gave birth to a daughter. This time her mother appeared at Miss Lippincott's Sanitarium, the only place to have a baby, and pronounced "Her name is Isabel." This baby, referred to as Belitta by her parents, had a wriggly, unsettled nature that kept everyone up at night with her frequent crying. Worn down by work and noisy child, Freddy developed pneumonia. At this point his mother, who was equally as strong-willed as the Stillmans, came and stole him away to a resort in Maine to nurse him back to health.

Years later, Isabel Jr. admitted to her namesake daughter that she would have left Freddy at that point, except she had no money of her own. (The public would never have believed Percy Rockefeller's daughter to be penniless, but her experience was—and still is—common practice among the wealthy. Young couples had to construct a semblance of a luxurious life, often accumulating debts, while awaiting the eventual inheritance of a trust fund.) Once again, Aunt Elsie Rockefeller saved the day by firing a telegram of outrage to Freddy, who shamefacedly caught the next train to rejoin his wife and infant daughter.

When adolescents rebel, they usually conform to available models of misbehavior. In the 1920s, other wealthy young men, like Fritz, made a mess of their college careers, gambled, and piled up debts. Wealthy young women, like Babs, became flappers. More often adolescents are too self-conscious to have the assurance to defy their parents so publicly. Rather, they display the normal troubles of maturation within conventional bounds. John 3rd felt gawky and shy. Isabel Jr. teased her admirers, gathered their proclamations of love, then deserted them. In time they shed these patterns. A few children flow through these transitions with ease. Fowler McCormick was one. Despite his unusual upbringing he passed into his adult years better than any of Senior's or William's grandchildren. Perhaps it was just the array of genes, his getting only the best qualities of his parental lines and none of the troublesome ones.

Of all the grandchildren on both sides of the family, however, only one left shards of her life that reveal some of the difficulty of growing up among the elite. She, too, was a rebel, but in a unique way. One can only wonder to what extent her siblings and cousins shared some of her poignant reflections on her position. True, she was very sensitive and so preoccupied with her dramatic views of Society that she was not typical. Nonetheless, being a poet she captured a chilling truth about her life, perhaps shared by others of her class, if not by her blood kin. She was Geraldine McAlpin, daughter of William Rockefeller's favorite child, Emma. She was named in honor of William's other daughter, Geraldine Rockefeller Dodge.

By 1915 Emma was probably worth more than Senior's children altogether, for her father lavished large sums upon her from early in her marriage. By 1920, she was averaging $200,000 a year income from the family trust. Her leavings to history are bound notebooks with her household management accounts: comments about servants; lengthy itemizations of linens and dining ware; details about shelves, mirrors, and racks; reminders to resupply waste baskets and mattresses in servants' rooms. A leatherbound *recette de cuisine* with labelling tabs entered in French recorded her favorite recipes. She kept separate accounts for the money spent on her children—their doctors, school tuition, clothes, and so forth. For years she listed all the important weddings of society, both to note gifts sent and to keep track of women's name changes. Most of the people in her address book had summer homes in Seal Harbor or Bar Harbor, where her family vacationed. Her check stubs showed small amounts written to charity, often ten dollar donations, with much larger sums to B. Altman, Lord and Taylor, Tiffany, Best and Co., Arnold and Constable—the purveyors to the rich. When she went to Europe, she rented a Rolls and bought French antiques, including rare toys that eventually went to the Museum of the City of New York.

Society shaped her life. She lived at a "good" address on Park Avenue. She dined often with her friends at the Colony Club, the first all-female private club in New York City. When war struck Europe, she participated in war relief projects sponsored by the Junior League and the YWCA. She saw that her children attended the right schools, had the "best" doctors, and took ballroom dance lessons. One of her homes, Brooklawn Manor in New Jersey, was a working farm, although unlike Alta Rockefeller she played no hand in operating it. In view of the practices of her peers, Emma was a good wife and caring mother, and nothing exists to suggest she was otherwise. There are only Geraldine's perceptions of her mother, and any good historian wants more than one source.

Early on, Geraldine did not find her lot fitting.[30] During her teen years, she wrote poems suffused with images of freedom: of gulls in flight, of ships calling to take her away anywhere, of honor to artists for providing messages of beauty, of longing for the spaciousness of the West with its silence and peace. Following graduation from the Westover School, Geraldine made her debut in 1920 and did not go on to college. After that, her writings hinted at broken romances and untrustworthy friends ("What people crave is pleasure") and hope in God. In a bitter and caustic poem about a wedding, she described fat old dowagers, drunken ushers, the parents unthanked by the bride:

> *Here's a modern wedding*
> *Lots of show*
> *Bride crowned with selfishness*
> *Sing heigh ho*

Her hunger for affection was touchingly expressed in a gift she made for Ivy Lee, the Rockefeller public relations advisor, who invited Geraldine to join his family on an automobile tour around the country in the early 1920s. On the way she filled a bound book with extensive descriptions of every stop and conversation, and pasted in dozens of postcards as illustration. The Lees must have been dumbstruck to receive this outpouring, more characteristic of a youngster than an adult woman.

Eventually Geraldine took courses in early childhood education, including Montessori training, and taught at a neighborhood nursery school. In 1930, she became the head of the Department of Educational Therapy at Babies Hospital of Columbian Presbyterian Hospital.

Modernism crept into her writing. Admiring the skies, she wondered "just how the average passerby/would look if seen through taxi's eye." In love, she advised, you should give your lips, not your heart to a man, for it is your body he wants. She fell in love with a "cad," to whom she wrote, you "held me in your arms but still above/My head, your eyes were gazing at her window full of love." Reflecting on a visit to the Dominican islands, she observed the women there danced for fertility while we "turn nature into jazz and shut it into stifling rooms"; while Dominican men dance for crops, city men dance for gold, "their dance a treadmill of bitterness."

She continued to live at home while resenting her parents. On one Mother's Day, she complained that Emma used money, power, and fear to keep her on the path she chose, to which Geraldine purposely rebelled by remaining unmarried. She derided her parents' reminders of their martyrdom and self-sacrifice on her behalf, their demands for senseless obedience and dependence. She sent some of these poems out to publishers and saved the rejection slips.

The last dated poem, completed in 1933, cried for forest and desert:

> Here I am imprisoned in a glassy car
> No freedom have to move or breathe or sing
> Caged in parental luxury. From far
> Circled by protection's magic ring.
>
> Always I'm yearning for a sense of space,
> For silence, color, form, where I can be
> Not the descendant of a wealthy race
> But simple, sincere and unassuming me.

Was it a plea others of her generation in the family would have shared?

In 1934, Geraldine became engaged to Jerome Pierce Webster, a plastic surgeon. Since her mother Emma was dying, the couple wed in the hospital by her bedside. Afterwards, Geraldine thanked John Jr. for his sympathy. While her mother "left us a heritage rich in courage, patience, gentleness, and high ideals," she admitted that she was relieved to be left with her father. When she moved with her husband to Riverdale on the Hudson, she thanked John Jr. for buying up the Jersey Palisades, for she would "never have to look out on a Mazola sign" across the river.

After giving birth to a daughter, she seemed more reconciled with her parents, and appreciative of the qualities she had always taken for granted. Then, two years later, while delivering twins, she died, an uncannily poetic ending for a tragic poet.

13

Sacrifices in Abundance

> *"Charge them that are rich in this world . . . that they do good, that they be rich in good works, ready to distribute, willing to communicate."*
>
> —I Timothy 6: 17-18

By the 1920s, Abby was rightfully proud of her husband's national recognition as a leading statesman much respected for his principles. Having spent so many years in the company of leading experts in finance, business, health, education, religion, art, industrial relations, and the social sciences, John Jr. was more confident in his grasp of the nation's needs and a vision for meeting them. Increasingly he was a leading voice for ethics in business, for racial and religious tolerance in society, and for faith in science to illumine and solve social problems. Abby was never one to take credit for her role in his achievements, but those closest to the couple knew the value of her frank, open-minded counsel.

As she had suggested at the time of the Ludlow Massacre, she had taken on more household decisions. Trusting staff at their several homes to do their work competently, she could oversee more creative domestic matters, such as interior design and gardening. Despite her many volunteer activities, Abby's priority was her family. Essential to nurturing, in her mind, was the shaping of an eye-appealing, comfortable, practical home and the lands around it. Had she lived in more recent times, she would have wondered about those who belittle homemaking as a calling. Besides, she acknowledged that her husband's authority in society extended her own, that her easing of his daily life freed him to fight for causes she supported.

Nonetheless, being so caring of her family and others, she could take on too many commitments and tax her health. She could not simply administer a project from afar. For example, during the 1920s she created a community house in Elizabeth, New Jersey, to serve the needs of working-class families. Besides choosing the site and overseeing the construction, she hired the staff, and appeared often just to be around the people served by Bayway Cottage. She lavished her affection on "twenty-five naked, squirming, cunning, fat little babies, some of whom took the occasion to drench me . . . [E]very once in a while they would all begin to howl at once."[1] She brought her own children along to join in the activities, and shared her own child-rearing problems with other mothers.

Though John Jr. was very judgmental of himself (and often family members), his position toward his associates was liberal. He thrived on opposition, and liked those who stood up to him. His great gift to those working on his many projects was his way of quieting discord through patience, clarity of view, and tact. His broad experience enabled him to find solutions to dampen the power plays and ego wars of specialists on the committees. One colleague's observations of John Jr. summed that of many who worked with him: "I have known him . . . to argue strongly against a proposed policy . . . and then when outvoted, I have seen him take the chairmanship of the committee appointed to put the policy into operation, and at the cost of hard work carry the matter he had voted against to a successful conclusion."[2]

The full story of John Jr.'s contributions has yet to be written, and this is not the place to go into detail. In considering his family life, one should keep in mind the complexity and seriousness of his daily activities away from home. His days were consumed with a level of meetings, trips around the country and abroad, speeches, and correspondence akin to that of corporate presidents. His initiatives included an interchurch world movement, the interdenominational Riverside Church, the creation of what became the Grand Teton National Park and preservation of forests in Yosemite, the purchase of Fort Tryon and the building of the Cloisters in New York City, continued involvement with colleges for African-Americans and the United Negro Fund, consulting with Margaret Sanger and quietly supporting her and others' efforts toward legalizing and disseminating birth control, the establishment of International Houses on several college campuses, support for the League of Nations, as well as membership on local city boards and councils. In addition, he continued his responsibilities to the extended family, such as overseeing improvements at Pocantico, running interference for Senior, making investment decisions, and dealing with his sisters' finances and problems.

Imagine being a boy with five siblings, four of them brothers, growing up under a father of such energy, talent, and renown. The competition for attention is great, the father an awesome model to match. The father, though, had been the only son, swaddled in a world of loving women of three generations. The father's five sons have just one female for nurturing, their mother, warm and fun to be sure, yet increasingly occupied with her own needs that take her out of the house. (Their only sister feels outnumbered by the boys' presence and does not add much big-sister adoration.) When the father comes home, desperate for quiet and a wise companion, he steals the mother away. No wonder several of John Jr.'s children as adults expressed resentment about his competing with them for Abby's attention. It is an old story common to many American families following industrialization, the circumstances heightened by this father's achievements and unusual need for their mother's attention. How many children accept the thought of their parents making love, metaphorically and literally?

Furthermore, the unrelenting activity undermined John Jr.'s health, which resulted in further separations from the children. He and Abby took several long trips during the 1920s, officially for one cause or another. Abby encouraged these journeys because she knew the only time her husband really rested was when he left the country. Pocantico was too close to the New York offices, and even at Seal Harbor he daily went through stacks of reports and correspondence. Unlike his father, who methodically scheduled daily rest or play as a necessary tonic, John Jr. could not relax without feeling anxious. Now and then he went on hunting trips, but one suspects from his chosen companions that conversations in the lodges turned to his projects. At best health, he suffered immobilizing headaches, sinus infections, and stomach troubles; at worst, he collapsed. Abby just as much required these respites away from home, for her own enormous work load provoked insomnia and hypertension. Given the family dynamic, though, it was John Jr.'s ailments that received the most attention.

Several times Abby simply commanded her husband quit working, for her recurring worry was "how many widows there are in the world . . . because their husbands worked too hard."[3] In late 1922 she urged him to go to Dr. Kellogg's Battle Creek Sanitarium for three weeks to recuperate from nervous exhaustion. Upon returning, he caught a debilitating flu, which led her to leave the children and accompany him to Senior's place in Florida. Even so, after several months there John Jr. eventually had to be hospitalized before he recovered fully. Although Abby hated being away from her youngsters, she admitted that it was "a great joy" to have some time alone with her husband, because even when they travelled other people surrounded them.[4]

While the children perceived their father to be monopolizing their mother—which in truth could not have been so extreme given his schedule—they neglected to consider that she consented to his requests. Abby obviously needed respite from her playful gang, her committee meetings, her partygoing and giving, as much as John Jr. did from his philanthropies. What extraordinary conversation he must have provided during their private moments! What relief she offered him as she wound up the Victrola and invited him to dance! Their opposite temperaments and inclinations in many areas must have added unexpected rhythms and riffs to their discussions.

Abby's most noted influence upon her husband was in art. After starting on his Chinese porcelain collection, he extended his interest to traditional paintings, principally of the early Italian period and the French eighteenth century, and to Oriental rugs. The craftsmanship of the porcelain particularly appealed to his pleasure in details. He studied and grew adept at noting the subtle changes in style that marked a shift in time or locale. The paintings drew upon his readiness to anchor himself deep in the past, to see a connection between modern day and earlier Western civilization.

His most frequently admired purchase was the extraordinary Unicorn tapestries now on display at the Cloisters in upper Manhattan. Woven in the late Middle Ages, these brilliant hangings depict the vitality of the hunt, amidst a colorful array of the flora and fauna of the setting. The images entice the viewer into the past, both through the particulars of medieval life and the universals of the unicorn myth. John Jr. hung them in a favorite retreat in the New York townhouse. They were so large that they covered the walls from ceiling to floor, and turned the corners to wrap the entire room, therefore the viewer, in their wondrous story and vision.

Having spurred her husband to purchase as well as admire art works, Abby could more easily spend her own Aldrich income on objects her husband disliked. John agreed a life surrounded with beauty was necessary, but he balked at his wife's broad conception of beauty. He appreciated her collection of Persian miniatures for their rich palette, realism, and skill. He happily gave her money to buy old Japanese prints, ancient Buddhist sculptures, and fine European china. What he could not bear was what she started bringing home during the 1920s: modern woodcuts, German Expressionists, Postimpressionists, and American folk art. "I showed Papa the [George Overbury Hart] pictures . . . and he thinks they are terrible beyond words," she wrote son Nelson.[5] Nor was he impressed with the tapestry Abby commissioned from Margaret Zorach, which incorporated scenes of their family life at Seal Harbor. He was so repulsed by some of Abby's choices that she set up her own gallery on the seventh floor of their house where she could show off her latest finds. The walls' light-wood panels had polished metal strips to allow a changing exhibit of the paintings and prints stored in cabinets. When friends or children came for tea, she took them up to her hideaway, pulled out a box of art works, and gave an informal lecture on the artists.

Abby's taste was unconventional, for few New Yorkers then acknowledged the significance of contemporary art. The sensational Armory Exhibition of 1913, with its show of Fauves, Cubists, and the Ash Can School, had only hardened major museum trustees against the incursion of contemporary styles with their emphasis upon expression over formal depiction, and their fascination with form, line, and color in themselves. Following the war, the Red Scare added a new objection, that modern art was Bolshevik, anarchist, or in another way politically suspect. To counter these forces, Gertrude Vanderbilt Whitney gave her fortunes to support living American artists and displayed their works at her Greenwich Village gallery. The other avant-garde Manhattan gallery owner was Edward Stieglitz, who was too competitive to consider working with Whitney toward their common cause.

Since most curators and gallery owners remained conservative, collectors like Abby often developed new tastes by happenstance. Through social contacts they met an artist or scholar who would educate them and break down any resistance to modern aesthetics. In Abby's case, the first advisor was William R. Valentier, director of the Detroit Museum of Art, a close friend of many European artists and writers. He was also well informed in certain traditional periods, which made his presence at dinner palatable to John Jr.

Two of Abby's women friends were also collectors of modern works. One was Mary Quinn Sullivan, a lawyer's wife who did interior design and taught art. Mary helped locate prints for Abby to purchase. The other, Lillie Bliss, had begun to assemble her own contemporary collection well before Abby. She started with five important paintings from the Armory exhibit, and soon had major works by Renoir, Degas, Seurat, Pisarro, and Matisse. She had to hide the pictures in a storeroom, for her mother, with whom she lived, disapproved of them. When Lillie's mother died in 1922, she sold the family mansion and bought an apartment with a three-story gallery, where she proudly hung all her previously forbidden fruit.

Chance encounters abroad led the three friends to recognize they shared a dream. While travelling in Palestine, Lillie Bliss ran into Abby. While catching up with one another, each mentioned her wish for a gallery or museum that would foster contemporary art. After leaving Palestine, Abby encountered Mary Sullivan aboard the *Ile de France,* and reviewed her conversation with Lillie. Mary agreed the three should seriously pursue their idea.

Upon reaching home, Abby used the standard Rockefeller approach to any initiative: build a broad base, locate the best experts, negotiate disputes, and plan very carefully before acting. To assist in their plans, the women invited Conger Goodyear, a collector of French painters (who had recently been tossed off the board of the Albright Gallery in Buffalo for adding Picasso's *La Toilette* to its permanent collection). Goodyear accepted major responsibility for the daily footwork toward establishing what became the Museum of Modern Art, while the women turned to raising the requisite funds to start it.

Despite being married to the wealthiest Rockefeller—for by now Senior had divested himself of much of his fortune—Abby had to look outside her family for major donors to fund a building for her project. Her friends remarked on her husband's "granite indifference" to MOMA; her sons knew too well his objections to "Mother's museum."

John Jr.'s intransigence on this issue was unusual. Throughout his life he had been one to listen, to broaden his view, to reverse himself when proved wrong. Whatever his motives, some lively arguments resulted at 10 West Fifty-fourth, though never of the force to threaten the marriage. Each had a particular style of fighting. John Jr. pressed his position unrelentingly "like a bulldog," one of Abby's friends observed, while she fenced back, dodging this point or that, introducing surprise parries. Her son Nelson suspected she enjoyed a good fight, for at times she seemed to take glee in provoking them. Perhaps this impasse over modern art, which seemed heartless to those supporting Abby, was an essential ingredient to their marital satisfaction. John Jr. could bark all he wanted about how Abby should behave, hence feel he was living up to his patriarchal duty, while Abby could assert her right to her choices, which ultimately he knew were hers alone. The Victorian husband thus compromised with the egalitarian American in himself.

However grudgingly, John Jr. accompanied Abby to the opening of MOMA on November 8, 1929. Admission was free, as well it needed to be given the collapse of the stock market a week before. The initial show, a collection of French art that Goodyear had obtained on loan for the event, was a clever introduction to the founders' aims. The women had agreed upon a brilliant young art historian, Alfred Barr, whose catalogue was both accessible to lay viewers and addressed the interests of scholars. The next show, which featured contemporary American art, was however not well received, and the direction of the museum stayed on an international course. Consequently, when Gertrude Whitney, who with her indomitable and astute assistant Juliana Force, soon afterward established a museum devoted to American art, their effort was not duplicative. Despite the failure of MOMA's second show, and the more serious problem of the Depression's effects upon the pocketbooks of potential donors, Abby pushed forward. To compensate for her husband's lack of interest in MOMA, she found an enthusiast in her son Nelson, who would himself become a major collector and advocate for the museum.

It is easy to overestimate the impact of Abby and John Jr.'s disagreements over modern art on the relationship. For one, they readily set aside different parts of their homes for their favorite art works. For another, they collaborated on other projects during this time. For example, Abby added to her husband's concern for conservation by sponsoring activities toward roadside beautification. With the rapid availability of cheap automobiles, the byways of the nation became noted as much for their litter and blight as for their landscapes.[6] It may seem odd that Americans would require education about such things as roadside trash and attractive refreshment stands, but changes in behavior accompany any new technology. Henry Ford did not anticipate that the country's roadsides had lacked housewives to keep them clean!

More significant for some would be Abby's collaboration with John Jr. concerning the Williamsburg Preservation. In 1926, while visiting the nearby Hampton Institute, the couple accepted the invitation of Dr. William R.A. Goodwin, rector of a church in the colonial town. For some time Goodwin had unsuccessfully sought various patrons, including John Jr., to fulfill his dream of restoring the original State Capitol area into an educational site. This time, Goodwin's enthusiasm and guided tour of the site enchanted John Jr., who sponsored a feasibility study of the proposal. When his advisors affirmed that the project was worthwhile, he authorized Goodwin to purchase parcels in the area, without stipulating the actual buyer. By 1928, most of the townspeople supported the restoration, and learned of John Jr.'s role as its major donor. No project would absorb him so much as this one, for he loved working with plans, measuring walls, brooding over landscape choices, talking with carpenters, gardeners, architects, and historians.

So much did he and Abby love the restoration that they bought an adjoining 585-acre woodlands containing Bassett Hall, a modest eighteenth-century frame house with only two bedrooms, to which they added a dining room, guest rooms, and workers' quarters. Decorated in Abby's eclectic style, it became their favorite spring and fall residence. The interiors were more informal than their New York townhouse, and displayed a fascinating array of American weather vanes, chalkware, pottery, needlework, and pictures. Except for the areas immediately surrounding the house, they preserved the natural landscape of the 585-acre tract of rolling woodland. Like she had done at the Eyrie, Abby laid out and planted the flower gardens and shrubbery.

Two of Abby's most significant contributions to Williamsburg built on her previous volunteer experience. One was the development of the Williamsburg Inn, which would become one of the nation's premier hotels, and a frequent governmental choice for extending hospitality to foreign officials. After convincing her husband of the need for good lodging and dining nearby the historical site, she again collaborated with Mary Lindsley about all aspects of the hotel design, from ventilation to the location of the chauffeurs' lounge, to the Regency decor, and to selection of the final management.

Only affluent visitors could appreciate Abby's efforts at the Inn; a larger public benefitted from her support of American folk art. During the 1920s, beyond collecting modern works, Abby delighted in the works of untrained painters and sculptors, and also the crafts of often anonymous children, women, and workers from the nineteenth century. Her holdings greatly improved when Juliana Force, a major collector, fell into financial trouble and was forced to sell many of her treasured objects. She bought quilts, hooked rugs, sculptures, and drawings from Juliana's brilliant collection. In the early 1930s, Abby lent many of these works to galleries around the country, where they attracted much public interest if not always respect. Viewers questioned the "art" label attached to seemingly primitive paintings of farms and family, weather vanes, or samplers. In 1934, she decided to loan 250 pieces for exhibit in the restored Ludwell-Paradise House in Williamsburg. Over the next few years she consulted frequently with Williamsburg staff concerning placement of the art in various buildings, and made her contribution permanent in 1939.

For a time it appeared Edith would make her mark in the museum world as well. By the early 1920s, she decided to lend objects from her collections to the Art Institute of Chicago. She intended to bequeath the works to that museum, and wanted to share them with the public even before she died. (In a will written later that decade, she left her townhouse to the museum to house exhibits.)

Also among Edith's most noted purchases were tapestries. Best known were the three superb early sixteenth-century Tournai tapestries she had acquired in 1909 in Munich, and later hung in the entrance hall and dining room at Villa Turicum. "Verdure with Animals" was eleven by eighteen feet, a thicket of blossoms in red, blue, and yellow, among which were found doves, hawks, pheasants, peacocks, an owl, deer lions, wildcats, a fox, a griffon, and a dog. A scarlet border with garlands, urns, and scrolls framed the design. The colors were fresh and strong, the tapestry firm and unrepaired. Two other tapestries, each about eight feet square, depicted "The Boar Hunt" and "The Bear Hunt." Typical of such tapestries, the settings included precise depiction of plants such as heartsease, camomile, and poppies, along with various bird life and small mammals. These tapestries had been trimmed, and were slightly faded, yet otherwise were in excellent condition. Edith subsidized art historian Phyllis Ackerman to prepare a history and interpretation of the works, and paid for a finely produced limited edition of her study.

As Ackerman noted, the verdure design originated with one of the oldest symbols of most religions, the Tree of Life. The universe is depicted as a tree: the world its trunk, the abyss its roots, and the branches the sky. The gods associated with the tree are of the animal kingdom (horned animals, cats, serpents, and raptors most prominent) and have astral associations. Such designs can be found in the art of Mesopotamia, Greece, and Egypt, China, India and Scandinavia. Between the ninth and fifteenth centuries, Jesus became increasingly identified with the tree of life. ("I am the vine, ye are the branches.")

The universal theme of the Tournai imagery with its integration of base, carnal, and spiritual, reflected Edith's new philosophy of life as influenced by Carl Jung. In explaining her founding of the Chicago Zoological Gardens, she had declared, "We must get nearer the animal to reach the human soul."[7] She went beyond her mentor, however, in placing more credence upon the theories of astrology and reincarnation. Where Jung saw these systems as myth, Edith claimed them as valid. According to one story, perhaps apocryphal, she seemingly went into a trance and announced that she had lived previously as Seti I, the child wife of Tutankhamen. Though some snickered, enough admired Edith's erudition that Chicago society developed a cultist element ready to study and adopt her latest interests. More significantly, they turned to her for Jungian insight, and her home became known as a mecca for devotees of psychoanalysis.

Despite her eccentric behavior, Edith returned to her place as the social leader of the opera crowd, who sought invitations to her preperformance dinners. By now many societal matrons had dropped the trappings of aristocracy from their festivities. Following the war, experienced household staff were hard to find, large houses seemed too cumbersome to manage, and tastes grew more informal. In New York and other cities, families sold their mansions to skyscraper builders, moved into apartments, and used hotels and restaurants for large entertainments. Edith not only insisted on the highest traditional style, but purchased lots adjoining her house to prevent a highrise from casting a shadow across its turret windows. (In this regard, she was Chicago's equivalent of New York City's Grace Vanderbilt, the opera doyenne who retained Gilded Age style into the 1940s.)

Guests arrived at her Lake Shore house to have the doors of their cars opened by the footmen in plum-colored livery. The omniscient butler Denham supervised the many servants taking cloaks, seating guests, and waiting at table. Were a special guest being honored, the place setting would be the gilded silver service of Napoleon's brother-in-law, Prince Camillo Borghese. The 1,600 pieces weighed more than 725 pounds, and each bore the Borghese arms surmounted by the imperial crown of France. The menus were in French with raised gold letters. When it was time to leave for the performance, Edith was helped into an ermine cape of 275 skins and assisted into her plum-colored Rolls Royce by two footmen. The wearing of ostentatious jewels, for some time avoided by society, may have returned to Chicago as a result of Edith's wearing emeralds once owned by Catherine the Great, her $1 million diamond matching dog collar and tiara, or her $2 million pearls. Little did they guess that she was in debt for some of her gems.

Appropriate to her regal presentation was sincere *noblesse oblige.* Virtually everything she did in Chicago since returning from Zurich was to improve life in the city for working-class and middle-class residents. The zoo was her first effort, with others to follow. In 1925, she was chief sponsor of a short-lived attempt to organize a civic theater that produced classical and modern drama at reasonable prices. That year she also sponsored a modest Woman's World Fair to bring women from various countries together. Her greatest commitment, however, was to provide affordable housing.

In late 1923 Edith entered into business with her Swiss protégé Edwin Krenn and an old friend of his, Ernest A. Dato, "to provide homes for persons with limited means at a price within their reach."[8] The two men had been school friends in Switzerland, and may have had an intimate relationship as well.[9] Dato had been living in Chicago for some time, as an employee with International Harvester. According to him, one day while reading the papers, he came across Krenn's presence in the city, looked him up, and suggested their forming a partnership. To fund the operation, Edith placed $5.2 million in Standard Oil securities into a trust to underwrite the operations. Very quickly the partners bought almost two hundred acres on the lake shore near Highland Park, along with a new office building on land once owned by the Palmer family.

Newspaper editors praised her plans. One noted how wealthy men were now expected to work to maintain self-respect, while their sisters were not. Thus, Edith set a good new example. They thought her entry in real estate wise because it was a business requiring "intuition[,] traditionally a trait in which women are supposed to excel." They looked forward to the results of her holding her own in a business "accustomed to purely masculine competition."[10]

In discussing her investments, Dow, Jones & Co. estimated that Edith's total stock holdings were worth over $27 million. Based on current dividends, she was earning almost $1 million a year income. Considering these figures, the financial analysts concluded, Edith's decision to assign part of her funds to back the project was not flagrant. Real estate was booming, and smart money followed that action. The economists were unaware of Edith's continued spending on art, such as the "Emperor's Carpet," a 660-year-old Persian rug once the property of Peter the Great. Nor did most people anticipate the coming collapse of the economy, however much the signs were evident to more prudent observers.

One prudent observer was Senior, who asked to see the trust agreement so he could have it checked by his lawyers. He worried "you would find yourself the possessor of the things which they [Krenn and Dato] wanted to unload, and at prices at which you could not resell the same." Given her previous bad experience in business "with foreigners," he predicted "great disappointment . . . which would give us all great humiliation."[11] Edith was certain for once she could prove her father wrong, by demonstrating that she was a capable executive and deserving of his recognition for her achievements.

Although the evidence is spotty, Edith's partners appear to have operated astutely at first. In particular, Dato was skillful at marketing a product and motivating a sales force. They started small, with a taxicab driver working as a salesman on the side. By the end of their first year, they occupied a large three-story building and had sold out their first subdivision. This led to the purchase of more vacant prairie land, advertising sketches that depicted winding drives and beautiful parks, and illustrated brochures that tempted "Own a piece of the good earth." They herded prospective customers into auditoriums for sales presentations interspersed between free entertainment and refreshments. In time, Krenn & Dato became one of the nation's largest subdividers, with more than six-teen thousand Chicagoans purchasing lots worth over $28 million from the firm. In addition, they set up subsidiary corporations to provide engineering consulting and property management.

According to the trust agreement, the principals were to withdraw no profits, but only receive salaries. Krenn and Dato each drew forty thousand dollars annually. Yet Krenn lived in a luxurious suite at the Drake Hotel, employed a butler, and collected Chinese antiques. Part of his apparent wealth was from Edith, who had given him a million dollars in stocks to establish him as a man of prestige. It is also possible he and Dato siphoned additional money by leveraging properties to float loans for other investments.

Edith's role in the company is unclear. She continued to infuse money; she participated in board meetings; she met with Krenn daily. The only historical witness to her activities years later was Dato, who had reasons then to be very critical of her. She interfered with her unannounced visits to the office, he recalled. She insisted that the salesmen maintain a "proper appearance" and not smoke. She intruded on his time by having him handle trivial problems at her mansion. His remarks are compatible with Edith's arrogant side, yet may not present the entire picture of her contributions. Was she a meddler who interfered with their more important decisions, or was she part of the team?

Meanwhile, Harold McCormick had bought a house in Lake Forest, where he lived when he was not on the road with Ganna Walska. As planned from the start of the venture, he and Edith did turn the Chicago opera company over to a group of underwriting subscribers in 1923. This transfer saved each from losing so much of their annual income to the company, and removed their authority as well. Nonetheless, Edith's legacy of productions in English remained.

Now married to a holder of the International Harvester fortune, Ganna Walska found her appointment book filled with singing dates. It soon became apparent that some impresarios hired her to squeeze out McCormick funding for their productions. In 1924 she sang incognito for a travelling Wagnerian company and contributed $100,000 to cover expenses. Another time, a concert committee withdrew its booking when she refused to make a donation to the city's orchestra association. Others put her on the stage as a novelty. When it was obvious that she would not rise to stardom in America, she dragged Harold overseas to underwrite productions for her there. In Paris audiences tittered and whistled through her Verdi and Mozart arias. Critics in Berlin, New York, Detroit, Chicago, and many other cities mocked her. One of the most alluring and gorgeous performers ever to grace the opera stage, she ruined the vision upon singing her first phrase.[12]

Anita McCormick Blaine's sister-in-law had married Walter Damrosch, a noted young conductor, and appealed to him to cast Walska in his performance of Beethoven's Ninth Symphony. He apologized that he could not hire the "great beauty" because "her voice is absolutely devoid of charm. What a tragedy. If only she would leave art alone, she would be much happier."[13]

Walska blamed everyone but herself for her poor reviews. No one could take her seriously, she protested, because she had married rich men. The American press were out to undermine her, and Edith was behind the cancellation of some Chicago concerts. The power of her self-delusion was manifest in her autobiography, where she wrote of her trials as comparable to such martyrs as the immolated Jeanne d'Arc and the censored Tolstoi, among others.

When Walska decided to quit singing in the States, Harold followed her faithfully around Europe. By 1926, the marriage was over. Walska's colorful account exempted herself from the matter:

> Harold's mind was especially confused by an abnormal sense of what he thought were his responsibilities, almost a mental complex of his duties, and an entirely misguided idea of what his part should be as an important citizen of his beloved city, Chicago ... [An] idiosyncrasy led him to idolize the physical expression of love and he became insatiable in his search for the realization of the physical demands, insatiable because they were unattainable for him anymore.[14]

Walska said she loved Harold so much "for his soul" that she could not imagine his preferring "gross and limited pleasure" rather than her "divine companionship." If Harold had paid attention to Freud instead of Jung, she averred, he would have understood the weakness of giving in to "the dictates of lower instincts"!

Ganna Walska found "divine companionship" in mysticism, as inspired by Maharishee in India, Paul Brunton, Manly Hall, Swami Yogananda, Rudolf Steiner, Meher Baba, and others of that movement prominent in the 1930s. (Baba, she concluded, was like a "spoiled soprano" more interested in her money than in her soul.) She married a fellow spiritual seeker, and travelled about the resorts of Europe. That marriage did not last either. "During my travelling, if I ever saw in a field a Harvester International machine I always sent to it a feeling of love or with my finger a tiny kiss."[15] At her luxurious home in France, the Chateau de Gallius, she practiced healing by "singing each pure tone" to send "to the Infinite a Divine Messenger" to cure her clients. Into old age she continued to study voice and remained convinced she could yet be another Jenny Lind. When the next European war struck, she settled in Santa Barbara, California, naming her new estate "Tibetland."

In 1927 Edith McCormick was called to appear before the Real Estate Board of Illinois to explain her connection to Krenn & Dato. An unhappy tenant evicted from his apartment had filed a petition to revoke the firm's license. For weeks Edith resisted testifying until the court threatened her with contempt. On the stand, she swore she was not financially interested in the firm, nor had she authorized them to use her name in their advertising. Under cross-examination, she admitted that the firm was the sole agent for her properties and had a right to claim such. (Why she disavowed herself in her early testimony is puzzling.)

Krenn & Dato did not lose its license, but its troubles were just beginning. All over the country real estate booms were busting. The largest rush had been with land in Florida, which people treated like a second gold rush. In this case, they did not have to travel there personally and find the ore; they need only put money down on a mortgage and watch the value of the land rise. Then, in September 1926 a disastrous hurricane swept across the state and Gulf region, leaving eighteen thousand homeless and property losses at $80 million. The once-paradise now seemed a foolish place to live. School teachers, factory workers, and pensioners found themselves making payments on worthless plots of land. This was the first public hint of the disaster that would beach the national economy.

Less visible was the erosion of the farm economy, in which the McCormicks and International Harvester were unwitting players, having built the plows that killed the plains. During the war and afterwards, farm owners invested in machinery that led to large debts, overproduction, and less income. Plows also replaced tenant farmers, who were driven off to wander and pick the grapes of wrath. Eventually nature assisted the human foolishness. Unheard-of floods in the Mississippi Valley in 1927 made over 600,000 homeless and destroyed several hundred millions in crops. Then dust storms ravaged what remained of the eroded topsoil of the plains.

Few in the cities paid attention to the small farmer being forced off his land, and most ignored the gradual decline in real estate in their own neighborhoods. Edith and her partners knew too well what was happening, for their subdivisions no longer sold out and more tenants missed rent payments. At this point she turned to her father and John Jr., who had his staff examine the financial conditions of her various holdings. The review found many weaknesses in Krenn & Dato's accounts. For example, it was unclear whether certain claimed valuations were estimated appreciation or actual market value. The return on two large office buildings was negative. Although the firm had made a half million dollars in 1926, it was well over a million in debt for 1927.

Adding to its troubles, Krenn & Dato had recently floated a bond issue of $11 million in five-year notes that would return six percent. The partners hoped this influx of cash would save their investments. Labeled the "Edith Rockefeller McCormick Trust," the security backing up the issue was her bonds and securities, primarily Standard Oil of New Jersey, worth over $17 million. Small investors lined up to buy into the plan. What could be more secure than Standard Oil and Rockefeller money? John Jr. reminded Edith that this issue added to the firm's expenses in the long run, for they had to repay the bonds and the interest.

The real problem was out of the firm's hands. With property declining in value, John Jr. explained, "[Y]ou seem to be in a position whereby the more property you dispose of, the greater will be your deficit."[16] Yet holding on to the property guaranteed a loss as well, as there were annual taxes and assessments, maintenance, and management costs. His advice was to hold on in expectation that the downward cycle would end, the valuations increase again.

John Jr.'s recommendation may have been one he was taking himself. Although he never informed his sister, he too was investing in real estate. Having been given the Forest Hill property by his father, he thought it would be a good location to provide housing for young Cleveland executives. Consequently, he developed one section of the acreage for large lots with well-built brick homes. Unfortunately, they were priced at forty thousand dollars, beyond the range of his market, and few sold. John Jr. would have sought the best counsel as to his next move with regard to this investment, so his advice to his sister was well-informed.

Neither he, Senior, nor Edith imagined how drastically the economy would fall. As unemployment grew and more tenants could not pay rent,

Edith let them stay in their homes and apartments. She also insisted that the small investors receive the periodic income due on their bonds. Despite the stock market collapse, she remained optimistic. She had plans drawn to have an undeveloped site on the lake turned into a conference and retreat center where scholars on sabbatical could work and collaborate. To help her out, Edwin Krenn returned the million dollars she had given him several years before.

Although Edith's later years have been described as lonely, this was not necessarily the case. What had changed was her style of relating to people. In the mid-1920s, Chicago financier Samuel Insull gradually took control of the opera company and removed it from Louis Sullivan's beloved Auditorium. After that, Edith had no reason to give her lavish preperformance entertainments. Her friends were those who protected her privacy. She preferred small gatherings and even hosted coming-out parties at her house for favorite young women. She became enamored of the movies, which she attended almost daily in the afternoons with Edwin Krenn alongside, her bodyguards a few steps behind. Following his divorce from Ganna Walska, even Harold approached her door now and then, and always sent flowers on her birthday. And while Senior gave out shiny dimes, Edith went out on Christmas with gold pieces for the police.

William Rockefeller's line was hit hardest by the Depression. Despite inheriting millions from his father, during the 1920s Percy Rockefeller borrowed to invest in the skyrocketing stock markets. Unfortunately, he put himself in the hands of Ivan Kreuger, the "Match King." Kreuger built a reputation in international finance based upon, of all things, monopolies in matchbooks. He gave investors documents showing that governments around the world were requiring their citizens to buy only his approved matches. (If this seems a bizarre product for investment, one must recall the great popularity of cigarettes at the time.) What Kreuger held, however, were forged papers, and in time the entire enterprise collapsed. Percy lost so much money that he was sued for unpaid debts.

As if the matchbook scandal were not enough, the collapse of the stock market swallowed more of Percy's wealth. Two stories exist here. His family's version was that as a member of Skull and Bones, Yale's most elite fraternity, Percy had taken a lifetime pledge to come to the aid of fellow brothers in trouble. With the collapse of the market, many of these men lost their yachts, mansions, and capital, and therefore turned to Percy for help. Consequently, he raised cash by dumping his stocks and selling short. The government's account was that he purposely broke federal laws to benefit from the falling market. Whatever, Percy's health broke; he suffered a stroke and died in 1934 at age fifty-six. His family blamed Congress for his early death, and accused its investigating committees of harassing Percy needlessly over his precipitate stock sales.

Percy's widow Isabel died a year later of cancer, and left a trust worth $8 million divided among her five children. Some was in depressed real estate, and some went to taxes. Percy's five offspring were forced to tear down their childhood home, the fortresslike Owenoke, and sell the land to a subdivider. Isabel left nothing to charities. Thus Percy's descendants, like most of their cousins in the William Rockefeller line, would slip into comfortable obscurity, the life of private clubs and exclusive communities, but little of the wealth or social mission of their counterparts in John D.'s lineage.

The Depression less harmed Alta's or John Jr.'s family. Their Standard Oil stock declined in value, but the loss of income was not perceptible, and they had government securities to compensate. In fact, Mount Hope farm thrived as Parmalee's methods proved their worth. They had one of the top producing dairy herds in the country—their best cow needed four milkings a day. Their chickens lay eighteen thousand eggs a week, and they sold over thirty thousand of their specially bred chicks a year. Parmalee now raised chickens by a new method, in cages rather than free range, as he found their productivity went up when enclosed.

Alta must have worried about their finances nonetheless, for just before the stock market collapse they had moved into a new sixty-room brick Georgian mansion built at Mount Hope. The house had taken four years to construct, and did not seem an excessive expense during the high flying 1920s. As in the past, she hoped to use some of her father's unused possessions to lower her costs. Senior had passed 10 West Fifty-fourth on to John Jr., who had it closed and its furnishings covered in dust cloths. While Alta was preparing her new home, without asking anyone's permission she tried to remove some of her father's furnishings. Caretakers stopped her and informed John Jr. of her attempts. Kindly, and without chastisement, he let her "borrow" what she wanted.

The most immediate threat of the Depression to John Jr. was its undermining his Rockefeller Center project. The land, stretching for three blocks between Forty-eighth and Fifty-first streets along Fifth Avenue, was part of the original Columbia University, which had moved to Morningside Heights. In 1928, a group wishing to build a new Metropolitan Opera theater asked John Jr. to help in developing the land. Believing the change would be a civic improvement to the neighborhood, he took a lease option, purchased adjoining frontage, and sought corporations to develop and finance their own buildings on the site. Then the opera company withdrew its interest in the site, and the stock market failure wiped out other potential investors. John Jr. was left with an annual rent to Columbia University of over $3 million on property earning him a tenth of that.

In an audacious move for a period of economic collapse, he decided to invest in the nation by underwriting the full development himself. He was as usual knee-deep in mortar during the construction of the fourteen buildings that resulted in employment for over 200,000 workers. The vision of this extraordinary project was his expression of hope to the breadline unemployed and apple sellers. What had begun as a side project became a central endeavor, one that came to symbolize in stone and art deco bas relief the family's achievement. It took a member of the younger generation, Nelson, to convince his father to name the complex not Radio City, in honor of the major tenant NBC, but Rockefeller Center.

Nelson was the natural person to persuade this honoring of the family name. He was proud that he shared the same birthday as his illustrious grandfather John D. "It seems funny to think that today is Grandfather's 90th birthday and my 21st birthday. The 90 makes my 21 seem mighty small and insignificant, just like a little sapling standing by a mighty fir. But the sapling still has time to grow and develop and someday it might itself turn into a tree of some merit."[17] Of all the children, he was quickest to defend the family from attack, and wrote his senior thesis at Dartmouth to vindicate criticisms of Standard Oil. He made clear to his parents that he expected to do more than the clerking duties his older brother John 3rd had been assigned after college.

Always impatient, Nelson was the first to become engaged. It was somewhat of a surprise, because during his first three years in college he dated often. During a trip to Paris with his Aunt Lucy he wrote home of his meeting a Belgian princess and other wonderful young women. Nelson's brothers were amused by his fickleness. John 3rd teased about Nelson's car, how it was so well-trained it headed toward the nearest girl's college. Despite his playing the field, Nelson recognized that he kept returning to one, Mary Todhunter Clark, "Tod" to friends.

The Clark family, prominent in Philadelphia Main Line society, vacationed each summer at Seal Harbor, so Nelson had known Tod for many years. When he went on to Dartmouth, she went to the Sorbonne, and completed a degree there. She matured into a tall, slender brunette, with an elegant posture hinting at her expert horseback skills. She shared Nelson's high energy, which she expressed in play and sport; though high strung and excitable, she was quick to apologize after her temper flared.

In 1929 Abby and John Jr. invited Tod to accompany them and David on a trip to Egypt. Nelson wrote worrisome letters that another young man in the party would court Tod. He tried to forget her, but by the start of his senior year realized he was "really and truly desperately in love."[18] So was Tod.

The problem was that Nelson had not yet completed college. Abby calmed her furious husband down enough that he sent the couple down to Florida to meet Senior, where Tod played well enough on the golf course to gain the patriarch's approval. Her sense of fun and cleverness must have appealed to Senior as well.

Nelson and Tod married in the summer of 1930, right after his graduation, at a Main Line Episcopal church. The new prayer book, which omitted the word "obey," was used for the ceremony. Over 1,500 guests struggled through the crowds of curious to get to the reception. Favored guests were invited to view the display of gifts that covered the entire first floor of the Clark home. The presents, worth hundreds of thousands of dollars, included rare editions of the classics, a Chippendale bookcase, London silverware from the 1700s, a Sheffield tea set from the early 1800s, and rows of antique furniture. This display may have been the Main Line's one-upmanship, for a frequent story afterwards went that one local guest sneered, "Who is this fellow Nelson Rockefeller who is marrying into the Clark family?" The Rockefeller response was to send the couple on a yearlong honeymoon around the world.

John 3rd took longer to wed, only because he was so shy and naïve. Fortunately, he attracted a remarkable young woman, Blanchette Ferry Hooker, who appreciated his sensitivity and was willing to fight for him when necessary. Where Nelson found the family charge to service a joyful challenge, John 3rd felt a heavy sense of responsibility and spent many years drifting about various philanthropies in search of an identity of his own making. Following his college graduation, he had traveled to the Far East and, as a result, became committed to problems of worldwide population. Until the late 1950s, birth control remained a sensitive, impolite topic, yet he went on record in its support, and became the primary donor to Margaret Sanger's Research Bureau.

Blanchette was a Vassar graduate, active in Junior League social service activities, and a member of a family well known in "café society." She was the most reserved of four beautiful, sparkling sisters, who despite her public debutante appearance was unpretentious and studious. She shared with John Jr. an interest in politics, economics, and global affairs, and was a supporter of the League of Nations.

John Jr. had to encourage the courtship, by giving his timid son the key to a secluded cottage in Seal Harbor. During hikes there together, Blanchette realized that her suitor was like her, uninterested in social-climbing. Where she was confident and optimistic, however, he was insecure and a worrier. One evening he gave her a list of his faults, which amazed her. This difference in temperament would strengthen their relationship, not weaken it. Everyone around town agreed they were made for each other.

For Blanchette, the marriage brought the added pleasure of a relationship with Tod. She admired Tod's tomboy courage and clever humor, and the two would grow very close.

Following the usual wedding hyperbole—JOHN D. 3RD TO MARRY SOCIAL WORKER—Blanchette showed her compatibility with the Rockefeller conscience. Speaking before the Family Welfare Association of America, she presented a fresh analysis of lay people's role in charity. She bluntly criticized those who merely lent their names to pet organizations and bought tickets to social fundraising events. What charities need is the time and talent of contributors as well, she asserted. Papers nationwide and *Time* covered the speech, and she appeared on a "10 American women who attained fame list," alongside Shirley Temple.

Laurance was next to start a family, marrying Mary Billings French, descendent of an old, very conservative New England family. Laurance had an interesting mix of John Jr.'s reticent intellectualism and Nelson's exuberant practicality. At Princeton he took every philosophy course offered; at Harvard Law he sought knowledge that could serve him as a social activist.

Mary French was a longtime friend, for her brother had been Nelson's roommate at Dartmouth. She had attended Vassar, but rather than graduate went to England to study sculpture at Cambridge. Her religious upbringing was similar to that of the Rockefellers, and shaped her sensitivity to social causes. Her mother, like Laurance's, had been a leader in the YWCA, and she continued that service. Tall and stately, with glowing blue eyes, she was ready to join Laurance as an indefatigable worker, preferably anonymous, on behalf of his commitment to conservation, as well as her own concern for women's rights worldwide. This was another felicitous partnership.

In many American families, marriage symbolizes full independence from the parents. This is less the case among the wealthy, where investments and trusts encumber independence. Because their father resisted releasing his hold over their actions, the Rockefeller offspring were doubly dependent. The man who had matured to practice the liberal, tolerant ways of Christ in his public life retained the demeanor of the Old Testament Jehovah in private. For the older children, who had completed their schooling and were establishing their own families, his intrusion into their most mundane decisions ruined the ritual Sunday visits.

In a most remarkable move, all six children consulted privately and composed a letter sent on May 1, 1933, to their father. In it they reflected upon the "normal but difficult changes" they experienced with their parents.[19] They feared their previously intimate family relationship was "in jeopardy" because during visits "routine and even vexatious" issues came up, such as the merits of obtaining a particular apartment, of buying a Chrysler instead of a Buick, of arranging a reasonably priced vacation. Although they valued their parents' advice, they felt such business matters were interfering with "more fundamental questions of life," and respectfully requested an increase in their allowances. That way they would gain more experience in making their own decisions, and have more time during visits with their parents to discuss more interesting matters. They acknowledged they had never shown sufficient gratitude for all their parents had done in the past, and emphasized they valued their parents' guidance. Nonetheless, they thought the change necessary out of "our interest in the future of the family as a whole."

This carefully-worded request must have culminated lengthy and trying discussions on the siblings' part. The respect and even-tempered rhetoric was more effective than they anticipated. At first their father raised everyone's allowance. A few months later he gave his three oldest children 200,000 shares of Socony-Vacuum Stock, making each a millionaire. Recent changes in the tax laws, which now set estate taxes at sixty percent and gift taxes at forty-five percent, compelled him to set up trusts in 1934 to take advantage of tax incentives before the higher rates kicked in. The result was seven irrevocable trusts, initially valued at $18 million for Abby, $12 million for Babs, John 3rd, and Nelson, and fifty thousand dollars for the three youngest sons. In 1935, he increased the gifts to the latter to equalize the trusts for all five young men. Neither Abby nor Babs could invade their principal, while the sons could do so upon reaching age thirty. Furthermore, upon death of a beneficiary, the trust would split equally among any children, that is John Jr.'s grandchildren. As that generation died, its portion of the trust would be terminated, with the tax-free proceeds distributed to the great-grandchildren. This generation-skipping feature was a common way to preserve wealth within families.

This plan reshaped relationships among family members. Abby now had more income of her own and less need to cajole her husband. Babs and Dave Milton, an impecunious young lawyer now, were freed from persistent financial problems. The older sons felt somewhat less dominated by their father, though not completely, for they could not get to their funds until they reached age thirty. By selecting trust committee members congenial with his aims, John Jr. arranged that the youngest boys received only enough to cover their basic school and living expenses. Thus they remained under his control. As for the surplus, he saw it directed by the trustees into various philanthropic causes.

In general, the trust specifications reflected John Jr.'s reluctance to release his wealth prematurely. Senior had not begun a similar transfer until John Jr. was in his forties, and he had the added burden of making allotments to five ambitious sons without causing rancor among them. In his cautious way, in his attempt to find the precise formula to give enough help but not too much, he became even more distant. Like his mother had done with him, he showed his affection by sending homilies, tracts, and books of an uplifting nature. Despite his deserved public reputation as a man of progressive, democratic spirit, toward his own children John Jr. continued to insist his way was right. When angry, he never raised his voice, but took on a cold look, and spaced his words distinctly "as if he were snipping off the tail of each one with his teeth."[20] As his children realized the contradiction between their father's stated principles and his actions at home, conflicts naturally resulted.

Another way in which John Jr. continued to control his adult offspring and their families was his rule over Pocantico. For example, each family had only one master key that unlocked the gates to woodland trails. If a family member misplaced the key, everyone was out of luck. If someone wished to go horseback riding, he or she had to make an appointment at the stables. When Tod one day took her children to wade in the shallow garden pools, John Jr. ordered them out, claiming they were unsafe. As one longtime staff member concluded, the families had to live under rules one would expect at a scout camp.

John Jr. could show deep public affection to only two people in his life, his father and his wife. Father and son communicated constantly, and whenever they met now they embraced openly, a form of greeting not common to men of their class. His approach to Abby remained that of a young lover. One rare deviation from his stiff decorum was his giving in to the impulse to pinch his wife's legs when she mounted stairs ahead of him.

Abby was least affected by the changes brought on by the trusts. After all, to the extent that John Jr. refused to be flexible and undogmatic, she appeared the kinder, warmer parent. The children did not seem to recognize that she shared some of their father's seeming hypocrisies. For example, John 3rd was distressed to learn that workers at Pocantico did not receive overtime, pensions, or other favorable benefits that John Jr. preached and practiced outside the home. (John Jr.'s view was that their staff should save enough to carry their old age.) When he questioned his father for not granting liberal labor relations policies to family employees, he did not seem to consider that his mother was just as responsible for condoning these procedures. Surely Abby was aware of the stingy pay and benefits.

Most significant, Abby now could use her newfound money with impunity, and did so toward her favorite causes, whether modern art or a leftwing woman's labor group. She gradually transferred more art from her collection to MOMA, as she was more assured of its financial security. Lillie Bliss had died in 1931 and left the best of her collection to the museum, so Abby's donation during her lifetime challenged others to follow. The January 1936 exhibit of her first large gift to MOMA put her on the cover of *Time*. There she was compared favorably to Gertrude Vanderbilt Whitney for her support of living American artists. Unlike Whitney, who with Juliana Force controlled her museum, Abby remained the anonymous worker in the background at hers. Part of *Time*'s preference for Abby was her being "modest" and "reticent," in other words a more reputable model for other social matrons than bohemian Whitney. The comparison was unfair to both women, who each had prodded the museum-going public to look upon American artists as no less significant creators than their counterparts overseas. Still, regarding the quality of the collecting, Abby deserved first place, both for her unerring eye and her refusal to let sentiment guide some of her purchases.

Abby was among the first people Juliana Force approached with her intent to start a fifty-thousand-dollar fund to purchase works or make direct grants to needy artists. Abby immediately pledged five thousand dollars, and authorized Juliana to locate contemporary prints and drawings she could place in her own collection. With Abby's backing, Juliana set up an artists' cafeteria and experimented with a cooperative gallery. Before she had her own Rockefeller trust, though, Abby's contributions through Juliana had been smaller than she wished.

Her greatest coup in support of art, though, was in convincing John Jr. to cooperate in the development of a permanent home for MOMA. After much private discussion, Abby convinced him to sell his properties at 15, 17, and 19 West Fifty-third to the museum at a price of a quarter million dollars. Eventually he agreed to add property that extended to a seventy-foot frontage on West Fifty-fourth. Since the children were all grown, the couple decided to tear down their nine-story mansion to add that property to MOMA, and move to an apartment on Park Avenue.

These changes unsettled Alta, for her house adjoining the new museum had to shrink a bit when workmen realized the new building would compromise the security of her property. The constant noise of tearing down and construction over many months also annoyed her on her few visits to the city. It is doubtful she liked seeing her old-fashioned townhouse backed up against a stark, severe International Style monolith.

In submitting to her request for MOMA's new building, John Jr. exacted a hard price: that Abby should withdraw from involvement in the museum. The demand was not explicit, yet she could not miss his stated unhappiness over her committee meetings, phone consultations, and fundraising events. With her children off and establishing their own lives, she particularly enjoyed the young, sometimes disputatious staff of MOMA, whom she rewarded privately with gifts of money for work well done. John Jr. no longer had the children to compete with his time, and he did not want MOMA to draw Abby away from home any longer. Consequently, she eased son Nelson to take her place in the organization. She also recognized daughter-in-law Blanchette's abilities, and started to draw her into both YWCA and museum work as well. When Juliana Force sold her collection of Shaker furniture, Blanchette was the major purchaser.

Some of John Jr.'s opposition to Abby's museum work might have been out of concern for his wife's health. Now in her sixties, Abby had limited energy, and was temporarily disabled by several falls during the 1930s. She had high blood pressure and heart disease, though neither recognized how advanced it was. His migraines and blue periods continued as well. For the first time ever his investment income failed to match their regular living expenses, which meant this normally penny-pinching man could be even more aggravating in discussing expenditures with his family and his estate workers.

Unable to embrace modernity, John Jr. must have felt his life principles increasingly threatened in this time of rapid social transformation and economic readjustments. (No wonder the projects in Williamsburg, at the Cloisters, and Riverside Church entranced him.) Unfortunately, his children and wife were fully comfortable with the fast pace, seeming chaos, and complexity of the new era.

14

The Generations Pass

"O death, where is thy sting? O grave, where is thy victory?"

—I Corinthians 15: 55

*I*n 1930, Edith underwent surgery to remove a tumor. When the doctors were unsuccessful in excising all of it, the family agreed not to tell her some malignancy remained. Her illness prompted the return of her errant daughters, who decided to reconcile with her.

Mathilde brought Max and her two small children from Europe to meet Edith, who followed Senior's practice of welcoming the return of prodigal offspring. Perhaps at this time Mathilde admitted to her mother the terrible truth, that her husband had married her for her money after all. As Edith had forewarned, Max Oser's treatment of his wife was autocratic and uncaring. Yet Mathilde was not ready to leave the adopted country she loved, nor face the nasty publicity that would result if she did. In discussing her visit to Chicago, newspapers extolled her "happy marriage," a fiction she held up for the sake of her young children.

Muriel also made amends and told her mother of her upcoming plans to marry. Thus Edith, not Harold, made the public announcement of Muriel's engagement to Elisha Dyer Hubbard of Middletown, Connecticut. Muriel followed the pattern of her siblings in choosing a mate her parents' age. Her husband gave his occupation as "farmer," but he was really from an old, moneyed New England family. The two wed in Bar Harbor, at the McKinlock summer home where they first met. It was a small affair, with none of the McCormick or Rockefeller relatives present.

While Edith's family ties were reconnecting, her financial ones had become too entangled to manage on her own. In April 1931, she arranged through Cartier to sell some of her remarkable jewels. Because the value of her stocks had greatly declined, the banks were calling for more collateral on her loans. In December of that year, she asked her father to lend her a million dollars to carry her real estate business through the rough times. John Jr. urged his father against such help. To put money in, he advised, would "be only the beginning of a long, painful relationship with Edith's representatives, who would naturally feel that once we had come in with them the burden would be gradually put on us."[1] Senior agreed that his son had "the correct view."[2] (It is interesting that Senior had been willing to bail his son out years earlier when he lost a million dollars in the stock market. His actions implied that since Edith insisted on behaving independently, then she must take the consequences on her own. Still, Senior and John Jr. worried about the effects of Edith's situation on the family reputation, and potentially, upon other members' wealth.)

Although unwilling to help financially, John Jr. sent advisors to Chicago to perform an independent analysis of her situation. Bertram Cutler interviewed Edith, who explained how she was selling her valuables and reducing her charitable giving. She insisted she wanted a loan, not a gift, which she was confident in five years the firm could recover fully. John Jr.'s investigators noted that were it not for the Depression, Edith's income and stocks would have sufficed to cover her debts. Despite their obvious bias (a reference to her partners as "Jews"), they concluded that Krenn and Dato ran the company well in some respects. Part of the real estate holdings retained clear long-term value, but much needed to be liquidated or defaulted on. As a gesture of good faith to the family, Edith agreed to give up her personal real estate, art, and jewels toward the collateral required by the banks.[3]

Helping Edith was a prominent local banker who advised her without any fee. When asked why he was helping Edith *pro bono*, he explained that the year before, when his son died in an accident, she had done more than anyone to console him. Initially he advised Edith to just pull out of the whole mess and claim bankruptcy. To his amazement, she replied, "I am having the best experience of my life. I have had everything before and have never known what it is to want for anything and not be able to satisfy my longing. I am learning and having a much greater feeling toward others."[4] To John Jr. she confessed full responsibility for the situation, which of course was not so. She appealed to his compassion, "I have gone through so much in my life and am so tired and weary and need some encouragement from your helping hand." Could he not buy some of her jewelry or furniture at least? He would not. Nor would Harold McCormick, whom she approached to buy Villa Turicum, take even a share in it.

Part of Edith's weariness was a side effect of the radiation treatment for the cancer, and may have spurred her accepting her brother's eventual offer to help. In a meticulously detailed letter he enumerated her personal accounts, which included over $100,000 in overdue taxes, unpaid bills of almost the same, and close to fifty thousand dollars in annual mortgage interest on her two homes. After going over expenditures, he asked her to cut her donations in half, and move into a hotel, taking minimal staff. By his figures, she needed $322,000 for the next year to cover her expenses and outstanding bills, most of which consisted of back taxes. However, he made "this proposal contingent upon the success of your negotiations with the trust company . . . . A complete program of relief is what I want to see brought about."[5] In other words, she had to give up her hopes to continue the business. In announcing her move, the papers headlined MRS. EDITH MCCORMICK SACRIFICES MILLIONS TO PROTECT POOR.

Despite the contretemps with her brother and father, Edith joined in a show of family loyalty on another matter, prohibition. On June 7, 1932, John Jr. released a press statement stating his withdrawal of support for the nationwide ban on alcohol. Having been with his father among the most noted temperance figures in the country, John Jr.'s reversal turned a trend into a tidal wave. He admitted that total abstinence was the wisest choice an individual could take, but acknowledged that it could not come about through legal coercion. The 18th Amendment, though well intentioned, had caused a greater evil, the corruption of respect for law. Several days later Edith seconded his stance, with an addition. She offered as a compromise that the government should control the manufacture, sale, and distribution of alcohol, and receive all the revenues from its sale. She would have no time to lobby for this clever idea.

John Jr. was well aware of the impact of Edith's cancer. "Her x-ray treatments will last a year longer. It makes her dreadfully sick to ride on a train. . . . She is very anxious to see her father," an associate had recently informed him.[6] Surprisingly, his letters expressed no compassion for her private trauma. In a cold-blooded postscript to his proposal to help her, he noted that "under the circumstances" he and his executors were curious to know "what disposition you are making of your property by will."[7] Discussing the matter with an aide later, he remarked on how "if either of us was apparently being cruel, we were being cruel to be kind."[8]

Muriel did not agree, and made a rare show of loyalty on her mother's behalf. When she learned of her uncle's refusal to save Krenn & Dato through a direct loan, she complained angrily. She disagreed with him that when her mother died only Krenn and Dato personally would bear the consequences of the company's collapse. She wanted more efforts by her Rockefeller relatives to see that her mother's reputation would not be sullied following her death.[9]

Soon after moving into the Drake Hotel, Edith's health declined so rapidly that all her family gradually gathered to be with her. Fowler of course had never neglected his mother, and came with new wife Fifi. In recent years, Harold had become a wanderer, disabled by arthritis, and anguished over having left Edith for such an inferior successor. Fowler knew his parents still loved each other, and watched their poignant struggle to ignore the terrible rift in the past. Father and son spent day and night with Edith through her suffering, and invited Edward Krenn to join them at her bedside.

By the time Mathilde arrived at the deathbed, Edith was in a coma, yet responded to desperate treatment to greet her favorite daughter for the last time. Finally, John Jr. and Abby came, although Edith did not seem to recognize anyone by then. For days she rallied and collapsed, her strong spirit amazing her nurses and doctors. Then, "death came peacefully," announced Muriel to the press. "All members of her family were with her at the end." She died without fulfilling her wish to see her father, whom she had not seen in twenty years.

The funeral resembled many Rockefeller family weddings. The ceremony took place before a select group of several dozen family and closest friends in the Empire Room of 1000 Lake Shore Drive, the home John Jr. had forced her to leave. Edith's coffin sat before the large fireplace, a blanket of 12,000 lilies of the valley draped over the bier. Sprays of 400 orchids, 5,000 roses in festoons, borders of 1,000 gardenias, vases of 750 tuberoses, ferns, and tubs of palm trees hid the walls of the three public rooms. (Seven truckloads of flowers flown in from New York went to the cemetery, and were donated afterwards to a hospital.) A string quartet hidden behind drapes played some of her favorite music; a Presbyterian choir sang hymns she may not have heard since childhood. The minister read brief selections from the Bible and led the Lord's Prayer. Afterwards, a crowd of two thousand watched outside the mansion to glimpse the eight pallbearers, who included Edward Krenn and members of the family. Alta was present, along with some of John Jr. and Abby's children. A crippled Harold limped out on the arm of his older brother Cyrus. Senior, now ninety-three, felt too frail to travel from Florida.

Edith's surviving sister and brother must have been amazed by the sight of police controlling the thousands more who lined the roads to the cemetery. This scene, more resembling the death of royalty or a high-level politician, was visible proof of the affection average Chicago residents felt for their sister. The mourners gathered in a small cemetery chapel, where the casket was set in a crypt until arrangements for its permanent placement were completed. It would be many years before Edith's body would find its permanent rest.

Chicago papers lauded her memory by recalling her many civic contributions to the city and her efforts to provide housing for residents of all classes. Old friends gave affectionate reminiscences, recalling her empathy and generosity with emotional and financial support. Her longtime servants gave interviews, praising her professionalism in running the household and how easy it was to work for her. A local historian later summarized, "She was a great original, and we have never had too many of those. . . . If there are ghosts in Chicago, surely one of the most curious and touching must be that of Edith Rockefeller McCormick."[10]

John Jr.'s treatment of his sister in her final years may seem callous, and it was because he let his role as financial advisor prevent him from being the loving and playful brother of their youth. He later recalled not her suffering, but how "the completest and most beautiful reconciliation between her and her children and former husband and his family has turned our sorrow into rejoicing."[11] Part of his coolness was his hostility toward the "foreigners," Edith's partners, in particular Edward Krenn. In refusing to save Edith's business, however, he was following his father's practice of allowing people to make their own mistakes and live with the consequences. All the Rockefeller family advisors encouraged this response (and many people today would do the same with their own relatives). Furthermore, it must have been very exasperating, given his own worries and problems—Rockefeller Center, Williamsburg, the foundations, his children—to find himself at middle-age still being asked to handle the responsibilities of his older, grown sisters. In colluding with his father to keep the women distanced from family wealth and public influence, he ensured continuation of this unhappy rule over their lives.

Abby told her sister that Edith had a splendid trust company executor, which meant that John Jr. would not have to deal any more with the complicated business affairs of her private estate or Krenn and Dato. This was not true. Edith's will, rewritten three weeks before her death, reflected her determination to do things her way, for certainly her capable lawyers did not recommend its odd disbursements. She divided her estate into twelfths, with four-twelfths to go to Muriel, two-twelfths to Mathilde, one-twelfth to Fowler, and five-twelfths to Edwin Krenn. The large proportion to Krenn was to return the money he had put into the company in recent months in a futile move to save it.

Even as Edith lay dying, John Jr. and his advisors were busy pressuring Krenn to accept a buyout instead of his share of her estate. Parmalee Prentice helped in negotiations by which Dato got sole ownership of the real estate firm while Krenn accepted an annuity of two thousand dollars for life. In this way the real estate muddle was totally separated from Edith's personal estate, and the family's aides would have to deal only with Dato, the better businessman of the two surviving partners. Krenn was just as pleased to be freed from the humiliation he often felt when around Edith's Rockefeller relatives and their assistants. (The Mc-Cormicks were much more appreciative of his special friendship with Edith, but had no authority in the settlement of her estate.)

Once Krenn was removed from the matter, John Jr. had to deal with Muriel's continued displeasure over his actions. According to the generation-skipping trust established by Senior on Edith's behalf, her three children were her only heirs and were to receive equal shares of the trust. Based on 1932 dividend rates, each would earn about $120,000 a year in income from the investments. Muriel balked that she must seek the intercession of trustees to gain access to this money. She wanted her full share of the trust upfront and full control of its use. Following much haggling, she agreed to accept one-half of her share outright, with the other half to be put in a separate trust. She continued to bombard John Jr., who was one of her trustees, with long letters explaining why she needed to invade the principal. (The trustees had the opposite problem with Mathilde, who was too proud to ask for money directly, and even re-sisted suggestions she cut into her principal when they thought she had good reason to do so.)

Against her trustees' advice, Muriel spent heavily on her homes, which included a new estate at Palm Beach, and neglected the wisdom of experience. Thus, Senior's financial largesse would invite one grandchild onto a path of self-destructive misery.[12] In rejecting these experts, Muriel turned her back on some of the most astute financial minds in the country.

Edith's death had unfortunate fallout for the bondholders who had bought into her investment trust. Many wrote to John Jr., who may never have read these individual pleas for help, though he clearly approved the response to them.[13] A Mrs. O'Malley had invested her life's savings. A Gus Rahn, aged seventy-one, with an invalid wife, had bought the bonds "with confidence in the Rockefeller name." A teacher had put all her re-tirement in these investments, which had paid regularly until Edith's death. Now all learned there was no possibility of further income, let alone the return of their principal. Could not John Jr. help? His office responded with a terse note explaining that his sister's business was separate from his own, and thus he must decline any assistance.

Meanwhile, something had to be done with Edith's estate proper. Creditors, taxing officials, and mortgage holders clamored for payment. There followed the auctioning of her personal property, her furnishings, jewelry, book and manuscript collection, and art works. The Art Institute of Chicago had to return exhibits on loan from her that it had once expected to own outright. Given the poor economy, the auctions brought in much less than would have occurred under normal circumstances.

Villa Turicum, which Edith had not lived in since before 1913, was placed on the market, but no one had the income or desire to maintain such a luxurious estate. It took almost ten years to find a buyer, who could not afford to restore it. It sat unused for many years and vandals took off with its walnut paneling, defaced its oil-painted ceilings, and its mosaics. Too decrepit for anyone to save, it fell to the demolishers in 1956. In fact, Edith's probate took nineteen years to settle completely, with the secondary creditors gaining only sixty cents on the dollar in payment.

Circumstances would next implicate John Jr. in the matters of yet another family member, his niece Margaret Strong. Though John D. Rockefeller had accomplished all he wished in life, he was denied his one remaining goal, to live to one hundred. In mid-May of 1937 Senior had chronic difficulties sleeping and showed an unusual restlessness, but his doctor was not concerned. Despite episodes of weakness, he was in good spirits and joked with his staff. Then, just before sunrise on May 23, 1937, his heart gave out after ninety-eight years. In his final months, apart from his weak heart, which restricted him to a wheelchair, he had remained vigorous in voice, hearing, sight, and appetite. He had continued his daily automobile rides and basking in the sun, often accompanied by visitors to his home in Florida.

Senior's body was taken to the Pocantico Hills Union Church for the funeral service. Characteristically, these were plain and brief, with only immediate family and a few friends invited. Following the ceremony, the staff filed past the bier for a last look at their employer. Around the country, in the offices and factories of the Standard Oil empire, at the hour the services began all work ceased for five minutes. The body went by rail to Cleveland for burial in Lakeview Cemetery beside Laura and their daughter Alice. Nearby rest the bodies of old friends and associates:

Stephen Harkness, Oliver Payne, Mark Hanna, John Jay, and lesser-known congregants of his beloved Euclid Avenue Baptist Church.

At his death, Senior owned only one share of Standard stock, No. I, a sentimental keepsake from his past. All else he had given away, mostly to his many philanthropies and to his son. His estate of $26 million was predominantly in U. S. Treasury Notes. Taxes took $16 million. After dispensing to John Jr. all his personal effects (furnishings, automobiles, art works, horses, and such), the remainder went in trust to his grand-daughter Margaret.

When Senior died, Margaret was in Italy, and thus heard of his be-quest to her through phone calls from reporters. After all expenses and taxes were paid, she received about $6 million outright, much less than the $26 million the press reported, but hardly a pittance. When writing his will in 1925, Senior singled out Margaret to make up what she might have received through her mother had she lived to 1917, when he had set up large trusts for his remaining children. Still, some family members may have wondered why he had chosen to stay with this decision. His doing so was further evidence of Senior's deep family loyalty and trust in indi-vidual redemption, for Margaret had been consistently spendthrift.

Margaret had come into her maturity in 1918, and as a result already controlled income inherited from her deceased mother.[14] By 1919, she added over $2 million that Senior had recently given her, thus was a well-to-do young woman. She visited New York that year for her American social debut, which Emma Rockefeller McAlpin hosted for her. This ap-pearance was just a gesture, however, for she returned to France where she could live in splendor apart from any Rockefeller interference. Now es-tranged from her father, she seemed a most fortunate young woman, free to enjoy the vibrant expatriate community of Paris in the 1920s.

Several years later Senior and his son were dismayed to learn that Mar-garet was wasteful with her money. She ran frequent overdrafts on her bank accounts, and during her visits to the States accumulated debts against Abby's charge accounts. Senior usually covered these bills, but ex-pected payment eventually, and kept a record of her debts. Margaret was a likeable young woman he could not refuse. He also may not have wanted to punish her for the failure of her father to raise her "like a Rockefeller."

Despite the family's counselling, Margaret continued her spendthrift habits. One year she subscribed to over 300,000 shares of Standard Oil of New Jersey, while falling in arrears with Revillon Freres furriers and Cartier jewelers. When she bought herself a mink coat for one thousand dollars, she was thoughtful enough to buy a wrap for her maid at five hundred dollars. Unfortunately, she neglected to pay for the maid's mink. Finally, Senior's advisor Bertram Cutler recommended that Margaret's funds be placed in the hands of a trustee such as himself to prevent further plundering. To sweeten the deal for Margaret, he recommended that Senior add several hundred thousand dollars to her capital. Fowler Mc-Cormick agreed to persuade Margaret to accept the agreement. She balked, and said she would accept a trust only if it could be revoked later. Senior rejected this stipulation, so the two were at an impasse.

In August of 1927, Margaret married Jorge [George] de Cuevas, whom she met while living in Paris. De Cuevas was born in Chile to a Danish mother and Spanish father, who took the dubious title Marquis de Piedrablanca de Guana. He was a charmer, like Margaret small in stature, debonair in looks and style. Paris then was a haven for aristocrats who had lost land and titles during the recent European war and revolutions. Somehow George emigrated there, where he met Russian Prince Felix Yusupov, one of the murderers of Rasputin. The two opened a dress shop known as Irse, conveniently located around the corner from the posh Ritz Carlton. There titled but often impoverished refugees gathered, perhaps more for introductions to the beautiful models than for the clothes.

Almost twenty years older than his wife, de Cuevas might seem a fortune hunter. Margaret informed her grandfather that George was handling all her financial matters because "in Europe when a woman arranges these things everybody tries to profit." Soon after, Margaret changed her mind about Senior's offer of a trust. She said that George supported the proposal, and that they would accept Bertram Cutler holding their power of attorney. (George had persuaded Margaret to be less stubborn for she would be wealthier simply by accepting Senior's plan.) At that point, her monthly allowance was set at five thousand dollars, about half the actual income from her accounts. Trustee Cutler and Senior neglected to foresee that this limitation would fail for the simple reason that she and George could continue to charge.

On January 22, 1929, Margaret gave birth to Senior's first great-grandchild, Elizabeth "Bessie" de Cuevas. Given the prospect of raising a family, she and George decided a permanent move to the States was wise. They moved to an apartment at One Beekman Place in New York City, and took over her mother's original home in Lakewood, New Jersey as well. They joined the most exclusive clubs, hired servants, and ignored the economic deluge. In 1930, following a difficult pregnancy, Margaret gave birth to her second and last child, a son appropriately named John.

Despite their differences in age and culture, Margaret and George de

Cuevas were highly compatible. They loved luxury and lived well beyond their income. In 1931, when she was finally permitted more control of her own trust, Margaret was forced to use part of it to defray her many debts to Senior. He generously accepted as payment a collection of securities to pay back a debt of $100,000, even though the securities were actually worthless. So high were the couple's debts that in 1932 they sent furniture, rugs, and jewelry to auction, sublet their home, and moved to a small, less expensive suite in a hotel. Bertram Cutler tried to help them through these difficulties, as he had done previously for Edith, but the couple simply could not control their impulses. In 1933, John Jr. drafted a letter for Senior reminding Margaret that he "should not want any member of the family to adopt a standard of living which was in any way related to what he might expect to receive from my estate after death."[15] Yet the next year George wrote self-pitying letters concerning his unpaid Colony Club dues, and the unbearable indignity that being ejected from membership would bring him.

Perhaps to avoid creditors, the de Cuevas family returned to Europe. There Charles Strong, very sick and virtually penniless, reconciled with his only child. Yet Margaret's letters to Bertram Cutler naïvely broadcast her continued profligacy. She complained that she had no money to buy a new dress to attend the wedding of Don Juan, Prince of Austria. Later she pawned her jewelry to do so and asked Cutler for $1,800 to redeem it. Then Margaret was attached to scandal when her chauffeur-driven car struck an Italian boy and killed him. Rather than make a settlement with the child's family, George unwisely and unsuccessfully tried to use the influence of a friend close to Mussolini to sway the court against a fine.

Nonetheless, Margaret and George retained Senior's good will. It helped that they were taking steps for the entire family to obtain American citizenship. When Margaret married George, she was fortunate that Congress had recently changed the law such that women who married foreigners did not lose their citizenship, so she remained an American. Having been born in France, however, daughter Bessie held her father's citizenship, that of Chile. Having been born in New York, son John was American. Given the restrictive immigration and naturalization laws of the time, the couple had to find a way to get American citizenship for George and Bessie. George decided it would help him in the process to first obtain Spanish citizenship by making claims to his family's dubious title there. As a result, he became the Marquis de Cuevas. (Although the press from that point referred to the two with their aristocratic titles, they seldom used them.) His complicated maneuver worked, and he became a naturalized American with his daughter.

Senior was also sympathetic because Margaret and George had chronic health problems, yet never let them interfere with their children's needs. Though both tended toward hypochondria, Margaret had repeated, disabling depressions, while George had painful arthritis. Despite being raised by two narcissistic parents, Bessie and John appeared to others healthy, happy, and with lovely manners. Senior welcomed their visits and notes. "I love you and your beautiful letter and mother and father and so do the rest of us," he wrote his de Cuevas grandchildren. "You are the dearest we have on earth. We love you with tenderest affection."[16]

As one might expect, following receipt of Senior's bequest Margaret and George did not harness their spending habits. John Jr. had to dissuade her from buying Senior's sizeable estate with golf course in Lakewood, and urged her to dispose of some of her other residences. Perhaps because of growing up with little permanence, the couple could not resist adding properties, and ended up with homes in France, Florence, New York City, and Lakeport. Most of the time now, however, they lived quietly in Westchester. Margaret dressed like a Spanish duenna in plain, dark dresses. Their parties were intimate, and their few evenings out were to nightclubs with Brazilian singer Paloma and George's Spanish friends.

In 1939, the New York World's Fair gave the couple an opportunity to use their funds in a way John Jr. approved. He had agreed to lend some of his art collection to an exhibit at the Fair. He was pleased to learn that Margaret was the exhibit's chief backer, that she had provided $175,000 in hopes a twenty-five-cent admission fee would recoup the costs. Though crippled with an undiagnosed infection, George hobbled about the construction site and created the interior design. After visiting the pavilion, John Jr. wrote a letter of praise, unusual for him, commending their contribution.

As with so much at that remarkable fair, the venture was a great financial loss. Furthermore, the news articles about the de Cuevas donation brought piles of mail to the Marquis with requests for aid, or worse, statements of abuse. "Aren't you ashamed to throw your money around like that and sit there in your luxury while other people don't know how to pay the rent."[17] To still the criticism, George invited a reporter over and gave a public accounting of their income. They earned about $200,000 a year, of which seventy-five percent went to income taxes. This meant they had to "struggle" on fifty thousand dollars. "Why do we have to have four homes. My dear fellow, we can't get rid of them! Then there are our relatives and friends in Spain, who have been impoverished by the civil war. One can't close one's eyes to suffering." It was not an explanation to appease Depression-weary Americans. Soon the houses amounted to five, as the couple added a place in Palm Beach, and also land in Connecticut.

In 1939, the gathering clouds of another major European war gave Mathilde Oser an excuse finally to leave Switzerland and move her two children, now adolescents, to the States. She settled in southern California, where Harold McCormick lived with his third wife, Adah Wilson. (Wilson had been his visiting nurse for several years when he proposed.) Two years later, word came from Switzerland that Max Oser was dead of a heart attack at age sixty-five. In informing John Jr. of the news, Fowler requested that he send Mathilde no sympathy note, for she had been separated from her husband for years.

This was not the only death notice Fowler had to convey to family in 1941. That October Harold McCormick died of a cerebral hemorrhage at age sixty-nine. All three children were by his side in the hospital, along with his wife. Though crippled by his arthritis, to the end Harold was busy on behalf of International Harvester and his various musical philanthropies. (Following the disastrous collapse of the Chicago Grand Opera under Samuel Insull's patronage, in 1934 Harold helped organize the Chicago Opera Company, which grew to the world prominence it enjoys today.)

By the 1940s Fowler was proving the best expression of Rockefeller-McCormick liberal values. Committed to correcting past injustices brought upon African-Americans, he was a major fundraiser for such groups as the United Negro College Fund Campaign and the Committee on Race Relations. As head of International Harvester, he formed a research division on labor-management relations, and was in the forefront of American businesses in establishing antidiscriminatory hiring policies. His uncle John's industrial-relations philosophy clearly influenced his projects, except he more distanced himself from corporate class interests. Although John Jr. acknowledged the rights of labor, he was resistant to unionism and ultimately favored management. Fowler was less antithetical toward unions, and in his dealings with them urged a model to balance the needs of consumers, stockholders, and employees. John Jr. saw the corporation as an entity unto itself, with considerable autonomy. Fowler argued that once a business grew to a certain size, it was an influential social institution that should not be run with the interests of only one group, the stockholders, in mind.

Against all odds and public expectations, Fowler's marriage to Fifi proved strong. They gradually pursued ranching, starting with a small spread in Illinois. As they spent less time in Chicago, they developed a cattle ranch in southern California, and near Scottsdale, Arizona, which became their favorite home in their later years. As an outdoors woman, Fifi thrived working on their various spreads, and calmed her fiery temperament. Fowler raised Fifi's younger children as though they were his own. When her offspring had all moved away, Fifi acquired Indian art with the idea of establishing a museum for that purpose. On their Arizona ranch, she built hogans to house master artisans, and supported them and their families. She also sought out historic objects to assemble a comprehensive collection for the education of others. Her devotion to Indian art was exceptional, for few then thought their creations more than trinkets or "primitive."

When the United States entered World War II, Abby and John Jr. had five sturdy sons ready to serve. Since achieving financial independence from their father, they each pursued their separate interests with more seriousness. During the late 1930s, when attacks on capitalists were more heated, the Rockefeller brothers presented an exception from the common belief that sons of the rich turned out badly. John 3rd was on the boards of many organizations his father had started. Nelson had already made the cover of *Time* for his work on behalf of MOMA, and was learning as much as he could about Latin America. Laurance was exploring investments, and more important, formulating philanthropic work in worldwide conservation. Winthrop, the least settled of the five, nonetheless continued his interest in the oil business. David, the most scholarly, after graduating from Harvard had studied at the London School of Economics, then went on to earn a Ph.D. in Economics from the University of Chicago.

The greatest satisfaction to their father, though, was in September 1940, when they invited him to lunch and announced their formation of the Rockefeller Brothers Fund. It was a way the brothers, now going very different ways as adults, affirmed the continued unity of the family. Most significant to John Jr., that unity was committed to continued civic and philanthropic service.

Even before Pearl Harbor, bon vivant Winthrop was first to enlist. Starting as a private in the Army, he worked his way up to enter officers' candidate school. His service included some horrific battles on the Pacific front. President Franklin Roosevelt put Nelson, thirty-two, in charge of the Office for Coordination of Commercial and Cultural Relations Between American Republics. John 3rd, a naval reserve officer, sat behind a desk in the Bureau of Personnel in Washington. He and his wife Blanchette were active in the British War Relief Committee, and subscribed to care for two London boys during the duration of the conflict. Laurance, also in the Navy, coordinated aircraft plant production. David signed up for the Army, trained in intelligence, and went overseas. During his two-year absence, his wife Peggy grew particularly close to Abby—and became the source of yet more jealousy for John Jr.

David had married Margaret "Peggy" McGrath in 1940. They had met seven years earlier, when he was a freshman at Harvard and she a student at Chapin. Vivacious, fun-loving, and outspoken, Peggy had the least sheltered background of this group of daughters-in-law. Her father was an attorney in Mount Kisco, a suburb of New York less formal than Greenwich or Bronxville. She had heard stories of her ancestors' struggle as immigrants, the women straining their backs over sewing machines. Although a hard worker, David was the most easygoing of the brothers, quick to smile, overpolite toward everyone, and gifted in solving disputes and reading others' moods. While David was the most erudite of the brothers (and modest about showing his knowledge), Peggy had not gone to college. She had a quick mind that would make that lack of advanced training irrelevant. Abby and John Jr. could smile yet again that a son had found so compatible a partner.

Now in her late sixties and slowed by her ailing heart, Abby remained in high spirits and dove into the war effort. She helped the USO and found excuses to have young men on leave over for dinner. She gave the College of William and Mary benches for the soldiers to sit on while they ogled coeds. Riding about New York or Williamsburg, she had her chauffeur pick up men in uniform and give them a lift. She worked to fund the Emergency Rescue Committee, which helped to get European artists, particularly Jews and antifascists, and their art works into the States. She consulted on key decisions at MOMA. Among these was her critical role in the firing of director Alfred Barr, who no longer seemed the right person to run the growing museum. In 1944, she gave nearly all her money to the institution, almost $600,000.

In 1943, amidst the war excitement and museum intrigues, came the news that Babs was going to Reno to divorce Dave Milton. Their differences in temperament had become too great. Dave loved farming, and had developed a working spread just beyond the Pocantico estate, but Babs was really a city person. More troublesome for her, in recent years he was away from home for weeks following up one or another "deal." Babs acknowledged that Dave was a good person, a thoughtful father—when he was around—but she needed more steady, devoted companionship. Her father, who believed divorce to be a sin, fought her plans. Only after Abby's softening did he accept his daughter's decision. Typical of John

Jr., he also told Dave that he would always be considered a member of the family.

Following the divorce, Babs needed to consult a doctor. A friend introduced her to Dr. Irving Pardee, and in time she began to date him. They married in 1946, with both of her parents' full blessing and approval. Pardee proved the considerate, devoted, supportive man Babs had hoped for. Three years later he died of leukemia.

Following years of relative anonymity, in 1944 Margaret and George de Cuevas went public with a most surprising and unexpected plan, the establishment of a ballet company. Initially known as Ballet Internationale, the company was to reside in New York, performing at a theater the couple were renovating on Columbus Circle. Although both Ballet Theater and the Ballet de Monte Carlo were active in the city then, George explained Ballet Internationale would go on the road whenever the others were in production. Along with the company would be a school "to uphold the technique and tradition of the classical ballet, and to help in the creation and development of the modern American ballet."[18] Used to watching ballet in Europe with its lengthy tradition, he was disappointed in performances he had seen recently in the States. His analysis was correct—the art form was in its stumbling youth here, and standards not yet consistent. "If you like ballet you notice that it is not perfect. I want perfect." Toward that end Margaret placed $1 million into the company endowment, with the stipulation that any profits earned be returned to the project and shared by the collaborative artists.

Their social circle of friends, which included expatriated dancers, artists, and composers, along with promising young American artists, contributed to the cleverness of Ballet Internationale. This was evident from its debut in October 1944. The participants include figures familiar to balletomanes even today. The choreography included a staging of the classical *Les Sylphides* by Mme. Fokine and a modern work by Nijinska. Salvador Dali designed the stage set for a dance to a score by Paul Bowles. George Balanchine and Leonid Massine were soon among those choreographing for the company. Among de Cuevas's intents was to develop young dancers into stars, because other American companies preferred to hire well-known Europeans for the top places. His early rosters included many dancers who later achieved fame, such as André Eglevsky, Rosella Hightower, Marie Jeanne, Viola Essen, John Taras, and William Dollar.

Awestruck by the glamorous theater interior, the audience applauded loudly even before the dancing began. The 1,300-seat hall, designed decades earlier by Stanford White, had been completely redone to evoke an intimate, luxurious atmosphere. The chandelier's 27,000 pieces of brilliant crystals overhead outshone the jewels of the women below. Afterwards, Edwin Denby, the noted *Times* dance reviewer, saw promise in the performances, but thought the company needed to find its own style. Nonetheless, he was pleased to see evidence that the dancers had been well-rehearsed, and the orchestra play with sensitivity and accuracy. Overall, he thought de Cuevas's intentions were good, that with time the company would mature to distinction. Following its initial New York run, the group toured to other cities in the United States and in Mexico.

Ballet Internationale was not a New York resident for long. In 1947, it combined with a company from Monte Carlo, and relocated its base in France. From there it travelled all over the world, and was unusual in giving its performers full-time work based upon rehearsal periods interspersed with forty weeks of performances a year. De Cuevas also featured Americans in his overseas roster.[19] By ensuring sufficient rehearsing, the entire company, from corps through soloists, were of high technical skill. This was a break from the usual practice of touring companies, which often depended then, as today, on underrehearsed stars to draw the audience. The departure from New York City proved wise. De Cuevas could not compete with the larger companies there, in particular the growing influence of choreographer George Balanchine. In fact, de Cuevas offered the Columbus Circle theater to Balanchine in 1947, and gave both him and his wife, ballerina Maria Tallchief, work during breaks in their own company.[20]

The significance of de Cuevas's ballet contributions was little understood in the States because most of the publicity surrounding him related to his flamboyant publicity stunts. An irrepressible showoff, George played up being eccentric artist to the press because it gained easy, free publicity. In announcing his company's move to Monte Carlo, he held a levee, the royal greeting of people from his bed. There guests found him surrounded by fifteenth-century Spanish furniture, a chair covered in zebra skin, walls hung with Dali paintings, and two petrified tree trunks flanking the massive wrought iron bed. During the event he reportedly answered two telephones, speaking in six different languages, threw orders at several secretaries, and handed his wrist to his physician to monitor his pulse. (Margaret appeared briefly with their pet Pekingeses Boo-boo and Susie.)

Behind all the glitter and smiles, George and Margaret faced problems common to parents of any background. The most troublesome occurred in 1948 when their daughter Bessie, who was about to enter Vassar, instead married against her parents' wishes. (This time John Jr. played a role once common to his father, of urging parents to be more tolerant and accepting of their wayward child. He sent the newlyweds one thousand dollars, and later helped Bessie's husband get a job.)

In later years in Europe George threw fantastic costume parties and staged a "duel" with choreographer Serge Lifar. At his most famous ball, held in Biarritz in 1953, five orchestras entertained two thousand guests dressed in eighteenth-century costumes. His plans to transform the country club there into a château took ten months, and at the last minute sheep and cows borrowed from a local convent decorated the lawn. Dancer Zizi Jeanmarie rode almost naked upon a camel. Lady Ashley, former wife of Clark Gable, wore only flowers. The famed partygiver, chubby Elsa Maxwell, rode in on a donkey as Sancho Panza. Aly Kahn brought actress Gene Tierney. Humorist Art Buchwald dressed as an Indian bearing the tattoo "US Go Home." While some magazines gushed over the event as vicarious entertainment, more sober journalists decried the extravagance during a time when France was still recovering from the devastation of war. Similarly, the Vatican condemned the "feast of ostentation, vanity, immorality in all its aspect, whose only justification lies in decadence and paganism."

Away from reporters, George showed more substance. Wherever he went, he was very popular—admired for his warmth, generosity, sensitivity, and artistic vision. One observer remarked approvingly on his having the "wit of [Oscar] Wilde, impetuous, cruel, and polished."[21] He had continental charm, and greeted people with enthusiastic kisses. In other words, he fit well with the French, who awarded him the Legion of Honor in 1952 for his artistic contributions to the culture.

As George found his life's meaning as a dance impresario, Margaret's melancholy increased. George did not know what to do with his sad wife. He wrote John Jr., "I am not very happy about Margaret's condition. She is too depressed and I feel that she has a total lack of courage to face life." It is not clear whether her bouts of illness were a possible motive for or a consequence of his creating a career in art. Margaret had been austere and pious as a young girl, given to solitude, and withdrew completely from the world as her husband discovered a very public place within it.

When World War II ended, Abby and John Jr. were relieved that all their sons were alive and had acquitted themselves well in their various assignments. Now in their seventies, both kept busy with their philanthropies.

John Jr. tried to rein Abby in from the museum and parties and, as usual, she managed to slip away from his control. Further competing with him for her attention were seventeen grandchildren, with more on the way.

In 1947, John Jr. fulfilled a longtime wish for a protracted time alone with his wife, though not out of her willing compliance. Concerned over her health, her doctor ordered her to spend the winter in Arizona, which meant separation from her children and grandchildren. She had little opportunity to socialize with other guests at the Arizona Inn where they stayed, for her husband found ways to keep her inactive, even secluded. In letters to her sister Lucy, she often used the word "persuade" to describe her efforts to involve her husband in picnics, teas, and dinners. Occasionally she shared her husband's dislike for particular company. They welcomed Lord Astor for tea, and were relieved that Lady Astor was not available because she did "not make for peaceful conversation."[22] A more welcome visitor was their longtime friend, birth-control activist Margaret Sanger.

John Jr.'s favorite companion in Arizona apart from Abby was Marcellus Hartley Dodge, husband of William Rockefeller's daughter Ethel Geraldine. A tragedy many years previously had separated this once-happy couple. Their showplace estate in New Jersey, Geralda Farms, sprawled with woodlands, deer park, fields, and dog kennels. Though extremely wealthy, instead of leading a leisure life, Marcellus preferred running Remington Arms and investing in Wall Street. (In one of his best-known coups, he floated an issue called Midvale Ordnance and netted $24 million overnight in profits.) The couple seemed content and well matched.

Uncharacteristic of the Rockefellers, Geraldine had only one child, Marcellus Dodge, Jr. In 1930, he died in an automobile accident in France. Geraldine became so unhinged that she kept the coffin with her son's remains in her drawing room for weeks. Unable to convince his wife that she was not responsible for her son's death, Marcellus left her. Although they never divorced, they maintained separate residences from that point. Geraldine then devoted her life to dogs. She bred them, sponsored dog shows, started kennel clubs and dog warden services in New Jersey, and coauthored a book on German shepherds.

Abby also entertained Margaret de Cuevas and her son John, who were staying in Arizona that winter. In her usual astute way, Abby quickly captured the essence of the boy, finding him brilliant, with a "seething underneath." John de Cuevas was in love with a ballet dancer and choreographer he would later marry.

During this time Abby was particularly concerned about son Winthrop, whose name continued as in the past to appear in the gossip columns. Over the years he had been pictured winning a dance contest with Mary Martin and out dancing with movie stars like Ginger Rogers and Joan Blondell. He frequented café society hangouts—El Morocco, the Stork Club, 21, the Copacabana. While he reassured his parents that the columnists were writing fiction pressed upon them by publicity agents, they knew he was drinking and smoking, and that some element of the stories were true. Abby remained nonchalant, and praised Winthrop for his success with friends, while his father carefully avoided mentioning the topic of his son's nightlife.

This time the publicity was true and sensational. In October 1947 Barbara "Bobo" Sears had gone to Reno for a quickie divorce from her diplomat husband Richard. Soon afterward reporters learned her likely new mate was Winthrop Rockefeller. With her fair, blonde beauty, and nickname, she seemed a fortune seeker. The public was certain of this when they learned her real name was Jievute Paulekiute, and her parents were Lithuanian immigrants. She had started on the road to upward mobility as a model posing for the Montgomery Ward catalogue. Actually, she was very bright, witty, and a popular guest among both the conservative rich and the devotees of flashier café society. John Jr. disapproved of Bobo being a divorcée, but Abby thought this intelligent and sensible woman would make her wandering son a good wife.

In early February 1948, during a phone call interrupting a lunch, Laurance broke the news to his parents that Winthrop's plane en route to Florida had crash-landed at sea. Following several terrible hours of waiting, a reporter called to reassure them that all the passengers had survived. Several days later Winthrop married Bobo—a surprise to the public, if not to his family. Because Florida had a three-day waiting period, the ceremony occurred at midnight at the end of the third day. Their guests included the Duke and Duchess of Windsor, "Prince" Mike Romanoff, assorted Astors and Vanderbilts, and other well-known socialites. The reason for the sudden marriage, they explained, was the shock of reality brought on by Winthrop's accident. But seven months later son Winthrop Paul Rockefeller Jr. was born.

Following news of the wedding, Abby made clear to family members that Bobo was not responsible for all the media hoopla. She thought it good to introduce some Slavic blood into the family, and noted that the Lithuanians were a courageous, sympathetic people. She wrote to Bobo's mother in admiration of her daughter's "sweet, charming disposition and friendly spirit."

Abby would never see her latest grandson and Winthrop's heir. After returning to Pocantico that spring, on April 3 she and John Jr. held a family reunion. All six children, eighteen grandchildren, and various in-laws gathered for lunch. The weather was agreeable, the gardens starting to bloom. On Sunday morning she rode back to New York City accompanied by her son David and his daughter Peggy, who sat in her lap. She stopped to visit with Bobo, who had been too ill to attend the festivities in Pocantico. Before going to sleep, she phoned her sister Lucy to share her excitement over the family visits. The next morning she awoke with a stomach upset, and died of heart failure while the doctor was examining her.

John Jr. collapsed, and was unable to fathom Abby's death. The man who could not bear to have his mother's body moved from her bed demanded his wife's body leave at once. "Take this blow away," he begged, and had her lifeless form cremated the same day. His children and their spouses gathered around helplessly to watch him struggle through the grief of losing his companion of forty-seven years. Only after their insistence would he accept a memorial service, which was held in May at the interdenominational Riverside Church. In late June he consented to take her ashes to a private burial spot in Pocantico the two had chosen earlier, where preset headstones awaited them. The native plants Abby loved, as well as flowering shrubs like dogwood and rhododendron encircled the ground. In recent years the couple had come to treat this spot as a sacred place, for meditation and private talk. The family arranged a simple prayer ceremony led by a minister. John Jr. wrote in his journal, "There were no tears shed for we all felt that the dear wife, mother, and grandmother, although invisible, was a member of the group that gathered there and we talked of her simply, naturally, as though she were present with us."[23]

Abby's estate, including the art works, was modest, little more than a million dollars. In recent years she had given away most of her art. The oriental miniatures, which she had kept, eventually went to Harvard's Fogg Museum. Virtually everything else went to MOMA. At the time of her death, she had been consulting on plans for a print room, was adding to her original contribution of 1,600 works for the facility. Consequently, the museum completed her project in her honor.

Wounded by awareness of his insensitivity toward modern art and Abby's museum, John Jr. gave MOMA in her memory shares of stock valued at $4 million. He also funded a center in Colonial Williamsburg to hold her American folk art collection. Those objects had been the source of some controversy among the staff in recent years, because most were of a later period—the nineteenth century—than the reconstructed buildings where she had placed them. He chose for the center a site next to the Williamsburg Inn she inspired. (In 1992 the center expanded considerably to support its large collection, research facilities, and educational services.)

One other memorial was created, one that would have particularly pleased Abby. Through the intercession of Alfred Barr, Henri Matisse accepted a commission for a work to be placed at the Union Church in Pocantico Hills. Matisse was bedridden, and had resorted in his final years to creating compositions from paper cutouts, some of which were translated into stained glass. The family hoped he could do something similar in Abby's honor, and finally convinced him to take the assignment, which he completed the final days of his life. The result was elegant and brilliant, like Abby herself.

With Abby gone, John Jr. followed his father's model and took solace in the companionship of women friends. Two were his daughters-in-law Blanchette and Mary Tod. During a stay at the Eyrie, he took such comfort in the companionship of another young woman, Margaretta Murphy, that he wanted her and her physician husband Robin close by. He invited the Murphys to build their winter home at Pocantico Hills, and helped Robin gain a position at the Rockefeller Institute. Doubtless John Jr. never imagined that this chance acquaintanceship in Maine, and subsequent invitation to become part of the family's circle of friends, would result in Margaretta becoming his daughter-in-law. It may not have been coincidence that Nelson Rockefeller waited until his father was dead before going public with his love for Mrs. Murphy.

Now in their eighties, Alta and Parmalee anticipated their deaths with equanimity. Parmalee fell and broke a hip and had failing eyesight. While less enfeebled than her husband, Alta was a realist. One day they sent John Jr. precise instructions to carry out in case of their death: who to call along with the phone numbers, their choice of undertaker, and their request for cremation. The funeral was to be private, with no public notice of death, no procession or hearse with the undertaker's name upon it, and interment in Vermont where they had bought plots in the early thirties. They specified that Rev. John Strong conduct the service, though without his clerical attire, that no music or poetry of any sort be included. Furthermore, there were to be no prayers for the dead. If a benediction was given, it was to be only for the living present. Unwritten was the message that Alta had rejected her family's beliefs, for this bleak document denied hope of resurrection.

Following Abby's death, John Jr. showed more interest in Parmalee's work for reducing hunger and increasing food production. They cordially debated the problem. John Jr. sent copies of Margaret Sanger's latest essay to argue that birth control was "the only alternative to an ultimate world population covering so large a part of the earth as to leave too small an area on which to produce the necessary food for its support."[24] Further signs of softening occurred between the two brothers-in-law. He accepted Parmalee's views at times, and sent him articles of interest, such as one on the potential organic productivity of the sea. Parmalee found some merit in his brother-in-law's emphasis upon birth control because he equated population growth with crowding, therefore an inevitable reduction in human freedom.

Both men agreed that Alta was a wonderful person. In a rare admission of praise, Parmalee wrote John Jr. of her eighty-first birthday:

> [W]hat a life she has made of it, for she has given no attention whatever to the things to which most people give chief prominence—publicity, etc. Her attention has been confined to those things which have been worth doing . . . . When I refused the Legion of Honor in France, I did it right along the line of Alta's outlook. A ribbon or a name is nothing to her. Something that will make the world better is everything and that is what has taken her attention—largely the interest of increasing the production of food and by decreasing the consumption of food, as in the case of refusing to maintain inadequately productive animals.[25]

John Jr. described her similarly to friends, as generous, kindly, and unselfish, although privately he often wished she had given more to "large" causes rather than local ones.

In December 1955 Parmalee died, earning posthumous admiration for his work in agriculture and the elimination of world hunger. Afterwards, strangers who wanted to buy his now classic Marmon "16" Phaetons besieged Alta, but she held onto them. One wonders if, in her grief, she referred to the spiritual comforts of her youth.

The Rockefeller longevity was serving the remaining brother and sister well. In 1951, at age seventy-seven, John Jr. remarried. His wife, Martha Baird Allen, twenty years younger, was a recent widow, her husband having been a Brown classmate and lifelong friend of John Jr.'s. A talented musician, as a young adult she had debuted with Sir Thomas Beecham and the London Symphony. Though she had given up her career for marriage, she remained vitally interested in musical causes. John Jr.'s children were grateful to have her join the family, for she was such a balm for their father. Perhaps having learned from his experience with Abby, even before the wedding he gave Martha a large trust fund so she could give to musical causes without his interference.

The booming economy of the war years had reinvigorated the family investments. One consequence was that John Jr. revived his high level of giving to favorite causes, particularly Williamsburg, interdenominational activities, the restoration of Hudson River Valley historic sites (Philipse Manor, Van Cortlandt Manor, and Sunnyside, Washington Irving's home). The other result was his giving yet more money to some of his children. In 1948 he had sold his share of Rockefeller Center to his sons. In 1952 he significantly added to the trusts of John 3rd, Nelson, Laurance, and David.

The unequal treatment of Winthrop and Babs was not new. Winthrop's lifestyle contradicted all that was expected of the Rockefeller children. His hasty marriage to Bobo did not last. Their backgrounds were too difficult, their temperaments bristled. His family, particularly David and Peggy, tried to make Bobo feel welcome, but she shared too little of the other wives' experiences to feel comfortable. The couple tried valiantly to resolve their differences, but were unable to get beyond raucous fights, often following heavy drinking, that eventually occurred in public. Winthrop withdrew, went on long business trips without his wife, and after eighteen months locked her out of their Park Avenue duplex. The gossip columnists followed every step of the marriage disintegration with glee.

Despite what it seemed to the misled public, money was not a factor in the breakup, just as it had not been Bobo's motive in the marriage. She wanted to continue working on the marriage, and only after she realized Winthrop was unwilling to reconcile did she force a large settlement. For five years lawyers battled before she came away with the largest record in any court to that date, over $6 million in cash, trust funds for herself and their son, and property. When it was all over, Winthrop moved to Arkansas, where he finally found some stability as a leader in that impoverished state.

Despite his notorious behavior, Winthrop received larger gifts than his sister Babs from their father because at least he had a philanthropic streak. Even so, after Winthrop moved to Arkansas, where he made a new life as a successful rancher, John Jr. always found excuses to keep from visiting the spread. If he wanted to see his father, Winthrop had to make the trip.

Babs lost out in John Jr.'s eyes less because she was female than for rejecting religion and divorcing a "good man." Worst of all, she refused to give to charity. Her father reviewed her annual tax returns every March and was incensed to see that she would rather pay large taxes than share her wealth and enjoy a tax break as well. It was not until her father died that Babs began to give money away in large amounts.

Even in his final years John Jr. exerted control, occasionally at the expense of his children's feelings. In a noted example, he encouraged John 3rd's involvement in Williamsburg, then sided with those whose agenda differed with his son's. It humiliated John 3rd, now middle-aged, to be so publicly countered by his father, who thought his son was going in the wrong direction with the restoration project. This intrusion was not special to the man, for such ruling over adult children's lives (as has been seen within the families of James Stillman and William Rockefeller) is common among the well-to-do, where blood and money are so interconnected. For some children, those more self-confident and assured, one like Nelson, this parental control was an annoyance to work around; for hesitant and vulnerable offspring, one such as John 3rd, it was a debilitation. At least Blanchette understood her husband's self-doubts, and washed away the hurt from her father-in-law's criticism with gentle, constant encouragement.

John Jr.'s life continued to follow the cycles set decades earlier. His daily schedule began at seven, followed by a prompt breakfast at eight, work until noon, lunch and a nap, more work, then a drive or other relaxation. His main home remained Kykuit in Pocantico, which meant he went to New York on weekdays to work at his office in Rockefeller Center. On Sundays, following worship, he expected as many of his children and grandchildren as possible to show up for dinner. For several weeks each spring and fall he and Martha went to Williamsburg. Summer took them briefly to Seal Harbor, where he worked at his favorite keyhole desk with a view overlooking the Atlantic. Winter brought a stay at the Tucson Inn.

He remained comfortable with old ways. In 1952 a visitor was amazed to see this noted philanthropist wore high-buttoned shoes. Another guest found him delighted to have just bought and packed up twenty-two Bibles for his grandchildren. In this regard he resembled his father, except that he was never able to slacken his pace nor seek out moments of folly. He remained more like his mother to the end, prim and sincerely committed to the life of service and piety.

In 1959, now eighty-five, John Jr. had a prostate operation. Those close to him watched a slow, irrevocable decline. His skin hung on his form, his bones pronounced themselves. He developed a palsy in his hands and had difficulty writing. With frailty he preferred solitude and meditation. He no longer wanted his family or friends about for conversation. When they did come, they would find him bundled under a blanket in a chair placed by a sunlit window. Still, his death on May 11, 1960, was a surprise.

At the time John Jr. died, his grandson John D. Rockefeller IV was studying in Japan, yet chose to return to New York for the services. He later recalled, "It was quite powerful, the whole experience of grandfather's death. I remember feeling strongly the idea that more than my grandfather had died. It was the end of an era. It was history itself passing on."[26]

15

Legacies

"Train up a child in the way he should go: and when he is old he will not depart from it."

—Proverbs 22:6

*I*n truth, the era of Senior and John Jr. was not over until Alta died in June 1962 at age ninety-one. As she requested, there was only a small, private service, her ashes set next to Parmalee's. In Cleveland, where Alta House still served its neighborhood, its patroness was forgotten. She bequeathed Mount Hope farm to Lenox Hill Hospital, and her New York townhouse to MOMA for use in later expansion. Though never interested in modern art, Alta had included the bequest on the urging of her brother. These gifts were also her final acts of obedience to her parents, her being true to the Rockefeller conscience.

Now few remained in the family who had known Senior during his prime.

His first adult grandchild to die had been Mathilde McCormick Oser, who succumbed following cancer surgery in 1947. She was forty-one, too young to enjoy the fruits of her attentive mothering.

Several years later, Fowler McCormick reunited the bodies of his family. Edith's coffin, along with those of her children Jack and Editha, were removed from the crypt in Graylawn Cemetery. Harold's went from its resting place in Forest Lawn to the McCormick plot in Chicago where his parents rest. There Edith and the children were placed as well. Fowler explained he was fulfilling his parents' wish to him that they be near one another in death.

Granddaughter Muriel McCormick Hubbard died in 1959, and despite her spendthrift ways left an estate of over $9 million. She also placed four small children, adopted late in life, under the guardianship of a close friend. The original source of her money was the 1917 trust that Senior had established for her mother Edith. John 3rd was chair of the trust committee, and wanted the money for the development of Lincoln

Center. Consequently, he argued that the four young children Muriel had adopted late in life were technically not "legal," meaning biological issue, as specified in Muriel's will. The children's representative sued John 3rd and the trustees; the court case dragged on so long that the inheritance grew by $4 million more. In the end, the court awarded money to both the children and to Lincoln Center. Thus Muriel, who had never realized her hope to be an actress and start a theater, after death contributed to this major American performing arts facility.

George de Cuevas died in 1961, at age seventy-five. Days before, his appearance at his company's performance of "The Sleeping Beauty" had brought him great applause of appreciation from the audience, which knew he was mortally ill. "This is my last ballet," he announced. "I've put everything into it—my money, my health, my passion." Starring as the Prince was a recent Soviet defector, Rudolph Nureyev. Several months earlier, when the dancer escaped from his Soviet guards in Paris, George had been quick to offer assistance.

At the time of his death, George and Margaret were separated. Nasty stories had been appearing concerning his leaving her. These became more sensational when a male protégé sued George's estate. The name "Rockefeller" seldom appeared in the reports, and the scandals were short-lived. George's strange behavior during these final years suggests he had lost full control of his mental faculties and was vulnerable to others' manipulation.

Apart from a noted purchase in 1965 to save two New York landmark buildings, Margaret remained out of the public eye. In 1977, at age eighty, she married dancer and choreographer Raymundo de Larrain, who was forty years her junior. Like her first husband, De Larrain was Chilean, and had been a member of George's ballet company since 1952, taking it over after his death. Margaret died eight years later, leaving little estate, having given most of it away to ballet.

Fifi Potter Stillman McCormick died in 1969 at age eighty-nine. Her devoted husband Fowler, though eighteen years younger, died just four years later. Fowler was the only one of Edith and Harold's three children to live a full, satisfying life. He remained a close friend of Carl Jung, and was among those present during the psychologist's final days. Unfortunately, Fifi's plans for a museum of Southwest Indian art never materialized, and following Fowler's death, the heirs sent her collection to an auction house.

The first of John Jr.'s children to die was Winthrop, in 1973 at age sixty. Following his divorce from Bobo, he married Jeannette Edris, daughter of a Seattle industrialist and millionaire. Her youth had been as rebellious and wild as Winthrop's, and included three marriages in rapid succession. By her late thirties, she had matured into an independent, frank, and earthy woman well-suited to her fourth husband. Jeannette joined her husband in his devotion to improving Arkansas. When he founded the Arkansas Art Center in Little Rock, she travelled throughout the state to organize local chapters of that organization. When her children from previous marriages chose to attend public school, she struck out to raise funds for new buildings, upgrade the curriculum, and encourage farm children to go to college.

Unfortunately, even following his achievements in ranching, in Arkansas-related philanthropy, and in politics, Winthrop remained doubtful that he was living up to Rockefeller standards. Essentially a shy and sensitive man, his responsibilities required constant public exposure where he was expected to put on an appearance of toughness. His use of liquor to silence his private conflicts became well-known, the cause for rumor. In Arkansas, a dry, Baptist state, everyone who wished to do so drank, just as those who wished to gamble went to Hot Springs. Never satisfied with his performance, Winthrop took on too much work, especially as governor, and Jeannette felt neglected. After fourteen years of marriage, she decided to leave him while they could part friends. Soon afterward, Winthrop was diagnosed with cancer, and he died in the adopted state he had done so much to advance.

Next to pass was Babs, in 1976 at age seventy-two. She had married a third time, to banker Jean Mauzé, but was a widow by the time of her death. Living on the sidelines, she always retained her brothers' affection and protection. While she was still alive, in her honor they established the Abby Rockefeller Mauzé professorship at Massachusetts Institute of Technology, with the chair to go to a distinguished woman scholar.

Following her father's death, Babs took on various charitable activities, as though she had to be free of his judgment to express her charitableness. Her interests included her mother's beloved MOMA, the Asia Society, and the New York Zoological Society. In 1971, she spent $6 million to build Greenacre Park, a restful retreat on East Fifty-first Street in New York City, and included an endowment to maintain it in perpetuity. Her greatest efforts were for the Sloan-Kettering Cancer Center, to which she donated millions of dollars, and served as a trustee. Ironically, it was cancer that finally took Babs's life, which ended as she wished it, in her own bed in her apartment at One Beekman Place. Her will's major bequests were to medical organizations. Her two daughters inherited the trust provided by John Jr. in 1934.

* * *

Three of William Rockefeller's children had died in the mid-1930s. The youngest, Ethel Geraldine Rockefeller Dodge, spent her last years under nursing care, with her finances managed by a guardian. Despite having been separated from her husband for many years, she inherited his estate. Being childless, various people kept a death watch, not always tastefully, in anticipation of controlling her legacy. Her fanaticism for dogs and animal welfare did not strike everyone in her family or social class as a worthy crusade. In her final years, challenges to the support provided by her trustees succeeded in conserving more of her capital for future heirs.

One of Geraldine's eccentricities had been a constant embarrassment to the family: an odd-looking mansion combined with dog kennel in the heart of the East Side, on Fifth Avenue at Sixty-first Street, facing Central Park. Once completed, she seldom occupied it, and caretakers lived in the basement quarters to keep squatters out. Neighbors and relatives tried to force her to sell the place, which was an eyesore with its weed-ridden yard and gradually dilapidated exterior, but she refused.

Geraldine died at age ninety-one in 1973. She left $85 million in trust, under the control of her kennel master at Geralda Farms. The family did not question the formation of the trust, but two of her nephews went to court to have Rockefeller kin replace the kennel master as trustee. Having been told to expect her estate, the canine lovers sought their just due. Five law firms shared in the litigations, their combined fees of a half million dollars forming the largest in New Jersey history to that date. While this suit was in litigation, one nephew, William Avery Rockefeller II, the son of William G. and Elsie, committed suicide with a bullet to his head. When all the court wrangling was over, Geraldine's 1955 will, which left the bulk of her money to an animal shelter, was found invalid, and a 1962 will with broader stipulations was implemented.

Geralda Farms eventually became a corporate retreat. Most of her inheritance went toward the funding of advancements in secondary education, along with animal welfare and protection. Decades later viewers of public television would see on program credits the assistance of the "Geraldine R. [Rockefeller] Dodge Foundation." She was the only one of William's four children to pass significant resources to public use.

William's descendants did not suffer a fall from class. The Great Depression, taxes, and the absence of anything like the office of advisors at Rockefeller Center meant some deterioration of that line's wealth. Where Kykuit, John D.'s home, was preserved and is now open for public viewing, Rockwood Hall fell to the demolishers. Part of William's estate on the Hudson became a corporate facility, and his children's homes vanished as well. Nevertheless, his descendants resided in exclusive Connecticut communities, sent their children to elite schools, and intermarried with others in the Social Register. Unlike Senior's line, their names and faces seldom appeared in the newspapers, and none of those living today are well-known. That privacy is their choice, and most characteristic of Old Money.

One of William's grandchildren suffered posthumous notoriety. Isabel Stillman and Percy Rockefeller's third child, Winifred, was so insecure and plain-looking that after three days she married the first man to pay attention to her. Brooks Emeny was a brilliant political scientist, overly proud of his family background with its ties to Pennsylvania Railroad wealth. Self-important, he apparently viewed the marriage as a convenience necessary for his career, for he was seldom home. His career advanced rapidly to include teaching at Yale, a position with the U.S. State Department, and eventually presidency of the Foreign Policy Association.

While Brooks pursued fame, Winifred raised their four daughters virtually on her own. Even when their child Betty came down with a fatal cancer, Brooks was seldom around to comfort the family. What would have been stressful for people of normal temperament was hellish for Winifred, who suffered from manic-depression. Relatives referred to her intermittent spells of wakefulness and melancholy as the "Stillman disease," a reference to those characteristics of James Stillman that affected some of his descendants.

In the spring of 1951, Brooks Emeny went on a lecture tour of the Midwest, accompanied by his oldest daughter. On March 15, Winifred gave her governess, cook, and maid the day off. Later she went to her regular psychiatry appointment, where her doctor wrote up an optimistic report on her condition. She then drove to the Greenwich School to pick up Wendy, twelve, and Jo-Jo, six. Back home, she gave the girls a snack and suggested a drive through the country. The girls fell asleep during the drive, for their mother had laced their milk with sleeping pills. Winifred drove back to the house, locked the roll-down garage doors and the two doors leading into the home, stuffed blankets around the jambs, and kept the automobile running.

Early that evening the girls' governess returned from New York and wondered why the house was dark and locked up. Hearing the automobile engine, and lacking a key, she contacted Winifred's brother Avery, who called the police. Upon breaking into the garage, they found all three dead. Particularly horrible was the sight of Wendy. That child had not been drugged well enough by her mother. The position of her body showed that she had awakened to discover the deadly trap and tried unsuccessfully to break down a door before she succumbed to the fumes.

As if the loss of their troubled sister were not enough, Winifred's siblings felt society's sting of ostracism. The family minister refused to perform a service, not even for the two girls, the murder victims. When the family took the ashes to Tarrytown to place near William Rockefeller's mausoleum at Sleepy Hollow, however, they were consoled by the presence of so many of John D.'s descendants. The two lines did not mix much socially or in business, yet the bond of the two originating brothers extended through the generations, where it continues today.

One of Isabel and Percy's other daughters, Faith, had a tragic life as well, though without such shocking consequences. Like her sister Winifred, Faith chose a spouse unwisely. A wholesome, outdoor type, she was considered old for the time, thirty-one, when she married Jean Model, a Belgian refugee six years her junior. His shallow motives soon emerged, for he used his connection to the Rockefeller name and fortune as a first-class ticket into café society. Their first child was severely retarded and placed in an institution, but their next two children were healthy. In 1955, at age forty, Jean died during a polio epidemic. In 1960, Faith died of breast cancer. She had apparently known about the tumor for several years yet refused to tell anyone. "A form of suicide," the doctors concluded, suggesting her choice may have been modelled upon her mother's similar form of dying.

One of those troubled by the suicides was William Rockefeller's great-granddaughter Bel (really Isabel III). Bel followed her mother's interest in science and like her worked at the Sloan-Kettering Memorial Center at times. During the 1950s, she married Basil "Buzz" Elmer, of the prominent Lincoln clan that included Parmalee Prentice. Bel could not get her parents' permission to marry Buzz until they checked his bloodlines in the Social Register!

The couple settled in the insular world of Greenwich, where Bel had four children in five years (including Isabel IV). Her life was like that of so many homebound mothers of the 1950s, except of course she had household help. Like so many men born to or married into William Rockefeller's family, Buzz rode the train to the city, where he traded stocks on Wall Street.

Though Bel's ulcer and Buzz's migraines were symptoms of dissatisfaction, they retained their lifestyle. Bel later recalled:

> The thing that seemed to help somewhat was to spend a great deal of time with . . . aunts and uncles and quite a few of my thirty-four first cousins and their spouses. There always seemed to be something going on—a wedding, a christening, an engage-

ment, or a wedding. The premise with the Rockefellers and the Lincolns—and it's true of many clannish families—is that if you huddle together enough, nothing on the outside can hurt you. Inside the stronghold's walls, aberrations were winked at ... [T]he family nonetheless contrived to "not see" them.[1]

With the history of a grandmother and two aunts being suicidal, Bel could no longer ignore the danger to her own stability.

When after ten years Buzz lost his job, the value of the clan was apparent, for family connections soon found him a position with another investment firm. "We talked about our anxieties and our emptiness, but there didn't seem to be any way of resolving such things; people in our walk of life just didn't do that." One day they attended a Billy Graham event, and felt some temptation to pursue religion more seriously, but they continued their usual ways. In 1963, they happened upon a Congregational Church, one "decidedly untypical of Greenwich, where Episcopalians lived up to their reputation as God's Frozen People." Still, it was some months before they felt able to desert the family Episcopal congregation.

Several years later, at a Christian healing workshop, during her meditation Bel thought she heard the voice of God saying, "I have called you for my purposes. The money that you will have, I have entrusted to you, to accomplish My will." These words, stated often in John D.'s family, were uncommon among William's bloodline.

Because of their encounter with charismatic Christianity, Buzz and Bel quit their jobs and Greenwich. They moved their family to the Community of Jesus in Cape Cod, a communal organization devoted to education and charitable works.

John Jr.'s greatest legacy was not his estate, worth $157 million, but his commitment to stewardship.[2] As we have seen, it was the family's resolution of a contradiction that emerged during the time of his grandparents, namely, their highly concentrated wealth in what was supposedly an egalitarian republic. His grandparents, forging a bond between Christianity and capitalism, urged their children to rise in the world economically to practice Christian service more munificently. His father and mother honed and polished this interesting fusion of the material and spiritual.

What seemed a natural blend in the 1800s appeared insoluble by the early 1900s. The critics' voices labelled the religious rationale for wealth "hypocrisy," and government agreed that a totally unregulated economy led to unacceptable inequalities and harm. John Jr. had early sensed the contrariness of his parents' philosophy when he chose philanthropy over business as his main activity. But John Jr. could neither fully ignore nor avoid the capitalism. His father's sense of righteousness argued that the family was specially chosen to be stewards for the nation. If, as Senior once said, God gave him the money, then the family had a God-given duty to continue raising money to give away.

Because Senior lived so long, and oversaw the functionaries who invested the family wealth, John Jr. did not have to concern himself much with finances. Only when the Depression hit was he forced to see the possibility that the funds could run out, as they had for his sister Edith and some members of his uncle William Rockefeller's family. John Jr.'s pressure upon his sons to succeed may have been to alleviate anxiety that the family philanthropies would decline. He reminded them constantly "that every right implies a responsibility; every opportunity, an obligation; every possession, a duty."[3]

John Jr. had little reason to fear. His sons would surpass his expectations, both in finance and stewardship. Had she lived longer, the more trustful Abby would have been less surprised to see them rise to prominence in their careers, for she, not their father, was their real lodestone. John 3rd, the most insecure and overwhelmed by his father, in later life rose to prominence in Asian-American relations. He also devoted fourteen years to the long gestation of Lincoln Center for the Performing Arts in New York.[4] More an Aldrich than a Rockefeller, Nelson proved as adept and powerful a politician as his Senator grandfather, governed New York for three terms and served as vice president under Gerald Ford. He continued his mother's devotion to modern art and MOMA. More the business executive, Laurance developed luxury resorts, stimulated research in environmental policy, and supported cancer research. The late bloomer, Winthrop, found success in Arkansas, first as a rancher, then as the first Republican and reformist governor of that state in ninety-four years. David rejuvenated Chase Manhattan Bank, developed real estate, championed civil rights, and became an international leader in world banking. (A joke went that for David Rockefeller to become President of the United States would be a demotion.)

With five Rockefeller men active in the top levels of finance, politics, and philanthropy, public perception of family unity was greater than the reality. Sibling alliances and animosities remained. Laurance and Nelson were the closest, yet had different priorities in life. Nelson's position as governor could prove useful, as when he worked with John 3rd to ensure Lincoln Center's realization, but Nelson's egotism rubbed his siblings raw.

Still smarting from childhood teasing, Winthrop chose self-isolation in Arkansas. David and Laurance were world travellers with extensive agendas of their own. In other words, the adult siblings were typical of other American families that had emphasized individuality over kin relations.

With age, the Brothers' differences increased, which meant shared decisions involved lengthy negotiation, complicated by problems in coordinating overtaxed schedules. Furthermore, these needs to consult as a unit were few, most often related to probate or the disposal of joint property. When a Congressional committee was investigating the long reach of the Rockefeller influence, Laurance refuted the idea of the family having an "empire." The family did have ties that bound it together, he agreed, but these had almost exclusively "to do with a shared set of common experiences." An examination of individual members proved "that most have succeeded in finding a way to do his or her 'own thing' rather than a 'family thing.' "[5]

Adding to the false public perception of cohesion was the attachment of the family name to significant institutions. They owned a minority, not a majority, of Rockefeller Center. Their father had ensured that the Rockefeller philanthropies allowed family participation, yet minimized family influence or interference. (When it became known in later years that some wealthy people used foundations as tax dodges, John Jr. and John 3rd both backed legislation to require the separation of interests.) Consequently, the revelation that Nelson took large writeoffs for donations of art was a particular embarrassment to his brothers. The larger philanthropies grew into staid bureaucracies, afflicted at times by the usual power plays, rituals, and secret agendas that so effectively quash outside influences. The winners of the ego clashes among scientists in their research organizations had more influence than any family member trustee.[6]

The Brothers were connected to major centers of power, but their interests were not always compatible. Nor were they a "power elite" in the sense of consistently coordinating their actions to further one another's interests. They did contribute many millions over the years to Nelson's political campaigns, and some critics thought David's power at Chase Manhattan Bank gave the Brothers a great advantage over other elites.[7] More often Wall Street analysts noted that the family holdings were not sufficiently concentrated to give the Brothers much influence in the management of various corporations. Furthermore, the Brothers were too individual in temperament and interests to submit to decisions requiring the approval of all. What they did have was the palace guard, the functionaries in Room 5600 at Rockefeller Center, who could move smoothly in private whenever a family member contemplated a new project. The Brothers retained Senior's gift for identifying highly competent experts, advisors, and managers who could advance their purpose. It was this organizational army that made them fearsome to opponents.

The Brothers did not, on the other hand, share Senior's certainty that their acts were graced by God, His working through them for the betterment of the world. Money is a tool, Nelson once explained, that can be used constructively to facilitate many things, but it can also be sharply destructive. As the Brothers aged, they had to face at times that "good works" do not always bring good results, but can inflict unintended damage. This understanding of the complexity of social life had been caused partly by Rockefeller investments in the social sciences. Sociologists now revealed how well-intentioned motives could disguise and maintain imperialism, racism, oligarchical power, and other threats to egalitarian democracy. Thus, the Rockefeller dynasty, one built upon Christian piety, unintentionally sponsored the development of social theories that challenged some of that religious dicta. Both their theology and their understanding of social life grew more sophisticated as a result.

Referring to Abby Rockefeller's legacy, the *New York Times* observed "Hers was the spirit that held them [the family] together." Her unifying influence extended beyond that of her husband and children to her sons- and daughters-in-law. She nurtured her daughters-in-law in particular. In her tactful, determined way, Abby passed on to them the female version of the Rockefeller conscience.

Even before these women joined the family, Abby served as a model of a wife that spurred her sons to choose their marriage partners wisely. Blanchette, Mary French, Mary Tod, and Peggy were all attuned to the demands placed upon wives of prominent men. They were sensible, unaffected, and unassuming—"skirt-and-sweater" women who avoided the Café Society of the 1930s. They wanted to create comfortable homes, stay out of public view, and raise their children as normally as "Rockefeller" offspring could be. If there was unity across the male siblings, it was through their wives.

Leaving aside Winthrop's wives, the daughters-in-law started their families during the hard Depression years, when women were expected to leave jobs to the underemployed men. The advancements toward equality accomplished by the suffrage movement receded. Where in the first decades of the century young affluent women entered college at increasing rates and joined the professions, in the thirties they were even advised against attending college. (Blanchette, the oldest daughter-in-law, graduated from Vassar, while Peggy, who came of age late in the 1930s, did not go to college.)

All the Brothers' wives valued the domesticity. They understood they were to be the key child rearers during years their husbands were often away on business, war work, or philanthropy. (Blanchette admitted that her husband was so busy during one period that their children almost needed to make appointments to see him.) As the men grew more successful, though, the wives had to accompany them on trips, the ceremonial spouse to be entertained by someone else's ceremonial spouse. Childcare nurses, often European in background, were common.

Once the children matured, however, the wives sought ways to express their talents away from the home. Just as John Jr. inspired his sons to continue one of his key interests in life—conservation, art, social policy, medicine, historic preservation—so Abby encouraged her daughters-in-law to cultivate their own pursuits. She watched them closely to identify their nascent talents and carefully directed their growth. As illness forced her to give up beloved activities, she found ways to engage various daughters-in-law in her place. Yet she also understood that large responsibilities required large amounts of time, and did not push the women too quickly, before they had finished raising their children. Consequently, each Brother's wife entered middle age ready to strike out in an area of service of her own.

Blanchette inherited Abby's place at MOMA. Her prominence there grew in 1949, when Nelson asked her to create a Junior Council to bring new blood into the museum. Very quickly Blanchette attracted several dozen younger people to initiate programs such as an art lending service. By 1955, she was a trustee, and had started the International Council. Among this committee's programs was the circulation of exhibits worldwide, so that modern American art could make an impression all over the globe. In 1959, when the museum was about to start a $25 million fund drive, several major officers had to leave. Blanchette was elected president, and in her typically humble way explained, "I think the justification of having a woman president is that the men are too busy."[8] Blanchette held that office for thirteen years, after which she was elected chair of the board of trustees.

Abby also inspired Blanchette to collect art. "I think I started out because I wanted something to cut loose on," she recalled. Her first purchase was a bronze horse by Marino Marini, which she had ordered from Italy on the basis of a photograph. Several months later two burly men appeared with the piece, which was out of scale and out of place in their traditional English-style drawing room. Worse, John 3rd had the same antipathy to abstract art as his father had, and did not appreciate her hanging works of such artists as Mark Rothko.

Blanchette had advantages her mother-in-law lacked, in that she controlled a sizeable income of her own from the Hooker chemical fortune. She could not only buy larger and more important works of art, but even hire an architect to design a gallery separate from her home in New York. She selected Philip Johnson, who as first director of the architecture department at MOMA had proselytized the austere International Style. On a property Blanchette had purchased on East Fifty-second Street, Johnson placed a gallery/guest house of elegant serenity, where artworks would not compete with carved woodwork and chintz. Blanchette quickly filled the rooms with avant-garde paintings and sculpture. (Her children dubbed a Giacometti skinny six-foot man with spectral finger "No Dessert.")

One disadvantage Blanchette had compared to Abby was less opportunity to separate her museum work and her private life. By the 1950s, museums like MOMA and the Whitney Museum had become chic institutions that offered social prestige to patrons in exchange for their money. Self-made business leaders wishing recognition from elite society gravitated to the balls and dinner parties, where they jockeyed for an invitation to the boards of trustees. Now that she had her guest house, so convenient to MOMA, Blanchette felt more pressure to sponsor receptions and dinners on the museum's behalf. John 3rd, still self-conscious, crept about the edges of the gatherings, while Blanchette, almost as shy, forced herself to circulate and introduce people, which she did with grace. By middle age she was elegant and regal, without the sense of superiority that can accompany that appearance.

Thanks to a government assignment, Blanchette and John 3rd developed a mutual interest in Asian art. In 1951, he became a cultural advisor on the Peace Treaty Mission in Japan. While there, he and his wife discussed the importance of trying to undo the hatred between Japan and the United States. When they returned, Blanchette took graduate courses in Oriental history at Columbia, and encouraged her husband to continue visiting Asia. Out of these visits, John 3rd conceived two organizations, the Asia Society and the Japan Society. He was so pleased with Blanchette's acquisitions there, the woodblock prints, the Balinese temple carvings, the Buddhas from various countries, that he softened his stance toward some abstract art. Her collections grew so rapidly that she had

Philip Johnson convert the basement of the Pocantico home into a small gallery. John 3rd added pieces of his own selection, usually the more disciplined and formal examples of Asian art.

In the 1960s, John 3rd recognized that the many Asian visitors they entertained saw only European or Asian art at his homes, and almost nothing by Americans. Deciding that works of his native land should be on view, he became absorbed in this new part of the collection. American art was still a virgin territory, which allowed him to acquire both the famous names and the little-known who were temporarily out of fashion. Their first purchase, Winslow Homer's study of two women, *Backgammon*, was quite different in composition and coloration from his usual outdoors scenes. What mattered to the couple was not the typicality or potential investment in a work but their personal response. In a very short time they assembled almost two hundred paintings, and in the process awakened interest among other collectors and museums in earlier American art. (This collection is now a permanent holding of the de Young Museum in San Francisco.)

Few outside the art world were familiar with Blanchette's efforts on behalf of MOMA, as an art collector, as a valued contributor to performing arts boards, or as a fundraiser for schools like Vassar and Juilliard. Nor were many acquainted with the contributions of her sisters-in-law.

The most private wife was Tod, who was temperamentally seclusive, yet had practical reasons to keep out of the newspapers. Visible achievements were less important to her than camping, golfing, horseback riding, sailing, and tennis with her five children and friends, who loved her sense of humor. Slim, muscled, face weathered pleasingly from the sports, Tod showed a contented smile to the world. When Nelson became governor in 1958, she played the political wife role so well that none guessed the couple had been estranged for almost twenty years. She appeared beside him at rallies, answered impertinent questions from reporters, and convinced women magazine readers that theirs was an ideal family. In agreement that divorce was inappropriate, they chose to live separate lives, and maintained separate bedrooms. Ironically, this most private of the sisters-in-law was to face the most public exposure.

Laurance's wife Mary was more visible, partly because the couple participated in high society. His main business venture was the development of prestige resorts, so it was important that they mix and mingle with potential clients. They were pictured at charity galas, and their dinners were described in columns. Mary was comfortable with the demands placed on executives' wives at the time to be exemplary hostesses, yet she also followed her mother-in-law's model of service. Mary's endeavors were wide-ranging, devoted to racial justice, foreign policy education, Christian education, preservation of her hometown Woodstock, Spelman College, and more. She served on the boards of the Metropolitan Museum of Art, MOMA, and the Whitney, for which she worked twenty-five years. Negotiating agreements among the contentious partisans of the art world takes great diplomacy, which she had in abundance.

Perhaps most important to Mary was the YWCA, an organization she strengthened on both international and local levels.[9] While accompanying Laurance on his constant world travels to study environmental issues, she would break away to visit hospitals, slums, and schools. Dressed in sheath and heels, she sought out the most backwater projects, from scratch poor farms in Uruguay to *favelas* in Rio. Her formal dress did not reflect her attitude, which, like Abby's, was embracing of the culture. She returned from these trips moved by the spirit of the Y community workers in their fight against illiteracy, for vocational training, and for women's political participation. Through sharing the knowledge of their separate jaunts, Mary and Laurance came to a richer understanding of the interconnections among resource conservation, women's status, and economic development. The result of this partnership could be very practical, as in their seeing how the YWCA could implement conservation programs, and broad, as in their influence with international policy makers.

David's wife Peggy was also less intimidated by public attention. Unlike Mary, her name was seldom in the society pages. An accomplished and serious gardener, her philanthropy emphasized farmland preservation, the Maine Coast Heritage Trust, and the New York Botanical Society. It was this work, less glamorous than the museum world, that placed her picture in the papers. Often described as "down to earth" for her warm, easygoing nature, Peggy earned that description more literally. Farming so pleased her that she got a spread of her own, 2,972 acres in the Hudson Valley, where she operated six farms to raise 550 head of cattle, along with corn, soybean, wheat, rye, alfalfa, and grasses. In her late seventies she still drove the tractor to cut hay. In 1992, she and David placed the land in an agricultural trust. Asked whether she would get a tax benefit from the agreement, she said, "Since I give all I can give now, it won't make any difference."[10]

She also joined her husband in gathering an impressive array of Impressionist artworks. Their interest was spurred by Margaret Barr, wife of MOMA curator Alfred Barr. Following the war, unlike his brothers, David set his family in a townhouse on the fashionable Upper East Side of New York. Peggy filled it with old English furniture, family artifacts, and eighteenth-century art, all of which suited David fine. Although he had become a trustee at MOMA, he did so more for his mother's sake than out of his own interest. The Barrs suggested that the couple consider modern art to add excitement to the traditional ambience of their home. The first significant purchase was in 1951, a seminude by Renoir entitled *Gabriel.*

A major purpose behind their purchases was to educate their six children in the appreciation of beauty. Visitors would find one son shooting his ray-gun in the foyer under the shadow of a Degas, while a daughter bounded up the sweeping staircase past water colors by Arthur B. Davies and Japanese prints. In the living room, a self-possessed nobleman by Sully stared across at Cezanne's sullen *Boy in a Red Waistcoat.* Other furnishings included eighteenth-century Chinese wallpapers, English porcelains originally collected by Lucy Aldrich, and Louis XV chairs. The paintings became vogue, and worth much more than they had spent for them, but the David Rockefellers bought for enjoyment, not gain. Of course, it helped not to have to worry about the prices. When asked about one noted purchase she made at auction, a thirty-one-thousand-dollar Signac, Peggy explained, "I just raised my hand and kept it up until I reached my top price. Fortunately, the other bidding had stopped and the painting was mine."[11] If history is any predictor, Signac and their other extraordinary objects will one day be on permanent display in a public museum.

By the 1960s, the Rockefeller Brothers' children, the Cousins as they came to refer to themselves, were coming of age. They grew up according to certain Rockefeller traditions, such as doing menial chores to earn money, which their great-great-grandmother Eliza had originated over a hundred years before. They moved with the seasons among family holdings in New York City, Pocantico, and the Maine coast. On the other hand, religion held less sway. Laura and Senior would have been dismayed to know some of their great grandchildren did not attend church weekly, let alone be Sunday School teachers. Also, the Cousins' mothers were away from home more, accompanying their husbands for ceremonial purposes to fulfill the decorative spouse role. Pocantico was lovely, but in a shrinking world, some Cousins felt isolated there. (Always one to keep her distance from the family name, Babs raised her daughters on Long Island.) There were no common keepers of the flame, no Senior with Laura, no John Jr. with Abby, to inculcate dynastic values. In the background, nonetheless, remained the drum beat of service, of using the family's great wealth to transform society.

Numbers alone ensured more diversity among the Cousins. There were twenty-three born between 1928 and 1967, with most appearing in the late 1930s and early 1940s. In an interesting reversal of their fathers' generation, females predominated. Lacking the need to carry the Rockefeller name through life, they could be more resistant to family pressures. Their rebelliousness would help some of their brothers and male Cousins to challenge the family mystique as well.

Most of the Cousins grew up just when a separate youth culture emerged in America. They had their own music and entertainment, a looser sexual ethic than their parents, and a readiness to question authority. Where their grandfather and fathers learned to question Social Darwinism and the principle of an unregulated economy, the Cousins questioned capitalism itself and exposed contradictions in the actions of business and political leaders. Some Cousins resisted this radical criticism, and easily adopted their parents' life choices. Others had "identity crises," as did so many youth coming of age in the fifties and sixties, meaning they felt disaffiliated with what America practiced. Like their less-affluent peers, these Cousins attacked racism, sexism, nuclear arms control, the Vietnam War, ecological destruction, colonialism, imperialism, and governmental duplicity. As happened in middle-class households, some spoke out and argued with their parents over dinner, and showed signs of disrespect. Some attacked their parents' investments in South Africa, developments in precious wildlife areas, or support of government policies toward Vietnam.

Further complicating the troubled Cousins' search for clarity was the knowledge, however unstated during the turmoil, that their parents had also done substantial good. As Laura Rockefeller explained, "the deepest conflict has been between a desire to disappear, become anonymous, invisible, to run away, and a wish to be known, recognized, appreciated."[12] Rockefeller fortunes, though built on concentration of industrial power, had resulted in schools improved, diseases cured, opportunities increased for the racially and ethnically oppressed, wilderness areas saved, art placed for all to see, historical sites preserved, and more. The impact of all this philanthropy was multiplied, for the Cousins saw it expressed by their aunts and uncles as well as their parents.

Although the Cousins chose different paths out of their shared dilemma, they retained the awesome Rockefeller conscience. On the most extreme left was David's daughter Abby. Among the most radical feminists of her day, she belonged to a group that called itself Cell 16. Its members favored black martial-arts dress, and criticized other feminists for being too soft. Abby wrote about sexuality's role in gender oppression, and urged that women stop having sex with anyone. She also contributed funds to the Boston Draft Resistance and the Socialist Workers Party. When social activism receded, she turned to environmentalism, and purchased the rights to manufacture and sell a flushless toilet called the Clivis Multrum in America. She later married and raised a family while devoting her resources to popularizing this idea ahead of its time. The onetime Marxist turned entrepreneur.

Even the best-known of the Cousins to date, John IV, better known as Jay, did not settle upon his life's course readily. This handsome, lanky, personable man first considered becoming an Oriental scholar. After working with Sargent Shriver in the office of the Peace Corps, he became a Kennedy Democrat. From there he joined the antipoverty movement in West Virginia, where he later served as governor and Democratic senator. Typical of men in his family, he married a strong, talented woman, Sharon Percy, who made a name for herself in public broadcasting administration.

During her college days, Laura Rockefeller was a member of Students for a Democratic Society. In time, she came to accept family values, and trained to be a licensed psychiatric social worker. Her favorite philanthropies followed the path of her namesake great-grandmother. First, she has served as a trustee of Spelman College. In that role she met Marian Wright Edelman, president of the Children's Defense Fund. The CDF lobbies bills on behalf of all children, but particularly pushes those that will affect the poorest and minority youth. Laura came to terms with her money by separating her own earned from inherited funds. She gives much away anonymously, without taking a tax writeoff. "People who make a lot of money and don't give it away just enrage me. To not return to the system which allowed you to receive this bounty some portion, not even what you get a tax writeoff for, makes me very angry."[13]

At least one Cousin made spiritual concerns his center. In seeking a simpler life, Nelson's son Steven married a Norwegian household worker. The engagement and Cinderella marriage filled pages of newsprint. As in past generations, the public approved. For some, Steven's marrying "down" was evidence that romance could reduce class equality. For others, more cynical, his actions brought the family "down" with him. Regardless, theirs was among the first celebrity weddings in which the television reporters caused a traffic jam, causing the couple to escape through an unknown entrance to the estate.

In typical Rockefeller style, Tod and Nelson fully accepted Anne Marie Rasmussen, for she demonstrated that principles were more important than social status. Unfortunately, Steven and Anne Marie soon discovered they had chosen each other for opposite reasons. He admired her growing up on a remote island lacking even electricity, while she thought he would offer an escape into the cosmopolitan life of his family. When he expressed his interest in seminary training, she realized they were incompatible, and they eventually divorced. After graduating from Union Theological Seminary, Steven completed a Ph.D. in philosophy at Columbia University. He became a noted scholar of religion, a college professor and dean, and later remarried. Anne Marie wrote a thoughtful book about her experiences that did not blame the family for her marital problems.

Other Cousins chose service-oriented careers, such as medicine, psychotherapy, conservation law, and art. Not surprisingly, the females are as well educated as the males. Laurance's daughter Lucy graduated with an M.D. in psychiatry from Columbia Medical School. Some, like David Jr., assumed a direct role in Rockefeller-funded activities, although this meant less time for his first love, music. The diversity of occupations reflects the American underpinnings of the family, the striking of a balance between the "family thing" and one's "own thing," of group welfare and individualism.

Whatever the Cousins' private lifestyles—whether chauffeured car or rusting Honda—almost all make philanthropy a major avocation. The expression varies, of course. Some are grassroots workers in their communities, where they can maintain their privacy and relative anonymity. John 3rd's daughter Alida prefers this route, giving to small groups that do not have access to United Way or foundations. Among these have been a radio station owned by Oglala Indians on the Pine Ridge reservation in South Dakota. Others serve on boards and work for large institutions, such as Laurance's daughter Laura. Others follow their parents' model in identifying new initiatives, seeking out appropriate experts, and creating new national or worldwide organizations. While still in her twenties, David's daughter Eileen created the Institute for the Advancement of Health, which researched mind-body healing. As a result of this interest, she realized that American children suffer with regard to emotional self-understanding, and established a group for the development of school curricula on emotional literacy. Her broad vision and knack for how to develop successful programs seems inborn, but is the result of growing up among masters in philanthropy. She and others in her generation absorbed stewardship much as medieval apprentices acquired their crafts.

Some Cousins invest so much money in their charities that they are withdrawing from the principals of their trusts. They do so aware that their own children, the eventual beneficiaries in the generation-jumping trusts, will inherit much less. There seems a purposeful decline in economic status, though of course the Cousins' children will hardly return to middle-class levels.

Certain of the Cousins' endeavors seem correctives for some of the earlier philanthropies' actions. For example, radical historians criticized the Rockefeller role in underwriting modern medical education with its narrow emphasis upon drug and surgical treatment. There is some wisdom in their critique, although hindsight is always easier. Unlike philanthropists funding the arts, those sponsoring science take a greater risk that a discovery can result in an application resulting in widespread harm. Today, several descendants of Big Bill, the travelling doctor touting herbal cures, are committed to expanding medical practice to include mind-body principles, Oriental medicine, and "natural healing." There have been instances where children have funded a group protesting their parents' latest business venture. Similar to their fathers, who once announced their independence from John Jr. by forming the Rockefeller Brothers Fund, in 1967 the Cousins created the Rockefeller Family Fund.

While the Cousins were coming of age, scandals attached to the reputation of one of the Brothers, Nelson. He was always brash and strong-willed, but with public office he grew in hubris. The resulting egoism led to his acting in ways that a family unusually prickly over negative publicity would deplore.

The first instance came in 1961 when an accident revealed his marital difficulties. On March 3, late at night the gubernatorial mansion caught fire, and onlookers observed how firefighters escorted Mary Tod from a wing opposite her husband's. She left Albany and never returned. On November 17, Nelson, fifty-three, announced the decision to leave his wife of thirty years.

Two days later came cruel news of the disappearance of their son Michael, twenty-three, presumably drowned in New Guinea. Nelson and Michael's twin, Mary, flew to New Guinea to piece the story of the tragedy together. When they returned, they explained what they had learned to the other children and Tod. In her characteristic way, Tod mourned in private, while her estranged husband gathered his collection of primitive art, so loved by Michael, and gave it to the Metropolitan Museum.

Tod did not quarrel with Nelson's request to end the marriage, and at the proper time went to a dude ranch in Nevada to spend the six weeks required before divorcing there. Still in grief over her son, she spent most of her days on solitary horseback rides or hikes. She suggested that locals tell nosey reporters, "I'm a homely old lady." As the end of her stay neared, she became more outgoing, and gained the admiration of the community. On the day of the hearing, seeming smaller than usual in her dark tweed coat and close-fitting hat, she appeared at the court house with son Rodman by her side for support. When she left the building at the end of the ten-minute ceremony, she was in tears.

After the divorce was final, Nelson refused to address rumors concerning another woman in his life, Margaretta "Happy" Murphy, thirty-six, the mother of four children. Nelson had been acquainted with Happy for many years, ever since his father had invited her family to live in Pocantico. Happy's marriage with microbiologist husband Robin was stormy, and it would be natural that she and Nelson, each in a loveless relationship, would find common sympathies. Her husband, however, refused to give her a divorce, and finally agreed to let her go only if he kept legal custody of the children. Following months of anguish and therapy, Happy accepted his demands.

Although Nelson's political advisors and his family warned him against the marriage, he was bullheadedly confident the American voters would not punish him for doing so. (Nelson later learned what other politicians were to face in subsequent years: that the public held its leaders to higher standards than it followed itself.) It did not help that Happy was a dazzling blond, younger looking than her years, in contrast to the thin, pain-faced, obviously older Tod. Worse, Happy had given up custody of her four young children, which made her seem a heartless mother. In fact, she was to keep the children more than half the time and did not neglect them, as the newswriters often implied.

Most of the brothers and their wives, and even Nelson's children, avoided the 1963 wedding. They all loved Tod for herself and for her fidelity to her family. She had honored Nelson throughout his career, and lost more from their private separation than he had. He seemed all the more dishonorable for breaking that pact now. However, Laurance, always closest to this most ambitious brother, allowed the ceremony to be held in his living room at Pocantico. Afterwards, Nelson moved Happy to Kykuit, which he had taken over since his divorce.

To outside observers, the marriage was a success. When Nelson was running for the Republican nomination for president in 1964, he flew home on weekends to be with his new wife, who was pregnant. Happy gave birth just before primary day, a time for intense final campaigning, and he was by her side. (Nelson lost to Barry Goldwater, for reasons beyond the morality issue of his private life, and earned grudging respect from some when he spoke out against Republican extremism.) Happy found Nelson gentle in comparison to her first husband. She resembled Tod in being very private, which led others to conclude she wanted Nelson to quit public life. She denied such, and admitted to lobbying him hard for women's issues, such as the legalization of abortion in New York.

A more serious attack on the family came in 1974, when Gerald Ford, who rose to the presidency following Nixon's resignation, nominated Nelson for vice president. The subsequent Senate hearings on the nomination were lengthy and acrimonious. Some senators were stunned by the size of his wealth: "one dollar every minute going back to the year 1627," calculated Robert Byrd. His experience and depth of knowledge impressed them, however, and he seemed an easy appointment. Then a series of press leaks exposed Nelson's political gift-giving, which included $50,000 to Henry Kissinger, $625,000 to the head of the powerful New York Port Authority, and $176,000 to an urban development chief, and many others. He was quick to forgive loans of over $100,000 to others. Those close to Nelson explained that he was simply a generous man, naïve about the appearance of these kindnesses. Others saw wealth used to corrupt power, particularly after the revelation that Laurance had financed Victor Lasky's hatchet-job biography of Arthur Goldberg, Nelson's opponent for governor in 1970. IRS information disclosed how that agency had disallowed sizeable deductions in the past, and that in 1970 Nelson had paid no income tax at all. Polls showed that most of the public did not want to see Nelson as president one day, yet they split about whether he should be vice president.

In the midst of this front-page drama, a grim-faced Nelson called a news conference. Happy had discovered a lump in her breast and underwent an operation for cancer. Even more surprising was the news five weeks later that she had undergone a second mastectomy. This very human story shifted the focus away from Nelson's questionable ethics to Happy's courage. Nelson was seen taking her presents and spending much time with her during the recuperation. "She's a very strong person, a wonderful person. And great strength of character and great moral strength," he reported.[14]

Betty Ford had undergone a mastectomy only weeks before Happy's operation. Until their disclosures, so close together, breast cancer was a taboo topic. The disease conjured up unfeminine disfigurement followed by death. These prominent women's frank announcements of their mutual ordeal made them feminist heroines. Happy welcomed journalists to interview her about her experience, for she wanted to encourage other women to be less fearful and more realistic about the disease. If it should happen to you, she advised *Reader's Digest* women, go for treatment and do not dwell on the loss.[15] As a result of her candor, much of the previous irrationality concerning breast cancer was replaced by fact and balanced discussion.

Possibly Happy's condition restrained some critical senators. By late November, Nelson displayed his willingness to do whatever was necessary to prevent future conflicts of interest. On December 8, by a Senate vote of 90–7, his nomination was confirmed. His achievement came at great cost to the extended family. It was easy for others to assume that Nelson's tax-machinations and his use of money for political influence was common to all other Rockefellers. Laurance's collaboration with Nelson on some questionable activities reinforced this conclusion. It was a difficult time for the Brothers, who preferred the appearance of a united front. Fortunately, Nelson handled his office as vice president well and without much controversy.

Nelson's embarrassment of the family was not over. Late on the evening of January 26, 1979, he died of a massive heart attack in his parents' first home, 13 West Fifty-fourth Street. The news was delayed, and the details of his death initially obscured. Later, reporters revealed that an attractive blond, twenty-five-year-old Megan Marshack, had been present with him at the time. Described as an assistant on an art book he was writing at the time, Marshack's income, sixty thousand dollars a year, suggested to cynics that she was more than a researcher. A local television personality and friend of Marshack's, Ponchitta Pierce, revealed it was she who had called 911. Apparently, when Nelson collapsed, Marshack called her friend, and administered CPR until Pierce arrived at the apartment. Innuendo and speculation spread concerning the circumstances of Nelson's final hour. Worse, his will revealed cancellation of a forty-five-thousand-dollar loan to Marshack, who had used the money toward buying an apartment in New York.

To the public eye, the family did "not see." Nelson's children released a statement in support of Marshack for doing all that she could. The doctors verified he had died quickly of a single massive cardiac arrest. Privately, though, the family acted differently, and saw Marshack removed from the Rockefeller payroll. Afterwards, she found establishing a career in writing very difficult, but eventually found a place as an independent newswriter and producer. Never married, she continued to draw notoriety from gossip columnists, who intimated her involvement with various older men, including the late cartoonist Charles Addams, and Pat Brown, ex-governor of California.[16] She continued to reside close by the town-house where the fated evening passed.

However humiliated some family members, Nelson's death was for average Americans a morality play. He had sinned, and he was brought to a fall. As often happens, sick jokes referring to the incident became part of daily conversation. And any woman in Marshack's position, if completely innocent of what others were whispering and laughing about, could never keep her integrity. The widow, so cruelly belittled by her husband's apparent infidelity, would have found much support among the public, had she chosen to show herself. That was not Happy's way, however, and she receded into the protection of the family, just as her predecessor Tod had done.

Nelson's death was shocking as well because the family was mourning the loss of John 3rd, six months earlier, to an auto accident on a country road near Pocantico. John 3rd had struggled for years of torment with the fear that he could never meet his father's standards in philanthropy. In his softspoken way he had become a statesman, an advocate of the "third sector," of private nonprofit activity beside business and government. As Jay noted during the memorial service, his father "never sought recognition for himself, but he would fight to the ends of the earth for what he believed in."[17]

Blanchette survived her husband by fourteen years. After her husband's death, she led a major campaign to free MOMA from its dependence on the Rockefeller family and private support, and increased corporate and government contributions. She supported selling air rights to a developer who built a fifty-two-story apartment at the site, and gave the museum more space on its lower floors. She urged this controversial plan because it secured the museum's future without compromising its purpose. Other institutions later copied the practice. Until 1980, Blanchette filled her days with her many philanthropies, calling herself a "lay administrator."

As she cut back her activities, the life seemed to be cut out of her as well. Her behavior became odd. Normally sedate, she grew strangely unsettled, unable to sit still. She lost her patience for the Handel and Mozart music she had always loved. In 1986, she was diagnosed with Alzheimer's disease, and her condition deteriorated rapidly. She would wake up in the middle of the night, don one dress on top of another, wake up the staff, and ask for breakfast. After being returned to bed, two hours later she would repeat the same pattern. Like many afflicted with the disorder, she could have violent spells in which her strength seemed superhuman. The family hired two fulltime nurses who were specialists in Alzheimer's care, at $100,000 a year.

Towards the end, she was in and out of hospitals, where she fought such treatments as a feeding tube being forced down her mouth. Though unable to speak her mind clearly, she communicated through her eyes and gestures. When son Jay rested his head in her lap, she stroked his hair. Yet she would not look him in the eye, because "she felt demeaned by the disease. She felt she was a shell of a person."[18] Her friends thought it terribly unfair that so creative and life-embracing a woman die in 1993 abased and in agony.

Alzheimer's has become a modern scourge, one many families have endured in secret. Just as once one never mentioned breast cancer as the reason for a woman's suffering, so today one hesitates to admit to others or in an obituary the presence of the personality-destroying disease. (This masking and denial may be self-protective, because the disorder is believed to have a genetic component.)

It was fully characteristic that the Rockefellers not disguise the cause of Blanchette's withdrawal from society and eventual death, that they describe her struggle to others. Characteristically, they understood how fortunate they were in caring for her. "My family had the resources," recounted Jay, "but most people can't afford that kind of care. . . . My mother had a wonderful life. But she died a perfectly terrible death—one that a lot of other people will face. I'm not alone in my pain." One hears Blanchette in this language, an honoring of the truth, of *caritas* and community.

16

Revisionings

"My father began talking to me about philanthropy when I was five years old."

—Alida Rockefeller

Steven Rockefeller once commented, "My feeling is that the family as an institution was the creation of a certain culture and a certain time in the history of this nation. It has had its day. Once the original generating energy goes out of an institution, it just dies. That's the way it is and ought to be."[1] He was wrong—the generating energy of the Rockefellers has not yet dissipated.

His remark reflects a wish-fulfillment that critics of the Rockefellers share: that the wealth disappear, the influence vanish. It is this deathwish that underlies public fascination with the wealthy and, in more recent times, the searching for private lapses as well as public ones. If we cannot force elites to redistribute their money—to pour and not just trickle down their wealth—then we will strip them of their reputation and dignity. These attacks against the Rockefellers began during the 1890s, then subsided between the 1920s and 1940s. With the 1950s, however, criticism resurged.

Most exposés had limited circulation. Some were academic papers by scholars; more often they were one-sided rhetorical attacks aimed at one or another extremist audience. The imprints were not major publishers.

In 1976, however, there appeared *The Rockefellers*, an entertaining panoramic narrative of four generations of the family by Peter Collier and David Horowitz, then Marxist-leaning journalists (who have since turned neoconservative). Its spicy prose, radical critique, and snatches of exposé easily propelled the book to the bestseller list. Well annotated, and seemingly based upon material in the Rockefeller family archives, it appeared to historians the definitive biography. In truth, the writers had limited access to the family's official and personal records. Much material had yet to be catalogued, organized, or even unpacked. The many factual errors stated in *The Rockefellers* did not become apparent until the papers were processed and moved to the research center at Pocantico, where scholars could study the full range of the catalogue. Given Collier and Horowitz's blitz, a more-balanced and insightful study by Alvin Moscow, *The Rockefeller Inheritance,* was ignored by reviewers and readers when it appeared soon afterward.

Particularly sensational was the role of the Cousins, some of whom cooperated with Collier and Horowitz. The writers easily cultivated the sympathies of more rebellious offspring. (One author was intimately involved with a Rockefeller daughter when he did the study.) Even some more traditional Cousins resented their fathers' resistance to pass on more responsibility and autonomy, just as their fathers had been in the 1930s when they challenged John Jr. A careful reading of *The Rockefellers* shows that most of the Cousins either did not give interviews or may have expressed opinions inconsistent with the writers' slant. The poor sampling was irrelevant—Middle America discovered that the children of the rich were as troublesome as their own.

Yet even as radical analysts, Collier and Horowitz misled their readers. They were poor historians, who ignored the context in which the Rockefellers acted. To judge the behavior a hundred years ago based on present-day beliefs and experience is wrong. As has been demonstrated here and by other scholars, members of the family were in the vanguard of those pushing for racial equality, improved public health, expanded employee rights, quality education for the poor, interdenominationalism, environmental preservation, avant-garde art movements, women's issues, sexual enlightenment, and more. The arc of John Jr.'s career was toward increased liberalism, in the broadest sense of that term. Though less visible, the women inspired and reinforced the men's broad-minded and far-seeing philanthropic initiatives, and several women made significant advances in their own right. What was forward-thinking in those early years, however, seemed reactionary to those used to the activism of the 1960s.

In fact, over the years conservative forces had regularly condemned the family and its institutions. The most noted attack was during the McCarthy era, when Congress held over a hundred investigations into possible communist infiltration of various sectors of society. The right-wing's targets included the tax-exempt foundations run by the "eastern liberal establishment." These organizations' internationalist orientation threatened Cold War isolationists. The Rockefeller Foundation came under scrutiny because it supported the Institute for Pacific Relations, which was being blamed unfairly for the loss of China to communism. Other Congressional hearings condemned the Foundation for sponsoring Kinsey's research on sexuality, for its General Education Board, and for giving fellowships to twenty-six "leftists." Years later, when Nelson started his futile march to the presidency, a major obstacle was the Southern electorate, whose long memory connected anyone with the name Rockefeller to racial equality and other liberal causes. Collier and Horowitz omitted discussion of these and similar political assaults.[2] Their revisionist history missed the mark.

If Collier and Horowitz were far from definitive, they did reaffirm the public's need to scrutinize those in power, however much they may object. The Rockefellers are not unusual in their sensitivity to public criticism. Well-functioning families care about how they appear in their communities, for scandal harms innocents. (One wonders how Tod and Happy handled their children's questions and discomforts surrounding their father's death.) In a free, democratic, purportedly egalitarian society, however, the powerful rightfully lose some protection of privacy.

Philanthropy and nonprofit organizations are a significant power base today, one the family did so much to expand. Because these activities are "good works," it is easy to assume they are exempt from intrusive review. The laws of nonprofit corporation are supposed to ensure public accountability. Yet anyone who has worked in the nonprofit sector knows how inadequate the laws are in protecting the public's right to know and prevent abuse.

What is interesting is that this privacy-driven family has opened so many of its files concerning its charitable works. As a result, since the codifying of the archives, scholars have already mined dozens of studies that address harder questions, ones that do not titillate the public. They have explored the biases of those appointed to manage the Rockefeller philanthropies, and considered how those biases affected public policy. They have traced the influence of now outmoded ideas, such as eugenics, on Rockefeller-sponsored medical research. Their work is building a model of this third sector of power, and reminds us that elites influence our lives in ways other than in business or politics.

As has been shown here, the women in the family were excluded from an active role in these activities, and had to find other ways to express their stewardship. Their choice depended upon the particular limited options society allowed during their lifetimes. They could work for religious, cultural, and family causes, not scientific, medical, political, or economic ones. The women-run activities were not always free from male interference. They were part of the larger tide that allowed women, even wealthy ones, to leave home if the purpose was elevated and noble, as the men defined such. As a result, women from elite families today have the option to do lay administration, primarily in cultural organizations. Nevertheless, their options are smaller than those from nonaffluent families.

Part of the Cousins' rebellion, which Collier and Horowitz so misunderstood, has been to live as though less advantaged. By doing so, the women in particular gained more power than had they adopted the insular ways of Old Money. No brother or husband or father, however loved, can inhibit them. Though little known to them, their great-aunt Edith, not Laura or Abby, is their spiritual forebearer.

The Rockefellers call to mind the Kennedys, particularly in their staunch loyalty to one another in confronting trouble and in their encouraging individual pursuits. Both are quintessentially American. Because wealth exaggerates, both families dramatize the unifying themes and conflicts of American culture. Where the Rockefellers reflect the Protestant Yankee strain that shaped the major principles of the nation, the Kennedys are the immigrant experience writ large. Both lines were established by patriarchs whose strong drive and need for great achievement came from their mothers. Both had a staunch religious identification, and welcomed members of the respective clergy as family advisors. Both lines forged grand visions, the highest expectations of success.

The Kennedys, however, were ruled by a dictatorial patriarch, who viewed money as the route to power, resources, and self-aggrandizement. Though supportive of one another's interests, family members were to serve the father above all, next, the eldest son, who was to advance the status of the clan. They sacrificed three men in the process, and pressed members of the next generation to continue the charge. When a member has come under public scrutiny for questionable private behavior, the family has appeared in numbers to defend the accused. Although firmly Catholic in identity, they do not appear troubled by obvious breaches of Catholic doctrine and standards of behavior.

In contrast, the Rockefeller descendants have been loyal to the ideal established by Senior and Laura, later perpetuated by John Jr. and Abby. Although in keeping with the times they did not encourage their daughters to participate in business, they expected them to make a mark in charity. The Rockefellers were inculcated to follow their inner voice, a stern conscience, one that the Cousins still voice sincerely. Unlike the Kennedys, some have been uncomfortable carrying the family name and its too ready connection with money.

Their attitude toward their homes and property further reflect the differences in the families. The Kennedys have kept tightly guarded compounds. Even Jackie fought with a local Indian tribe over rights to land adjoining her Cape Cod estate. The Rockefellers fenced and gated only a small portion of Pocantico, and opened the rest of the lands to the public. For decades, hikers and horseback riders could encounter members of the family along the trails.[3] Much of that land is now a state park. Today, even part of the private compound, Kykuit, along with eighty-six surrounding acres, is open to visitors under the management of the National Trust for Historic Preservation. Most of the Cousins live modestly, even by the unassuming, unostentatious standards of Old Money, and mix easily within their local communities.

What this comparison clarifies is the significance of the values that define a family's identity. How do parents measure achievement? What means to success do they encourage? Joe and Rose Kennedy's children learned to seek fame and power, to think of themselves as special. In the process, they failed to develop the ability to be close to those who were not family members, and had disastrous marriages as a result. In small ways—the treatment of staff, the attention to their personal effects— they were thoughtless. Yet, if one questioned the family members, they would probably be satisfied that they had for the most part fulfilled the family's demands.

The vision began in Senior's family line was more high-minded on the surface. His children and theirs learned to avoid frivolity, and honor the family through service. The motive remained fame, though of a different kind, and power, more subtle and independent of public control.

The most striking difference between the two dynasties is the women's place. The Kennedy women generally played supporting and secondary roles. Rose, usually portrayed as the wonderful matriarch and superb mother, was often absent when her children were growing up and when around was emotionally distant. It took an outsider, Jacqueline Bouvier, to introduce a more compassionate model of family life, and insist on individuality for herself and her children. It is good to belong to a clan, she seemed to say, but not submit one's life to the clan. Only one daughter, Eunice, became noted for her philanthropic work, which has addressed the study and treatment of mental retardation. There are no Kennedy wings of museums or permanent collections of beautiful objects. Jackie, the most devoted to her family, was the most active in charities, especially historic preservation, ballet, and other performing arts.

In contrast, the leading Rockefeller matriarch, Eliza, prepared her sons for a full life, one with material success, spiritual richness, and consideration of the larger public welfare. John D. Rockefeller was a distant, if loving father, who backed his wife Laura's strong influence on their son. John

Jr.'s strong dependence upon his mother was further increased by society, which at the time venerated women's moral education of their boys. ("Momism," the purported deleterious effect of mothers upon sons, did not come into cultural consciousness until the 1950s.) As the youngest child and only boy in a family with sisters, grandmothers, and an aunt, John Jr. adopted female ideals of piety and charity. Only when he reached college did he realize how different his ideals were from those of his fun-loving, frivolous-seeming upper-class peers.

Although conforming to the model of "the lady," the efficient domestic manager, Laura participated in the nascent women-run organizations emerging after the Civil War. The YWCA, WCTU, and Baptist women's missionary groups all eased the public expression of her beliefs. Through these activities, she introduced her children to the importance of social action, and exposed them to people of different backgrounds and needs. Her involvement inspired her children, for she practiced what she preached, the daily living of a life guided by social Christian principles. From her, John Jr. formed so strong a sense of responsibility that he failed to see the necessity of leisure and its regenerating effects.

While still restricted to domestic life, Laura's daughters felt able to break away from some parental values. What mattered most here was the men they married. Edith, the most fortunate in marrying a wealthy man, was free to use her income in the service of music, art, and psychological health. Harold McCormick had been raised by a strong-minded mother who took over the family business, so he supported Edith's efforts to make her own way. Even when the marriage was falling apart, he defended her entrepreneurial activities before her family critics.

Alta was less cosmopolitan than Edith, and would not gravitate toward grand plans, such as founding a major opera company or reading all there was to read on Goethe. She found fulfillment in a return to the land, in feeding chickens and swine and studying livestock inheritance charts. Contributing to the cultural and economic life of Williamstown was more than enough to satisfy her. She likely had a richer life being married to Parmalee than had she wed a business executive and lived in the city. Parmalee was demanding and rigorous, but Alta molded herself to his temperament and thrived.

The major inhibitors for Edith and Alta were not their husbands and domestic demands, but their father and brother. Both men excluded them from full participation in the family-identified philanthropies. Both criticized and even condemned each woman's choice of charities and style of giving. The sisters could never win full respect as a result. Expected to meet high standards of service, they could not achieve those standards as father and brother defined them. Living a more secluded life, Alta was less rebuked than her younger sister. It is ironic that Edith, who was essentially ostracized by the family, was willing to do what no one else was, to give everything away.

Before casting blame solely on those two men, however, remember that a third person, Laura, was an unseen hand. Because her letters to her daughters no longer exist, it is impossible to draw sure conclusions. Nevertheless, she was the heart of the family for both Senior and John Jr. It was she who affirmed their Baptist call to stewardship, and raised her precious son accordingly. To some extent the patriarchal demands of the father and son must reflect her approval. That she sent two of her daughters to Dr. Silas Weir, known for his success in turning troublesome young women into "normal," seconds the point. As the times changed, as the suffragists spoke out and Progressive women grabbed more public roles, Laura (and her sister Lute) clung happily to older ways. She would not have her daughters paddle their own canoes.

The contrast with William Rockefeller's line is striking. In choosing the life of Gilded Age barons, they severed their historic roots to New England austerity, reform, and Christian service. Their offspring emulated that part of the upper class whose lives center on exclusive clubs, communities, and resorts. This shift to consumption and comfort was more typical of Americans in the late 1800s, for what better proof of the young nation's superiority than the material advantages of its citizens? William required no temperance pledge of his sons, and one became an alcoholic. Mira raised her daughters to be wives of wealthy men, a complicated job requiring the management of multiple households with large staffs. Studying such private existence is difficult, and best left to the insight of novelists. What stands out, nonetheless, is the lack of this lineage's significance in philanthropy.

William's line was more characteristic of the descendants of Robber Barons. In the Vanderbilt and Whitney lines, for example, wealth did not vanish, but the sense of a call to service, whether as business, political, or cultural leaders dissipated. Such families were pious in the first and second generations, but by the third, religious activity became separated from the rest of life, a matter of Sunday morning ritual. The later generations of men did not repeat the achievements of the patriarch, nor did it seem they often wanted to. They already had much more money than most Americans, and little motivation to seek more. The names receded from recognition, with a few exceptions—the drunken rogue, the inventor of contract bridge, the governor, the yachtsman. The women who earned celebrity did so on their own merits, as philanthropists, artists, and business people. Importantly, these women—Gertrude Vanderbilt Whitney, Gloria Vanderbilt, Flora Whitney Miller, Flora Biddle—lacked exposure to the stern patriarchy Senior and John Jr. represented.

One question is, how could the sons of John Jr., who also grew up in the shadow of their eminent grandfather, reject the familiar pattern? The answer is of course Abby Aldrich. It is hard to imagine the Rockefeller family today without her. She introduced a sense of fun and a modern outlook. Her marriage to John Jr. was often frustrating for her, but she responded to his idiosyncrasies with wisdom rather than rancor. Abby was blessed in being the favorite of a powerful man who encouraged her talents and independence. She had secretly resented her passive, melancholy mother and avoided turning into that kind of adult. So no matter how much her husband protested, she had her way, whether it meant bearing many children, traveling on YWCA business, buying strange and shocking art, wearing funny hats, or joining Polish folk dances. She simply resisted his paternalism, tossed it aside, and fought with him when need be.

While reading about John Jr.'s dominating ways, it is easy to forget that for the most part Abby shared and reinforced his stern principles. In raising her children, she communicated her husband's deepest commitments to what is called "character" today, but was less prim in their expression. She challenged her children to find their individual purpose, which should include service to others, and accept no less than excellence, whatever the endeavor. They were never to take their wealth for granted, but as a hair shirt to remind them of their destiny.

If Abby were around today, one wonders if she would regret her relationship with Babs. Once the sons started coming, Abby could not help but favor them. She admitted to a friend that she preferred the more boisterous mischief of the boys. Possibly because John Jr. was so attached to his daughter, Abby thought the situation balanced. Neither parent recognized Babs's sense of being lost in the corner of the room. Nonetheless, Babs did pass through her brief rebellion to shape the life she wanted, apart from the Rockefeller name. Judged on her own terms, raising two daughters well, doing no harm to others, Babs was a success.

Abby's priorities were clear: family first, then service. She inspired her daughters-in-law accordingly. She absorbed them into her heart and awakened their talents. Blanchette said it best:

> I may have been influenced by Johnny's mother, who had begun collecting on her own; the Museum of Modern Art grew out of that. All of us girls really adored our mother-in-law. Nelson's

wife was the first, then me, then Laurance's wife, then David's. She was such a human person, and so interested in her daughters-in-law. We'd sit and knit and talk about things.[4]

This language reflects woman's talk, its reference to individual persons, to sitting in a circle and sharing thoughts. No one writes it down (unless she keeps a diary afterwards), no one can trace its intellectual genealogy directly, as one traces footnotes in publications. Invisible, its force is nonetheless powerful.

Life was so much more rewarding, Abby seemed to say, when it is complicated. Why restrict oneself to similar people and predictable ritual, however pleasant and secure? Why not strike out for yourself, even if your beloved objects? Her daughters-in-law listened, and sought opportunities for leadership before the last child was out of diapers. They in turn passed the Rockefeller conscience onto their offspring, who make different choices while remaining true to the family spirit.

The dynasty continues.

ACKNOWLEDGMENTS

My greatest debt is to the Rockefeller Archives Center, among the most congenial and efficient places I have ever done research. Harold Oakhill was particularly helpful in preparing me for my visits. Tom Rosenbaum proved a wise and constantly resourceful guide while I was combing the mass of manuscripts. During research breaks Tom listened to my developing interpretations attentively, responding with thoughtful questions and ideas. Other scholars working at the Archives who provided important guidance were James Anderson, Donald Fisher, and John B. Sharpless.

As usual, the Reuban Salazar Library at Sonoma State University provided outstanding interlibrary loan services along with basic reference materials. George Yetter and Mark Wegner at the Colonial Williamsburg Foundation, helped me understand the Rockefeller role at that site, and assisted my viewing Basset Hall before it was opened to the public. Other institutions that facilitated my work include the State Historical Society of Wisconsin, University Library of the University of Illinois, Chicago Historical Society, New York Historical Society, Women's Resource and Research Center of Spelman College, Case Western Reserve University, Western Reserve Historical Society, Green Library at Stanford University, and University of California at Los Angeles.

Partial financial support came from the Rockefeller Archives Center, which provided a travel fellowship, and Sonoma State University, which awarded a grant for research assistance and expenses.

Bernice Kert, who had just completed her own study of Abby Aldrich Rockefeller, gave warm support and assistance. She kindly introduced me to Eileen Rockefeller Growald, who verified some factual details on recent generations. Flora Biddle, who has been a leader in the world of New York museum philanthropy, illuminated an area of life so outside my own experiences.

Members of my graduate seminar on biography proved an astute source of ideas and criticism: Janet Rider, Gregg Saxon, Rick Jones, Tad Curtis, Judy Johnson, and Steve Cunninghame. Three of these, Gretchen Grufman, Jan Andres, and Benét Johnson, also worked as able research assistants collecting secondary data. Michael Caldwell served me well investigating archives in Chicago and the Wisconsin Historical Society.

Two people gave quick and able help providing photographs, Melissa Smith at the Rockefeller Archives Center and Cynthia Knight at the State Historical Society of Wisconsin.

Special thanks go to those who supplied housing and companionship during the lengthy stays away from home. Marlise and Bob Tellander convinced Krista Hurty to lend me her apartment and delightful feline companion Ansgar gratis for a month's stay in New York City. The late Charles Moore let me use his Sea Ranch condominium during the early writing of the manuscript. It was while rummaging through Charles's eclectic library that I found the original 1829 edition of Ann Judson's diary exactly on the day it proved useful. Others who offered respite on the road were my brother James Stasz, J. J. Wilson, Thelma and Bob Zener, Nona and Gary Schwartz, and William Phillips.

Members of the Douglas Street Fine Arts and Adventure Society were my major emotional support and tryout readers. Among those who commented on early drafts were Denise Cushing, Kristi Jacobs, Linda Lipps, Richard Morehead, and Virgina Reuter. Others offering encouragement were Steve Jacobs, Doug McCasland, and Vicki Lima.

My dear friends Candy and Jim Donnelly also gave astute reading of the drafts. Candy's frankness delighted me for its pointing out patterns of weakness in my writing I had never noticed before.

My Internet buddy, Susan Gatti, conversed with me daily over the electronic highways. She kept me in good humor and returned my perspective on days when I thought this was a totally impossible task of questionable value.

Editor Charles Spicer inspired my following up *The Vanderbilt Women* with this comparison study. I knew virtually nothing about the Rockefellers, and appreciate his confidence I could take on the venture, and enjoy it.

Any deficiencies or errors are fully my own. There comes a day to close the files, and tell the story. No work is definitive, especially one where so much research material is available. If my errors or biases provoke others to respond with counter argument, I will be most gratified—though of course I hope any insights inspire some to further study of the themes discussed here.

My husband would rather have gone trout fishing, and as usual gave up a vacation to help me on one of my research trips. My sister Cathy, with whom I was in tremendous sibling rivalry for decades, has turned into my biggest supporter. I figure it is long overdue I dedicate a book to the two of them.

NOTES

Abbreviations Used

Proper names:

AAR	Abby Aldrich Rockefeller
Alta	Alta Rockefeller Prentice
Edith	Edith Rockefeller McCormick
Senior	John D. Rockefeller, Sr.
Jr	John D. Rockefeller, Jr.
HMcC	Harold McCormick
LSR	Laura Spelman Rockefeller

References to Rockefeller Family Papers, Rockefeller Archive Center:

AAR Papers	Office of Messrs Rockefeller General Files, RG2, Abby Aldrich Rockefeller Papers.
Fosdick	Office of Messrs Rockefeller General Files, RG2, John D. Rockefeller, Jr. Papers, Series 7, Manuscript and Research Materials for Raymond B. Fosdick's biography.
Inglis	John D. Rockefeller Papers, William O. Inglis interview and research materials, RG1, Series I.
JDR Jr.	Office of Messrs Rockefeller General Files, RG2, John D. Rockefeller, Jr. Personal Papers.
JDR	John D. Rockefeller Papers, RG I.
OMR	Office of Messrs Rockefeller General Files, RG2.
Spelman	John D. Rockefeller Papers, Spelman Family, RG1, Series S.
WR	William Rockefeller Papers, RG50.

Footnotes

Foreword

1. Allan Nevins, *John D. Rockefeller*, Vol. I, 223.

Chapter One: Eliza Davison, a Good Woman

1. This was the New Madrid quake, the greatest ever recorded in the history of the United States. Although loss of life was small, destruction of the environment was catastrophic. See James Pennick, Jr., *The New Madrid Earthquakes of 1811–1812*.

2. Helpful overviews of agrarian women's labor may be found in Susan Strasser, *Never Done*, chaps. 1–6, and Jack Larkin, *The Shaping of Everyday Life, 1790–1840*, chaps. 2 and 3.

3. Several of Eliza Davison's letters survive from late in her life. Their grammar and spelling is poor. One letter with correct language use was in another hand, possibly that of Lucy Spelman.

4. On the early family life of the Rockefellers that follows: Virtually all information is taken from notes made by William O. Inglis in 1917. Inglis interviewed John D. Rockefeller as well as neighbors in Moravia and Owego still alive at the time, and did research in the archives of Tioga County. Allan Nevins referred to this material extensively in preparing *John D. Rockefeller: The Heroic Age of American Enterprise*, 1940, and of the many biographers since, he remains the best source on the early years of the family.

5. I have no direct evidence that Bill voted, let alone that he was a Whig. I speak of Whiggery here as a cultural current that permeated the country beyond the membership of the party. Taken in this context, the Rockefeller family can be seen as representative of its day, not unique, as famous man biographies are wont to do. To my knowledge, no other biographer has drawn this connection to Whiggery.

6. Jesse Buel, *The Farmer's Companion*, as abridged in Carl Bode, ed., *American Life in the 1840s*. Buel's work, published in 1840, also refers to agriculture as the nation's "nursing mother" and "the salt which preserves from moral corruption," among other functions.

7. E. Douglas Branch, *The Sentimental Years, 1836–1860*, 35.

8. Inglis interview with Samuel Steele, a Moravian resident. Steele was born in 1837 and would likely have heard this story from a parent. Inglis, B4, F8.

9. In the course of writing this book, I repeatedly encountered associates or strangers who volunteered the same story when I mentioned I was writing about the early Rockefeller family. The response was characteristically, "Oh, Rockefeller [or his father] was a horse thief [or a crook]. I heard this growing up there [or my uncle who lives there told me all about this]." These were identical to the stories William Inglis heard when he visited the region over sixty years ago. While one can find many reasons to dispute the truth of these tales, I have lived most of my life in small towns and have learned such historical gossip has an element of truth. Distortions do occur, such as confusing Bill and John D. Rockefeller, but the tales cannot be tossed out completely.

10. John D. Rockefeller's cousin, Mrs. John Wilcox, gave the details of Nancy Brown to Inglis. Her father was Jacob Rockefeller, Bill's brother. Samuel Steele also remarked on Cornelia's resemblance to Bill. Inglis, B4, F8.

11. "Antecedents and Childhood," Inglis, B5.

12. Quotes from John D. Rockefeller in this section are taken from the Inglis interviews with him, B1.

13. Interview with Cyrus McNeil LaMonte, Inglis, B4, F8.

14. This and subsequent quotes attributed to Eliza come from the interview with Mrs. John Wilcox, Inglis, B4, F8.

15. I am inferring from general knowledge about the Baptists, Sunday Schools, and the social milieu here, and do not have direct proof that the Rockefeller children were so explicitly taught. However, their later actions and beliefs as adolescents imply such conscious promulgation was taking place earlier, by Eliza, the local church, or both. See Anne M. Boylan, *Sunday School*, and William Henry Brackney, *The Baptists* for an introduction to this material.

16. Most of this discussion is based upon Ann's published journals as they were edited in J. D. Knowles, *The Journals of Ann H. Judson*, 1829. Further background on Hudson's significance is in Carma Van Liere, *Hallowed Fire*.

17. Knowles, 10.

18. Knowles, 353.

19. On the rape charges of 1849: Inglis located the original indictments (Inglis, B4, F8), while Nevins (1940, Chapter III) uncovered related criminal and civil records.

Chapter Two: Cradled in Capitalism

1. Later members of the Rockefeller line, the best-known being Nelson Rockefeller, had this learning disability.

2. For more on the boy culture of the period, see E. Anthony Rotundo, "Boy Culture: Middle-Class Boyhood in Nineteenth-Century America," in E. Anthony Rotundo, *Meanings for Manhood*, 1990.

3. From *Nature*, in Brooks Atkinson, editor, *The Selected Writings of Ralph Waldo Emerson*, 6. John D. would not agree with Emerson's religious ideas. Nonetheless, much of the essayist's philosophy with regard to the significance of nature and a man's character are so consistent with Rockefeller's personal philosophy to lend credibility that he became familiar with the writings at Owego Academy.

4. Blockson, *The Underground Railroad*, 212.

5. LSR, "Keeping Back Part of the Price," a speech presented at the annual meeting of the Woman's Baptist Foreign Missionary Society in 1894. Although no author appears in the printed version, which is in pamphlet form, a copy she sent to her son identifies herself as the author. JDR Jr., B19.

6. See William Inglis interview with Lucy Spelman, Inglis, B21.

7. The full text of this address is in Spelman, B2, which contains other materials from her schooling.

8. William Chalmers Whitcomb, *The True Consoler,* as quoted in Karen Haltunnen, *Confidence Men and Painted Women,* 131.

9. The history of Oread is detailed in Nancy Read, *The Story of Spelman College,* Chapter I.

10. Cettie [Laura] Spelman to Mrs. Hawley, 16 March 1858, Spelman, B2, F8.

11. Cettie to Mrs. H[awley], 23 March 1859, Spelman, B2, F8.

12. Cettie to Mrs. Hawley, 12 July 1858, Spelman, B2, F8.

13. Lute [Lucy Spelman] to Mrs. Hawley, 22 August 1858, Spelman, B2, F8.

14. Cettie to Mrs. Hawley, 12 July 1858, Spelman, B2, F8.

15. Lucy and Cettie to Mrs. Hawley, 8 June 1858, Spelman, B2, F8.

16. The full copy of "Vox Oreadum" described here is in Spelman, B2, F11.

17. Cettie to My Dear Friend [Mrs. Hawley], 26 June 1859, Spelman, B2, F8.

18. Lute to Mrs. Hawley, 2 September 1859, Spelman, B2, F8.

19. Cettie to My Dear Friend [Mrs. Hawley], 30 April 1860, Spelman Family, B2, F8.

Chapter Three: The Storm King and the Zephyr

1. Nancy Read, *The Story of Spelman College,* 22–3.

2. Spelman, B1, F4.

3. Reverand Matthew Sorin, *The Domestic Circle, or, Moral and Social Duties Explained and Enforced,* first published in 1840, abridged in Carl Bode, *American Life in the 1840s,* 63.

4. Susan Strasser, *Never Done,* 62.

5. Harvey Green, *The Light of the Home,* 76.

6. Donald E. Sutherland, *The Expansion of Everyday Life, 1860–1876,* 80.

7. Two other brothers coming of age then, Cornelius II and William K. Vanderbilt, similarly patterned their behavior. Cornelius II was a devout communicant at St. Bartholemew's Episcopal Church in New York, and raised his children more according to the practices of middle-class piety. William K. chose the more profligate life, and was more unscrupulous in business. See my comparison of these two families as narrated in *The Vanderbilt Women.*

Chapter Four: Cleveland: A Promised Land

1. Josiah Holland, *Titcomb's Letters to Young People, Single and Married,* 200–1.

2. Inglis interview with Lucy Spelman, Inglis, B21.

3. Edith to Senior, 9 September 1922, OMR, B33, F257.

4. For an overview of literature on this late nineteenth-century phenomenon, see Margaret Marsh, "Suburban Men and Masculine Domesticity, 1870–1915," *American Quarterly* (June 1988): 165–86.

5. Jan Cigliano, *Showplace of America,* 200–1.

6. As quoted in Grace Gouldner, *John D. Rockefeller, The Cleveland Years*, 84.

7. As quoted in Cigliano, 10.

8. Cigliano, 229.

9. The source of the money, he asserted in a speech at the University of Chicago, was God. This was said with humility, not the arrogance some have read into the statement when taken out of context. Allan Nevins, *Study in Power*, Vol II, 435.

10. Cigliano, 292.

11. Inglis, B4, F13.

12. Inglis, B1 502–3.

13. Inglis, B2, F5, 846.

14. Inglis notes, 1037–Q.

15. Inglis notes, 298–300, 493.

16. LSR, "Keeping Back Part of the Price," JDR Jr, B19.

17. Gouldner, 100.

18. Senior to LSR, 17 March 1872, JDR, B36.

19. Mary Sims, *The Natural History of a Social Institution*, 18.

20. Jed Dannenbaum, *Drink and Disorder*, 221.

21. Dannenbaum, 220.

22. Inglis notes, 274.

23. Senior to LSR, 30 November 1871, JDR, B36.

24. Senior to LSR, 15 December 1871, JDR, B36.

25. Senior to LSR, 20 January 1872, JDR, B36.

26. Senior to LSR, 20 January 1872, JDR, B36.

27. Senior to LSR, 1 December 1871, JDR, B36.

28. Senior to LSR, 13 January 1872, JDR, B36.

29. Senior to LSR, 17 March 1872, JDR, B36.

30. Senior to LSR, 22 March 1872, JDR, B36.

31. LSR to Jr, 28 January 1897, JDR Jr, B20.

Chapter Five: God's Precious Jewels

1. JDR Jr, B21.

2. LSR as quoted in Grace Gouldner, *John D. Rockefeller*, 140.

3. The evidence for this is in various account books kept by John Jr., which list daily fines against family members. Senior appears more often than all the others combined.

4. Helen Chisholm Hord to Gouldner, 125–126.

5. 1887 Trip Diary, JDR Jr, B37.

6. Spelman, B1, F3. Address book, entry dated September 1887.

7. Raymond Fosdick, *John D. Rockefeller, Jr.*, 43.

8. Edith to Senior, 9 September 1922, JDR, B33, F257.

9. James Anderson, *The Education of Blacks in the South*, 281.

10. Anderson, 281.

11. Anderson, 5.

12. Anderson, 18.

13. Anderson, 40.

14. Nancy Read, *The Story of Spelman College*, 38.

15. Read, 80.

16. Read, 82.

17. Laura to Mr. and Mrs. Dixon, 5 December 1883, JDR Jr, B44, F2.

18. Jr, 1884 Diary, 17 February, JDR Jr, B8.

19. Essay, "A Hundred Years Hence," dated 13 February 1885, JDR Jr, B1.

20. Jr, 1885 diary, 24 July, B3.

21. Jr, 1886 trip diary, B37.

22. John Briggs, *Requiem for a Yellow Brick Brewery*, 6.

23. Jr, 1887 trip diary, B37.

24. LSR, "Keeping Back Part of the Price," JDR Jr, B19.

Chapter Six: Angelic Invalids

1. Raymond Fosdick, *John D. Rockefeller Jr.*, 39.

2. An unidentified physician as quoted by S. Weir Mitchell, *Wear and Tear*, 17.

3. Health reformer J. H. Kellogg, as quoted in Carroll Smith-Rosenberg, *Disorderly Conduct*, 184.

4. Physician Walter Taylor as quoted in Smith-Rosenberg, 192.

5. Edward Tilt as quoted in Smith-Rosenberg, 192.

6. D. C. Potter to Jr, 17 October 1887, JDR Jr, B19, Miscellaneous correspondence 1882–1936. Similar themes may be found in other letters the adolescent John Jr. received from older male advisors.

7. Senior to Jr, 28 November 1887, B21.

8. Senior to Jr, 19 November 1887, B21.

9. Alta to Jr, 12 February 1881, OMR, RG III2H, B97, F740.

10. Alta to Jr, 12 April 1887, OMR, RG III2H, B97, F740.

11. "Life as It Seemed to Me, Described by Mrs. McCormick," *New York Evening Journal*, 30 August 1932.

12. Hardly any information exists in the family archives on Bessie. Only a handful of her letters survive, and the letters among the family say little to give insight to her personality.

13. Allan Nevins, *John D. Rockefeller*, vol II, 171.

14. Jr to Bessie, 18 October 1890.

15. Gilbert A. Harrison, *A Timeless Affair*, 28. The speaker is Nettie's daughter Anita McCormick Blaine.

16. Harrison, 198–9. This information is from one of Stanley's later psychiatrists. Since Harold and Stanley were raised almost like twins, it is possible the governess seduced Harold as well.

17. Stella Roderick, *Nettie Fowler McCormick*, 179.

18. Alta to Jr, 28 January 1890, OMR, RG III2H, B97, F740.

19. Alta to Jr, 13 December 1891, OMR, RG III2H, B97, F740.

20. Alta to Jr, 13 April 1890, OMR, RG III2H, B97, F740.

21. Raymond Fosdick, *John D. Rockefeller, Jr.*, 32.

22. Diary, JDR Jr, B3.

23. Inglis, B4.

24. Senior to Jr, 13 November 1891.

25. Senior to Jr, 2 March 1892, JDR Jr, B21.

26. S. Weir Mitchell, *Fat and Blood*, 29–31.

27. Apart from the self-starvation, contemporary cases of anorexia exhibit symptoms distinctly different from those of the Gilded Age. For a better understanding of why this is so, see Joan Jacobs Blumberg, *Fasting Girls*, especially chapters 4–5. For a social history of the emergence of thinness as a standard of beauty for women in America, see Hillel Schwartz, *Never Satisfied*; chapter 4 discusses the "social decline of fatness" around the turn of the century.

28. One of Mitchell's patients, Charlotte Perkins Stetson, was so upset with his paradoxical suggestion she do nothing that she determined to be the opposite. She is better known as Charlotte Perkins Gilman, who remains one of the most insightful feminist writers to date. Her novella *The Yellow Wallpaper* captures the claustrophobia of the conventional woman's role at its extreme.

29. For example, Carroll Smith-Rosenberg, "The Hysterical Woman: Sex Roles and Role Conflict in Nineteenth-Century America," *Disorderly Conduct*, 197–216. In an otherwise astute analysis, Smith-Rosenberg at times errs in ignoring subtleties, hence skews the position taken by Mitchell and other medical writers to fit her hypothesis. Her charge may apply, however, to insensitive followers of Mitchell whose idea of shocking the women into action included practices such as dunking them in ice water.

30. From an 1875 *Ladies Home Journal* article, as quoted in Schwartz, *Never Satisfied*, 92.

31. The particulars of Bessie's illness are missing, so it is difficult to discern whether she

had a congenital heart defect, a rheumatic heart as the result of scarlet fever, or another systemic illness.

32. Nevins, Vol. II, 119–120.

33. Nevins, Vol. II, 148.

34. Another lawsuit from Ohio, and another testimony of "not recalling" took place in 1897. This time the state tried to prove that Standard Oil of Ohio was in fact still part of a trust under a different umbrella. This time the attorney general failed, partly because of alleged burning of the books by the company. This action spurred the final organization of SONJ as the holding company.

35. Andrew Carnegie, "Wealth," *North America Review*, 148 (June 1889), 653–64, and 149 (December 1889), 682–98.

36. Senior's nervous illness in response to a career crisis can be found in the biographies of other noted men of his day, including William and Henry James, Theodore Dreiser, and Louis Sullivan. Doctors diagnosed wealthier men differently from the less-affluent, whose symptoms were seen as related to enlarged appetites for sex, alcohol, or drugs. See F. G. Gosling, *Before Freud*, for an analysis of cases from this period.

37. Henry Adams, *The Education of Henry Adams*, 342–3. In researching the exposition, I found various sources referring to Adams's metaphor of the dynamo and the virgin as being developed during this fair. In fact, he conceived this idea during the Great Exposition of 1900, and is clear on this in his book, which is arranged chronologically. But later commentators sometimes confuse his 1900 experience as applying to that of 1893.

38. John 10: 16.

39. Robert Herrick, *The Memoirs of an American Citizen*, as quoted in Edward Wagenknecht, *Chicago*, 19.

40. Ernest Poole, as quoted in Wagenknecht, 19.

Chapter Seven: Come Into My Garden

1. Anthony Rotundo, *American Manhood*, 224. For more on the role of print media in popularizing the virile blond hero of the turn of the century, see Theodore P. Greene, *America's Heroes*.

2. Notes on John at Brown, Fosdick, B44.

3. Jr, Notes on Speeches, 18 March 1894, Fosdick, B49, F25.

4. Jr, Notes on Speeches, 18 March 1894, Fosdick, B44.

5. Jr to LSR, 6 January 1895, JDR Jr, B19.

6. LSR to Jr, 27 January 1895, JDR Jr, B19.

7. Jr to LSR, 6 January 1895, JDR Jr, B19.

8. As copied in Jr to LSR, 25 June 1895, JDR Jr, B19.

9. Jr to LSR, 17 June 1895, JDR Jr, B19.

10. Jr to LSR, 14 July 1895, JDR Jr, B19.

11. HMcC to Senior, 28 September 1895, "Miscellaneous Correspondence," JDR Jr, B19.

12. In my study of this episode in *The Vanderbilt Women,* I argue otherwise, that Consuelo was more a willing participant than gossip implied. In later years she was a key source in reinforcing these original rumors, despite strong evidence to the contrary of their validity.

13. Stella Roderick, *Nettie Fowler McCormick,* 191.

14. HMcC to Andy Imbrie, 4 April 1905, Harold McCormick Papers, Historical Society of Wisconsin.

15. *Idem.*

16. Senior to LSR, 27 February 1897, Spelman, B1, F9.

17. LSR to Jr, 13 June 1897, JDR Jr, B20.

18. Jr to LSR, 24 January 1897, JDR Jr, B36.

19. As reported to Bernice Kert, *Abby Aldrich Rockefeller,* 66.

20. LSR to Senior, 1 March 1897, JDR, B19.

21. Jr recollections of his father, Inglis, B21.

22. Jr to Senior, 11 November 1899, as quoted in Raymond Fosdick, *John D. Rockefeller, Jr.,* 91.

23. Fosdick, 111.

24. John D. Rockefeller, *Random Reminiscences of Men and Events,* 34.

25. Allan Nevins, *John D. Rockefeller,* vol. II, 448.

26. Ronald M. Deutsch, *The Nuts Among the Berries,* 118.

27. Fosdick, 99.

28. Edith to Jr, 17 October 1900, as copied from unavailable original by Fosdick, JDR Jr., B49, F23.

29. Alta to Jr, 11 May 1990, OMR, Family Series, B97, F740.

30. Harvey Warren Zorbaugh, *The Gold Coast and the Slum,* 48. This classic sociological study is perhaps the only one to analyze an urban elite neighborhood on the basis of extensive interviews with its members. Chapter III included a map of the area along with lengthy quotes from its residents. Interestingly, part of the support for the research came from the Laura Spelman Rockefeller Foundation.

31. "Life as it Seemed to Me, by Mrs. McCormick," *New York Evening Journal,* 31 August 1932.

32. Untitled, undated clipping, c. 1925, *Chicago Tribune,* Edith McCormick files, Chicago Historical Society.

33. Roderick, 228.

34. Edith to Senior, 11 October 1905, JDR Jr., Biography, B49, F23.

35. Malcolm Forbes, *What Happened to Their Kids,* 221. See also Stephen Birmingham, *The Grande Dames,* in which his chapter on Edith repeats this and other scurrilous gossip. Peter Collier and David Horowitz similarly caricature Edith, *The Rockefellers,* 72. The source of these stories can be placed on Bertha Baur, a Chicago socialite who spread them in the late twenties and thirties. Baur was angry that Edith did not do some social favors for her.

36. Mira Rockefeller to Emma, 28 February 1895, WR, B2.

37. Idem.

38. Mira to Emma, 7 June 1895, WR, B2.

39. William to Emma, 26 April 1894, WR, B2.

40. Mira to Emma, 5 March 1895, WR, B2.

41. LSR to Emma, 16 August 1895, WR, B2.

42. John K. Winkler, *The First Billions,* 137.

Chapter Eight: "Being Married Is Perfect."

1. Jr to LSR, 24 August, 1901, JDR Jr, B20.

2. Bernice Kert, *Abby Aldrich Rockefeller,* 80.

3. Jr to Aunt Lute, 14 October 1901, JDR Jr, B20.

4. Laura tracked her illnesses in brief journal notes, Spelman, B2. Lacking these, one would not suspect how seriously ill she was much of her later years.

5. Jr to LSR, 16 October 1901, JDR Jr. B20.

6. Mary Ellen Chase, *Abby Aldrich Rockefeller,* 4.

7. Allan Nevins, *John D. Rockefeller, Vol. II,* 459.

8. Chase, 47.

9. Chase, 48.

10. Raymond Fosdick, *John D. Rockefeller, Jr.,* 112.

11. Henry St. George Tucker, president of Washington and Lee University, as quoted in Fosdick, 117.

12. Bernice Kert, *Abby Aldrich Rockefeller,* 120.

13. Kathleen Brady, *Ida Tarbell,* 22.

14. Henry Demerast Lloyd, as quoted in Brady, 132.

15. According to the reporters of the New York *World,* William Avery Rockefeller died at a cottage in Freeport, Illinois, on May 11, 1906. Allan Nevins was told by Frank Rockefeller's daughters that he died on his Dakota ranch in the summer of 1909 at age one hundred.

16. Ida M. Tarbell "John D. Rockefeller: A Character Study," *McClure's Magazine,* August 1905, 386–7.

17. Tarbell, 391.

18. Tarbell, 394.

19. LSR, Journal notes, 1904, Spelman, B2.

20. LSR to Jr, 24 January 1905, JDR Jr., B19.

21. David Rockefeller as told to Bernice Kert, 174.

22. Alta to Senior, 30 November 1910, JDR Papers, B30, F234.

23. Alta to Senior, 8 July 1911, JDR, B30, F235.

24. HMcC to Morris L. Johnston, 3 September 1904, Harold McCormick Papers, State Historical Society of Wisconsin.

25. Unhappily for Katherine, although the research on schizophrenia did not reveal a cure. Late in life, after Stanley died, she was a major supporter of Margaret Sanger and the key donor in the work of Dr. John Rock and his discovery of the birth control pill.

26. HMcC to Charles Coolidge, 20 August 1906, Harold McCormick collection, State Historical Society of Wisconsin.

Chapter Nine: Earthly Trials

1. LSR journal, 1908, Spelman, B2.

2. This description hardly captures the brilliance of the work by architect William Welles Bosworth, much of which remains today. See his discussion and plans in his article "The Garden at Pocantico Hills," *American Architect*, 4 January 1911, 1–10.

3. I could not discern the identity of Harold's mistresses. Reference to his philandering occurred in enough different sources to presume he was adulterous.

4. Harold McCormick was a confidante to many high-level politicians, possibly because of his sharp analytical mind and willingness to see all sides of an issue, as well as his heading a major corporation.

5. Emma Jung's letters show her to be struggling to keep her identity despite Jung's dominance. Biographies of her husband implicitly reinforce his view of her as his *hausfrau*, when in fact she was an intellectual confidant, an astute and insightful woman in her own right.

6. Gilbert A. Harrison, *A Timeless Affair*, 189.

7. Ronald L. David, *Opera in Chicago*, 85.

8. Ibid, 88–9.

9. Ibid, 90.

10. Edith Rockefeller McCormick, "Four Family Divisions," *Delineator*, October 1911, 259.

11. For floor plans, photographs, and landscape information, see "The Renaissance Villa of Italy Developed into a Complete Residential Type for Use in America," *Architectural Record*, March 1912, Vol. XXXI, 220–225.

12. HMcC to Senior, 28 December 1913, JDR, B32, F249.

13. Two sources inform on Edith's intellectual activity. Following her death, S. M. Melamed, a Chicago scholar, examined her library and prepared an essay, "Edith Rockefeller McCormick's Intellectual Personality," OMR, B80, F608. Also informative is the auction catalogue, "The Splendid Library of the Late Mrs. Rockefeller McCormick," American Art Association, Anderson Galleries, 1934. This sale did not include her full library, as significant materials described by Melamed, such as her Kantiana, were not included, and presumably sold privately.

14. Melamed, 7.

15. HMcC to Senior, 28 December 1913, JDR, B32, F249.

16. Senior to Nettie McCormick, 6 October 1918, JDR, B32, F250.

17. Bernice Kert, *Abby Aldrich Rockefeller,* 142.

18. David Rockefeller as told to Bernice Kert, 143.

19. Spelman Prentice to Bernice Kert, 163.

20. Nelson Aldrich, Jr., *Old Money,* 165.

21. Between 1900 and 1919 the father and son gave over $350,000 to the Anti-Saloon cause. John was the more keen, and once unsuccessfully tried to persuade his father to increase a donation because "Intemperance is the cause of so many human ills . . . ." Raymond Fosdick, *John D. Rockefeller, Jr.,* 250.

22. One reason for Parmalee's relatively uneven income as a lawyer could be that he accompanied Alta for several months each year when she took her treatments. These long absences would have precluded his taking certain cases.

23. JDR Jr, B22. This explanation was to accompany the 1925 will, which divided Senior's estate between the Laura Spelman Rockefeller Foundation and John.

24. Jr to Senior, 15 March 1922, JDR, B21.

25. Jr to LSR, 29 July 1908, JDR Jr, B20.

26. Fosdick, 335. This request was made in 1915, when the collection of J. P. Morgan, then on loan to the Metropolitan Museum, came on the market. Senior at first demurred, but John Jr. persisted and won his point.

27. Edith to Senior, 4 September 1915, JDR, B32, F250.

28. Jr to Starr Murphy, 10 April 1913, Spelman, B1. In light of surrounding correspondence, the date may be a misprint, for the discussion fits more logically as taking place in 1912.

Chapter Ten: The Call of the Carpenter

1. John Ensor Harr and Peter J. Johnson, *The Rockefeller Century,* 86.

2. Bouck White, *The Call of the Carpenter,* 312.

3. Susan Curtis, "The Son of Man and the Gospel of the Father," in Mark C. Carnes and Clyde Griffin, *Meanings for Manhood,* 77.

4. President of Brown Elisha Benjamin Andrews, Harr and Johnson, 46.

5. Harr and Johnson, 49.

6. *Salt Lake City Herald*, 9 December 1902.

7. 7 July 1885 Diary, JDR Jr., B3.

8. Harr and Johnson, 128. It is noteworthy that most of Congress did not support the United Mine Workers here either, and that even the national UMW leadership eventually disavowed itself from the provocative acts of its workers at CFI.

9. AAR to Jr., 4 October 1914, JDR Jr., B55.

10. Harr and Johnson, 137.

11. HMcC to Senior, 3 October 1914, JDR, Family, B32, F249.

12. Alta to Senior, 4 February 1915, JDR, Family, B31, F237.

13. LSR to Jr, 7 April 1914, JDR Jr, B20.

14. Nevins, *John D. Rockefeller*, Vol. II, 677.

15. Report written by Laura's nurses, Catherine Kearney and Jessie Mitchell, Spelman, B2, F4.

16. Edith to Senior, 14 March 1915, JDR, Family, B33, F250.

17. Edith to Abby, 22 September 1915, AAR, B15.

18. This incident occurred in 1917, but was not revealed until 1923. See "Says Mrs. M'Cormick Freed French Ace," *New York Times*, 12 April 1923.

19. Here hard evidence does not exist. My claims here are based upon Jung's biographers, who do not supply particulars as to the extent of her financial support or exactly what translations she paid for.

20. HMcC to Senior, 1 September 1915, JDR, Family, B32, F250.

21. Edith to Senior, 23 February 1922, JDR, Family, B33, F256.

22. HMcC to Senior, 31 October 1915, JDR, Family, B32, F250. For Jung's eventual full development of his theory, see his *Psychological Types*, volume 6 of his *Collected Works*, published in 1921. Some readers may be familiar with this model as expanded by later therapists into the Myers-Briggs typology.

23. Edith to Senior, 13 May 1915, JDR, Family, B32, F250.

24. Edith to Senior, 22 October 1915, JDR, Family, B32, F250.

25. Edith to Senior, 31 January 1916, JDR, Family, B33, F252.

26. Edith to Senior, 24 January 1918, JDR, Family, B32, F251.

27. Senior to Edith, 4 March 1916, JDR, Family, B32, F251.

28. Edith to Senior, 22 June 1917, JDR, Family, B33, F252.

29. Jr to Senior, 28 June 1912, JDR, Family, B30, F235.

30. HMcC to Jr, 25 April 1915, JDR Jr, Biography, B49, F23.

31. Jr to HMcC, 3 June 1915, JDR Jr, Biography, B49, F23.

32. As reprinted in *Report of the Williamstown Food Commission*, Williamstown, 1919, OMR, B96, F736.

33. From a letter to William Inglis, as quoted in Nevins, *John D. Rockefeller*, Vol. II, 698.

34. Kert, 162.

35. Raymond Fosdick, *John D. Rockefeller, Jr.*, 406.

36. Fosdick, 403.

Chapter Eleven: By Their Fruits Be Known

1. Allan Nevins, *John D. Rockefeller*, Vol. II, 696.

2. Vincent Brome, *Jung*, 176.

3. Jung to Patricia Hutchins, as quoted in Brome, 177.

4. James Joyce to Frank Budgeon, 3 January 1920, Stuart Gilbert, ed., *Letters of James Joyce*, I, 134.

5. James Joyce to Frank Budgeon, Gilbert, 144.

6. James Joyce to Stanislaus Joyce, 25 July 1920, Richard Ellmann, ed., *Letters of James Joyce*, II, 10.

7. James Joyce to Daniel Brody, 29 August 1932, Gilbert, 324.

8. Walska's autobiography, *Always Room at the Top*, is very free with chronology, so exact dating of her first encounters with Harold, among other events not publicized in papers, is hard to make.

9. Ganna Walska, *Always Room at the Top*, 26 passim.

10. Walska, 131.

11. Edith to Senior, 27 March 1919, JDR, Family, B33, F253.

12. For the full account, see HMcC to Senior, 19 January 1920, JDR, Family, B22, F254.

13. Carl Jung as quoted in HMcC to Senior, 9 February 1920, JDR, Family, B33, F254.

14. Edith to Senior, 24 September 1920, JDR, Family, B33, F254.

15. Cyrus McCormick to Senior, 6 September 1921, JDR, Family, B33, F255.

16. Abby A. Rockefeller, "The Young Women's Christian Association and Legislation," *Association Monthly*, March 1920, 121.

17. *Pasadena Star News*, 23 May 1922.

18. AAR to Mary Lindsley, 4 May 1922, AAR Papers, B28.

19. Edith to Senior, 19 November 1921, JDR, Family, B33, F255.

20. Jr to Judge Cutting, 20 December 1921, ORM, B80, F613.

21. Harrison, *A Timeless Affair*, 191.

22. *New York Times*, 25 June 1922.

23. A telling history of the Stillman sisters and their Rockefeller husbands is Isabel Lincoln Elmer, *Cinderella Rockefeller*. Elmer is a great-granddaughter of William Rockefeller, and a granddaughter of Percy and Isabel Rockefeller.

Chapter Twelve: As Plants Grown Up

1. Senior to Fritz, 15 March 1918, JDR, Family, B31, F240.

2. Alta to Senior, 24 January 1923, JDR, Family, B32, F244.

3. Senior to Alta, 25 February 1920, JDR, Family, B31, F242.

4. Senior to Alta, 19 February 1921, JDR, Family, B31, F243.

5. Alta to Senior, 15 March 1921, JDR, Family, B31, F243.

6. Senior to Alta, 21 December 1922, JDR, Family, B32, F244.

7. Senior to Alta, 10 May 1920, Family, B31, F242. Italics are added because in other places in this letter JDR refers to "the family" as a corporate unit with regard to financial matters.

8. For example, in 1920 he praised her for having such low income taxes and gave her $25,000 to use on the farm. Several months later he gave her $200,000 to invest in government bonds. Two years later he added $90,000 to her security accounts to make up for "losses," that is, drops in value as part of the normal cycle.

9. Alta to Senior, 24 January 1923, JDR, Family, B20, F236.

10. Senior to Fritz, 2 February 1923, JDR, Family, B32, F246.

11. Muriel to Senior, 21 February 1922, JDR, Family, B33, F256.

12. Fowler to Senior, 21 February 1922, JDR, Family, B33, F256.

13. Edith to Mathilde, as recopied in a letter to Senior, 23 February 1922, JDR, Family, B33, F256.

14. Harold to Senior, 24 February 1922, JDR, Family, B33, F256.

15. Anita McCormick Blaine to Max Oser, 1 March 1922, State Historical Society of Wisconsin.

16. Edith to Senior, 25 February 1922, JDR, Family, B33, F256.

17. HMcC to Senior, 31 October 1922, JDR, Family, B33, F257.

18. Muriel to Senior, 8 November, 1922, JDR, Family, B33, F257.

19. Pyle, 43.

20. *New York Times*, April 1926.

21. *New York Times*, 1 October 1925.

22. Edith to Senior, JDR, 20 October 1922, Family, B22, F257.

23. Morris, *Nelson Rockefeller*, 77.

24. Bernice Kert, *Abby Aldrich Rockefeller*, 171.

25. Lucy Aldrich, "A Week-end With Chinese Bandits," *Atlantic Monthly*.

26. Kert, 192.

27. Kert, 205.

28. Kert, 206.

29. Tom Pyle, *Pocantico*, 82.

30. Emma Rockefeller papers, WR, B8, contain Geraldine's notebooks and poems.

Chapter Thirteen: Sacrifices in Abundance

1. Bernice Kert, *Abby Aldrich Rockefeller*, 180–1.

2. Harry Emerson Fosdick, *The Living of These Days*, 179. Fosdick was asked by John Jr. to be the first minister of the interdenominational Riverside Church.

3. Abby to Lucy, 29 November 1992, *Abby Aldrich Rockefeller Letters to Her Sister Lucy Letters*, 85.

4. For detailed descriptions of Abby's dealing with John Jr.'s illness, her absence from her children, and the conflicting needs all put on her, see her late 1922 and early 1923 letters to her sister Lucy, 84–102.

5. Kert, *Abby Aldrich Rockefeller*, 252. Hart was a self-taught American artist, a wanderer who depicted whimsical scenes from his world travels.

6. See, for example Mrs. John D. Rockefeller, Jr., "Small Wayside Refreshment Stand Competition," *Ladies Home Journal*, November 1930: 30.

7. *New York Times*, 27 January 1923.

8. Undated or identified news clipping provided by Ivy Lee to Senior, OMR, B81, F619.

9. The possible homosexual tie between Krenn and Dato is from Chicago gossip columns of the day, which insinuate their living together at Krenn's apartment. Lacking other evidence, this remains speculative.

10. *New York Herald*, 24 December 1923.

11. Senior to Edith, 27 December 1923, JDR, Family, B33, F258.

12. One has to wonder whether the young Orson Welles became familiar with the Walska-McCormick story. Reading the reviews of Walska's performances brings immediately to mind the famous opera sequence in *Citizen Kane*. Harold, of course, was no Kane, for it was Walska who pushed him, and not the opposite.

13. Walter Damrosch to Anita McCormick Blaine, 16 October 1923, State Historical Society of Wisconsin.

14. Ganna Walska, *Always Room at the Top*, 199–102.

15. Walska, 404.

16. Jr to Edith, 23 July 1928, OMR, B81, F619.

17. Peter Collier and David Horowitz, *The Rockefellers: An American Dynasty*, 197.

18. Morris, 79.

19. Babs, John, Nelson, Laurance, Winthrop, and David to Jr, 1 May 1933, JDR Jr. papers, B19, miscellaneous correspondence 1882–1936. Although the letter is addressed "Dear Father," the content continually refers to both John Jr. and Abby jointly in the matter.

20. Pyle, 180.

Chapter Fourteen: The Generations Pass

1. Jr to Senior, 24 December 1931, OMR, B80, F608.

2. Senior to Jr, 29 December 1931, OMR, B80, F608.

3. "Chicago Study," OMR, B81, F619.

4. "Analysis of Chicago Properties," 23 April 1932, OMR, B81, F621.

5. Jr to Edith, 1 July 1932, OMR, B81, F621.

6. Bertram Cutler to Jr, 5 March 1932, OMR, B80, F608.

7. Jr to Edith, 1 July 1932, OMR, B81, F621.

8. Jr to Tom [Thomas M. Debevoise], 1 September 1932, OMR, B80, F616.

9. See Thomas E. Debevoise to Jr, 9 August 1932, OMR, B81, F621 for his description of a meeting with Muriel over the matter. This correspondence also documents how John Jr. was working behind the scenes regarding Edith's estate even before her death.

10. Michael Ebner, *Creating Chicago's North Shore*, 199.

11. Jr to Tom [Thomas E. Debevoise], 1 September 1932, OMR, B80, F616.

12. Muriel McCormick Hubbard's papers are closed to protect the privacy of others. In the course of reading other files, I came across material that suggested why this was the case and could construct the outlines of what her private papers likely detailed. Nonetheless, in respect to those desiring confidentiality, I decided to honor the principle rather than take advantage of the materials that happened to appear elsewhere in the archives. Let it be noted that Muriel apparently became an alcoholic and an addictive gambler, whose less than rational decisions brought confusion and sometimes pain to those close to her.

13. See OMR, B81, F618 and F619, for details.

14. For evidence on Margaret Strong's financial problems, see OMR, B112, F850.

15. 15 February 1933, OMR, B112, F850.

16. Senior to Bessie and John deCuevas, 17 May 1935, OMR, B112, F850.

17. *New York Post*, 13 September 1939.

18. *New York Herald Tribune*, 20 June 1944.

19. To be precise, Ballet Imperial existed only one season, at a cost of $600,000, after which George mounted productions in New York. Based upon his reputation, he was offered the Ballet Nouveau de Monte Carlo, to which he added his previous dancers to become the Ballet de Monte Carlo, later the Grand Ballet du Marquis de Cuevas.

20. The offer of the theater on Columbus Square was aborted without explanation. As Lincoln Kirstein noted in his diaries, one day Nelson Rockefeller called him to his office with the opportunity to house Balanchine's group. Kirstein thought it was "too good to be true," and was not surprised when nothing came of the matter.

21. *London Times*, 1 September 1957.

22. Bernice Kert, *Abby Aldrich Rockefeller*, 470.

23. Alvin Moscow, *The Rockefeller Inheritance*, 209.

24. Jr to Parmalee, 29 February 1952, OMR, B96, F734.

25. Parmalee to Jr, 10 April 1952, OMR, B96, F734.

26. Peter Collier and David Horowitz, *The Rockefellers: An American Dynasty*, 336.

Chapter Fifteen: Legacies

1. Isabel Elmer, *Cinderella Rockefeller*, 154.

2. John Jr.'s personal assets were distributed as follows: $48 million to his wife Martha, $72 million to the Rockefeller Brothers Fund, and $12 million in state and federal taxes. Various real estate and personal property was divided among Martha and the sons.

3. This is from John Jr.'s ten statements of belief he had composed for Rockefeller Center. Visitors today are given cards with the full text, which emphasizes his philosophy of individualism grounded in duty, social justice, opportunity, honor, thrift, love, and belief in God.

4. The Asian art went to the Asia Society, an organization to which he devoted much time over the years; the American collection went to the deYoung Museum in San Francisco. The collections are properly named after both John 3rd and his wife Blanchette, who was a partner in the acquisitions.

5. Vance Packard, *The Ultra Rich*, 84.

6. A good example here is Rockefeller University, which in the early 1990s suffered in-fighting around its president's support of a scholar who had fabricated her data. He eventually resigned, but not before other key scientists quit in protest. A more laudable example of scientific conflict within a philanthropy is described by Gerald Jonas, *The Circuit Riders*. There he unfolds how during the 1920s and 1930s key people in the Rockefeller Foundation resisted the rational-sounding racists and eugenicists.

7. For a leftist critique, see Myer Kutz, *Rockefeller Power*, New York: Pinnacle, 1974. An interesting contrast is Gary Allen, *The Rockefeller File*, Seal Beach, CA: '76 Press, 1976. Allen argues the family's "psychopathic lust for monopolistic power" subsidizes Communism and intends to impose a Communist-style government.

8. "Modest President," *The New Yorker*, 2 January 1960, 21.

9. See Mary French Rockefeller, "YWCA International Success Story," *National Geographic*, December 1963, 904–933; Mary and Laurance Rockefeller, "Parks, Plans, and People," *National Geographic*, January 1967: 74–119.

10. "Rockefellers Move to Preserve 2,972 Acres of Hudson Farms," *New York Times*, 24 June 1992.

11. Aline Saarinen, *The Proud Possessors*, 379.

12. Vance Packard, *The Ultra Rich*, 82.

13. Packard, 83.

14. Packard, 84.

15. "Happy's Brush With Cancer," *Newsweek*, 28 October 1974, 29.

16. Phoebe Eaton, "The Woman Who Was There," *New York Magazine*, 14 January 1991, 23.

17. Critics have a rich topic here, the examination of the proper place of this third sector in an egalitarian democracy. What dangers and benefits are there in heavily-funded private foundations? To what extent do they preserve the interests of the privileged, whether the funders themselves or the experts employed by the organizations? What opportunities do they have to evade public accountability and to serve aims inconsistent with American values? Who is excluded, who served? What are the rights of the donors to express themselves? What regulation should there be beyond current tax-law restrictions? How are the large nonprofits different from grassroots nonprofits, which are built upon human capital more than monetary capital? These questions are more pressing today for the fact of the Rockefellers and their role in the shaping of philanthropy in American life.

18. "Jay Rockefeller: 'She Was Regal,' " *People*, 27 February 1995, 37.

Chapter Sixteen: Revisionings

1. Vance Packard, *The Ultra Rich*, 84.

2. For more detail here, see John Ensor Harr and Peter J. Johnson, *The Rockefeller Conscience*, chap. 3.

3. This public access also increased maintenance and security costs. At night, for example, the dark and winding roads became a favorite spot for illicit and illegal activities. For insight here, see Tom Pyle, *Pocantico*. Pyle held a variety of positions for both Fifi Stillman and the Rockefellers.

4. "Modest President," *The New Yorker*, 2 January 1960, 20.

SELECT BIBLIOGRAPHY

Ackerman, Phyllis. *Three Early Sixteenth-Century Tapestries: With a Discussion of the History of the Tree of Life.* New York: Oxford University Press, 1932.

Adams, Henry. *The Education of Henry Adams.* New York: Modern Library, 1931.

Akin, Edward N. *Flagler: Rockefeller Partner and Florida Baron.* Kent, Ohio: Kent State University Press, 1988.

Alcott, William A. *The Young Husband, or Duties of Man in the Relation of Marriage.* Boston: George W. Light, 1939.

Aldrich, Nelson W., Jr. *Old Money: The Mythology of America's Upper Class.* New York: Vintage, 1988.

Anderson, James D. *The Education of Blacks in the South: 1860–1935.* Chapel Hill: University of North Carolina Press, 1988.

Andrews, Wayne. *Battle for Chicago.* New York: Harcourt, Brace and Co., 1946.

Atkinson, Brooks, ed. *The Selected Writings of Ralph Waldo Emerson.* New York: Modern Library, 1992.

Bailey, Beth L. *From Front Porch to Back Seat: Courtship in Twentieth Century America.* Baltimore: Johns Hopkins, 1988.

Barbour, Fannie Cooly Williams. *Spelman Genealogy: The English Ancestry and American Descendants of Richard Spelman of Middletown, Connecticut, 1700.* New York: Frank Allaben Genealolgical Company, 1910.

Beecher, Catherine E. and Harriet Beecher Stowe. *American Woman's Home.* New York: J. B. Ford, 1869.

Bello, Joaquin Edwards. *El Marques de Cuevas Y Su Tiempo.* Santiago, Chile: Nascimento, 1974.

Berman, Avis. *Rebels on Eighth Street: Juliana Force and the Whitney Museum of American Art.* New York: Atheneum, 1990.

Birmingham, Stephen. *The Grandes Dames.* New York: Simon and Schuster, 1982.

Bittar, Helen. *The YWCA and the City of New York, 1970 to 1920.* Doctoral dissertation, New York University, 1979.

Blockson, Charles. *The Underground Railroad.* New York: Prentice-Hall, 1987.

Bode, Carl, editor. *American Life in the 1840s.* Garden City: Doubleday, 1967.

————. *Midcentury America: Life in the 1850s.* Carbondale: Southern Illinois University Press, 1972.

Bordin, Ruth Birgitta Anderson. *Frances Willard: A Biography.* Chapel Hill: University of North Carolina Press, 1986.

Boylan, Anne M. *Sunday School: The Formation of an American Institution, 1790–1880.* New Haven: Yale University Press, 1988.

Brackney, William Henry. *The Baptists.* New York: Greenwood Press, 1988.

Brady, Kathleen. *Ida Tarbell: Portrait of a Muckraker.* New York: Seaview/Putnam, 1984.

Branch, E. Douglas. *The Sentimental Years, 1836–1860.* New York: Hill and Wang, 1934.

Bremner, Robert H. *American Philanthropy.* Chicago: University of Chicago Press, 1960.

————. *From the Depths: The Discovery of Poverty in the United States.* New York: New York University Press, 1964.

Briggs, John. *Requiem for a Yellow Brick Brewery.* Boston: Little, Brown, 1969.

Brown, E. Richard. *Rockefeller Medicine Men: Medicine and Capitalism in America.* Berkeley: University of California Press, 1979.

Brumberg, Joan Jacobs. *Fasting Girls: The History of Anorexia Nervosa.* New York: Plume, 1989.

Burgess, Charles O. *Nettie Fowler McCormick: Profile of an American Philanthropist.* Madison: State Historical Society of Wisconsin, 1962.

Burlingham, Michael John. *The Last Tiffany.* New York: Antheaneum, 1989.

Carnes, Mark C. and Clyde Griffin, editors. *Meanings for Manhood: Constructions of Masculinity in Victorian America.* Chicago: University of Chicago Press, 1990.

Cayleff, Susan E. *Wash and Be Healed: The Water Cure Movement and Women's Health.* Philadelphia: Temple University Press, 1987.

Chase, Mary Ellen. *Abby Aldrich Rockefeller.* New York: MacMillan, 1950.

Chesler, Ellen. *Woman of Valor: Margaret Sanger and the Birth Control Movement in America.* New York: Simon & Schuster, 1992.

Child, Lydia Maria. *The American Frugal Housewife.* New York: Samuel and William Wood, 1860.

Cigliano, Jan. *Showplace of America: Cleveland's Euclid Avenue, 1850–1910.* Kent, Ohio: Kent State University Press, 1991.

Collier, Peter, and David Horowitz. *The Rockefellers: An American Dynasty.* New York: Signet, 1977.

Cooper, John Milton, Jr. *Pivotal Decades: The United States 1900–1920.* New York: W. W. Norton, 1990.

Cross, Whitney. *The Burned-Over District: The Social and Intellectual History of Enthusiastic Religion in Western New York, 1800–1850.* New York: Harper & Row, 1965.

Dannenbaum, Jed. *Drink and Disorder: Temperance Reform in Cincinnati from the Washington Revival to the WCTU.* Urbana: University of Illinois, 1984.

Davis, Ronald L. *Opera in Chicago.* New York: Appleton-Century, 1966.

Dedman, Emmett. *Fabulous Chicago.* New York: Random House, 1953.

Douglas, Claire. *Translate this Darkness: The Life of Christiana Morgan.* New York: Simon & Schuster, 1993.

———. *The Woman in the Mirror: Analytical Psychology and the Feminine.* Boston: Sigo Press, 1990.

Douglas, Emily Taft. *Margaret Sanger: Pioneer of the Future.* New York: Holt, Rinehart, and Winston, 1970.

Drinka, George Frederick. *The Birth of Neurosis: Myth, Malady, and the Victorians.* New York: Simon & Schuster, 1984.

Earhart, Mary, *Frances Willard: From Prayer to Politics.* Chicago: University of Chicago Press, 1944.

Ebner, Michael H. *Creating Chicago's North Shore: A Suburban History.* Chicago: University of Chicago, 1988.

Ehrenreich, Barbara and Deirdre English, *For Her Own Good: 150 Years of the Experts' Advice to Women,* Garden City: Anchor Press, 1978.

Ellmann, Richard, editor. *Letters of James Joyce,* Volumes II and III. New York: Viking Press, 1966.

Elmer, Isabel Lincoln. *Cinderella Rockefeller: A Wealth Beyond All Knowing.* New York: Freundlich, 1987.

Filene, Peter Gabriel. *Him/Her/Self: Sex Roles in Modern America.* New York: Signet, 1975.

Finke, Roger and Rodney Stark. *The Churching of America, 1776–1990.* New Brunswick: Rutgers University Press, 1992.

Forbes, Malcolm, with Jeffrey Bloch. *What Happened to Their Children?* New York: Simon & Schuster, 1990.

Fosdick, Harry Emerson. *The Living of These Days: An Autobiography.* New York: Harper & Brothers, 1956.

Fosdick, Raymond B. *John D. Rockefeller, Jr.: A Portrait.* New York: Harper & Brothers, 1956.

Frost, Dick. *The Rockefeller Encyclopedia.* Chicago: Aquarius Rising Press, copyright 1987.

Gilbert, Stuart, editor. *Letters of James Joyce.* New York: Viking, 1957.

Gosling, Francis G. *Before Freud: Neurasthenia and the American Medical Community, 1870–1910.* Urbana: University of Illinois, 1987.

Gouldner, Grace. *John D. Rockefeller: The Cleveland Years.* Cleveland: Western Reserve Historical Society, 1972.

Green, Harvey. *The Light of the Home: An Intimate View of the Lives of Women in Victorian America.* New York: Pantheon Books, 1983.

Greene, Theodore P. *American Heroes: The Changing Models of Success in American Magazines.* New York: Oxford University Press, 1970.

Halttunen, Karen. *Confidence Men and Painted Women: A Study of Middle-class Culture in America, 1830–1870.* New Haven: Yale University Press, 1982.

Harr, John Ensor and Peter J. Johnson. *The Rockefeller Century.* New York: Charles Scribner's Sons, 1988.

———. *The Rockefeller Conscience.* New York: Scribner's, 1991.

Harrison, Gilbert A. *A Timeless Affair: The Life of Anita McCormick Blaine.* Chicago: University of Chicago Press, 1979.

Hawke, David Freeman. *John D.: The Founding Father of the Rockefellers,* New York: Harper & Row, 1980.

Holland, Josiah Gilbert. *Titcomb's Letters to Young People, Single and Married.* New York: Charles Scribner, 1858.

Horowitz, Helen Lefkowitz. *Culture and the City: Cultural Philanthropy in Chicago from the 1880s to 1917.* Lexington: University Press of Kentucky, 1976.

Hughes, Adella Prentiss. *Music is My Life.* New York: World Publishing, 1947.

Jonas, Gerald. *The Circuit Riders: Rockefeller Money and the Rise of Modern Science.* New York: W. W. Norton, 1989.

Jung, C. G. *Memories, Dreams, and Reflections.* New York: Vintage, 1965.

Kasson, John F. *Rudeness and Civility: Manners in Nineteenth-Century Urban America.* New York: Hill and Wang, 1990.

Kerr, John. *A Most Dangerous Method: The Story of Jung, Freud, and Sabina Spielrein.* New York: Alfred A. Knopf, 1993.

Kert, Bernice. *Abby Aldrich Rockefeller: The Woman in the Family.* New York: Random House, 1993.

Knowles, J. D. *Memoir of Ann H. Judson.* Boston: Gould, Kendall & Lincoln, 1829.

Kramer, Michael, and Sam Roberts. *"I Never Wanted to Be Vice-President of Anything!" An Investigative Biography of Nelson Rockefeller.* New York: Basic Books, 1976.

Larkin, Jack. *The Reshaping of Everyday Life, 1790–1840.* New York: Harper & Row, 1988.

Leamer, Lawrence. *The Kennedy Women: The Saga of An American Family.* New York: Villard, 1994.

Lord, Russell. *The Care of the Earth: A History of Husbandry.* New York: Thomas Nelson & Sons, 1962.

Marquis, Alice Goldfarb. *Alfred H. Barr Jr.: Missionary for the Modern.* Chicago: Contemporary Books, 1889.

Matthews, Glenna. *"Just a Housewife": The Rise and Fall of Domesticity in America.* New York: Oxford, 1987.

McCarthy, Kathleen D. *Women's Culture: American Philanthropy and Art, 1830-1930.* Chicago: University of Chicago, 1991.

McGuire, William, and R. F. C. Hull, editors. *C. G. Jung Speaking: Interviews and Encounters.* Princeton: Princeton University Press, 1977.

Mitchell, S. Weir. *Fat and Blood: How to Make Them, 2nd ed.* Philadelphia: J. B. Lippincott, 1877.

————. *Wear and Tear, or Hints for the Overworked, 5th ed.* Philadelphia: J. B. Lippincott, 1887.

————. *Lectures on Diseases of the Nervous System, Especially in Women.* Philadelphia: H. C. Lea's Son & Co., 1881.

Morris, Joe Alex. *Nelson Rockefeller: A Biography.* New York: Harper, 1960.

Morris, Lloyd. *Incredible New York.* New York: Random House, 1951.

Moscow, Alvin. *The Rockefeller Inheritance.* Garden City: Doubleday, 1977.

Nevins, Allan. *John D. Rockefeller: The Heroic Age of American Enterprise.* New York: Charles Scribner's Sons, 1940.

————. *Study in Power: John D. Rockefeller, Industrialist and Philanthropist.* New York: Scribner, 1953.

Packard, Vance. *The Ultra Rich: How Much is Too Much?* Boston: Little, Brown, 1989.

Portman, David N., editor. *Early Reform in American Higher Education.* Chicago: Nelson-Hall, 1972.

Prentice, E. Parmalee. *Farming for Famine.* Garden City: Doubleday, Doran, 1936.

————. *Hunger and History: The Influence of Hunger on Human History.* New York: Harper & Brothers, 1939.

Pyle, Tom. *Pocantico: Fifty Years on the Rockefeller Domain.* New York: Duell, Sloan, and Pearce, 1964.

Rockefeller, John D. *Random Reminiscences of Men and Events.* Tarrytown: Sleepy Hollow Press and Rockefeller Archive Center, 1984.

Read, Florence Matilda. *The Story of Spelman College.* Atlanta: n.p., 1961.

Robinson, Marian O. *Eight Women of the YWCA.* New York: National Board of the YWCA of the USA, 1966.

Rockefeller, Abby Aldrich. *Abby Aldrich Rockefeller's Letters to Her Sister Lucy.* New York: n.p., 1957.

Roderick, Stella Virginia. *Nettie Fowler McCormick.* Rindge, New Hampshire: Richard R. Smith, 1956.

Rotundo, E. Anthony. *American Manhood: Transformations in Masculinity from the Revolution to the Modern Era.* New York: Basic Books, 1993.

Ryan, Mary P. *The Empire of the Mother: American Writing about Domesticity, 1830–1860.* New York: Institute for Research in History and Haworth Press, 1972.

Saarinen, Aline B. *The Proud Possessors: The Lives, Times, and Tastes of Some Adventurous American Art Collectors.* New York: Random House, 1958.

Schwartz, Hillel. *Never Satisfied: A Cultural History of Diets, Fantasies, and Fat.* New York: Doubleday, 1986.

Shclereth, Thomas J. *Victorian America: Transformation in Everyday Life, 1876–1915.* New York: HarperCollins, 1991.

Sims, Mary. *The Natural History of a Social Institution [the YWCA].* New York: The Womans Press, 1936.

Sklar, Kathryn Kish. *Catharine Beecher: A Study in American Domesticity.* New Haven: Yale University Press, 1973.

Smith-Rosenberg, Carroll. *Disorderly Conduct: Visions of Gender in Victorian America.* New York: Alfred A. Knopf, 1985.

Stasz, Clarice. *The Vanderbilt Women: Dynasty of Wealth, Glamour, and Tragedy.* New York: St. Martin's Press, 1991.

Stephenson, Nathaniel Wright. *Nelson W. Aldrich: A Leader in American Politics.* New York: C. Scribner's Sons, 1930.

Stevens, Louise L. *Scholarly Means to Evangelical Ends: The New Haven Scholars and the Transformation of Higher Learning in America, 1830–1860.* Baltimore: Johns Hopkins University Press, 1986.

Strasser, Susan. *Never Done: A History of American Housework.* New York: Pantheon, 1982.

Sullivan, Mark. *Our Times: The United States 1900–1925, vols I-VI.* New York: Charles Scribner's Sons, 1927.

Sutherland, Daniel E. *The Expansion of Everyday Life, 1860–1876.* New York: Harper & Row, 1989.

Tarbell, Ida. *The History of the Standard Oil Company.* New York: McClure, Phillips, 1904.

Torbet, Robert G. *A History of the Baptists, Revised Edition.* Valley Forge, Pennsylvania: Judson Press, 1969.

Van Liere, Carma. *Hallowed Fire: Faith Motivation of Early Women Activists.* Valley Forge: Judson Press, 1991.

Van Tassel, David D. and John J. Grabowski. *The Encyclopedia of Cleveland.* Bloomington: Indiana University Press, 1987.

Veblen, Thorstein. *The Theory of the Leisure Class.* New York: Macmillan, 1899.

Veith, Ilza. *Hysteria: The History of a Disease.* Chicago: University of Chicago Press, 1965.

Wagenknecht, Edward. *Chicago.* Norman, Oklahoma: University of Oklahoma Press, 1964.

Wall, Joseph Frazier. *Andrew Carnegie.* Pittsburgh: University of Pittsburgh Press, 1970.

Walska, Ganna. *Always Room at the Top.* New York: Richard R. Smith, 1943.

Wechter, Dixon. *The Saga of American Society: A Record of Social Aspiration, 1607–1937.* New York: Charles Scribner's Sons, 1937.

Weimann, Jeanne Madeline. *The Fair Women.* Chicago: Academy, 1981.

White, Bouck. *The Call of the Carpenter.* Garden City: Doubleday, 1914.

Winkler, John K. *The First Billion: The Stillmans and the National City Bank.* New York: Vanguard Press, 1934.

Yergin, Daniel. *The Prize: The Epic Quest of Oil, Money, and Power.* New York: Simon & Schuster, 1993.

Zorbaugh, Harvey Warren. *The Gold Coast and the Slum.* Chicago: University of Chicago, 1929.

INDEX